THE AFRICAN COLONIZATION MOVEMENT
1816–1865

The *AFRICAN COLONIZATION MOVEMENT 1816 - 1865*

by

P. J. Staudenraus

COLUMBIA UNIVERSITY PRESS

NEW YORK · 1961

Copyright © 1961 Columbia University Press, New York

Library of Congress Catalog Card Number: 61-8071
Manufactured in the United States of America

to
Joseph and Margaret Staudenraus

PREFACE

—◆◆◆◆—

PROFESSOR Hermann von Holst of the University of Freiburg once described the American Colonization Society as a "swindle" without parallel, a "piece of Don Quixoterie," a vicious, hypocritical plot by the "slavocracy" to strengthen slavery by ridding the United States of free Negroes. Southerners, the chief villains in von Holst's tale, "laughed in their sleeve" at their success in deluding the "philanthropists of the north" who thought colonization would Christianize Africa. At length the northern friends of freedom detected the ruse and exposed the "hypocrisy and falsehood" of colonization. Von Holst sorrowfully concluded that colonization was part of "a farcial interlude in the terrible tragedy, which hastened with giant steps towards its issue."

Von Holst's stern judgment exemplified the post–Civil War interpretation of African colonization, and the same theme filled many histories, encyclopedias, and textbooks. Von Holst notwithstanding, the American Colonization Society was not a conspiracy to strengthen the chains of slavery. Colonizationists, like most Americans of the early nineteenth century, were troubled by slavery and wished an end to it. But slavery was not the central problem. From Jefferson forward, colonizationists believed—and they persuaded a great many Americans to their view—that the race question was more fundamental than that of chattel slavery. Once this problem was solved, Negro slavery would disappear.

The American Colonization Society, like its many sister "benevolent" societies of the nineteenth century, argued that a ruling Providence guided nations to ruin or salvation. Nations, unlike mortals, received their punishments and rewards on earth. "The fortunes of a nation are not under the control of blind destiny," a prominent historian asserted. "A favoring Providence" was leading the country "to its present happiness and glory." For George Bancroft and many other Americans, God was immanent in the affairs of every nation. Obedience to God's ordinances meant growth, power, triumph; rejection brought decay, defeat, misery. With the conspicuous cooperation of Providence, the American nation could root out its social and political deficiencies, atone for past misdeeds, and shape the course of unborn generations.

The social "evil" which most concerned the American Colonization Society was the presence of a second race, a socially inferior and repressed nation dragged to the Western Hemisphere in chains and abused with impunity. Negro slavery was but a symbol of a grievous transgression against God's rulership over the universe. The presence of an alien nation in America was evidence of man's inhumanity to man and threatened the peace and stability of society. Removal of the alien race would atone for the African slave trade, root out slavery, restore the "Africans" to their divinely ordained home, civilize the dark continent, and hasten the coming of the American nation's millennium when "one happy, united, homogeneous race of freedmen" would tread the land.

The story of the African colonization movement in ante bellum United States embodies the plans, hopes, and achievements of men, inspired by many motives, who sought to rid the country of an unwanted race. The American Colonization Society, organized in 1817, claimed the endorsement of well-known men and with them wove a social movement that penetrated every part of the Union. In addition, the society established its own colony of Liberia as a pilot study to show that African colonization was practicable and to persuade the federal and state governments to underwrite a far larger project.

Like slavery, secession, and the compact theory, African colonization became a historical exhibit in a museum of curiosities from a bygone age, for the Civil War, the Republicans, and reconstruction forged a new nation that was to be bi-racial. The Negro, no longer looked upon as an "African," became a citizen. In this new context, African colonization schemes assumed the "visionary" and "Quixotic" overtones jeered in later years by von Holst, and only stray cranks could embrace preposterous schemes to deport millions of fellow Americans.

I owe thanks to many people for their assistance in the research and writing stages. I am indebted to the librarians in the Manuscripts Division of the Library of Congress, the Maryland Historical Society, the Howard University Library, and the State Historical Society of Wisconsin. The hospitality of the latter institution was extraordinary. I wish to thank Benton H. Wilcox, John Colson, Ruth Davis, June Johnson, Mrs. Esther Nelson, Don Oehlerts, Mrs. Herbert Kellar, Josephine L. Harper, Jacqueline Jurkins, Mrs. Dorothy B. Porter, and Elisabeth Joan Doyle for their help. John Hope Franklin of Brooklyn College read the entire manuscript and offered valuable suggestions. Irwin Wyllie of the University of Wisconsin corrected several errors. Larry Gara of Grove City College, Frank L. Byrne of The Creighton University, Clifford S. Griffin of the University of Kansas, and Ernest J. Isaacs, my colleagues at the University of Wisconsin, offered assistance and encouragement. The University of Kansas City assisted in typing a portion of the manuscript. Professor Emeritus Clifford H. Moore of Ripon College and my wife Nancy were helpful in more ways than they know. They have my affectionate thanks.

Finally, I wish to express profound gratitude to Professor William B. Hesseltine of the University of Wisconsin. Professor Hesseltine carefully studied the manuscript and cheerfully jotted, scrawled, and scratched many useful and often pungent remarks in the margins and footnotes, between lines, and across whole pages. I am deeply grateful for his fatherly forbearance, his friendship, and his sturdy devotion to history.

P. J. S.

Davis, California
December 28, 1960

CONTENTS

————◆•••▷————

I

TAPROOTS OF COLONIZATION

———◄•••►———

"AMONG THE ROMANS emancipation required but one effort," Thomas Jefferson observed in 1781. "The slave, when made free, might mix with, without staining the blood of his master. But with us a second [step] is necessary, unknown to history. When freed, he is to be removed beyond the reach of mixture." In his neat, rounded handwriting Jefferson was preparing a brief against Negro slavery. He later published it in his *Notes on Virginia,* wishing to persuade his fellow Virginians that slavery was a "great political and moral evil" and that a large and growing Negro population, whether slave or free, was a "blot in this country."

In 1776 Jefferson had penned the ringing words that "all men are created equal." But time and experience had modified his outlook. "I advance it . . . as a suspicion only, that the blacks, whether originally a distinct race, or made distinct by time and circumstances, are inferior to the whites in the endowments of both body and mind." Experience and reason taught him that "different species of the same genus, or varieties of the same species, may possess different qualifications." Color, "that immoveable veil of black," whatever its cause, drew a sharp line between the races. There were noticeable anatomical differences —skin glands that gave off a "very strong and disagreeable odour," a greater tolerance of heat and less of cold, a different "pulmonary apparatus," and a capacity to live on less sleep. As planter and slaveowner, Jefferson found Negro imagination often tended to be "dull, tasteless, and anomalous." Though "more generally gifted" in music and equal to whites in "moral sense," they lacked artistic, oratorical, and poetic talents. Even the American Indians "carve figures on their pipes, not destitute of design and merit" and "astonish you with strokes of sublime oratory." Compared with harshly restricted slaves of ancient times, American slaves were ungifted. "It is not their condition then, but nature, which has produced the distinction."

As a member of the Virginia Assembly, Jefferson had proposed an emancipation plan, calling for freeing all slaves after they reached maturity. This was the *post nati* plan. But differences of color and talent presented a "powerful obstacle" to all emancipation schemes, and antislavery sentiment in Virginia ripened slowly. There were those, including Jefferson, who feared that any effort to equality would result in "convulsions which will probably never end but in the extermination of the one or the other race." Those who rejected coexistence demanded, "What further is to be done with them?" Jefferson provided a solution—colonization of emancipated slaves in a faraway place, selected "as the circumstances of the time should render most proper." The state would train the freedmen in "tillage, arts or sciences, according to their geniusses" until adulthood and, declaring them a "free and independent people," send them out "with arms, implements of household and of handicraft arts, seeds, pairs of the useful domestic animals."

Emancipation and removal of Negro slaves were urgent. Jefferson detected a steady increase in the Negro population foreboding "a revolution of the wheel of fortune" that could reverse the roles of master and slave and bring tragic paroxysm to the land. "I tremble for my country when I reflect that God is just: that his justice cannot sleep for ever." [1]

Six years after Jefferson unveiled his colonization plan, a fellow Virginian lent the honored name of Fairfax to a similar scheme. In 1790 Ferdinando Fairfax drew fresh attention to the pitfalls of emancipation. Though he wished an end to slavery in Virginia, he did not endorse Jefferson's call for state laws abolishing slavery outright. He deemed such legislation "the height of injustice" to property rights. Instead, he favored individual manumission as the best procedure for ending slavery in Virginia and other states.

Fairfax shared Jefferson's fears that racial lines would force sharp cleavages and precipitate the total disruption of society.

The two races could never live side by side in harmony and equality. Legislation guaranteeing equal rights could not wipe out ancient, "insurmountable" prejudices. Social and economic inferiority inevitably would follow. The existence of a distinct social group within the community promised only to "endanger the peace of society." Intermarriage was one way of securing a homogeneous society, but he rejected it as being "very repugnant to the general feelings."

Fairfax held that the best solution was the wholesale removal of free Negroes "to a distance from this country." He proposed that Congress acquire a colony in Africa and transport free blacks from each state. Such a program would induce slaveholders to manumit their slaves, for they could feel assured that freedom of the blacks would neither "injure themselves nor the community."

Africa was the most desirable site for a Negro colony, Fairfax argued, because it was the Negroes' "native climate" and far enough away to forestall rivalries and antagonisms between the races. Also, American Negroes could carry Christian teachings to Africa's "rude race of men." Finally, American traders and merchants could reap valuable advantages from a tropical colony under American supervision. Such a colony would repay in profits all expenses of transporting colonists and at the same time assure the colony's eventual independence.[2]

Jefferson and Fairfax had wide influence. In 1796 St. George Tucker, professor of law at William and Mary College and an outspoken critic of slavery, warned that free Negroes, if they remained in the United States, would become "the caterpillars of the earth, and the tigers of the human race." But he was not convinced that colonization, even under the sponsorship of the federal government, was really feasible. Surely, he noted, Jefferson "could not have weighed the difficulties and expense of an attempt to colonize 300,000 persons." Tucker hoped that freedmen would voluntary emigrate in small numbers and thus avoid the problems of mass deportation which would bring "death by famine, by disease, and other accumulated miseries." He agreed with Governor James Sullivan of Massachusetts, who, noting the large cost of colonization, gloomily commented that "We have in history but one picture of a similar enterprise, and there we see it was necessary not only to open the sea by a miracle, for them to pass, but more necessary to close it again, in order to prevent their return." The acquisition of Louisiana gave Tucker new hope. Colonization was a "Utopian idea" deserving careful study, and he recommended an experiment in lower Louisiana, where the climate was "more favourable for the African constitution than any part of the United States." In addition, colonization would induce slave states to relax "rigid laws" against manumission and aid in rehabilitating criminals.[3]

During Jefferson's presidency, Philadelphia Quaker John Parrish urged adoption of Jefferson's twin plans of emancipation and colonization. He insisted that Congress had sufficient authority to set aside a portion of the "western wildness . . . where there are millions of acres likely to continue many ages unoccupied" and distribute homesteads of one or two hundred acres to each Negro family. Free Negroes would flock to the west, and sympathetic slaveowners would liberate their slaves "on condition of their so removing." Thus freed of "this dreadful evil," the nation could enjoy "that sabbath which is prepared for all those who do justly, love mercy, and walk humbly with their God." [4]

In 1801–1802 the Virginia House of Delegates briefly discussed the creation of a penal colony for rebellious slaves and free Negro criminals. The abortive Gabriel insurrection near Richmond prompted worried legislators to ask Governor James Monroe to sound out President Jefferson on the subject of setting aside a special territory for Negroes. Monroe looked upon the scheme as a humanitarian gesture, pointing out that capital punishment was the alternative. He hoped that all free Negroes residing in Virginia would eventually move to such a colony. The House took no action, however, and the correspondence between Monroe and Jefferson remained secret and unnoticed in the state archives.[5]

A different colonization plan, based on voluntary emigration, sprouted in New England. It originated before the Revolution as a plan to send missionaries to Africa. In April, 1773, Congregational clergyman Samuel Hopkins of Rhode Island, the chief exponent of the still novel doctrine of benevolence, called upon the Reverend Dr. Ezra Stiles, later president of Yale College, and unfolded his plan for training two missionaries for Africa. Hopkins was eager to test his theological concept of a dynamic evangelical Calvinism that would carry Christianity to the unredeemed throughout the world. The dark continent offered vast numbers of pagans and infidels, and Stiles suggested that they enlarge the project, organize a society, and send thirty or forty "well instructed Negroes . . . inspired with the Spirit of Martyrdom." In this way whites could compensate for "injury and injustice" of the slave trade, "that unhallowed Commerce of traffic in the Souls of Men."

Hopkins tutored free Negroes in theology, encouraging them to prepare for missionary labors in Africa. He also cast about for financial aid and secured small sums from the Society for Promoting Christian Knowledge at Edinburgh, Scotland. Some New England clergymen were hostile to Hopkins's plan, charging that he wished merely to experiment with some of his controversial theological tenets that had already provoked debate among Congregationalists. One foe sneered that the Africans "had better continue in Paganism." Hopkins appeased critics by sending two prospective missionaries to Princeton College for theological training. Shortly after, the Revolution interrupted all plans, and one of Hopkins's more important disciples, John Quamine, lost his life in combat. After the Revolution, Hopkins merged his long-delayed missionary plan with a larger colonization project sponsored by William Thornton, a well-to-do Quaker physician recently come from England.[6]

Self-assured, intelligent, and well-groomed, Thornton wore his Quaker label lightly. His coreligionists called him a "wet Quaker" because he wore a powdered wig, silver buckles, and other accouterments frowned upon by the Friends. His clothing and manners betrayed a characteristic tendency to shun modesty. He searched the large towns for a wealthy wife and won his way into the upper circles of New York city society. His "vivacity and his agreeable manners" delighted the French visitor Brissot de Warville, who insisted that Thornton was at heart a Frenchman.[7]

Young Thornton soon earned a reputation as a humanitarian. In England he had been a junior member of a fashionable circle of humanitarian reformers that included John Coakley Lettsom, celebrated London physician, and Dr. Samuel Fothergill, "the great apostle of philanthropy." After coming to the United States Thornton fancied himself a "Cosmopolite" whose only home was "where my services may be the most acceptable."

In 1785 an unexpected inheritance of a number of West Indian slaves provided Thornton with an opportunity to devise his own humanitarian scheme—a colonization plan. Dr. Fothergill had talked of such an undertaking for free blacks living in England. By settling his slaves on a self-sustaining plantation, either in the West Indies or Africa, Thorton hoped to dispose of them in a humane but profitable manner. There they would labor as before, but with the difference that their accumulated earnings would gradually buy freedom. Authorities in the West Indies discouraged the plan. They did not want free Negroes living near the slave population. Turning his attention to the west coast of Africa, Thornton consulted the Reverend Dr. Hopkins and revised his project to include the clergyman's religious-minded free Negroes. They could teach the unlettered West Indians the value of industry, morality, and proper behavior—the "blessings of civilization." In turn, the West Indians could provide the colony with special knowledge necessary to operate a tropical plantation and insure its financial success.

Thornton now thought of the colony as a "black commonwealth" for all free Negroes living in the United States. He was certain that they had no permanent place in American society. "This ardent friend of the Blacks is persuaded," Brissot de Warville recorded after his meeting with Thornton, "that we cannot hope to see sincere union between them and the Whites." Free Negroes found prejudice "an insurmountable barrier" to their advancement. They lived as if "condemned to drag out their days in a state of servility" while the whites reproached them for want of cleanliness and enterprise. Such a situation would foment "unceasing suspicions, jealousies, and partialities." He imagined an independent African nation with himself as the bounteous, farseeing benefactor. "I think by proper laws they may be made a good and happy people," he declared. "The minds of many Africans are ripe, and their understanding clear." He addressed scores of "regular industrious" free Negroes in New York, Boston, Providence, and Newport, whom he found to be "very desirous of reaching the coast of Guinea." They dreamed of a commonwealth where "their own laws are alone to be regarded . . . and where a man that Nature cloathed with a white skin, shall not, merely on that account, have the right of wielding a rod of iron."

In a manner reminiscent of an earlier Quaker patron-proprietor, William Penn, Thornton combined philanthropy and profit. He would show free Negroes how to achieve independence and wealth along Africa's commercially rich Ivory Coast and, at the same time, show masters a practical means of emancipation. A thriving colony could throttle the slave trade at its source by outbidding the slavers. The rescued Africans, suitably Christianized and apprenticed to the colonists, would work to repay their ransom price. American traders could purchase tropical products hitherto imported from the West Indies. Spices, gold dust, ivory, gums, and dyes would swell the commerce between the United States and Africa. "By proper encouragement and perseverance, a most valuable country would soon become the seat of commerce, of arts and the manufactures, of plenty, of peace, and happiness!" [8]

Anticipating the need of friendly aid from the great sea powers, Thornton proposed to make his "black commonwealth" a neutral nation. He busily wrote to friends in London and Paris and forwarded James Madison's unreserved endorsement to French humanitarians. Emancipation without colonization, Madison stated, would fail to promote the public good or guarantee happiness to the Negro. Prejudice forbade "a compleat incorporation" of the freedman into American society. Color was a "permanent and insuperable" obstacle. "Some proper external receptacle," such as an African colony, was the only solution. Colonization would "forward the abolition of slavery in America." [9]

Thornton's project never materialized. Although Samuel Adams, with whom Thornton said he was "very intimate," gave his endorsement, Thornton failed to persuade Massachusetts legislators to appropriate money for a colony not on the North American continent. Negotiations with French philanthropists produced nothing. His British friends considered the plan immature and rash and begged him not to squander his inheritance on visionary schemes. Recognizing that his motives "spring from a laudable desire," Dr. Lettsom gently reproved Thornton for devising a project "as if all were as virtuous and systematic as thyself: every day will exhibit to thy understanding, the impracticability of that moral perfection of government, which thy imagination has painted." [10]

Meanwhile, Thornton's British friends were organizing an African colonization project that established Sierra Leone. It began as a humanitarian gesture at cleaning up London's slums. In 1786 a group of wealthy philanthropists, led by Granville Sharp, hired Henry Smeathman to recruit the "black poor" of London and lead them to the banks of the Sierra Leone river. The "black poor" consisted of several hundred American slaves freed by British forces during the Revolution. Smeathman had lived on the African coast for a number of years, and for several years he had cherished his own plan for colonization. He once asked Benjamin Franklin's advice about raising money. Franklin told him to take his plan to Boston, where it would receive immediate attention. But Smeathman demurred, saying that he could not "carry my poor brat a-begging from continent to continent on uncertainties." For a time he considered making balloon ascensions, a new and startling wonder of the age, to raise money and advertise his colonization scheme.[11]

Smeathman persuaded a few hundred poverty-stricken Negroes to seek plenty and happiness in Africa. The London philanthropists chartered ships and loaded them with provisions. They also supplied the colonists with wives recruited from red-light districts. The ship delayed sailing when Smeathman suddenly died from a "putrid fever" contracted in the slums. After waiting many weeks on board ship the panicky colonists became fearful that their true destination was the newly established penal colony at Botany Bay. Alarm blurred distinction between colonization and "transportation." The philanthropists, however, insisted there was a distinction and declined to allow their wards to leave ship. Finally, in February of 1787, 350 half-starved and balky emigrants, virtual captives of the London philanthropists, sailed for Africa.[12]

Sierra Leone's early history was even less auspicious than its origin. The London philanthropists, discovering that colonization was far more complex and expensive than prison reform or almsgiving, soon lost control of the colony. Mass desertions, death-dealing fever, hostile natives, and rancorous quarrels among the surviving colonists forced them to surrender the settlement to an English trading company. The new owners promptly revoked all land rights and set about to regiment the colony with counting-house precision. The trading company also failed. In 1794 a French war squadron raided and destroyed the settlement. Frequent insurrections among the perennially dissatisfied settlers brought the company to near-bankruptcy. Before complete ruin struck, the company succeeded in unloading the faltering colony on the British government. After 1808, Sierra Leone operated as a crown colony.[13]

The African Institution, established in 1807, exerted great influence in Sierra Leone's affairs. It was a private society professing charitable interest in the welfare of Africans and the suppression of the slave trade. Many of its members and officers included former shareholders in the defunct trading company. By courtesy of the British government, the African Institution managed the colony's trade and preserved it for British interests. As a consequence, American traders found themselves excluded or restricted. Failure to come to terms with the directors of the African Institution meant confiscation or heavy fines.[14]

One American trader attempted to penetrate the British market at Sierra Leone with an offer to bring free Negro emigrants from the United States. Paul Cuffee, a half-Negro, half-Indian Quaker from Cuttyhunk Island, Massachusetts, began his career as the captain of a small coasting vessel that plied the rivers of Connecticut, Virginia, and Maryland. Shrewd, brawny, and accustomed to hard work, he had prospered—sometimes as a plaster of Paris or wheat merchant and sometimes as a cod fisherman and whaler. In time he had risen to the ownership of a large ocean ship. In 1808 he began looking to Africa for markets.[15]

"The travail of my soul is that Africa's inhabitants may be favored with reformation," Cuffee once declared. He corresponded with members of the African Institution and in 1811 visited Sierra Leone and England. He persuaded officers of the African Institution that Sierra Leone needed "good sober steady characters" to hasten prosperity. He volunteered to carry Negro farmers, artisans, and mechanics from the United States in return for trading privileges at the colony. The African Institution agreed to the plan and induced the British government to grant Cuffee a trading license. Cuffee thereupon formed the Friendly Society at Sierra Leone headed by John Kizell, a Sierra Leone merchant and former American slave. The society served as Cuffee's commercial depot in Africa.[16]

Cuffee returned to the United States and unveiled his scheme to free Negro spokesmen in New York, Philadelphia, and Baltimore. Daniel Coker, a teacher in the African School in Baltimore, James Forten, a prosperous sailmaker in Philadelphia, and the Reverend Peter Williams, Jr., of New York, organized miniature African Institutions in each place. They urged free Negroes to emigrate to Africa. Cuffee planned one voyage a year, but the War of 1812 delayed his sailing.

Undaunted, Cuffee petitioned Congress for special permission to trade with the enemy's colony. He argued that his was to be a voyage of benevolence designed to "promote habits of industry, sobriety, and frugality, among the natives of that country." On January 10, 1814, Senator Christopher Gore of Massachusetts brought in a bill granting Cuffee's request. Gore's bill passed the Senate and went to the House of Representatives, where it survived two readings, but a committee deemed it "impolitic" to relax the embargo for an individual project, however benevolent. Defenders and opponents hotly debated the bill's merits. Proponents, led by Congressman Timothy Pickering of Massachusetts, pictured Cuffee as a noble-minded philanthropist. The creation of "an institution which would invite the emigration of free blacks" would directly benefit the United States in ridding the land of "a part of our population which we could well spare." Opponents sneered that it was unnecessary to carry a cargo in order to propagate the Gospel. They sarcastically observed that Sierra Leone could procure benevolent deeds from Great Britain, the "bulwark of our religion." Besides, they reasoned, the enemy government would never consent to receive Cuffee's ship unless it was advantageous to do so. In the final vote, the House killed the bill, 65 to 72. Cuffee had to wait until the end of the war to carry out his scheme.[17]

By that time conditions had changed. Early in 1816, when Captain Cuffee landed thirty-eight American Negroes at Freetown, he found that his trading concessions had evaporated. The governor accepted the emigrants and issued land grants near Freetown, but for Cuffee there was nothing. The peace treaty excluded American vessels from the British colonial trade. He risked confiscation of his ship by being in British waters. He hastily departed to avoid seizure. In all the luckless venture cost him $4,000. A few months later, in September, 1817, death overtook him. His friends praised his "purest motives of benevolence" in shipping Negroes to the "land of his forefathers." Philanthropists eulogized his work as proof that free Negroes desired to emigrate.[18] More important, Cuffee had reached a large audience with arguments favoring colonization. Even as he lay dying, a group of benevolent-minded men were building a society to colonize free Negroes in Africa. Had Cuffee lived another decade he would have seen a large colonization movement spread across the republic.

II

THIS SCHEME IS FROM GOD

————◆•••◆————

IN THE YEARS following the War of 1812 scores of meliorative or "benevolent" societies were spilling over the country. A decade before only a handful of missionary and charitable societies ministered to the irreligious, the destitute, and the friendless. But by 1820 there were hundreds of local Sunday school, tract, Bible, charitable, and domestic and foreign missionary societies. National organizations, staffed by professional executive secretaries, traveling agents, and skillful editors and supported by numerous auxiliaries in every state, were just coming into existence. By 1830 the American Bible Society, one of the larger voluntary associations, claimed 645 auxiliaries. Other "American" organizations included the American Sunday School Union, the American Tract Society, the American Peace Society, the American Temperance Union, the American Board of Commissioners for Foreign Missions, the American Education Society, the American Home Missionary Society, the American Seamen's Friend Society, and the American Society for Meliorating the Condition of the Jews.

The rise of the benevolent societies was part of the evangelical zeal that inspired nineteenth-century Calvinism. The Great Awakening had spawned a generation of clerical and lay leaders who rejected passionless Calvinism for a new, evangelical emphasis. At first revivals were prime tools in spreading the faith. In many communities periodic awakenings built large congregations and strong churches. But revivals were too sporadic and limited in scope to assure continuity and rhythmic growth. Voluntary associations, such as missionary, Bible, and Sunday school societies, eventually took precedence in the task of extending the faith. These church-related groups enjoyed continuous existence, reached larger audiences through the printed word, and gathered ample donations from well-wishers.

A theological doctrine formulated before the turn of the century gave forward impetus to the benevolent society movement. The Reverend Dr. Samuel Hopkins of Rhode Island, who had briefly experimented with Negro colonization, was the disciple of Jonathan Edwards. He elaborated and popularized Edwards's theological tenets and taught that the quintessence of God's moral nature was selfless or "disinterested" love for his creatures. His elect shared this altruistic disposition. Good works betokened a man's true moral nature, but they had to be "disinterested"—that is, free from any taint of personal benefit. This was the doctrine of "disinterested benevolence." An act of seeming generosity, one of Hopkins's followers warned, "even when it does real good . . . is of no avail to him who performs it" if it originated from some "sinister motive."

The measure of disinterested benevolence was the degree to which the good deed promoted the "public good" or "general welfare." Truly disinterested benevolence, Hopkins said, "is pleased with the public interest, the greatest good and happiness of the whole." Thus benevolence had social utility, and in effect Hopkins was using the rhetoric of theology to explain basic social concepts. He cast his definition of social perfection in terms of the long-awaited millennium. This was the hackneyed "Redeemer's kingdom" so loved by sermon writers; "the last grand scene of the drama of human existence," as one Princeton-bred clergyman termed it; "the season of universal change and perfect reformation," said another. The new era would begin when mankind accepted God's moral leadership. The world would ripen into a vast theocracy directed by divinely appointed magistrates, and in the new order clergymen would command places of power. In Hopkins's perfect society there would be no poverty, intemperance, or ignorance of Christianity; no infidelity, doctrinal disputes, slavery, war, or crime. These evils were major obstacles to the achievement of the millennial era. It was the duty of every benevolent man to improve society and remove the evils that clogged the way to holy perfection.[1]

The melioristic doctrine of benevolence, ideological ancestor of a later "Social Gospel," was a powerful summons for deeds promoting the general welfare. Only collective action (what Tocqueville called "the principle of association," the Reverend Dr. William Channing termed "the principle of combination," and the Presbyterian General Assembly named "the social principle") was needed to make a social movement. When institutionalized in scores of societies, the doctrine of benevolence became a potent tool for systematically evangelizing thousands and exerting a degree of influence over the body politic seldom attempted in the United States.[2] It released a deep-flowing current of evangelical zeal. With martial fervor, benevolent societies fixed upon infidelity, indigence, and ignorance of Christian teachings as prime targets in the crusade to win the Redeemer's kingdom. One Congregationalist clergyman joyously hailed the new societies as evidence that "the peaceful banner of Jesus is again unfurled." Christians were girding themselves for a mighty battle, and each society was a weapon in the arsenal of orthodoxy.

Self-appointed almoners concentrated on the poor classes of the cities and towns. There were societies to prevent pauperism, intemperance, vice, and immorality. The blind, the deaf-mute, the crippled, orphans, widows, and fallen women were objects of benevolent associations. Other meliorative agencies concentrated on sailors who loitered in port cities, Indians who dwelt in ignorance of evangelical Calvinism, and Jews who had not embraced Christian teachings. Church missionary societies sent young clergymen to carry the message of salvation to Burma, Ceylon, Smyrna, and "Owyhee." At home the societies distributed Bibles and tracts and conducted Sunday schools for adults and children. Others built asylums. Some distributed old clothing, operated soup kitchens, or collected money for the new seminaries at Andover and Princeton. Ladies' auxiliaries sewed garments and held bazaars.[3]

In short, the evangelical-inspired societies attempted to touch every class or group that did not fit into the ideal of a homogeneous, Protestant, Bible-reading, industrious society. One clergyman summed up the movement as a militant campaign pledged to leave "no degree of vice unreclaimed, and no form of misery unrelieved;

to throw into every hut of poverty, and into every retreat of ignorance . . . the comforts and blessings of religion, the salutary
restraints of moral discipline, and the knowledge and worship of
the only true God." A renegade member of the crusading societies, the Reverend Calvin Colton, charged that the societies sought
to create a "dynasty of opinion" by manipulating "the two capital
conservative elements indispensable to the permanency of the
American Government and its institutions"—education and religion. The societies were a "stupendous spiritual dynasty" working
to supplant the authority of the government with Calvinist tenets.[4]

The Reverend Robert Finley of Baskingridge, New Jersey, took
note of the growing number of free blacks in his neighborhood
and wondered how religious men could prevent them from falling
into pauperism, vice, and infidelity. He was dismayed to find that
free blacks in his parish lacked any knowledge of the Bible, the
sheet anchor of society, and were unable to read the tracts which
he occasionally distributed among the poor. "Their number in-
creases greatly," he observed in 1816, "and their wretchedness
too." [5] More than 1,500 free Negroes lived in Finley's Somerset
county—more than any other county in New Jersey. In a thirty-
year period, New Jersey's free black population had almost quad-
rupled, and the same trend was evident in other states. In 1790
there had been less than sixty thousand free Negroes in the United
States. By 1820 there were a quarter million.[6]

Finley found that distributing Bibles and tracts did not alter
the Negroes' social status or bestow equality. "Every thing connected with their condition, including their colour, is against
them," he asserted. Removal from the United States was the only
solution. Among friends in Princeton, New York, and Philadelphia, Finley spoke of establishing a great benevolent society
for colonizing free Negroes in Africa.

Robert Finley was the son of an immigrant Scottish yarn merchant. His father was a close friend of John Witherspoon, president of Princeton College, and in 1783, at the age of eleven, young
Finley enrolled at Nassau Hall. The teachings of the venerable
Witherspoon, his son-in-law Samuel Smith, and Ashbel Green,
then a tutor, persuaded Finley to make his career in the Presbyterian church. After ordination in 1795, he took a small church in

Baskingridge, not far from Princeton, and there he served for twenty-two years as minister of the congregation and master of the local academy. Some of his students later became national figures—Samuel Southard, secretary of the Navy, senator, and governor of New Jersey; Theodore Frelinghuysen, senator from New Jersey, candidate for United States vice-president in 1844, and afterwards president of Rutgers; Robert Field Stockton, aggressive naval officer who won fame in the Mexican war as the captor of Los Angeles and later senator from New Jersey. Finley's boys learned their lessons from the Bible. It was the textbook in all his courses, and he once threatened to run another schoolmaster out of town unless he too adopted the Bible. The country academy prospered. Enrollment rose to fifty, and the school in 1800 moved into a new, brick building.[7]

Finley's reputation as a dynamic clergyman also grew. By leading occasional revivals he built the slim congregation at Baskingridge into one of the strongest churches in the New Brunswick presbytery. The Presbyterian General Assembly of 1815 praised Finley's work. His wife brought him a dowry of influential connections within the church that smoothed the way to greater distinction. Esther Caldwell Finley was the daughter of the Reverend and Mrs. James Caldwell, church martyrs killed by the British. Her foster father was New Jersey's wealthy Elias Boudinot, onetime president of Congress, an associate of Alexander Hamilton, and a Federalist officeholder under Washington. Since the turn of the century Boudinot had turned to church activities, becoming the foremost layman in Presbyterian councils. For many years he held the presidency of the Presbyterian General Assembly and dominated Princeton's board of trustees. In 1815 the assembly made Finley a director of Princeton's new theological seminary.[8]

The rapid growth of the benevolent societies attracted Finley's attention. Many of his associates and relatives were building the great meliorative societies. In 1816, Elias Boudinot founded the large and influential American Bible Society, and Finley's brother-in-law, John E. Caldwell of New York city, edited a weekly journal that advertised scores of charitable and benevolent societies. Caldwell was Boudinot's chief lieutenant in the Bible society. Finley's colleagues, Edward Dorr Griffin, John Brodhead Romeyn, and Gardiner Spring, were busily engaged in promoting benevolent works. The General Assembly often praised the growing societies, rapturously noting that they proliferated with undreamed "vigor, extension, and success." "The social principle is mighty in its operations," the Assembly intoned. "It constitutes a powerful law of nature. When sanctioned by religion, and consecrated to the immediate service of God, what results of high importance and holy advantage may not be expected from it?" [9]

By 1816 Finley was looking for a benevolent cause with which he might identify himself. Early that year he told Professor Archibald Alexander of Princeton that "When I consider what many others have effected for the benefit of their suffering fellow-creatures at an earlier age than mine, I am humbled and mortified to think how little I have done." Not long thereafter he announced that he intended to establish a colonization society that would meliorate the condition of free Negroes by removing them to Africa. He sought advice and aid from rich men in Philadelphia and New York. He told wealthy John P. Mumford of New York city, a friend of benevolent causes, that methodical colonization of free Negroes would both improve their condition and solve the larger problem of their future in America. A colony similar to Sierra Leone, with regular packet lines, would induce many to go. Our forefathers, he remarked, brought the Negroes to American soil and "we are bound if possible to repair the injuries" inflicted on Africa. Colonization would have a threefold effect: "We should be cleared of them," Africa would receive "partially civilized and Christianized" settlers, and the Negroes could enjoy a "better situation." He asked Mumford to consider uniting a substantial number of "rich and benevolent" men in a colonization society. Colonization, he said, was a monumental effort requiring a grand system and careful planning—a task perfectly suited to a benevolent association. Skeptics told him the plan was visionary, but he resolutely answered, "I know this scheme is from God!" [10]

For the next few months Finley spent his spare moments elaborating his colonization plan and seeking support from colleagues engaged in other works of benevolence. In the fall of 1816 he unveiled his ideas to the New York and New Jersey Synod. The synod had created the African Education Society for the purpose of opening a training school for Negro preachers and teachers. Their primary work would be "correcting the morals and manners of their brethren in our cities and large towns." At Finley's request the school's directors agreed also to train missionaries and magistrates for his proposed African colony. They pictured the Niger as the future home of a civilization rivaling that of the Thames. There "sable hands will strike the lyre, and weave the silken web." [11]

The agent selected to raise money for the African Education Society was Samuel John Mills. At thirty-three he was a professional traveling agent for numerous benevolent societies and perhaps the best-known money gatherer of his time. From youth he was interested in missionary work. His father, a Congregational clergyman, edited the *Connecticut Evangelical Magazine,* an early missionary journal. In his student days at Williams, Yale, and later Andover Theological Seminary, young Mills had ignited revivals and devised missionary projects. With three other students he petitioned the Massachusetts General Association of Congregational Churches to establish the first foreign missionary society in the United States, the mammoth American Board of Commissioners for Foreign Missions. His classmates were among the earliest American missionaries to India, Ceylon, and Burma. By the time of his ordination in 1815, he had twice toured the American West for several domestic missionary and Bible societies. Benevolent society work was his métier. He helped organize the United Foreign Society and the Presbyterian Missionary Society. In 1816 he cooperated with Elias Boudinot in founding the American Bible Society, bewailing the scarcity of Bibles in the West as a "foul blot on our national character." Mills's attention next turned to the "new missionary field" among the urban poor. In New York city he launched a Marine Bible Society and looked into projects for meliorating the condition of free blacks.

His attitude toward social problems accorded with the doctrine of benevolence. "If an evil exists in a community," he warned, "a remedy must be sought, especially if it be an evil generally and necessarily increasing in its unhappy effect." Without exertions "to redress the grievance," the problem would only become "more hopeless." His opinion that the free Negro was an anomaly in American society exactly paralleled Robert Finley's. He too believed that systematic colonization would strengthen society and benefit the emigrating blacks. Two years before, he had toyed with the idea of a Negro colony in Ohio, Indiana, or Illinois. Such an experiment would prepare Negro leaders for the task of founding a larger colony beyond the Mississippi or along the African coast. He asked Paul Cuffee's opinion and discussed the plan with a few free Negroes. Learning of Finley's plan to create a benevolent society, he agreed to advertise it on his tour for the African Education Society. He found that collections were larger when he stressed the link between the African school and colonization.[12]

While Mills toured the middle Atlantic states and spread the news that a colonization society was forthcoming, Robert Finley polished his arguments for colonization. He solicited Paul Cuffee's advice and consulted his Princeton friends. In November, 1816, at a small meeting of townspeople, professors, and students at Princeton, Finley unveiled his scheme. His society was to be unique among benevolent associations in that it would depend largely on federal assistance. He proposed to establish the national society in Washington, D.C., among politicians and men of influence. The society would ask Congress and the president to secure suitable territory in Africa and help finance the removal of all volunteer emigrants. The college audience promptly responded with resolutions declaring that colonization would help free blacks "rise to that condition to which they are entitled by the laws of God and nature." It voted to petition the New Jersey legislature to seek congressional adoption of Finley's scheme. Another audience at Trenton gave blessings to the plan.[13]

Melioration played a large part in Finley's brief for colonization. Declaring that Negroes were capable of improvement and self-government, Finley stated that equality was impossible as long as they remained among whites. They were sons of Africa by color, temperament, and fortune, and God had destined them to dwell in Africa. "The friends of man will strive in vain to raise them to a proper level while they remain among us," he warned. Entrenched prejudice and a sense of inferiority conspired against any real improvement. Only in Africa, the "land of their fathers," could "Africans," as Finley insisted on calling all Negroes, find true freedom and equality. There they could enjoy unimpeded incentive to become industrious and virtuous. "Their contracted minds will then expand and their natures rise." A new hope for "place and power" would "create the feeling that they are men."

Removal of free Negroes would also forward the "general good." "If there is not reason to believe that it would be for the general benefit," he asserted, "the idea ought to be given up and the scheme rejected." The free Negro population was "unfavorable to our industry and morals" and removal would save society from "many a pang," such as "the intermixture of the different colours" and the burden of pauperism. He argued that colonization would benefit every state, especially southern states. Besides removing the blacks, colonization would be a "happy and progressive" means for ending slavery—one that would avoid southern fears that emancipation was dangerous.

Finley also urged colonization as a method of carrying the germs of civilization and Christianity to Africa. Viewed as a missionary enterprise, it would fix "a seat of liberal learning in Africa from which the rays of knowledge might dart across those benighted regions." Africa was a grieving mother who would "forget her sorrows . . . and . . . bless the hands of her benefactors" for returning her kidnapped children. Americans owed a moral debt which they could pay by transporting thousands of African progeny "who have learned the arts of life and are softened by the power of true religion." They could tame "the wild and wandering people who now roam over that great section of the globe."

Finley pointed to Sierra Leone as a providentially inspired experiment "designed by God to obviate every difficulty, to silence objections, and point out the way in which every obstacle may be removed." A private society of "virtuous and pious" men could begin a colony, just as British philanthropists had launched Sierra Leone, but responsibility for sustaining the colony ultimately belonged to the entire nation. The whole nation shared national guilt for slavery, "the great violation of the laws of nature." Only the nation's representatives could make the "atoning sacrifice" and correct "injuries done to humanity by our ancestors." Moreover, only the councils of the federal government were sagacious enough to adjust "the various interests which ought to be consulted" in so important an undertaking.

He waved aside all doubts as to the propriety of colonial holdings by a nation so recently freed from foreign shackles and dedicated in war to oppose colonialism. The colonies of ancient Greece and Rome gave "strength and lustre" to the metropoles, he said. Modern nations, such as Spain, France, Portugal, and Great Britain, maintained African stations near the rivers Gambia, Senegal, Sierra Leone, and Congo. The United States was destined to "extend the empire of liberty and Christian blessings to surrounding nations." Americans could throttle any international "jealousies" with appeals to justice and humanity.

The Baskingridge clergyman ventured no guess as to the possible cost of removal and colonization, but he conceded that it might prove "considerable." It was up to Congress to discover "some means of lightening," perhaps of "re-paying" the initial cost. Free Negroes with property could finance their own emigration and American warships could transport them. The very poor could buy passage by indenting themselves. Finally, the colony, "if wisely formed," could bring profits in the form of trade and commerce. Commercial penetration of the vast African interior promised returns that would "more than compensate for every expense." As evidence, he cited the African Institution's reports about Sierra Leone. Exclusive of the slave trade, imports and exports for that single colony nearly equaled the value of trade with the whole coast of Africa prior to the abolition of the slave trade.

Finley rounded off his arguments with earnest appeals to patriotism and benevolence. The age was "big with events." Man was learning the lesson of freedom and happiness. America already enjoyed "every blessing civil and religious," Europe was slowly reforming her corrupt governments, and in Asia "gloomy and dread superstitions" were tottering before the blows of Christian missionaries. Now it was Africa's turn, and Africa looked to America for salvation. Her bosom "begins to warm with hope and her heart to beat with expectation and desire." The "land of liberty" could not disappoint a sorrowful mother "panting for the return of her absent sons and daughters." "Happy America," chanted Finley, "if she shall endeavor not only to rival other nations in arts and arms, but to equal and exceed them in the great cause of humanity." [14]

His many-faceted arguments appealed to those who wished to uplift free Negroes, those who hoped to expand missionary work to all corners of the globe, those who groped for painless systems of emancipation, and those who perceived the glint of commercial advantage beneath the froth of religious phrases. The success of the whole scheme depended on federal sponsorship. The Reverend Mr. Finley tucked his manuscript plan for bettering American society into his waistcoat and journeyed to Washington, D.C., to woo the "representatives of this great and free people."

III

CLOSE TO THE NATIONAL VAULTS

WHEN Robert Finley arrived in Washington city in December, 1816, the nation's capital still bore many signs of a growing village. The valiant efforts of Americans to ape imperial splendor of European cities amused foreign visitors. Americans might call it republican simplicity, but the exaggeratedly broad vacant streets, the grassy avenues, the infinite stretches of weedy parks and empty *plaisances*, and the unfinished Capitol and public buildings bearing the scars of a British demolition squad brought smiles to the faces of European visitors. The Portuguese minister remarked somewhat tactfully that Washington was a "city of magnificent spaces." Houses and buildings clustered about Pennsylvania Avenue, a raw, muddy strip one hundred and sixty feet wide, reaching about a mile from Capitol Hill to the darkened ruins of the executive mansion. The mall added to the sense of spaciousness even if its marshy quality did not suggest grandeur. The low, wet places nurtured "bilious fevers" that periodically racked the inhabitants. Most of Washington's eight thousand inhabitants were poor Irish laborers and Negroes.

The larger, wealthier cities of New York, Philadelphia, Baltimore, and Boston were most suitable centers for Finley's benevolent society. Rich commercial and trading classes in those cities provided the sinews of associations dependent upon voluntary gifts and donations. Washington was not a commercial center. Its leading citizens were landed gentry, public functionaries, and politicians. From its creation Washington was a city dedicated to political matters.

Even the capital's social life revolved around politics. Each year the city languished until the politicians returned from the hustings. Their arrival in December, 1816, coinciding with the meeting of Congress, signaled the opening of the social season. The president's "drawing room evening" assembled the highest officers of the republic. Social arbiters followed suit with endless rounds of parties, levees, and teas. Their guests consumed sweetmeats, ices, chilled wines, and steaming negus concocted from sweetened wines, fruit juices, and spices. For daytime diversion the elite, with almost studied effeteness, lounged in the galleries of Congress and listened to their favorite orators debate the momentarily controversial Salary Act.[1]

The preeminence of political matters and the whirrings of social affairs did not lend Washington the air of a community with pious or holy pretensions. One visiting clergyman tartly asserted that piety among congressmen ebbed low. "The wickedness of Congress, and the horrible effect of its influence is described by all as truly awful." The religious, he alleged, were "tired, disgusted, and horrified." [2]

Unlikely as Washington may have been, the Reverend Robert Finley had chosen his base deliberately. His proposed benevolent society would require large amounts of money for the titanic task of colonizing thousands of Negroes in Africa. He would erect his society close to the vaults of the United States treasury, and, if possible, recruit its guardians as members.

Finley carried letters of introduction to President James Madison, a fellow Princetonian, and other department heads. His most helpful and influential ally proved to be his brother-in-law, Elias Boudinot Caldwell, Clerk of the Supreme Court. Together they called a meeting of prominent businessmen, politicians, planters, and clergymen in the Washington area.

Finley was fortunate in having the help of a man of Caldwell's position and sympathy. Forty years old, dignified and mannerly, Elias Caldwell had grown up and prospered under the careful tutelage of his namesake, Elias Boudinot of New Jersey. Caldwell attended Princeton, studied law with his venerable patron, and secured an appointment as assistant clerk of the Supreme Court. In 1800, at twenty-four, he became chief clerk. For the next quarter century Caldwell served the court, practiced law, and entered business affairs in the District. He met all of the prominent lawyers and politicians who came to Washington between 1800 and 1824. His offices in the Capitol placed him in the heart of the Republic's political affairs. From his fashionable home on Pennsylvania Avenue he enlarged his influence. Henry Clay, John Calhoun, Daniel Webster, and General Lafayette dined at his table. When the British burned the Capitol in 1814, he converted his home into temporary quarters for the Supreme Court, and the justices continued to meet there until the Capitol was rebuilt.[3]

Caldwell shared Finley's attitudes and convictions, ardently supporting the evangelical crusade. As the son of a martyr-hero of the Presbyterian Church and the foster son of its foremost layman, Caldwell had imbibed deeply at the fountain of Calvinist orthodoxy. Following Boudinot's leadership, he guided the local Bible society and joined various charitable organizations in the District. He conducted revival meetings that more staid Presbyterians found rather "methodist" in style and fervor.[4]

Upon hearing Finley's colonization proposal Caldwell agreed to forward the project. He enlisted his close friend Francis Scott Key, a well-to-do lawyer in the District. Slim, clean-shaven, well-attired, the thirty-eight-year-old Key bore a distinctly aristocratic air reflecting his background. Son of a wealthy patriot and nephew of Philip Barton Key, a rich loyalist turned Federalist, young Key had known only wealth, prestige, and distinction. After attending aristocratic St. John's College in Annapolis, he took up law, married the granddaughter of Maryland's royal governor Edward Lloyd, and moved to modish Georgetown, where he inherited his uncle's prosperous law practice. His fame as author of "The Star-spangled Banner" outlived his reputation as an attorney. By 1816 Key was one of the chief citizens of the District.[5]

Like Caldwell, Key was interested in the benevolent society movement. As a young man he had looked for a career in politics. His uncle was a Federalist sachem and his brother-in-law, Roger B. Taney, was a promising Federalist politician in Frederick, Maryland. But the War of 1812 and the eclipse of the Federalists dashed Key's ambitions. He regarded politics, with its party maneuvering and factional bloodletting, as slightly below gentlemen of breeding and grace. He considered the ministry or college teaching but eventually accepted John Randolph of Roanoke's advice to stand by the law. Key agreed with the gloomy Randolph that "the state of society is radically vicious" and that demogogues and rascals had made politics an anathema for talented men. Such a condition of society, Key concluded, craved the healing balm of virtue, order, and faith that only farsighted men could provide. He called for the building of Lancasterian schools, the resuscitation of churches, and the exaltation of the "benevolent, religious man." He recommended that "every country gentleman of worth" provide his neighbors with examples of benevolence. "Legislate not for the next elections, but for the next century," he cried.[6] Key followed his own prescription for reforming his countrymen. He became a pillar of the American Bible Society, of which he was a vice-president for twenty-five years, the American Sunday School Union, of which he was a manager, and the American Colonization Society, in which he played a major part for many years.

Prior to Finley's arrival in Washington, Caldwell and Key won a measure of renown as friends of the free blacks. When Philadelphia physician Jesse Torrey, Jr., came to Washington in 1816 to sue for the freedom of a group of free Negroes kidnapped into slavery, Key volunteered his legal services. Caldwell and others advertised the case and took up collections among Washington's leading citizens.[7]

In December, 1816, Caldwell, Key, and Finley joined talents in raising support for a colonization society. Finley published his *Thoughts on Colonization* and distributed the pamphlet among congressmen and senators. He delivered colonization sermons in nearby Georgetown and Alexandria. He persuaded aging Stephen B. Balch, Presbyterian clergyman at Georgetown and graduate of Princeton, to join the movement. David English, formerly Finley's assistant at the Baskingridge Academy and now a Georgetown banker, promised his aid. Caldwell and Key filled the *National Intelligencer* with colonization publicity. A long letter signed "Penn" argued that colonization was a "great national object" that deserved federal assistance. The *Intelligencer* urged men in and near the District to push the project.[8]

Caldwell and Key succeeded in enlisting high-ranking politicians. Eager to associate the revered name of Washington with the movement, Caldwell persuaded Bushrod Washington, veteran Supreme Court justice and present squire of Mount Vernon, to endorse colonization. He also approached the Speaker of the House of Representatives, the shrewd and worldly-wise Henry Clay. At first Clay was skeptical and wished to decline to attend an organizational meeting, but he yielded to persuasion. Key approached his old friend, John Randolph of Roanoke, who consented to attend the same conference.[9]

After several days of intensive canvassing, Finley, Key, and Caldwell secured enough names to assure a meeting. A terse advertisement in the *Intelligencer* extended a general invitation to gentlemen living in Washington, Georgetown, Alexandria, Baltimore, Annapolis, Frederick, and Fredericksburg "who are friendly to the promotion of a plan for colonizing the free blacks of the United States." The meeting took place at the Davis Hotel, December 21, 1816.[10]

A score of men of rank and renown gathered in a small, smoky room in the two-storied brick tavern, the finest in the city. Those present included congressmen, senators, clergymen, and wealthy citizens of the District. Henry Clay presided. Near by sat John Randolph of Roanoke, Richard Bland Lee, younger brother of the illustrious Light Horse Harry, and another brother, Edmund I. Lee, mayor of Alexandria. Congressman Robert Wright of Maryland, John Carlyle Herbert, well-to-do planter and congressman, John Lee, wealthy proprietor of an estate, "Needwood," near Frederick, Maryland, and Senator Robert H. Goldsborough, Maryland Federalist and scion of a famous family, added luster to the assemblage. General Walter Jones, famed as a militia officer in the District and talented constitutional lawyer, John I. Stull, Georgetown banker, Ferdinando Fairfax, early proponent of African colonization, and Thomas Dougherty, Clerk of the House of Representatives, were there. Solemn-faced Daniel Webster was then serving out his last term as a Federalist congressman from New Hampshire.

Several clergymen lent their names to the list of the distinguished. The Reverend William Meade, energetic young Episcopalian and later Bishop of Virginia, brought his friend the Reverend William H. Wilmer, rector of St. Paul's, Alexandria, and soon after one of the founders of the Virginia Theological Seminary. Square-jawed Stephen B. Balch, the District's Presbyterian patriarch, had ridden over from Georgetown. Samuel J. Mills had reached Washington only the night before. On his arrival he had joined Finley, Caldwell, and Key in a small prayer meeting for the success of the society they were about to launch.[11]

The men who sat before Henry Clay were sedate, honorable, judicious gentlemen. Nothing in their characters betokened a visionary or impractical turn of mind. As lawyers, politicians, clergymen, and businessmen—as aristocrats and leaders of opinion—they appreciated well-formed judgments and cautious assertions. Many probably shared Clay's impulse to dismiss colonization as well-meaning but impractical. They attended the meeting because they hoped to find a painless way to remove the Negro from the United States.

Clay called the meeting to order and gave a speech that echoed Finley's *Thoughts on Colonization*. He frankly observed that free Negroes "neither enjoyed the immunities of freemen, nor were they subject to the incapacities of slaves." Their condition and "unconquerable prejudices" prevented amalgamation with whites. It was "desirable . . . both as it respected them, and the residue of the population of the country, to drain them off." There was a "peculiar moral fitness" in restoring them to "the land of their fathers." He pointed to Sierra Leone's "gradual and steady progress" as a working model for American colonizationists. "We have their experience before us," he said. "Can there be a nobler cause," he demanded in peroration style, "than that which, whilst it proposed to rid our country of a useless and pernicious, if not dangerous portion of its population, contemplates the spreading of the arts of civilized life, and the possible redemption from ignorance and barbarism of a benighted quarter of the globe!"

In less flowery words Clay turned to slavery. Colonization was for free Negroes, not slaves. He bluntly warned that colonization must avoid the "delicate question" of emancipation. Men of the West and South, he asserted, had attended the meeting upon this important condition. Clay's plain-spoken warning was a rebuke to Finley's claim that colonization would eventually extinguish slavery.[12]

Elias Caldwell underscored Finley's arguments that colonization would benefit American civil institutions, morals, and habits. The free Negro population was "a monument of reproach to those sacred principles of civil liberty" and an explicit contradiction of the spirit of the Declaration of Independence. If Negroes remained in the United States, they would never become valuable citizens. Prejudice deprived them of incentives to make "great and noble achievements." Education, instead of making them industrious, moral men, would only imbue them with a "higher relish" for privileges and duties forever denied them. "The more you improve the condition of these people, the more you cultivate their minds," he lamented, "the more miserable you make them." The alternative—keeping them in permanent "degradation and ignorance" and brutish docility—was distasteful. Rather than adopt "such slavish doctrines" he urged colonization. He echoed Clay's dictum, assuring his listeners that Finley's plan carefully avoided "all those nice and delicate questions" of slavery.

John Randolph of Roanoke could not resist adding his remarks. Quite aside from "those higher and nobler motives" of benevolence, colonization would "materially tend to secure" slave property. Slaveowners believed that free blacks were "one of the greatest sources of insecurity, and also of unprofitableness" to slave labor. These "promoters of mischief" excited "a feeling of discontent" among slaves, served as couriers in insurrection plots, and acted as "depositories of stolen goods." Slaveowners had a special interest in "throwing this population out of the bosom of the people." John Taylor of Caroline, he noted, once called the free Negro a "bug-bear" to manumission, but colonization would open the door to hundreds of manumissions.[13]

With the area of activity defined, the men voted to establish a colonization society "for the purpose of collecting information" and assisting the federal government in formulating and launching a colony in Africa "or such other place as Congress shall deem most expedient." On December 28, 1816, they assembled in the hall of the House of Representatives, adopted a constitution, and took the title "American Society for Colonizing the Free People of Color in the United States." A few days later, fifty men signed the new constitution and elected officers. Bushrod Washington became president of the society. The thirteen vice-presidents were highly placed politicians or men of national reputation: Secretary of the Treasury William Crawford; Speaker of the House Henry Clay; William Phillips of Massachusetts; Colonel Henry Rutgers of New York; John Eager Howard, Samuel Smith, and John C. Herbert of Maryland; John Taylor of Caroline; General Andrew Jackson; Robert Ralston and Richard Rush, Pennsylvania; General John Mason, District of Columbia; and, in recognition of his early role, the Reverend Robert Finley.[14]

The actual responsibilities fell to the board of managers and the executive secretary. Board members included Francis S. Key, Walter Jones, the Reverend Stephen B. Balch, William Thornton, the Reverend James Laurie, Edmund I. Lee, John Peter, and the Reverend Obadiah Brown. Elias Caldwell was secretary, and David English, treasurer. In outward appearances the society was a national organization, but its inner core was exclusively local. The managers, secretary, and treasurer all lived in the District.[15]

Their first task was advertising the new society. Boston, Philadelphia, New York, and Baltimore newspapers printed minutes of the meetings signed by Henry Clay. The society's memorial to Congress carried Bushrod Washington's name. The Philadelphia *American Centinel* printed an anonymous letter flattering the new society as the agency for suppressing the slave trade and bringing eventual emancipation. The "insolent and domineering" free Negro would learn to value freedom. The Baltimore *Federal Republican* greeted the society as a move to improve the condition of free Negroes and destroy the slave trade. The editor praised John Randolph's "unanswerable arguments" that colonization safeguarded the slaveowner's property. "We are at a loss to imagine," he said, "what objections can be urged against a proposition, abounding with such genuine philanthropy." [16]

The Boston *Recorder,* a religious journal dedicated to benevolent society activities, fondly watched over the Colonization Society's progress, printed its constitution, memorial, and addresses, and gave space to African subjects, especially Sierra Leone's history, missionary work in West Africa, and curious native traditions. The *National Intelligencer* frequently opened its columns to sanguine articles on colonization prospects in Africa. Extraordinarily warm blessings came from the Georgetown *Messenger*. Colonization promised "a greater influence on the moral condition of the future people of this great Republic, than almost any measure which has been adopted." It would remove threats of insurrection and prevent intermarriage. "Who is there among us," the panegyrist demanded, "that can reconcile ourselves to the idea of such a posterity?" Colonization, compulsory if necessary, would purge the country of "inferior blood." [17]

The most distinguished endorsement came from Virginia's House of Delegates. While examining old records of the state legislature, Charles Fenton Mercer of Loudoun county discovered the hitherto unknown correspondence between President Jefferson and Governor Monroe concerning Virginia's efforts to establish a penal colony in 1801. Mercer disclosed the letters and pressed for the adoption of new resolutions endorsing a federal scheme of colonization similar to Robert Finley's. Meeting in December, 1816, behind closed doors and with the galleries cleared, the House of Delegates adopted Mercer's resolutions asserting that Virginia still advocated "an asylum, beyond the limits of the United States." A new period "when peace has healed the wounds of humanity" had settled upon the world, promising success to a colonization venture. The delegates asked the governor to consult the president for the purpose of obtaining a territory upon the coast of Africa, or upon the shore of the North Pacific "or any place not within the United States or its territories." They directed Virginia's senators and congressmen to work for federal adoption of a colonization scheme.[18]

The Virginia legislature's endorsement did not overawe critics of colonization. An anonymous writer in Washington parodied the society's memorial to Congress in a "counter-memorial." He challenged the colonizationists' motives and sneered that the "self-styled benefactors" had arrogated the right to "decree that other men are miserable." Despite their gentle assurances, he warned, they would not hesitate to make colonization compulsory. With an eye to arousing free Negro opposition, the satirist pictured Africa as a grim land cursed with a "burning sun and torturing insects—poisonous exhalations, corrupted water and unwholesome food." If the colonizationists really looked upon the Negro as an equal being, he asked, why did they not advocate amalgamation as the solution to the race problem? The *Intelligencer* printed the stinging attack, but its editors apologized for the gadfly and his "well-meant irony." [19]

Reaction among some free Negroes was immediate. The bogus "counter-memorial" found its way into the hands of free Negro leaders in Philadelphia, home of several thousand free blacks. James Forten, the Reverend Richard Allen, Absalom Jones, and Robert Douglass called a meeting of their brethren in Bethel Church and adopted resolutions deploring "the unmerited stigma attempted to be cast upon the reputation of the free people of color." They insisted that the United States was their true home. "We will never separate ourselves voluntarily from the slave population of this country." They called colonization a plan to dump free Negroes "into the savage wilds of Africa" and a "circuitous route" back to bondage.

The protest meeting surprised the Colonization Society, for only a year before some of the same Philadelphia Negro leaders had endorsed Paul Cuffee's emigration plan. James Forten, a well-to-do sailmaker, had assisted Cuffee and praised his work. In 1816 he told the British African Institution "we consider ourselves as merely instruments for the furtherance of your views" and he volunteered to serve "in the subordinate capacities" of an emigration agent. At the same time he sought "any exemptions . . . made in favor of this Institution [in Philadelphia], provided it should embark in any commercial enterprize desirable for the purpose of civilizing Africa." [20]

Realizing that the hostility of free Negroes would undermine a colonization project, the Reverend Robert Finley hastened to Philadelphia to allay all apprehensions. He spent several hours talking with leaders of the protest meeting. He came away feeling that the majority now saw colonization as the "fairest prospect" for their melioration. "The more enlightened they were," he reported to the managers, "the more decisively they expressed themselves on the desirableness of becoming a separate people." [21]

This was Finley's last service for the new society. During his December visit to Washington he began negotiations with William H. Crawford and other Georgians for the post of president of the University of Georgia. He accepted the position at the handsome salary of $2,000, but a few months after moving to Georgia he died of fever. Though Clay and others had insisted that colonization was not an emancipation device, Finley had clung to his original proposal and had believed that through it slavery would end in the United States.[22]

Finley's success in quieting free black opposition to colonization was momentary. During the summer of 1817, James Forten called another protest meeting attended by three thousand free Negroes. In an "Address to the Humane and Benevolent Inhabitants of the City and county of Philadelphia," they complained that colonization would deny the benefits of civil and religious instruction to freed slaves. Forten argued that removal would raise the price of slaves and discourage further manumission. "Let not a purpose be assisted which will stay the cause of the entire abolition of slavery." [23]

Philadelphia Quakers also resented the Colonization Society's intrusion upon Negro welfare projects. Since 1790 the Pennsylvania Abolition Society had concentrated on regulating the lives of free Negroes living in Philadelphia. Through a series of committees, especially the "apprenticing committee," it had supervised education, work, and activities of the poor black. Roberts Vaux, a distinguished Quaker abolitionist, flatly declared to Thomas Clarkson, the British philanthropist, that the Colonization Society "originated in the bosom of the Slave States" as a scheme for strengthening slavery. He sneered that "a few benevolent men" such as Caldwell and Key exerted small influence in the new society "compared with the mass of unfeeling men, by whom they are surrounded." [24]

Free Negro objections to colonization took a different turn in

Richmond. A "respectable portion" of the free black inhabitants issued a statement agreeing with the Colonization Society that separation would "ultimately tend to the benefit and advantage" of free Negroes, but they did not wish to go to Africa. Instead, they preferred a colony on the Missouri river or any place in the United States that Congress deemed "the most conducive to the public good, and our future welfare." [25]

Meanwhile, the society sped plans to secure federal adoption. On January 14, 1817, two weeks after the Colonization Society organized, John Randolph of Roanoke read the terse memorial signed by Bushrod Washington to the House of Representatives. Its sententious phrases exuded benevolence and patriotism. It spoke of the "low and hopeless condition" of free blacks, "baneful consequences" to society, "moral justice and philanthropy," and "political foresight and civil prudence." It begged Congress to create an African colony so that the whole Negro race may behold "the orient star revealing the best and highest attributes of man." [26]

The memorial went to the Committee on the Slave Trade. A month later, the committee brought in a report that turned down the scheme and suggested an alternative plan for cooperating with the British at Sierra Leone. Paul Cuffee had demonstrated that American Negroes would emigrate to that colony, and Sierra Leone had already surmounted the "first difficulties" and needed additional settlers. Cooperation with the British would save an "extraordinary expenditure of money" and forestall any "collisions and wars" between rival colonies. Sending American emigrants to Sierra Leone would "render its commerce an object of consideration" and therefore the British would have to open their trade to Americans. If the British turned down the proposal, American ministers in Europe could announce their government's intention of creating a neutral colony along the African coast.[27]

The House committee's report counseling delay greatly disappointed the colonizationists. In 1817 there was little reason to expect British consent to open Sierra Leone. Only a few months before, the British navy had seized American ships in Sierra Leone waters, and a British naval officer cruising the coast candidly referred to Americans as "the enemy." [28] Convinced that

Congress was too hesitant to take "efficient and decisive" steps, the managers of the Colonization Society decided to gather more precise information about the African coast and possible colonial sites. They set out to amass data and arguments that Congress could not ignore.

IV

ON AFRICA'S SHORES

———◆◆◆◆►———

THE COLONIZATION SOCIETY, resting all hopes on its formal sup-
plication to Congress, failed to persuade the nation's representatives to adopt African colonization as a national policy. But
momentary defeat in the House of Representatives did not destroy
the fledgling society. The leaders now laid plans to mend their
campaign and frame new arguments for the next Congress. They
agreed that the society had to persuade the "public mind" that
colonization was "both wise and practicable" and deserved "the
power, the aid, and the patronage of the National Government."
They further agreed that they needed first-hand information about
"that country to which all eyes are directed" to reassure both
Congress and the public that Africa was habitable, healthy, fertile, and the natives "well disposed to give every encouragement
to the establishment" of an American colony.

The task of amassing data and issuing publicity fell to the
board of managers. While President Bushrod Washington and
other dignitaries conferred prestige on the new society, lesser-
known men did the routine work and made the basic decisions.
Under the constitution the board of managers was to meet quarterly, collect and transmit data to Congress, and formulate operating policies subject to the approval of the annual meeting.
At first Henry Clay, Bushrod Washington, and William Crawford took turns at presiding, but as the board meetings became
more frequent they ceased to attend. Eventually most of the executive functions devolved upon Secretary Elias Caldwell, who
handled the society's correspondence and acted as liaison between
the board members and the national officers. In the beginning

there were no Colonization Society headquarters, and the managers usually met in the Indian Queen tavern or Brown's tavern.

The managers regarded the printed word as a powerful weapon in the struggle for public acceptance. They thought in terms of tracts rather than periodicals. In the spring of 1817, they issued a neat, twenty-four-page pamphlet containing the society's constitution, its ill-fated memorial, proceedings of the original meetings, and a complimentary description of Sierra Leone—items that a regular reader of the *National Intelligencer* would quickly recognize. They stressed the benevolent purposes of colonization and boasted the names of the famous men who launched the society. They distributed copies among members of Congress and sent quantities for distribution to the society's vice-presidents in Georgia, Virginia, Maryland, New York, Pennsylvania, and Massachusetts.[1]

Simultaneously they set out to assemble information about Africa. They asked President Monroe to direct the American embassy in London to collect data from the African Institution. They wrote to William Wilberforce, the prime figure in England's large and rich benevolent societies. They asked the "distinguished philanthropist" Thomas Clarkson for specific information about colonial sites along the African coast. The renowned foe of the slave trade replied that there was an island one hundred miles southeast of Sierra Leone which was fertile, well-watered, and inhabited by weak tribes. He urged the American colonizationists to examine Sherbro Island.[2]

But gathering information by correspondence was slow and unsure. The men in England offered hearsay data. In March, 1817, the Reverend Samuel J. Mills, then traveling for the American Bible Society, offered to go to England and Africa on a "mission of inquiry." He would gather information from officials of the African Institution and personally inspect colonial sites, including Sherbro Island, and perhaps procure a parcel of land. He argued that an expedition to Africa would "help to keep the subject alive in the public mind" until the next session of Congress. He persuaded the managers, but they had no money. Estimating that the "mission of inquiry" would cost $5,000, the board issued a request for donations over Bushrod Washington's name. The mission would gather "unquestionable information" for Congress and carry Christianity to the heathen. Appealing to both patriotism and benevolence, the managers asked Americans to give in the name of "the love of our own country, and benevolence of the cause to our suffering fellow men." [3]

Donations came slowly. During the winter of 1816–1817 the first postwar collapse had struck. Handbills alone did not capture $5,000. When he completed his tour for the Bible Society, Mills turned to raising money for his "mission of inquiry." The managers granted him permission to beg money in Baltimore, Philadelphia, and New York. They sent urgent letters to the society's vice-presidents in those cities and importuned them to help Mills.

His method for gathering money was organizing local auxiliaries. In his career he had created scores of local auxiliaries for missionary and Bible societies. Auxiliaries made possible the great national associations that depended on the voluntary donations of individuals scattered over the land. During the summer of 1817, he planted auxiliaries in the rich commercial cities of Philadelphia, New York, and Baltimore. Though the managers looked upon them as expedients in the struggle for federal sponsorship, they conceded that auxiliaries were useful instruments for enlightening the "public mind" on colonization's "great and important objects."

Early in June, 1817, Francis S. Key worked with Mills to organize an auxiliary in Baltimore. They invited men of prestige and position to meet in the Presbyterian church. John Eager Howard, Revolutionary hero, former Federalist governor and senator, figurehead in local charitable associations, and vice-president of the Colonization Society, presided. The drama-loving Key gave a flowery oration in which he painted the glories of a future African civilization. He spoke of "spires of temples glittering in the sun," "harbors shaded by the snowy wings of departing and returning commerce," and "the hum of industry resounding in the streets." He warmed nationalist sentiment, saying that Africans would point to the star-spangled banner in deepest gratitude for the blessings of civilization. With Key's vivid metaphors fresh in mind, the Baltimore men voted to form an auxiliary and raise money for the "mission of inquiry." They named committees to canvass every ward for donations. Officers included John Eager Howard, General William H. Winder, and Robert Goodloe Harper.[4]

Harper was a former senator, Federalist chieftain, and the foremost lawyer in Baltimore. His aristocratic family ties—he was the son-in-law of the rich and venerable Charles Carroll of Carrollton—placed him at the top of Maryland society. Through his efforts Maryland became a colonization stronghold. Shortly after the Baltimore auxiliary formed, he published a lengthy analysis of the benefits of colonization. His *Letter from Gen. Harper, of Maryland, to Elias B. Caldwell, Esq.* elaborated the familiar arguments that prejudice confined free Negroes to an inferior social status, that they "corrupted" slaves and taught them "thievous" habits, that colonization would open "mutually advantageous" commerce with Africa, and that it promised to remove the "great moral and political evil" of slavery. He pointed to sharp economic differences between slave and non-slave states. "The change is seen the instant you cross the line," he declared. In the north labor was honorable, the citizens more prosperous, and public and private improvements more conspicuous. In the south labor was the badge of slavery, and slaves ate more and worked less than free laborers. Colonization was the first step to emancipation, one that would not "unhinge the whole frame of society." He predicted the movement would take root in the middle states and creep slowly to the south and southwest.[5]

While General Harper kept colonization interest burning in Baltimore, agent Mills appealed to Philadelphia for aid. He invited support from Bishop William White, venerable Episcopal leader and staunch supporter of Bible, Sunday school, and missionary societies; the Reverend Jacob Jones Janeway, foremost Presbyterian clergyman in Philadelphia and an official of the General Assembly; the Reverend William Staughton, well-known Baptist educator. They helped him form an auxiliary that claimed wealthy and influential Philadelphia citizens: bank president William Meredith; Samuel Archer, rich importer and China and India trader; Robert Ralston, a director of the bank of the United States and Archer's partner; Richard Dale, retired naval officer, once John Paul Jones's junior lieutenant on the *Bon Homme*

Richard, and now a well-to-do East India and China merchant; and Horace Binney, admirer of Bushrod Washington, constitutional lawyer, and undisputed leader of the Philadelphia bar.[6]

Like the Philadelphia auxiliary, the colonization society in New York city was no less bejeweled with men of prestige. It originated in the mayor's chambers and included men prominently associated with benevolent associations. Presiding was wealthy merchant Divie Bethune, conspicuous in local charity societies and son-in-law of Mrs. Isabella Graham, a pioneer in charity work. Other members were: the Reverend John B. Romeyn, secretary for domestic correspondence of the American Bible Society; the Reverend James Milnor, ex-Federalist congressman and early officer of the American Bible and American Tract societies; Dr. John Griscom, organizer of the Society for the Prevention of Pauperism and Crime and a professor at Queen's College. The Reverend Mr. Romeyn's nephew, John B. Beck, later famous as a physician, was recording secretary. For officers the New York auxiliary selected Henry Rutgers, property magnate and philanthropist; Jeremiah Thompson, one of the country's great ship owners; William B. Crosby, Rutgers's heir and a member of Bible and Seamen's Friends societies; Jonathan Goodhue, prosperous East Indies trader; and William Colgate, rich soap manufacturer who each year gave one-tenth of his net earnings to benevolent associations.[7]

One of the founders of the New York auxiliary, the Reverend Edward Dorr Griffin, was a friend of Robert Finley and secretary of the African Education Society. In a colonization sermon in 1817 he asserted that Negroes deserved the attention of benevolent societies. They were not inherently inferior. He attacked theorists who "cast the Africans into another species, and sorted them with the ape and ourang-outang." Climate, education, habits, customs, and laws shaped men, he declared, and slavery—whether white or black—degraded human beings and accounted for the "present depressed state of the African mind." Colonization could benefit the free Negroes. "The Almighty Deliverer is already on his march to relieve the woes of Africa," he intoned. "A bright day is arising on Africa." [8]

Despite the publicity by Griffin, Harper, Mills, Key, and other colonizationists, donations for the "mission of inquiry" were slow. Mills began to lose hope of reaching England before winter storms churned the Atlantic. Late in the summer of 1817 the managers solicited funds in Alexandria, Georgetown, and Washington. A delegation hopefully appealed to President Monroe to allow Mills to sail with the new American minister to Great Britain. But by the time Richard Rush sailed to his new post the Colonization Society still had not scraped together enough to buy Mills's passage.[9]

Meanwhile, Mills invited another son of Connecticut to accompany him to Africa. He assured Ebenezer Burgess, professor of mathematics and natural philosophy at Burlington College, Vermont, that his knowledge of Spanish would be "eminently useful" to the success of the mission. Burgess readily accepted the offer.[10]

By November, 1817, both men were impatient to sail. Mills proposed sending Burgess ahead while he canvassed New York and Philadelphia for enough money to buy a second passage. The managers ended further delays by borrowing $2,500 from Isaac McKim, "an opulent and public spirited" Baltimore shipper reputed to have a ship on every sea. Shortly after, McKim became a vice-president of the society. The last-minute loan enabled Mills and Burgess to sail together on the *Electra* with enough money to carry them to Africa. They had unshakable confidence that the board could raise enough to bring them back.[11]

The managers directed the pair to collect information in England and procure letters of introduction to the governor of Sierra Leone. Next, they were to visit the African coast near Sierra Leone, paying special attention to Sherbro Island, its soil, climate, and healthfulness. If possible they should get pledges from the Sherbro natives to accept colonists and sell enough land for a settlement. The agents should gather information on rivers and their sources and habitable areas not already claimed by European powers.[12]

Before sailing Mills and Burgess armed themselves with a letter of introduction, signed by Bushrod Washington, to the Duke of Gloucester, patron of the African Institution. Henry Clay supplied an introduction to Admiral Lord Gambier, whom he had met as a commissioner of peace in 1814. Manager William Thornton wrote to Sir Joseph Banks, president of the Royal Society, stressing the necessity of guaranteeing free trade with Africa as a means of infusing that "vast region of moral darkness" with civilization and Christianity. He commended Mills and Burgess as "two respectable Persons on a friendly mission" to the "humane and benevolent" people of England.[13]

Beginning with "a very boisterous passage" across the Atlantic, drama and excitement attended Mills's and Burgess's "mission of inquiry." Near the English channel, a "terrific gale" flayed the ship, drove it from its course, and nearly sank it. The captain ordered the masts cut and the anchor cast, but the cable snapped. The crippled ship floundered in the tempest until it neared a long, jagged reef that shot angry waves high into the air. The captain said a hasty farewell to the *Electra*'s passengers and abandoned ship in a small boat. Instead of crumbling on the snarling reef, the *Electra* glided into calmer waters and drifted three days before approaching the coast of France. Mills and Burgess finally debarked at St. Malo and two weeks later reached London.[14]

The Americans promptly went to work collecting information about Africa and colonization. They sought out William Wilberforce, a saintly figure in the eyes of evangelical crusader Samuel J. Mills. He was the mainspring of the Clapham sect, the gentlemen who oversaw the Church Missionary Society, Bible Society, Religious Tract Society, African Institution, and the campaign to abolish the slave trade. He received them cordially and arranged meetings with high-placed men. Lord Gambier chatted with the agents, expressing his wish that they would receive "every necessary assistance and kindness." Lord Bathurst, Secretary for War and the Colonies, handed them a letter of introduction to the governor of Sierra Leone. The Duke of Gloucester accepted Bushrod Washington's letter, listened to the story of their shipwreck, discussed population and race problems in the United States, and invited them to stop on their return from Africa when the members of the African Institution "would then know better in what manner they could aid the American Society." [15]

Mills and Burgess spent a month in England. On February 2, 1818, they sailed for Sierra Leone. Mills's health had wavered in

England's winter dampness, and he looked forward to the warmth of Africa. The tall, lean agent had a dry cough that betokened consumption. On the long voyage they spent many hours studying French, Spanish, Portuguese, and Arabic to "facilitate their intercourse" with colonial officials and tribal chieftains. They pored over a dozen or more travel books, hoping to glean a detailed picture of Africa. When their ship sighted the low, shelvy coast of Africa on March 12, 1818, Mills excitedly pencil-sketched the view, and, faithful to his instructions, he noted the military and commercial characteristics of each settlement along the coast. He compared the broad rivers to the great Mississippi and the African prairies to those he had crossed in Illinois and Indiana.[16]

Mills was less a collector of African data and more a student and admirer of British benevolence. From the moment he reached Sierra Leone he vibrated with missionary zeal. As the ship slid into the wide mouth of the Sierra Leone river, he spied a church high on Leicester mountain overlooking Freetown. He solemnly predicted that "the time is coming when the dwellers in these vales and on these mountains will sing hosannas to the Son of David." For a week the two Americans toured Freetown and its surrounding villages. They estimated that the whole population was twelve thousand and Freetown's population five thousand. The picture of thousands of well-fed, educated Africans rescued from slavers inspired the Americans. Schoolmasters and chaplains, supported by benevolent societies, gave two thousand students daily instruction in reading, writing, and arithmetic. Large congregations of "neatly dressed, sober, and reverential" blacks crowded the churches. Mills and Burgess lauded Sierra Leone as a monument to British benevolence and a lofty example for Americans.[17]

Having seen the British colony, they were eager to visit Sherbro Island and other likely colonial sites. They spread out their maps, consulted Sierra Leone traders who knew the coast, and drew up an itinerary. John Kizell, president of the Friendly Society and Paul Cuffee's partner, was eager to help. He had been a slave and lived in South Carolina until the Revolution when British soldiers carried him to Nova Scotia and later to Sierra Leone.

Kizell convinced the Americans that he was "anxious for the temporal and spiritual welfare of Americans" and shared their views on colonization. Mills joyfully dubbed him "a second Paul Cuffee." Kizell served as his interpreter. For six dollars a day Mills hired a small sloop manned by an African captain and six crewmen. The excursion lasted six weeks.[18]

Warned that African chieftains feared intrusions by powerful nations and opposed further colonization, Mills and Burgess thought it prudent to gather testimonials from men whom the natives trusted. They stopped first at the Banana Islands to call on the "headman," Thomas Caulker, a British ally. Caulker gave his endorsement to the Colonization Society and sent them to the Plaintain Islands to secure similar blessings from his nephew, British-educated George Caulker. The younger Caulker warned that the Sherbro chieftains would find pretexts to prevent another colony as powerful as Sierra Leone.

Mills and Burgess hurried to Sherbro Island, stopping first at Samo, a village of twenty huts. The natives were full of "civility and kindness," but they became distrustful when the Americans gathered specimens of rice, cotton, and sugar cane. The agents observed that Sherbro contained "great tracks" of uninhabited land. At the village of Bendou they met Kings Somano and Safah in the "palaver house," an open structure twenty feet in diameter and capped with a conical shaped thatch roof. The venerable Safah appeared in a silver-laced coat, three-corner hat, and long mantle that dropped to his bare feet. Somano wore a gown, pantaloons, hat, and shoes. Following custom, Mills and Burgess shook hands with each of the forty or fifty natives who gawked at the strangers. Also according to custom, they offered presents to the chieftains: trade cloth or "bafta," a keg of powder, bars of tobacco, and, finally, the indispensable bottle of rum. Mills noted disapprovingly that this "temporary conformity" with African protocol would cease as soon as American colonists could "wean them from their vicious customs."

The lone bottle of rum, however, did not meet royal requisites. The indignant kings insisted that custom demanded a bottle set before each, and they refused to begin the palaver until a second bottle was fetched from the schooner. The American visitors received no gifts in return, an oversight for which the kings pleaded poverty.

Because the chieftains wore rude, even ludicrous costumes, displayed exaggerated dignity, and prayed to heathen gods, the two Americans looked upon them as ignorant, undisciplined children. They explained that "wise and good men" in America wished to bring free black people to Africa. They would bring knowledge of the arts and agriculture; they would have things to trade and sell; the Sherbro people would enjoy a better life. Would the kings give or sell a quantity of their uninhabited real estate? The kings answered that they feared an American colony would grow strong and make war on the natives. Finally, after delays and haggling, Safah and Somano confessed that they were powerless to sell land without the consent of King Sherbro, the island's principal chieftain.

The palaver at Bendou taught Mills and Burgess their first lesson in African diplomacy. They had wasted their gifts and time on subalterns. After inspecting the "devil's house" and the "devil's bush" and other native shrines, the Americans held a prayer meeting. The bemused natives watched as Mills and Burgess sang "Salvation, oh the joyful sound." In each village they visited they sang and prayed for Africa's salvation.[19]

Next, the Americans arranged a meeting with King Sherbro, an elderly, barefoot monarch who carried a horsetail as his "regal badge" of office. After the customary handshaking and presentation of gifts, the agents explained the purposes of the Colonization Society and its desire to buy land. The king recessed the parley and sent for additional chieftains. Two days later they still had not arrived. "Despatch in business," Mills wearily observed, "is what African kings know nothing of." Additional delays—a native funeral, demands for more gifts, and, finally, the impossible request for a letter addressed personally to King Sherbro from Bushrod Washington—destroyed hopes for a pledge of land. The native kings did not intend to sell land, and they did not scruple to accept free bottles of rum while the Americans deduced the truth for themselves. After a week of delay, Kong Couber, the king's favorite son and chief minister, told the Americans that only the inhabitants of Sherbro could cede land. To Mills's request for a general assembly of all the natives, Couber replied simply that it was planting time and they were too busy. He bade them farewell, saying that his people could not refuse immigrants who wished to live with them. After preaching and singing more hymns, Mills and Burgess left the tiny island. Burgess noted regretfully that "these children of nature," acquainted only with perfidious slavers, could not grasp the meaning of benevolence.[20]

African chieftains in other villages along the coast were as wary as those at Sherbro. Mills and Burgess visited many villages, examined rivers, collected specimens of African flora, and held more palavers with headmen along the Boom, Deong, Baanga, Bagroo, and Yaltucker rivers. As before, land terms were vague. One chief agreed to provide homes for immigrants, but he refused to make a specific land cession, saying that "when a man was looking for a wife, he would not like to have another select for him." [21]

In mid-May, 1818, Mills and Burgess ended their "mission of inquiry." At Sierra Leone Governor Charles MacCarthy warned them that a private society could not sustain a colony without government assistance. A new settlement required armed guards, food supplies for a year, and regular shipping lines to the outside. The Americans thanked him for his advice and sailed for England on the brig *Success*. The name symbolized their own judgment of the mission. Mills had come to Africa with the conviction that African colonization was both practical and urgent. Nothing he had seen altered his opinion. "I am every day more convinced of the practicability and expediency of establishing American colonies on this coast."

On the return sea journey the agents began sorting out and assembling the "unquestionable information" desired by the managers in their campaign for Congressional assistance. Mills outlined a report strongly urging the early creation of a colony at Sherbro Island. As an economy measure, he recommended using native labor to clear land and build houses. If Paul Cuffee still lived, Mills said, he would not hesitate to appoint him governor. "But unless a judicious man of colour can be found, who will secure the confidence of all parties, it will be best to have a white Governor." He called for naval protection by the United States.

"A single sloop or brig, sent to execute the abolition [of slave trade] laws, would give to our settlement perfect security. If the people were troublesome, fire a big gun out in the bay, and they will all fly to the bush, and not an individual [will] be found." [22]

Before completing his report, Mills contracted fever, chills, and hiccoughs. On June 16, 1818, he died. [23] His partner sorrowfully prayed over the dead missionary, and crewmen of the *Success* dropped the gaunt corpse into the gray Atlantic. The important task of delivering the report of the "mission of inquiry" fell to Burgess. As he slowly journeyed home, the Colonization Society was busily intensifying its drive to capture government aid.

V

THE FOSTERING AID OF GOVERNMENT

IN THE MONTHS that Mills and Burgess gathered data in England and Africa, the board of managers continued their work of popularizing colonization. Secretary Caldwell stuffed the society's *Annual Reports* with testimonials from church and government bodies and advertised the famous men who endorsed colonization. He reprinted the Virginia assembly's resolutions of 1816, the Maryland legislature's unanimous call for the purchase of an African colony, and the Tennessee legislature's approval of a colony in "some distant country." The Presbyterian General Assembly, the Synod of Tennessee, the Presbytery of North Carolina, and conventions of the Episcopal church in Virginia and Maryland also endorsed colonization. "To labour in this work," intoned the Reverend William H. Wilmer, "is to co-work with God." Henry Clay revealed that Jefferson approved federal assistance, and Congressman Charles Fenton Mercer of Virginia happily added that President Monroe shared Jefferson's opinion.[1]

Backed by these distinguished endorsements, the society submitted another memorial to Congress, praying for prompt adoption of colonization. Congressman Mercer, the society's most loyal defender in the House, rose to request President Monroe to acquire "a suitable territory . . . on the coast of Africa, for colonizing such free people of colour of the United States as may be willing to avail themselves of such an asylum." The endorsements of Virginia, Maryland, and Tennessee, he said, were "sufficient ground for the interposition of the national legislature." [2]

Congress failed to act and the managers grew increasingly

impatient for Ebenezer Burgess's return. From the day the two agents sailed to Africa the managers assumed that the report of the "mission of inquiry" would be a sure weapon for a new and successful assault on the public treasury. Before Burgess set foot on American soil, the managers anticipated his good tidings and called the expedition a complete success. One asserted "There wants only the fostering aid of the government to carry the plans of the Society into full operation." [3]

Burgess did not disappoint them. He gave rapturous accounts of Africa. From his trunks he took "many curiosities"—native leather goods, sandals, blankets, mats, grain and cotton fiber. He told eager audiences that a few tobacco leaves purchased these products and that a few beads and bolts of cotton would readily buy thousands of acres of land. He emphasized that Africa was not an endless desert. It was rich and fertile, and blessed with broad rivers. Rice, sugar cane, pineapples, citrus fruit, bananas, yams, domesticated fowl and livestock, fish, and valuable spices such as ginger, cinnamon, and pepper abounded. Tales of poisonous insects, dangerous reptiles, and voracious beasts were exaggerations. A few European nations claimed fragments of the coast, but the whole interior was virtually unknown. There were unlimited opportunities for a rich trade in gold dust, gums, ivory, hides, beeswax, palm oil, and camwood. In all, the African coast was an ideal site for colonization.[4]

The most important part of Burgess's report dealt with the slave trade. Africa was waiting for "an honorable trade" but slavers obstructed commerce. In village after village the slave trade had drastically reduced the population. Once prosperous communities were decaying. The grass grew wild, and banana, orange, lime, and plantain trees were unattended. Lonely natives howled about the sacred trees of the dead. Many had forgotten how to raise cotton, indigo, and sugar cane. So long as as the slave trade continued, the land would be too poor to trade with American merchants. The governor of Sierra Leone asserted that two-thirds of the active slavers were American.

Burgess argued that colonization was the best remedy for the "scourge of Africa." It would teach natives to drive off greedy slavers and welcome American traders seeking tropical products.

Eventually, colonial settlements rimming the entire African coast would choke the illicit traffic at its source.[5]

Burgess's return marked the beginning of a campaign to trumpet colonization's utility in strangling the slave trade. The managers saw that measures for suppressing the slave trade might provide the entering wedge for federal assistance. With all its stark tragedy and gore, the slave trade was an excellent vehicle for propaganda. A generation before, Clarkson and Wilberforce had developed the technique in England. Congressman Mercer called for "a speedy termination of that traffic which has been so long the crime of Europe, the scourge of Africa, and the affliction and disgrace of America." [6]

Shortly after Burgess delivered his report, the managers submitted a statement to Speaker of the House Henry Clay. The findings of the "mission of inquiry" amply proved the practicability of African colonization, they said. "It is now reduced to the single question, whether the undertaking shall be adopted and patronized by the Government, so as to become essentially national in its means and objects." They handed the Speaker a bundle of documents purporting to reveal numerous violations of the slave trade laws. "There is good reason to conclude," they declared, "that the establishment of such a colony as has been projected by our Society, may prove an important and efficient adjunct to the other preventative checks provided by law." [7]

Taking his cue from the colonizationists' complaints against the "inefficiency of the present laws against this abominable traffic," Congressman Mercer introduced a bill which transferred the responsibility for disposing of rescued Africans from the states to the federal government. Mercer's bill gave President Monroe authority to "make such regulations and arrangements, as he may deem expedient, for the safeguarding, support, and removal" of rescued Africans stranded in the United States. It authorized the President to send a naval squadron to African waters and establish a government agency on the African coast for resettling victims of the slave trade. Congress appropriated $100,000 for the work. In the closing rush of the session, the "American Wilberforce" expertly guided the bill to approval. The Senate cut out a House amendment calling for the death penalty for slave traders, but passed the bill with little debate. On March 3, 1819, "An Act in addition to the acts prohibiting the Slave Trade" became law.[8]

Nowhere did Mercer mention colonization, but friends of the society warmly supported his measure. The managers looked upon the Slave Trade Act of 1819 as a boon to their cause. They immediately laid plans for securing President Monroe's friendly interpretation placing the $100,000 appropriation within their eager grasp. They hoped to make the government's African agency the nucleus for a colony.

On March 4, 1819, the day after Mercer's Slave Trade Act became law, the managers of the Colonization Society named Justice Bushrod Washington, Francis S. Key, John Mason, and General Walter Jones, all famed constitutional lawyers, a committee to consult President Monroe.[9] They urged him to interpret the act as granting authority to purchase territory and establish an African colony. General Jones reasoned that the act did not merely contemplate dumping rescued Africans on the shores but envisioned the creation of a special colony for their rehabilitation. They knew that Monroe personally approved colonization, and they hoped his own opinions could overcome any constitutional scruples. In later years Monroe was an officer of the Virginia auxiliary and gave money to the society, but in 1819 he was not as certain as General Jones that the new Slave Trade Act permitted him to purchase land in Africa.

In his cautious way, Monroe took the problem to his cabinet. At a cabinet meeting on March 12, 1819, he strongly endorsed African colonization and noted that the Virginia assembly's approval weighed heavily in its favor. He knew many Virginians ardently wished to destroy slavery. Some had eagerly freed their slaves after the Revolution, but the subsequent rise of the free black population convinced them that emancipation alone was not enough. He repeated the colonizationists' arguments that free Negroes constituted "a class of very dangerous people" who lived by thievery and corrupted the slaves. Colonization would encourage manumission and eventually remove the entire black population of Virginia.[10]

The President's query whether he could use the Slave Trade Act as the basis for an African colony drew strong objections from Secretary of State John Quincy Adams. Adams told the cabinet the act did not permit such a broad construction, and he challenged the whole concept of African colonization on constitutional grounds. It was unconstitutional to build and own colonies. The purchase of African territory was a step toward augmenting federal powers and "engrafting of a colonial establishment" on the Constitution.

Not all of Secretary Adams's objections were based on the Constitution. Some sprang from his growing political rivalry with Secretary of the Treasury William H. Crawford. Both men were aspirants to the Executive Mansion. Adams confided to his diary that the Colonization Society, of which Crawford was a vice-president and leading figure, was merely one of the Georgian's "traps for popularity." He was unwilling to forward his opponent's candidacy. The colonizationists acted from many motives—mostly bad ones. Some were "exceedingly humane, weak-minded" men who harbored no ulterior motives. Others were "speculators in official profits and honors," seeking appointments to colonial posts. Still others, "speculators in political popularity," merely wished to please antislavery sentiment while satisfying southern desires to rid the country of free blacks at public expense. He even suspected that a few were "cunning slave-holders" who hoped to raise the market price of slaves.[11]

Before the cabinet met again, a committee of the managers tried to persuade Adams that the purchase of African territory was entirely constitutional. General Jones assured him that the Louisiana Purchase and the settlement at the mouth of the Columbia river fully established the constitutionality of such a step. He argued that Congress did not intend to leave rescued Africans on unfamiliar shores without protection and livelihood. Adams steadfastly replied that the Slave Trade Act contained no provisions for the purchase of land. Africa was not contiguous with American possessions and purchase of land was not covered by precedent. An African colony could never attain equal status with the rest of the United States. Nothing in the Constitution warranted the "establishment of a colonial system of government subordinate to and dependent upon that of the United States."

He contemptuously dismissed General Jones's reasoning as akin to an Indian cosmogony—mounting the world upon an elephant and the elephant on a tortoise "with nothing for the tortoise to stand upon." [12]

John Quincy Adams convinced the cabinet. On March 16, 1819, Attorney General William Wirt, Secretary of War John C. Calhoun, and Secretary of the Navy Smith Thompson agreed that the Slave Trade Act of 1819 did not authorize the purchase of territory or the creation of an African colony. Monroe accepted the decision, telling the Colonization Society that he was powerless to aid it. [13]

The cabinet decision was a defeat for William H. Crawford as well as for the society. In the next months Crawford's actions bore out Adams's charge that colonization was one of his "traps for popularity." Crawford was impatient to launch the African agency, but as matters stood the government had no reason to begin the project until a number of rescued slaves had come under federal jurisdiction. In glancing over the columns of the *Augusta Chronicle,* his searching eye fell upon the notice of the impending sale of thirty or forty Africans seized from a Spanish slaver. In 1818, with Crawford's assent and in accordance with the Slave Trade Act of 1808, federal officers had surrendered them to the state of Georgia. The governor then ordered their sale. Crawford now saw an opportunity to bring them under federal jurisdiction, arguing that the Slave Trade Act of 1819 superceded the 1808 act and Georgia law. He urged Monroe's administration to take possession of the Africans for immediate removal to Africa. But Attorney General Wirt, with Secretary Adams's encouragement, answered that the new act was not retroactive and could not apply to the Africans already in Georgia's jurisdiction.

Without contesting the point, Crawford turned to another course. Under Georgia law, rescued Africans were to be sold unless the Colonization Society formally claimed them from the governor and paid all expenses incurred in their behalf. Crawford summoned the managers into special meeting and urged them to stop the sale. The auction date was May 3. The managers immediately commanded the Reverend William Meade to go to Georgia "with utmost alacrity." George Washington Parke Custis of "Arlington" offered Smith's Island in Chesapeake Bay as a temporary asylum for the Africans while they waited for transportation to Africa.[14]

The Reverend Mr. Meade rushed to Milledgeville, Georgia, without enough funds to redeem the Africans, but the governor agreed to postpone the sale until the Colonization Society could raise the money. The managers made private appeals, wrote newspaper articles, and issued public addresses dramatizing the plight of the Africans who faced perpetual slavery if the society failed to secure $5,000. Donations will test the sincerity of "those expressions of detestation so frequently uttered against the slave trade," they said. High officials in Washington pledged money. William H. Crawford led off the subscription list with fifty dollars. Attorney General Wirt contributed ten. Two managers, James Laurie of the Presbyterian church and William Hawley of the Episcopal church, called on John Quincy Adams and urged him to obey his Christian impulse, but he icily refused to give a cent.[15]

Meade's hasty trip to Georgia produced more publicity for the society than freedom for the Africans. Spanish claimants brought suit for the Africans, immuring them in a labyrinth of legal questions. Meade returned to Washington empty-handed, but he reported that the captives were in good spirits and well cared for. He praised the managers' prompt intervention as "a most opportune and favorable" move whose "novelty" widely advertised the colonization scheme and gave fresh assurances that "our Society was about to do something." [16]

Meanwhile, Burgess's report extolling African colonization stirred hopes that the society would soon send an expedition. Burgess brought back letters from Paul Cuffee's emigrants at Sierra Leone reproving free Negro leaders in Philadelphia who opposed colonization. "You cannot enjoy yourselves in America as free men . . . because you are captives in a strange land." A few free Negroes volunteered to become the society's first colonists. George Bowling of Fairfax county, Virginia, a man of "strong mind and good understanding," expressed his wish to go immediately. He planned to persuade nearly one hundred Negroes to accompany him. The corresponding secretary of the

African Missionary Society of Petersburg, Virginia, asserted that many free Negroes were eager to leave their "adopted [land] for our Colonial Asylum" and wanted "correct information . . . respecting the Country and the means of conveyance." Another society in Richmond asked to send two missionaries as advance agents for many prospective colonists. William M'Intosh of Illinois reported that his free Negro neighbors "would embrace the earliest opportunity to leave" and some had already begun to sell their property preparatory to emigrating. Another Illinois resident, Abraham Camp of Lamott, declared he preferred to "suffer hunger and nakedness for years" than to live in the United States without equality and freedom. Nineteen free Negroes in Philadelphia asked for "exact information" about the society's plan to send a ship and colonists to Africa. The managers happily announced that applications were flooding the society's offices.[17]

With interest in colonization growing, Crawford renewed his efforts to confer federal assistance upon the society. In the fall of 1819, he and Francis S. Key entreated and cajoled President Monroe to reconsider his decision not to give the new Slave Trade Act a generous interpretation. Key offered a new plan. "My idea is that the President will appoint an agent . . . send a ship of war to the coast, and probably a transport with the colored men from this country, as laborers, and some agricultural implements." Monroe did not wish to challenge the cabinet decision opposing the purchase of land, but he agreed to Key's proposal if the Colonization Society accepted responsibility for buying African territory.[18]

Before putting the plan into effect, however, Monroe asked Attorney General Wirt to draw up an official opinion approving the scheme. Wirt promptly replied that the executive could not use any part of the $100,000 to buy land, transport free Negroes, purchase tools or supplies, or pay the salary of the government agent until he actually arrived in Africa. He concluded the opinion declaring that as "a measure of cooperating with the colonization society" the Slave Trade Act of 1819 was "altogether inadequate." The colonizationists exploded with anger. "Mr. Crawford's fears are realized," Francis S. Key groaned. "The President has forgotten his promises, and what simple courtiers were we to suppose it would be otherwise. We have it all to go over again." [19]

At once the managers concentrated their forces on Wirt. Within hours after submitting his chilling opinion, he found himself beseiged by officials of the society. Secretary Caldwell begged for a broader interpretation. Francis S. Key came away from Wirt's office with the impression that the attorney general feared colonization would excite slaves in southern states. Wirt admitted that he was "uninformed" about colonization, but it was an impracticable scheme.

In the end, Crawford's cogent arguments triumphed. The persuasive Secretary of the Treasury insisted that the new Slave Trade Act allowed the President broad authority because Congress was unable to anticipate the details of creating and operating an African agency. The power to return rescued Africans was the principal power, he declared, and all else was incidental to it. Perhaps in the rush of the last days of the session, careless wording crept into the bill.

Under Crawford's hammering, Wirt grudgingly altered his opinion. He conceded that the President could establish an African agency, send carpenters to prepare shelters, protect and support the station, organize a government for the resettled Africans, and send free Negroes from the United States if such a course was essential to the "safe and comfortable removal" of the rescued Africans. He conscientiously added his regrets that Congress had thrown "so large a mass of powers" on the executive's shoulders. He counseled delay until Congress clarified its wishes.[20]

President Monroe did not wait. In his annual message of 1819, he announced that he was sending two agents to Africa with teams of laborers and mechanics to prepare the government's African station. In order to meld the project with the Colonization Society's plan, Monroe appointed federal agents designated by the society. Samuel Bacon, a zealous young Episcopal cleric, became the government's principal agent. For a few months he served as an agent of the Colonization Society and then transferred to the employ of the United States government.

Samuel Bacon had led a varied, aimless life. Born at Sturbridge, Massachusetts, in 1782, he attended Harvard, taught school, studied law, and edited a literary magazine at Lancaster, Pennsylvania. During the War of 1812, he served as a captain in the Marines and fought at the battle of Bladensburg. After the war he practiced law in York, Pennsylvania. He became interested in the Sunday school movement and helped establish twenty-six Sunday schools. Bishop White ordained him an Episcopal priest and sent him out as the traveling agent of the Missionary and Bible Society of Pennsylvania. He was engaged in this work when the Colonization Society called him to Washington.[21]

On the society's recommendation, the government also hired John P. Bankson as Bacon's assistant. After consulting President Monroe, members of the cabinet, and the board of managers, Bacon and Bankson hastened to New York city to prepare an expedition. Bacon chartered a three-ton merchantman, the *Elizabeth,* to serve as the supply ship. He purchased enough supplies to feed and equip three hundred rescued Africans for one year. The government paid for wagons, wheelbarrows, plows, iron work for a saw mill and a grist mill, two six-pound cannons, one hundred muskets, twelve kegs of powder, a fish seine, and a "four-oared barge." At the same time, Secretary of the Navy Smith Thompson ordered an American sloop of war, the *Cyane,* to convoy the *Elizabeth* to Africa. At Monroe's personal direction the government deposited several thousand dollars with Baring Brothers of London for the agents' use while in Africa.

Monroe's administration officially treated the expedition as a step toward suppressing the slave trade, but it was a thinly veiled colonization venture. The secretary of the navy stated that the mission to Africa was entirely distinct from colonization. His was a meaningless gesture. As government agent, Bacon hired free Negro carpenters and laborers who were really colonists. Of the eighty-six who sailed on the *Elizabeth,* only one-third were men. The rest were their wives and children. The women posed as seamstresses, nurses, and laundry women. They regarded themselves as colonists, and the Navy made no arrangements for their return voyage. The managers of the society looked upon the project as the beginning of the long-awaited colonization scheme. Their agent, Samuel Crozer, accompanied Bacon and Bankson to Africa. Crozer carried instructions to purchase land at Sherbro Island and to frame a government for the colonists. During the voyage he issued rules for parceling out land in the new colony among the ostensible carpenters and mechanics.[22]

On January 31, 1820, with appropriate fanfare and accolades, the government expedition set sail from New York harbor. During the weeks of preparation Bacon preached the glories of African colonization in several churches, and at the hour of embarkation hundreds of spectators swarmed the *Elizabeth*'s wharf on the North river. As the ship eased out of dock a prosperous merchant and friend of colonization, Gabriel Disosway, joyously raised his voice with the crowd's. "It was a happy moment of my life," he cried, "never to be forgotten." [23]

VI

AFRICAN ILIAD

———◆•••◆———

EARLY IN MARCH, 1820, after six weeks on the Atlantic, the *Elizabeth,* laden with prospective colonists, touched at Sierra Leone and proceeded to Sherbro Island. The U. S. S. *Cyane,* separated from the colonist ship in the crossing, did not reach the island for several days. The foremost task of the American agents was to find a colonial site. Neither the Colonization Society nor the American government owned a foot of land in all Africa. The managers of the society had ordered Samuel Crozer to buy land on Sherbro Island, accepting Ebenezer Burgess's extravagant reports of cheap, vacant, fertile land and poor, weak, friendly tribes. The Navy Department also directed its agents to build the government station at Sherbro.[1]

On the shores of the island, John Kizell, Cuffee's old partner and the interpreter of the Mills-Burgess "mission of inquiry," greeted Samuel Bacon, John Bankson, Samuel Crozer, and more than 80 immigrants. Kizell was overjoyed to see the Americans, and he admitted that the two year interlude since Mills's and Burgess's visit made him despair of their coming. After the two missionaries had left the island in 1818, he had purchased a stretch of land and built a small village of twenty thatched huts for the use of future American colonists. He now invited the Americans to stay at Campelar and make their permanent settlement on his lands. Bacon was happy to find a settlement ready for occupancy, but he agreed to house the colonists at Campelar only temporarily. Crozer was under orders to negotiate with the Sherbro chieftains for a larger tract of land.[2]

Campelar was a wretched place. It stood on a low, marshy strip surrounded by dense thickets, mango trees, and fetid streams. Drinking water was little more than chalybeate marsh water, and its brackish taste and strong odor made it "very offensive." Too late the Americans learned that Kizell imported all of his own drinking water, as well as most of his food, from the mainland. When the *Cyane* finally arrived, its officers glumly noted that the island was both unhealthy and infertile. They complained that shallow waters and lack of any harbor prevented war ships from approaching the island and the proposed American station. The British naval commander at Sierra Leone added his disapproval of the location. But Bacon's authority as principal agent was supreme, and he resolutely determined to remain at Campelar at least until the rainy season passed.[3]

During the next two weeks, Bacon and Bankson settled the colonists at Campelar and directed the unloading of the *Elizabeth*'s copious supplies. Because the merchantman could not approach the island, Bacon purchased a small schooner at Sierra Leone and laboriously relayed the supplies from ship to schooner to island. Meanwhile, Crozer began the patience-testing work of negotiating for land. The obliging but untrustworthy Kizell served as interpreter. The Sherbro kings proved as devious in their dealings with Crozer as they had been with Mills and Burgess. They accepted the Colonization Society's gifts and letters, but repeatedly postponed any final agreements.

Soon the torrential rains began. Disagreeable water, strange food, and sorry weather made the colonists miserable and quarrelsome. On board ship they had fought with the *Elizabeth*'s tactless officers who threatened to pitch a pet dog overboard. The incident nearly provoked mutiny. Now, at the sodden village of Campelar, the colonists complained about the lack of fresh meat and vegetables and decent housing. Before long they were sick. One by one they came down with the "African fever," the same malady that hastened Samuel J. Mills to his grave. Bacon dolefully described the disease as "bilious." Soon, forty victims were groaning in delirium. Sharp headaches made sleep impossible, and inflamed eyes added to the mounting misery. A few died. Crozer, the only man in the expedition with any medical knowledge, was absent holding fruitless palavers, unaware of impending tragedy. He returned to stricken Campelar and fell ill. John Bankson, John S. Townsend, an officer on the *Cyane,* and six crewmen assigned to aid the settlers all became sick. On April 15, 1820, Crozer died, and Townsend expired the following day. Both were buried with military honors. Bankson rallied, gained strength, but suddenly died.

Only Samuel Bacon was left to dispense medicine, food, and supplies to the ailing, and he too sickened. The captain of a British schooner reluctantly agreed to take the feverish agent to Sierra Leone, but as Bacon's native canoe rowed toward the schooner, it hastily weighed anchor and left the island. Bacon's native oarsmen rowed for several hours under the burning African sun in an effort to catch the fleeing ship. They finally landed the sick man, delirious from exposure, at the British mission at Cape Shilling. He died the next day.

The mysterious plague had suddenly and thoroughly destroyed the first colonial venture. After the disaster at Sherbro Island, the colonizationists were less grateful to Mills and Burgess for their joyous reports in 1818. "It is only to be regretted that those gentlemen had not spent a longer period in that country, explored the coast more extensively, and used the means of acquiring a more exact and certain knowledge of the different subjects on which they were obliged to report," one colonizationist bitterly commented. The managers had drawn their instructions for Bacon, Bankson, and Crozer "under the erroneous impression, as to the true state" of Sherbro Island and the African coast. "To this cause must be partially attributed the fatal miscarriage of the expedition." [4]

The sweep of death left chaos and dejection among the surviving colonists. The dying Crozer conferred his commission as agent of the Colonization Society on the Reverend Daniel Coker, a mulatto Methodist preacher from Baltimore and former associate of Paul Cuffee. Following Bacon's death, Coker acted as both government and society agent. The handful of survivors, several of whom declared they recognized no authority, divided their loyalties between Daniel Coker and John Kizell. Without power to resist, Coker watched the natives from near-by villages raid the unguarded stores while the rascally Kizell generously distributed the remainder as gifts to the Sherbro kings. Coker finally led a remnant of the settlers to Fourah Bay near Freetown where they lived for the next year as guests of the British. For want of an American station, United States war ships deposited recaptured Africans at Freetown.[5]

Following the disaster, President Monroe appointed new agents and ordered another expedition. The Reverend Ephraim Bacon, Samuel Bacon's brother, and Jonathan B. Winn received commissions as government agents. The Colonization Society sent two representatives, the Reverend Joseph R. Andrus and Christian Wiltberger. On January 23, 1821, the four agents and thirty-three emigrants sailed from Hampton Roads on the brig *Nautilus*. The board of managers fixed no specific place for the second colonizing attempt. It merely ordered its agents to consult the government agents in all matters concerning the selection of a site.[6]

The four agents hurried to Sierra Leone, interviewed Daniel Coker, and took stock of the remains of the first expedition. They unanimously agreed to establish the colony at any place but Sherbro Island. Next, they visited native villages along the coast south of Sierra Leone, searching for a new, healthful colonial site. In April, 1821, Andrus and Bacon signed a treaty with King Jack Ben of Grand Bassa ceding the society perhaps forty square miles of tribal lands. The managers, however, refused to accept a treaty provision calling for annual tributes of $300 to the king. They rebuked Andrus and appointed Dr. Eli Ayres of Baltimore principal agent. The government obligingly commissioned Ayres a surgeon in the Navy and promptly conveyed him to Africa on the United States schooner *Shark*.

Early in November, 1821, Ayres arrived in Africa to find Andrus and Winn dead of the African fever. Bacon, sick and crazed with fear, had fled to the West Indies to escape death. Only Wiltberger remained. Ayres assumed duties as agent for both the society and the government. The survivors at Fourah Bay were in a rebellious state, distrusting all American agents. Ayres immediately issued a stern edict threatening severe punishments for sedition, mutiny, insubordination, and disobedience, but even these threats could not induce some of the colonists to accompany him to a new colony.[7]

Almost two years had passed since President Monroe had sent the *Elizabeth* and *Cyane* to Africa, and the government still had no receptacle for Africans rescued from the slave trade nor the Colonization Society a foot of African soil. The board of managers persuaded the administration to send Lieutenant Robert Field Stockton to Africa to obtain land. Stockton was an adventurous naval officer and an alumnus of Robert Finley's academy at Baskingridge. The Stockton name carried great prestige in New Jersey. His grandfather had signed the Declaration of Independence and various relatives were leaders in national and state affairs. Lieutenant Stockton was friendly to African colonization and eager to give the Navy a larger role in national affairs. He badgered the secretary of the navy into assigning him the newly built schooner *Alligator* and ordering him to the African coast. Bushrod Washington, Francis S. Key, and other officers of the Colonization Society granted the naval officer *carte blanche* authority to purchase a strip of African territory.[8]

Stockton hastened to Africa, joined Ayres, and journeyed down the west coast in search of a colony. The British at Freetown strongly recommended Cape Mesurado on the Grain coast 225 miles south of Sierra Leone and near the mouth of the St. Paul's river in the Bassa country. A few months before, Andrus and Bacon had examined Cape Mesurado, pronouncing it healthful and fertile. They liked its harbor and the river route leading to the interior, but King Peter flatly refused to sell the cape. He returned the agent's gifts and declined to palaver, but Ayres and Stockton determined to visit the king and make the transaction.

On December 12, 1821, the Baltimore physician and the American naval officer landed at Cape Mesurado and asked to see King Peter. Armed natives gathered about the strangers. Ayres, a short tense man, explained to one of the tribal dignitaries that Americans wished to bring civilization and Christianity to them. In his high, cracked voice he described how American immigrants would build houses, make farms, erect schools, and trade with the tribes. The natives looked uneasy and worried. Like their cousins along the coast, they were suspicious of white men and their promises of a radical change in the native way of life. At the Americans' insistence, King Peter reluctantly agreed to a palaver. He arrived at the seashore, wearing a cotton toga with wide blue and white stripes. An attendant held an umbrella over the royal head. Ayres again explained the advantages that a proposed colony would bring, prudently omitting any mention of civilizing and Christianizing the natives. The king thanked the Americans for their gifts of rum and tobacco and apologized for not being able to sell the cape. If he did, he would meet quick death and "his women would cry aplenty." He agreed to meet the Americans the next day and "make a book" for the land; the Americans took this as a promise to arrange terms.[9]

The next day Stockton and Ayres waited at the seashore, but King Peter did not appear. A palaver with lesser officials led nowhere. The following day the Americans again waited at the shore, but King Peter still did not meet them. They sent word that they wished to see him, but the African monarch answered emphatically that he would not see them and he would not sell the cape.

Lieutenant Stockton was infuriated by this ill treatment. With some qualms about entering a strange and possibly hostile country, the two Americans set out for the king's village with the intention of forcing him to negotiate. Led by native guides they walked inland six or seven miles, wading through mud and water, climbing over stumps and jungle tangles, and chopping through dense, swampy thickets. When one or the other American lagged, the guides whispered, "Come along, come along—the devil will catch us."

At the king's village they waited an hour before King Peter appeared. Distressed and angry, he shed all formalities. His first words were: "What do you want that land for?" Ayres began to repeat his explanation, but several natives around the palaver circle noisily interrupted, shouting accusations and brandishing threats. One called them the kidnappers of King Bassa's son. Another shouted that they were the men who provoked quarrels and fighting at Sherbro Island. A third pointed to the seething Stockton and denounced him for destroying the slave trade along the coast. The excited natives shrieked with anger and indignation. Stockton's excitable nature flared. He gravely drew a pistol, cocked it, and handed the weapon to Ayres with instructions to shoot if necessary. With equally dramatic deliberation he leveled another pistol at King Peter's head. The shocked natives cowered as Stockton peevishly told them that the Americans came as benefactors, not enemies, and that they wished only to confer great blessings on them and the entire country. As he spoke he solemnly raised his hand to heaven, and at that moment rays of sunshine burst through the clouds.

The pistol at King Peter's temple and the fortuitous flood of sunshine were enough to convince the natives of Lieutenant Stockton's authority. He sternly ordered the king and his aides to meet him the next day to sign the treaty of cession. On December 15, 1821, King Peter and five chieftains reluctantly deeded Cape Mesurado to the Colonization Society. In return they received muskets, beads, tobacco, gunpowder, clothing, looking glasses, food, and rum. Ayres and Stockton both signed on behalf of the Colonization Society. Stockton justified his action, saying "procrastination and perfidy have already done too much mischief, to allow me to practise the one or give an opportunity for the other to be practised on me." Ayres frankly admired his colleague's "dexterity at mixing flattery with a little well-timed threat." The cape cost less than $300.[10]

Through the direct intervention of an American naval officer and a navy surgeon, the society had seized a foothold in Africa. The small colony was named "Liberia" after the Latin *liber,* or freeman. The colonizationists were so grateful for the "fostering aid" of the federal government that they named the first permanent settlement "Monrovia" in honor of the President. General Harper said the gesture demonstrated "the gratitude of this Society to that venerable and distinguished individual, to whom it is more indebted than any single man. It is perfectly well-known," he told the annual meeting, "that but for the favourable use he has been pleased to make of the great powers confided to him (a use as wise as it was liberal), all our attempts and efforts must have been unavailing. No means that we possessed, or could have procured, would have proved adequate without his aid." [11]

There was a limit, however, to President Monroe's aid. He had to treat the African station at Cape Mesurado as a separate operation from colonization. Tacit aid fell short of total acceptance of the principle of government-sponsored colonization. At the beginning of 1822, the managers could rejoice at having won a measure of aid and a larger measure of sympathy from federal officials, but they could not ignore the fact that the Colonization Society was still a private agency, a mendicant no different from the many benevolent societies of the time. The status of the colony was roughly equivalent to colonies of private trading companies of the eighteenth century. It could not claim government protection or subsidy. Its governing policies, laws, and officials, as well as all financial support, came from a group of private citizens.

At the outset the managers determined to make the new colony a model establishment, and they began by legislating harmony and order. Though unfamiliar with the tasks of administering and sustaining a colony thousands of miles from their cramped rooms opposite Williamson's hotel in Washington, they framed colonial laws and issued regulations. The colonial constitution, issued before Ayres and Stockton bought Cape Mesurado, reserved every vestige of authority to the managers and their agents "until they shall withdraw . . . and leave the settlers to the government of themselves" at some unspecified date in the future. The board promulgated the common law, "as in force and modified in the United States," outlawed slavery, and forbade "spiritous liquors." It also issued rules for probating wills, holding jury trials, distributing land, and trading with native tribes. Whites could not own land, and missionaries could not reside in the colony without the express permission of the managers. The edicts of the colonial agent were law. He served as governor, judge, law-giver, and military commander. The colonists received no bill of rights, but the managers promised to treat them as American citizens. Even the town plan came from Washington. Architect William Thornton drew up a precise master design for the "chief town" which Ayres was to follow in building a settlement. With this blueprint for an orderly, well-managed colony, the board turned to making it a reality.[12]

Dreams of a placid administration collapsed as soon as the first colonists reached Cape Mesurado. In the spring of 1822, Dr. Ayres shepherded the immigrants at Fourah Bay to the sloping shores of the Mesurado river. Survival was the immediate goal.

The cape was a narrow tongue of high land three miles wide and thirty-six miles long, bordered by the Junk and the Mesurado rivers and the ocean, and covered with an inhospitable forest and dense thickets. The climate was hot and rainy. Ayres directed the colonists in clearing the land and throwing up a cluster of thatched huts. From the start they lacked sufficient food and equipment. A disastrous fire destroyed precious stores, implements, and utensils. The colonists found they could not raise enough food, and they disliked African dishes, preferring pork, flour, coffee, and other components of their American diet. Ayres urgently and repeatedly begged the managers to send additional supplies, warning that the colony faced starvation. Then, with the coming of the rainy or "sickly" season, the African fever halted all work. At the same time, King Peter's people, resentful of the American colony and hinting at war, demanded tributes from the impoverished pioneers and threatened to sell them into slavery.[13]

Despite all, the colony survived and grew. In August, 1822, the brig *Strong*, chartered by the United States government to carry eighteen rescued Africans, also brought thirty-seven immigrants to Cape Mesurado. Ayres made a hasty trip to the United States to obtain more supplies and more settlers. The *Oswego* sailed from Baltimore in the fall, 1822, and the *Fidelity* followed with more emigrants and stores. By mid-1823, 150 colonists were huddled on the shores of Cape Mesurado.[14]

The managers' responsibilities grew as the colony grew. All but the liberated Africans depended on the society's lean treasury for supplies, food, tools, and firearms. During 1820–1821, the managers paid out nearly $6,000 for supplies. The following year they spent an additional $4,000. Each expedition was a strain, and they urgently appealed for donations of food, clothing, goods, and implements to send with each ship and each batch of emigrants. In 1821, agents Joseph Andrus and Ephraim Bacon found that their major duty in organizing the *Nautilus* expedition was begging cash and goods. At Baltimore, New York, Boston, and Petersburg, they begged charitable individuals and mercantile firms to give barrels of flour, sugar, nails, knives, axes, blankets, garments, and medicine. Other donations included shoes, soap, castor oil, pewter plates, horse collars, and gin. In Baltimore, the

Young Men's Bible Society, with an eye to the colonists' spiritual diet, gave twenty-five Bibles and fifty New Testaments, and the local tract society added one thousand pamphlets.[15]

Supplies raised at each sailing considerably off-set the expenses faced by the managers. In the beginning, they met their obligations with little difficulty. At the time Ayres led the first settlers to Cape Mesurado, the society had $2,500 in its treasury. The colony's voracious appetite at once consumed the slim account. Simultaneously, contributions tapered off. In 1822, the society took in less than $800. The managers discovered that donations were more generous for removing free Negroes from the United States than for maintaining them in Africa.[16]

Dwindling income and mounting expenses quickly shoved the Colonization Society to the brink of bankruptcy. Within a year of Liberia's birth, the treasury was depleted and the managers unable to send a steady stream of supplies to Africa. The project hung in balance. If the managers were to recruit, equip, and transport more colonists and feed those already in Liberia, they required far larger resources than they commanded. In distress they called for a thorough examination of ways to secure massive aid either from the federal government or from private benevolence.

VII

EXPLORING THE VOLUNTARY SYSTEM

———◀•••▶———

FROM ITS INCEPTION, the Colonization Society was dedicated to securing federal support for its program. In this important respect it differed from the numerous meliorative or benevolent societies of the day. The others relied exclusively on a network of auxiliaries for systematic collections that swelled the coffers of each national organization. They employed special agents to tour the land, create local auxiliaries, distribute publicity, and trumpet their societies' glad tidings. This was the voluntary system. The Colonization Society, however, needed auxiliaries and agents only as means to enroll the names of the famous on its rosters. It cherished the testimonials of a few national heroes and politicians—Henry Clay, Bushrod Washington, William H. Crawford, John Randolph of Roanoke, General Lafayette, John Marshall, and hundreds of lesser figures who crowded its honor rolls—above an impressive array of state and local auxiliaries.

Believing auxiliaries to be merely supplemental to the larger goal of federal assistance, the colonizationists made only feeble and haphazard efforts to build local societies. For several years a handful of auxiliaries existed on paper, but they did not result from systematic campaigns. In 1817, Samuel J. Mills created a few auxiliaries for the special purpose of raising $5,000 to finance his "mission of inquiry." Though they boasted the names of foremost citizens of New York, Philadelphia, and Baltimore, they did not raise the money Mills needed. Afterwards they sank into quiescence. In the same year, Robert Finley founded an auxiliary in Trenton, New Jersey, but it promptly disappeared. A few months later, the Manumission and Colonizing Society of North

Carolina, a Quaker group, volunteered to affiliate with the American Colonization Society. The managers gave the uneasy alliance only slight encouragement, instinctively fearing confusion of Quaker abolition and colonization.[1]

In 1819, the managers made an effort to revive the fading auxiliaries and build new ones. As in 1817, they had an immediate purpose: to raise money to redeem rescued Africans in the custody of the state of Georgia. Francis S. Key organized a distinguished auxiliary in Annapolis that included Jeremiah Townley Chase, chief justice of the Maryland court of appeals, William Kilty, chancellor of Maryland, Roger Brooke Taney, successful lawyer and politician, and Governor Charles Goldsborough. Ninety subscribers, including a score of ladies, pledged nearly $500 to the parent society. The Baltimore society revived and pledged handsomely, merchant Isaac McKim topping the list with $500. Thirty distinguished men, including Charles Carroll of Carrollton, John Eager Howard, Philip E. Thomas, and Robert G. Harper, brought the total to $3,000.[2]

The Reverend William Meade nurtured the auxiliary society in Frederick county, Virginia. Its thirty-five members pledged over $6,000. In Loudoun county, seventy men led by John Mines, pastor of the Leesburg Presbyterian Church, Ludwell Lee, and Richard Henry Lee, respectively son and grandson of the Revolutionary hero, donated smaller sums.[3]

In Washington the managers sold life memberships to John Marshall, Bushrod Washington, Congressman Charles Marsh of Vermont, Congressman Charles F. Mercer of Virginia, Congressman John C. Herbert of Maryland, William H. Crawford, Henry Clay, and John Hartwell Cocke of Virginia. M. Hyde de Neuville, French minister to the United States, and Stratford Canning, the British minister, each gave $50.[4]

In May, 1819, Meade hastened to Georgia with orders to redeem the rescued Africans and to raise funds in various towns in Georgia, South Carolina, and North Carolina. Meade followed the traditional pattern. He visited men of wealth in each community, explained the colonization cause, placed their names on the subscription lists, called a meeting to organize a local auxiliary, hired a hall or church, appointed the most respectable citizen in town chairman, exhorted the audience to aid colonization, and took additional pledges from members and officers of the new auxiliary.[5]

Meade followed this pattern at Milledgeville where friends of colonization promised nearly $1,500 payable in five years. He also organized auxiliaries in Augusta, Savannah, Fayetteville, Raleigh, and Chapel Hill. In all, he amassed pledges totaling nearly $8,000 even though "a deep gloom" of hard times hung over every community.

Meade was as interested in impressive names as in donations. In Milledgeville ex-governor William Rabun, Governor John Clarke, state treasurer George R. Clayton, Congressman Joel Crawford, cousin of William H. Crawford, and surveyor general Daniel Sturges adorned the local society. In Savannah, Meade signed up Congressman Edward F. Tattnall, son of ex-governor Josias Tattnall, Judge James M. Wayne of the court of common pleas, and district attorney Robert Habersham. In Augusta, Judge J. H. Montgomery of the supreme courts of Georgia and Major Nicholas Ware, soon to be United States senator, endorsed colonization. One of the strongest auxiliaries in Georgia was an outgrowth of the Milledgeville society, the Putnam County Auxiliary Society, with Judge C. B. Strong of the supreme courts and Congressman John A. Cuthbert as officers. In Charleston he secured $50 pledges from Senator William Smith, diplomatist Joel Poinsett, and the Reverend Christopher Gadsen, rector of St. Philip's and later bishop of South Carolina. Serving as local agent, Gadsen collected over $500 from leading Charleston citizens, including $50 from Charles C. Pinckney.

Arriving in Raleigh during a session of the supreme court, Meade enlisted "the highest talents, authorities and wealth of the state" in his auxiliary. Governor John Branch was president, and other officers included Colonel William Polk, Chief Justice John L. Taylor, Justice Leonard Henderson, former congressman Archibald Henderson, and Joseph Gales, Sr., editor of the *Raleigh Register*. At Chapel Hill, the Reverend Dr. Joseph Caldwell, president of the university, was chief officer in the local auxiliary.

Occasionally Meade addressed free Negro audiences and explained the merits of African colonization. In Savannah, he exploded rumors that the society wished to make colonization compulsory, declaring that the Colonization Society was the "offspring of piety and benevolence." In Charleston he descanted on the missionary prospects of colonization. When his listeners declared their willingness to emigrate, he congratulated them for displaying "good sense, piety, sagacity, and information." In the same city a British-educated mulatto named Holman, a friend of Paul Cuffee, told Meade that at least forty free blacks wished to emigrate.[6]

Spurred by Meade's success in Georgia, North Carolina, and South Carolina, members of the board planted auxiliaries in Virginia and Maryland. Small societies sprang up at Harpers Ferry, Jefferson county, Shepardstown, Harrisonburg, and New London, Virginia, and in Prince George's county and Leonard Town, St. Mary's county, Maryland. Meanwhile, Secretary Caldwell journeyed to Philadelphia and New York to bolster the almost extinct auxiliaries and to collect overdue subscriptions. The Reverend Jacob Janeway, Bishop William White, the Reverend William A. Muhlenberg, lawyer Horace Binney, and trader Richard Dale contributed almost $300. At New York, friends of colonization promised Caldwell "a very handsome subscription." [7]

In the fall of 1819, the managers sent Meade to the eastern states to repeat the formula of success. He carried the colonizationists' tidings as far as Maine, laying the groundwork for numerous auxiliaries. Former Secretary of State Timothy Pickering advised him to use the newspapers "to excite public attention" and acquaint New Englanders with the scheme. Reminding Meade that New England wealth rested on commerce and concentrated in cities, he urged that he begin his tour at Boston, "our metropolis, where there is much wealth, much humane and Christian feeling, and great liberality." He hinted that Boston men would readily support colonization if they thought they were *taking the lead* in Massachusetts in this important business." [8]

At New Haven Meade enlisted Simeon Baldwin, son-in-law of Roger Sherman and former judge of the supreme court of errors, President Jeremiah Day of Yale College, and ex-senator David Daggett. At Hartford he collected money from Henry L. Ellsworth, son of Chief Justice Oliver Ellsworth and president of the Aetna Insurance Company, Seth Terry, pioneer worker with deaf-mutes, and William L. Stone, editor of the *Mirror*. At Providence, Rhode Island, and Newburyport, Massachusetts, smaller societies pledged their aid. Meade returned to Washington confident that the embryo groups would crystallize into large, wealthy associations.[9]

Meade's decision in 1820 to return to church duties was a serious injury for the Colonization Society. Too content with his bellwether success, the managers hired no replacement. For two years no agent prodded the men Meade pledged to the cause. Only occasional and meager publicity nourished the small auxiliaries. In 1820 the society published *An Essay on the Late Institution of the American Colonization Society* providing data on African geography, Biblical sanctions for missionary work in Africa, and prospects favoring colonial ventures. The pamphlet pronounced the birth of the society an historical event "fraught with more important consequences" than any since the Declaration of Independence or the adoption of the Constitution.[10] The *Annual Report* was the only regularly issued propaganda piece. It carried speeches, letters, editorials, and testimonials, plus lurid descriptions of the slave trade and miscellaneous facts about Africa. Friendly congressmen such as Charles F. Mercer scratched their franks on the society's mail.

In the spring of 1820, a young teacher whom Meade met in Maine persuaded the managers to issue a monthly journal. Jehudi Ashmun, born in Champlain, New York, alumnus of Burlington and Middlebury Colleges, once hoped to become a missionary to Africa. This ambition never entirely faded. After a brief, beclouded career as principal of a small academy at Bangor, Maine, he wandered, jobless and aimless, to Washington, D.C. He proposed to edit a journal that would give the public a "distinct, and exhaustive view of the great objects to which the exercise of African philanthropy may be most profitably directed." The managers cautiously agreed to subsidize his journal but they did not conceal their misgivings about the expense of publishing a periodical.

In July, 1820, the first issue of *The African Intelligencer* appeared. Its thirty-two pages contained sections on the slave trade, African geography, and the expedition of the *Elizabeth*, plus addresses, memorials, and the constitution of the society. Most of the copy came directly from the pages of the *National Intelligencer*. One number convinced the managers that there was not enough public support for the journal, and they promptly canceled their agreement with Ashmun.[11]

Want of system in building and sustaining auxiliaries and maintaining a flow of publicity mirrored the managers' administrative habits. They were busy men who spent only spare time doing the society's work. They left most matters to Secretary Caldwell. In his casual hands the society's publicity, correspondence, and records required no more than one or two desk drawers in his office in the Capitol. He kept no copies of outgoing letters, and with few exceptions he destroyed incoming letters once they received an answer. Only those containing publicity value survived in the *National Intelligencer* or the *Annual Report*. In addition, he was sapping his energies in leading religious revivals. "All day he goes from house to house, exhorting and praying, and every night at different meetings," Mrs. Samuel Harrison Smith observed. "As his health decreases, his zeal and labours increase." She did not approve of his "Methodist type meetings." "They are introducing all the habits and hymns, of the methodists into our presbyterian churches," she complained. "After the regular service is closed by the clergymen, the congregation rise, and strike up a methodist hymn, sung amidst the groans and sobs of the newly converted, or convicted, as they call them, then Mr. Caldwell calls on the *mourners* to come forward, and he and others pray over them." His neglect of the Colonization Society's affairs prevailed until 1823, when, paralyzed and dying, he surrendered routine duties to a clerk.[12]

With no traveling agents and insufficient publicity, the auxiliaries stagnated. In Georgia and South Carolina, the green stalk of colonization shriveled in the heat of the Missouri debates on slavery. No agent visited the auxiliaries and reassured them that African colonization was not a Trojan horse for "absolute abolition" and a northern plot to cripple the southern economy. Local colonizationists had to fall back on their own devices. The Putnam county society of Georgia hastily purged itself of any taint of abolitionism and tried to fashion distinctions between colonization and emancipation. It assured Georgians that southern men controlled the parent society, a fact which ought to "remove apprehension from the mind of the southern proprietor." The parent society could neither force free Negroes to emigrate or slave-owners to emancipate. Colonization actually made slaves more obedient by removing free blacks, "the most fruitful source of discontent." It knotted the "bond of servile fidelity" and thwarted "domestic insurrection, and the conflagration of cities." [13]

The *Missionary,* one of Georgia's strongest advocates of colonization, asserted that colonizationists did not question the right of property. The society, run by "some of the best and most enlightened men of our country," ranks "in importance with the Foreign Mission and American Bible Societies, and like them, is calculated to do great and extensive good." The moribund Putnam county society declared that colonization was the only "moderate, middle course" for preserving the Union. But distinctions between colonization and emancipation were too blurred in the public mind. One Georgia colonizationist privately warned colleagues to "proceed with utmost circumspection" and say nothing that can "excite apprehensions of improper inference with the slave population." The fledgling societies in Savannah, Augusta, and Milledgeville ceased to function, and the men who freely placed their names high on their rosters stayed away from meetings. Thousands of dollars pledged to the parent society never reached Washington.[14]

In Charleston, Charles C. Pinckney recanted his endorsement of colonization. The Charleston *Mercury* followed his move with a series of essays signed "Brutus" condemning colonization as "an insidious attack on the tranquility of the south" and a "nest egg" of abolitionists who wished to hatch "anxiety, inquietude and troubles to which there could be no end." The Colonization Society was "reprobated at the south, and justly regarded as murderous in its principles." [15]

The managers grieved over the southern attacks, but they had no effective system for countering critics and disentangling primary motives. Their feeble rejoinders that African colonization was benevolent and moderate tardily appeared in the *Annual Reports.* Any effort to "enlarge the stock of human happiness," they lamented, always attracted "sordid and degrading" adherents as well as "the most benevolent and exalted." Colonization should appeal to the "interest of the South, to the humanity of the North, and to the religion of the whole country." They deplored "that spirit of animosity which forms its judgments without distinctions of reason." [16]

These belated professions of good motives did not suffice in Georgia or South Carolina. Meanwhile, with no real encouragement from Washington, other auxilaries waned. Small societies in Rhode Island, Connecticut, Massachusetts, and Maine went into eclipse. In 1822, the managers sent young Ralph Randolph Gurley, a graduate of Yale College and licensed to preach, to retrace Meade's footsteps in New England. He received encouragement from the Reverend Joel Hawes in Hartford and the Reverend Dr. Edward Payson in Portland, but colonization's flame flickered so low that he was unable to collect more than his traveling expenses. In September, 1822, Boston men led by George Blake and Lewis Tappan publicly spurned colonization and formed the Society for the Suppression of the Slave Trade with Daniel Webster as president. Few slaveholders, the Boston men scolded, genuinely wished to free their slaves for colonization in Africa.

After 1822, the only thriving New England auxiliary was the Vermont Colonization Society, sponsored by Charles Marsh, a charter member of the parent society. Elijah Paine, former senator and judge of the district court, Cornelius Van Ness, soon after governor of the state, and General Abner Forbes lent glints of prestige. In four years the lone outpost in New England sent $1,500 to Washington.[17]

With only limited assistance from the government and no immediate prospects for complete acceptance in Congress, the American Colonization Society desperately needed private assistance. The steady growth of the colony and the rising colonial expenses sharpened the need. In the spring of 1823, with the society sliding toward the vortex of debt, the managers called a special meeting to decide the fate of the project. They asked friends of the society to diagnose its ailments and prescribe health-giving remedies. "The Society has arrived at a crisis . . . critical and important," they declared.[18]

On the appointed day in June, 1823, a handful of men gathered at City Hall, Washington, D.C. The majority were managers and officers of the society. Joseph Gales, Sr., who happened to be in town, represented the Raleigh auxiliary. Two delegates came from the Baptist General Convention, and two students traveled all the way from Andover Theological Seminary. The smallness of the gathering gave the conference the air of an inquest.[19] Doubt and confusion prevailed. The conferees examined the society's decayed finances and conceded that the situation was grave. But they could not agree on a plan of action. The real issue was whether the society could continue its work without government sponsorship. Some of the delegates did not believe the voluntary system could sustain a colonial establishment. They urged new applications to Congress for aid in sending more emigrants to Africa and perhaps granting territorial status to the new colony. Others were confident that a campaign for popular support would bring ample donations. They urged the society to flood the land with propaganda, station agents in every state, and build hundreds of auxiliaries.[20]

Young Leonard Bacon of Andover Seminary was the chief spokesman for the latter program. At Andover his report to the Society for Inquiry concerning Missions, in which he praised colonization as the vehicle for Christianizing Africa, had caused "uncommon excitement" among the missionary-minded students. He came to Washington with Solomon Peck, his classmate, as the representative of the Society for Inquiry. Bacon bluntly traced the Colonization Society's ills to careless, inept administration. The brash seminarist deplored the "want of that energy and business-like regularity of operations" that strengthened other benevolent associations. He criticized the managers' failure to maintain "constant communication with the public" and urged them to begin a periodical to be broadcast over the Union. He suggested the prompt appointment of traveling agents for every corner of the country, and the deliberate weaving of a vast network of auxiliaries. He asked the society to charter at least four emigrant ships that year, arguing that to load and outfit Africa-bound ships at Boston, Providence, New York, Norfolk, Petersburg, and Charleston would dramatize colonization and quicken donations.

He also recommended the creation of a special school where future colonists could learn how to build a colony and teach Christianity to the African tribes.[21]

Bacon's bold program was too sweeping for the conferees. Oppressed by an empty treasury, they tabled his motion for ships and shunted aside his missionary training school plan. Grudgingly the managers agreed to publish a periodical at some future time but only when the number of subscribers warranted. The conference adjourned without adopting further measures, except to beg the public for more donations.

Although the managers wished to believe the root of their trouble was financial starvation, they respected Bacon's searching criticism of the society's lax administration. More important, they accepted his suggestion that the society remodel itself as a self-sustaining benevolent society with a network of auxiliaries. They invited Bacon to come to Washington as Caldwell's assistant and eventual successor. But he declined, preferring to make his career in the church. He later took an active part in bringing the movement to New England. For many years articles praising colonization flowed from his busy pen.[22]

The managers next turned to their New England agent, twenty-five-year-old Ralph Randolph Gurley, son of a Connecticut Congregationalist minister and stepson of Revolutionary General Absalom Peters. Gurley's brother-in-law was secretary of the Maine Missionary Society. His brother, Henry Hosford Gurley, was a freshman member of Congress. A quiet, retiring young man of soft demeanor and unaffected simplicity, Ralph Gurley impressed all who came to know him. Friends admired his even, always serene temperament and his persistent fidelity to the African colonization cause. Congressman Elisha Whittlesey described him as "pure, upright and benevolent." Mrs. Samuel Harrison Smith of Washington, D.C., characterized him as "a most interesting man; in his looks, a hero of romance; in his temper and life, one of the most perfect Christians I ever knew." The managers voted to pay him $600 a year.[23]

Young Gurley eagerly identified himself with the struggling movement. In the beginning, his duties as resident agent were the routine, menial labors relegated to a clerk. The ailing Caldwell still retained full authority as Secretary, and all policy matters passed under his palsied hands. With devotion and vigor, Gurley opened an office and set about to bring "method, uniformity and system" to the parent society. He kept records of all routine expenditures and methodically preserved and indexed all incoming letters in bound books.[24] The important work of compiling the *Annual Report* fell to him. In the spring of 1824, he and Congressman Mercer assembled the largest report ever issued under the society's imprimatur. In his spare hours Gurley collected and arranged a small library of books and pamphlets about Africa, colonization, the Negro, and auxiliary society reports. Though confined to pettifogging work, he was serving his apprenticeship and digesting all details of operating the society.

The appointment of Ralph Gurley as resident agent marked a turning point. The managers were moving toward the voluntary system and seeking to build a systematic movement. They harkened to Bacon's call for traveling agents and many new auxiliaries. Pointing to a few small societies in Virginia and Maryland, they asked "And why may not similar auxiliary institutions be formed in most of the counties and towns throughout the Union?" In the summer of 1823, they commissioned agents to visit several states along the Atlantic. But none went below North Carolina, for the managers were convinced that an agent could no longer collect enough in South Carolina and Georgia to pay his keep. Instead, they looked to the eastern states where rich sister societies flourished. They urged their friends "possessed of zeal, industry, and perseverance" to forward the cause.[25]

During July, 1823, the Reverend Leonard Bacon and the Reverend Chester Wright, secretary of the faithful Vermont Colonization Society, toured New England. They held meetings in various Congregationalist churches and begged contributions. Their labors harvested small returns. They established no new auxiliaries, and Wright remitted only $60 from Boston men and $42 from Salem.[26]

In the fall of 1823, the managers shifted their attention to New York state where untilled fields invited colonization plowmen. They appointed Loring D. Dewey, thirty-year-old Presbyterian clergyman from New York and a friend of Leonard Bacon, agent for the entire state. He started his tour in New York city, refurbishing the auxiliary established by Mills in 1817. Philanthropist Henry Rutgers led off Dewey's subscription list with $100. Dewey persuaded the rejuvenated auxiliary to issue a pamphlet praising colonization as "the only possible means of gradually ridding ourselves of a mighty evil, and of obliterating the foulest stain upon our nation's honor." [27]

Lacking extensive knowledge of the colonization scheme and having access only to scattered *Annual Reports* and an occasional *Address,* traveling agents devised their arguments to fit local appeal. Colonization as a missionary project for the "degraded continent" was a standard argument. Another stressed the evils and heartaches of the slave trade. Another hailed colonization as an orderly, painless form of emancipation. Agent Dewey used these arguments and contributed a fresh one. For the practical minded he concocted elaborate calculations to show that in forty years colonization could remove all free Negroes living in the United States. He would radically reduce the free Negro increase by drawing off six thousand young men and women each year. By colonizing those reaching the age of reproduction, the society could beat the statistics. At the end of ten years, Dewey forecasted, the Colonization Society could slash the free Negro population by 100,000. At this rate, none but the aged and infirm would dwell in the United States in 1863.

The New York city auxiliary flourished similar calculations, arguing that the annual removal of thirty thousand Negroes—free and slave—could obliterate the entire black population in fifty years. With figures to prove that such a task was wholly practicable, Dewey and the New York city colonizationists renewed the call for extensive federal assistance. "The object is and ought to be a national one," they declared. An appropriation of $360,-000 a year would remove all free Negroes and $1,500,000 a year would remove the slave population as well. [28]

For several months Dewey toured the state, following the Hudson river as far as Albany, crossing and recrossing the river to call at villages on either bank, and establishing numerous auxiliaries. He broadcast the New York city pamphlet containing the computations of removal. He found it useful in awakening interest upstate. At Albany he created a society with Harmanus Bleecker, lawyer and former congressman, John Lansing, Jr., son of Chancellor John Lansing, Benjamin F. Butler, lawyer and politician, and Congressman Stephen Van Rensselaer, perhaps the state's foremost citizen and certainly its richest. Dewey urged the Albany men to sponsor an emigrant ship to Africa, but the infant auxiliary did not feel strong enough for this long step.[29]

Dewey was disappointed in his progress. He found that drum-beating for African colonization did not reverberate far. The excitement of politics and prior interest in the Greek cause and other well-entrenched benevolent enterprises drowned his bid for attention. Bad weather slowed his itinerary and discouraged large audiences. In all, he collected less than $900 in a year, and his salary of nearly $600 shrank his remittances to Washington. In several communities he encountered strong opposition. Some men told him the society was just "a scheme of the slaveholders to get rid of the free blacks and their surplus slaves." Others assumed the colonists perished as soon as they arrived in desert Africa.[30]

It was evident to Dewey that African colonization had to overcome prejudice and misinformation before it could draw substantial support from New York. The agent was losing enthusiasm just at the time the managers were hoping the voluntary system could save the society from bankruptcy and the colony from extinction.

VIII

CRISIS YEARS: 1823–1824

———————— ◄••► ————————

LORING DEWEY's dismay took a turn that shocked the board of managers and threatened the entire course of the African colonization movement. Dewey began thinking in terms of emigration rather than colonization. On his travels in New York he met several men, one a citizen of Haiti, who argued that Haiti was preferable to Africa because the climate was milder and an independent Negro republic already governed the island.

The Haitian emigration project was not new in 1824. New York newspapers had already pointed to Haiti as "a land of promise" more accessible and attractive than Africa. The New York *Statesman* had hopefully greeted the creation of the Colonization Society as an agency for fostering the "spirit of emigration" among free Negroes. It hoped thousands of Negroes would seek "liberty and property" not only at Cape Mesurado but at Madagascar, South Africa, Sierra Leone, Colombia, and Haiti. The rulers of Haiti encouraged immigration. President Alexandre Pétion and high officials of the small republic issued blanket invitations to free blacks "who groan under the dominion of barbarous prejudice." Artisans such as smiths, braziers, tinsmiths, carpenters, and boot– and shoemakers, one Haiti official asserted, could earn as much as twelve dollars a week. Agriculturalists could earn four dollars. The Haitians promised citizenship after one year's residence and called attention to their constitutional prohibition against slavery.[1]

While traveling in New York state, Loring Dewey wrote to President Pétion's successor, the bold, enterprising Jean Pierre Boyer, and inquired if Haiti still was prepared to grant "ample means" to stimulate emigration from the United States. Benevolent men lamented the "unhappy lot" of free Negroes but prejudice frustrated efforts to "elevate them in moral character." President Boyer, thinking Dewey represented the Colonization Society, promptly responded that his government would gladly cooperate with the society in providing transportation costs and homesteads for emigrants. He told Dewey his ideas exuded "the most perfect philanthropy," and he boasted that "the desire to serve the cause of humanity" animated his own deeds. He described Haiti as a land destined to be "a sacred asylum, where our unfortunate brethren . . . will see their wounds healed by the balm of equality." [2]

Boyer and his advisers privately viewed American emigration as a potent stimulant to the future prosperity of Haiti. After two decades of intermittent strife, the island was depopulated and its economy disrupted. The small republic was seeking both commercial ties and recognition as an independent nation. As a sugar processor looking for markets, Boyer expected emigration would "necessarily augment the Commerce of the United States with Hayti, both in imports and exports." He discredited African colonization, saying Africa was an arid land that would work desperate hardships on newcomers. The *Albany Gazette* pronounced Boyer's statements "plausible, and bespeak a feeling and a generous mind." It joined other newspapers in urging the Colonization Society to consider sending its colonists to Haiti. [3]

Ten days after Boyer's letter reached Dewey, Citizen Jonathan Granville, a special agent of the Haiti government, arrived in the United States with blanket instructions to cooperate with American "Philanthropists and Benevolent Societies" in hastening emigrants to Haiti. President Boyer supplied Granville with several thousand dollars for chartering emigrant ships and authorized him to send six thousand emigrants. Citizen Granville promised $40 for each passage, telling free Negro audiences in Philadelphia and New York that his government would give free land and provisions to each family. He flooded the newspapers with emigration literature, and by August, 1824, he was able to send thirty Negro families from Philadelphia. And more were preparing to leave. [4]

In the meantime, Dewey revealed his negotiations with President Boyer to the Colonization Society. The first response came from General Robert G. Harper who advised Dewey that blending colonization with emigration was inexpedient. He amiably suggested the creation of a separate, affiliated emigration society. The managers, however, took a less generous view. They saw the Haiti scheme as a dangerous rival. The board angrily reprimanded Dewey for his indiscretion "whilst acting as agent of this society." Secretary Caldwell ordered him to quit all plans that "contravene the fundamental object" of the Colonization Society. The managers sent letters to President Boyer, repudiating Dewey's correspondence as unauthorized and making it clear that the society did not intend to divert its attention from Africa to Haiti. They also begged the New York city auxiliary to "take no measures on behalf of Haitian emigration." [5]

Their exhortations came too late. Dewey adopted General Harper's suggestion and organized the Society for Promoting the Emigration of Free Persons of Colour to Hayti. It was affiliated to the extent that it drew its members from the New York city colonization society. Dewey converted patrons of benevolence such as Matthew Clarkson, Professor John Griscom, and William Colgate to the new association. They raised an auxiliary among free Negroes living in New York city, issued an emigration pamphlet, and solicited donations. In Philadelphia free Negro leader Richard Allen, foe of African colonization, served as president of the Haytien Emigration Society. Haitian emigration lured money from Quaker groups which did not wholly approve African colonization. Friends in North Carolina who once donated money to colonization now subsidized the rival project.[6]

Almost as quickly as it began, the emigration project collapsed. A year after launching the plan, President Boyer suddenly withdrew his assistance. He found that his American agents were absconding with the transportation funds. Also, the fear that large numbers of aliens would conspire against his rule chilled his ardor. The new settlers' restlessness and frank disillusionment gave substance to his fears. The American blacks complained that Haiti officials misused them and Haiti citizens stole their property with impunity. Despite President Boyer's eloquent promises, the differences of religion, law, language, and custom were large obstacles to happy readjustment. Sharp class lines wrecked dreams of equality. Quakers visiting the emigrants brought back the report that they preferred slavery in the United States to poverty and persecution in Haiti. Such rumors smothered all enthusiasm for Haiti. In 1825, two hundred emigrants returned to the United States, and in the next few years more trickled home.[7]

The managers of the Colonization Society took little public notice of Haitian emigration, though on one occasion Ralph Gurley hinted that it really was a plot to assist fugitive slaves out of the country.[8] But Dewey's defection and the mushrooming interest in Haiti genuinely alarmed them. In the summer of 1824, they sent two reliable agents to repair rents in Philadelphia and New York and to extend auxiliaries into New England. The managers turned to Dr. Eli Ayres of Baltimore, recently returned from the colony, as the person best equipped to scotch rumors that Africa was an endless desert infested with man-eating beasts and stung with man-killing climate. He was almost recovered from his bout with the African fever. They also invited the Reverend George Boyd, Episcopal rector of St. John's, Philadelphia, to accompany Ayres. Boyd had been a lawyer in New York before entering the ministry. As the son-in-law of Robert Livingstone he had influential connections in the state. In addition, he was a leading figure in the Pennsylvania diocese and he served as secretary and general agent of the Domestic Committee of the Board of Missions of the Protestant Episcopal Church.[9]

Ayres and Boyd began their tour at Philadelphia, paused in Princeton, and visited New York city. They found strong colonization sentiment in Finley's old home. Robert Field Stockton, Ayres's partner in seizing Cape Mesurado, presided at a meeting in Princeton's Presbyterian Church at which the New Jersey Colonization Society was formed. Several professors in the college and seminary were officers of the auxiliary—Professors John MacLean, Charles Hodge, Luther Halsey, and the Reverend Robert Baird. Stockton boldly declared that the "first and great object" of colonization was "a gradual abolition of Slavery." Attorney James S. Green, son of Princeton's President Ashbel Green, used business jargon to explain that slavery was a "moral debt" and colonization was the "sinking fund, by the gradual operation of which, this debt will be ultimately discharged." [10]

The New Jersey Colonization Society secured endorsement from Senator Theodore Frelinghuysen, a prominent actor in various benevolent societies. He lauded African colonization over Haitian emigration, saying the United States owed a special debt to Africa, not Haiti. The sins of the slave trade weighed heavily on the nation. "We have fed and nourished—yes, glutted the maw of this infernal Moloah," he declared. "It is recorded against us." [11]

Ayres and Boyd came away from Princeton with the conviction that the Colonization Society would have strong adherents in the orthodox Calvinist seminaries. They recommended that the parent society offer prizes to Princeton and Andover seminary students for the best essays on colonization. "Such a number of young men, returning annually to their homes, with minds stored with correct information, and warmed with zeal for the cause, must in a considerable degree promote the interests of the Society," they remarked.[12]

In larger communities, Haitian emigration still overshadowed all interest in colonization. In Philadelphia and New York, Ayres and Boyd found Citizen Granville monopolized all attention, and they did not even attempt public collections. They also encountered hostility to African colonization. Some men sneered that the Colonization Society was merely "an expedient devised by the holders of slaves" to get rid of free blacks. Ayres and Boyd replied that northern men fathered the scheme, pointing to the "enlightened zeal and indefatigable exertion" of New Jersey's Robert Finley, founder of the society.[13]

Their journey through New England succeeded only in planting a series of "Corresponding Committees" in New Haven, Hartford, Providence, and Boston. Men of wealth and prestige served on the committees: Nicholas Brown and the Reverend Stephen Gano in Providence; Henry L. Ellsworth, Dr. Mason Fitch Cogswell, and the Reverend Joel Hawes in Hartford; Timothy Dwight, the Reverend Harry Croswell, and Simeon Baldwin in New Haven; David Hale, Samuel Hubbard, and John Tappan in Boston. Ayres and Boyd hoped the committees would be nuclei for future auxiliaries in that section, but their hopes were not

high. They discovered that New Englanders, accustomed to giving to numerous benevolent societies and missionary enterprises
with headquarters in their region, expected colonization to derive
its support from the federal government. One New England congressman privately assured Ayres that he and his New England
colleagues would vote for any "definite proposal" by southern
Congressmen—if they promised to "hold themselves responsible"
for it. Hopes for federal subsidy discouraged large contributions.
The home of the great philanthropic societies failed to fill the
agents' pockets. They sadly concluded that "little dependence can
be placed upon any effectual or permanent pecuniary aid from
the Northern and Eastern sections of our country" until southerners took a strong stand for colonization.[14]

The flowering of a rival emigration scheme and the resistance
of eastern states to colonization were deadening blows to the
managers' hopes for wide popular support. Refusal to join forces
with Haitian emigration irrevocably committed the managers to
African colonization. Unfortunately, their small colony at Cape
Mesurado was facing waves of disaster that threatened to suf-
focate the settlement and discredit the African colonization principle. Unlike the Haitian emigration threat, these disasters did not
resolve themselves.

Dr. Ayres's long absence from Cape Mesurado in 1822 occurred when the new colony was beset with starvation, fever, and
hostile tribes. The situation had grown desperate when Jehudi
Ashmun stepped ashore in August, 1822. Following his brief and
fruitless association with the Colonization Society as editor of
The African Intelligencer, he drifted to different jobs—all without
success. He failed as the editor of the *Theological Repertory,* an
Episcopalian journal started by the Reverend William H. Wilmer
of Alexandria. He wrote an inspirational biography of Samuel
Bacon, the government's first agent to Africa, and hoped, in vain,
that royalties from the book would whittle down his large debts,
including a printing bill of $1,200.[15]

Suddenly, a "mercantile mania" gripped Ashmun. Under heavy
pressure from his creditors, he conceived a plan to trade with the
new colony at Cape Mesurado. He proposed to go to Africa to

open a trading station for the Baltimore Trading Company. He wanted the Colonization Society to grant him a monopoly patent for all trade with the colony. He would collect a fee of one-third on all shipments from Cape Mesurado. The pious-speaking Ashmun linked commercial plans with the spread of Christianity, insisting that "mercantile cupidity" did not dictate his plan, but rather "soundest policy" and "benevolence to the natives themselves." Trade conducted on a scrupulously honest plane, he argued, would wean the natives from their dealings with vicious slavers and instruct them in "the honorable exercise of industry." [16]

In May, 1822, Ashmun and his wife sailed to Africa in the brig *Strong*. They planned to remain a few weeks while he launched his commercial enterprise. But Ashmun remained six years, and his personality became an inextricable part of the colony's earliest history.

In 1822, the colony was totally unprepared for trade with the outside world. Its primary concern was survival. The feeble settlement barely subsisted. Ashmun, with doubtful authority, speedily assumed command in Dr. Ayres's absence and temporarily set aside his commercial dreams. By encouraging tribal jealousies and dissensions, he managed to delay an attack on the colony. Hurriedly he surveyed the colony's military resources. Of 135 settlers, only 35 were capable of bearing arms. In all, the pioneers possessed forty muskets and a few rusty field pieces. The self-appointed governor ordered the cannon cleaned and strategically mounted. He established the "Lieutenant's Corps" and drilled thirteen of the rescued Africans who had accompanied him on the *Strong*. He also supervised the building of small stockades around the gun emplacements and ordered the colonists to throw down a heavy carpet of tangles and thorns to impede the barefoot invaders.

Just as this important work began, Ashmun, his wife, and most of the *Strong*'s passengers came down with the dread "acclimating fever." Mrs. Ashmun died. Her husband, sometimes delirious, struggled to his feet each day to supervise the defense work. On August 31, he put the colony under martial law.[17]

For eight weeks the enclave dwelt in fear. When at last native informers brought word that an attack was impending, Ashmun rose from his sick bed to direct the defenders. At dawn, November 11, 1822, a throng of native warriors burst upon the frantic colonists. A sudden rush of hundreds of natives, shooting muskets, brandishing spears, and screaming vengeance, overwhelmed the team at the first mounted gun before it fired a shot. While the on-rushing invaders paused to plunder four houses in their path, Ashmun rallied his small forces. He aimed a rapid-firing brass cannon, double-shotted with ball and grape, squarely into the enemy's ranks. At thirty to sixty yards, with hundreds of warriors pressed shoulder to shoulder, the flashing cannon drove its lethal charge into a "solid mass of living flesh." The crowded ranks halted in confusion and horror. They struggled to turn away, but the massive host behind blocked their escape. The colonial defenders regained the lost cannon, and together the two field pieces raked the agonized invaders until they stumbled back to the forest.

The blood of the enemy drenched the small clearing on the river, and hundreds of their wounded, dead, and dying littered the tangled trails of the dark forest. The colonists grimly watched native canoes bear off scores of injured, and whenever their rescue squads came within range the cannon splattered them with more grape and ball. In the next weeks the putrefying dead stank in the thickets. The colonists' casualties were slight, but the natives had stolen seven children. Only half of the thirty-five defenders actually engaged in battle. They had enough powder to last one more hour.[18]

Peace did not come until a second, less bloody assault again turned to defeat for the natives. In the interval, the colonists had purchased needed supplies and ammunition from a passing British trader. Not long after, the British schooner *Prince Regent* from Sierra Leone negotiated an armistice. Major Alexander Gordon Laing, the British explorer, adjusted truce terms with the natives and made the governor of Sierra Leone arbitrator in future disputes. He left a squad of twelve men to maintain peace in the colony.

Native attacks ceased, but a more persistent enemy obstructed the work of building the colony. The African fever raged peri-

odically. Each newcomer was sure to suffer high fever and rack-
ing headaches. If the pestilence did not kill, it left the victims
debilitated for weeks. The least exertion assured a ferocious re-
currence. The colonists had no physician, but they applied
medicine-man nostrums to the sick and dying. The fever usually
was fatal to whites. Eight of Laing's men lasted less than four
weeks. In the spring of 1823, the U. S. S. *Cyane,* under Captain
Richard T. Spence, visited Cape Mesurado. Spence ordered part
of his crew to build the colony's defenses, including a stone tower.
Fever stopped the work. Spence removed his men, but it was too
late. Forty died at sea. Recurring attacks ate away at Ashmun's
strength, but he clung to his first judgment that "no situation in
western Africa can be more salubrious." Though he remained in
Africa six years, he never fully regained his health.[19]

The long interval of time and space separating the managers
from the Cape forced them to rely on their agent for their knowledge and understanding of colonial affairs. No manager ever
visited the colony. The colonial agent was the board's eyes and
ears, and in many cases the board could merely ratify decisions
that had been in effect for several months. Nevertheless, it retained
a lively proprietary interest, and though chained by inadequate
communication, it demanded close rapport with its agent in spirit
if not in fact.

The gaunt, half-sick Ashmun was not the managers' ideal of a
colonial agent. They knew him as an inept editor, a debt-ridden
failure, and an avowed adventurer seeking profits in the colony.
Distrust deepened when owners of the *Strong* presented Ashmun's
unauthorized draft on the society's treasury for $1,400 worth of
trade goods. He belatedly justified his action on the ground that
the society would gain by the investment when he sold the goods
to neighboring tribes. If the society preferred, he offered, it could
charge the trade goods to his salary and let him reap the profits.
Inasmuch as the managers had not voted him a salary and did not
intend to, they found Ashmun's behavior both galling and pre-
sumptuous.[20]

In 1823, the managers sent Dr. Ayres back to the colony on the
Oswego. He carried strict instructions to depose Ashmun. He also
carried perfunctory resolutions thanking Ashmun for his part in

the war, but he did not give Ashmun an appointment in the colonial administration. The managers strengthened Ayres's authority by putting the whole question of Ashmun's compensation for nine months' work in his hands.

Ashmun's eclipse was brief. He readily gave up his authority and remained in the colony. Meanwhile, Ayres began to lay out the townsite according to Dr. Thornton's plan. At the direction of the managers, he surveyed the land and assigned town lots to the settlers, but those who had built and defended their homes hotly resented the new arrangements. They were jealous of the newcomers who shared equally in the division and challenged the colonial agent's motives, charging that he had a personal interest in the property distribution. Dr. Ayres was a short-tempered, testy authoritarian. While the settlers were smarting under his sharp rebuke, he tactlessly announced that, at the order of the managers, he was terminating food rations after June 1, 1824. The managers, he explained, did not wish to encourage indolence and pauperism. The move was poorly timed. The colonists charged Ayres with supplying himself liberally with delicacies they could not draw from the society's storehouse. Before resentment erupted into open resistance, fever struck Ayres and killed eight of the *Oswego*'s sixty passengers. The outbreak paralyzed work on the townsite. Ayres fled Africa in shattered health, leaving Ashmun once more to govern the "very turbulent" and complaining colonists.[21]

Determined to please the managers by implementing their policies, Ashmun resumed the work of laying out town lots and re-ordering the clustered huts. The colonists challenged the rule requiring them to labor two days a week on public works. A dozen flatly refused to work on the town survey. When Ashmun accused them of indolence and threatened to withhold rations from the strikers, they answered by raiding the storehouse. Ashmun's regime was tottering.

In December, 1823, the colonists drafted a remonstrance and sent it to the board of managers. They complained that the colonial agent had a personal interest in the division of the town lots. They also complained that the board's land policy was too harsh in requiring two years' residence and specific improvements. They prayed for a new colonial agent unlike either Ayres or Ashmun. The managers replied with a stout defense of their policies. The town plan, they said, was designed to give a "free circulation of air," not to enrich the agents. They claimed their policies sprang from disinterested benevolence, saying "It is not for ourselves we are acting; it is for you, and your Children, and those of your brethren who may hereafter join you." [22]

Ashmun's next dispatch from Africa related how dissidents had rallied around the Baptist preacher, Lott Cary, a former warehouse-hand from Richmond, armed themselves, and seized food stores. The news took five months to reach Washington. Wrathfully, the managers denounced the "wicked combination and disgraceful proceedings," revoked Cary's license to preach until "time and circumstance had evinced the deepness and sincerity of his repentance," and bitterly censured Ashmun for failing to take drastic steps to punish insolence and abuse. The managers favored repressive measures. "In such cases you have a right to fine and imprison for contempt, immediately and without a jury," they told Ashmun. In secret instructions they directed him to arm himself and call upon near-by United States warships to suppress any disturbance. "Stop the rations of every one who refused to labour in the public service" and banish all chronic malcontents; "No idlers—no drones, must be suffered to live upon the industrious," they exclaimed. "Be ye wise as a serpent, and harmless as a Dove. . . . Be mild, calm, steady, and firm." They reproved the colonists in an address that catechized them on their duty to obey authority. "What is freedom? a government of laws! and who are supporters of these laws? the people." Obedience, they said, was the essence of patriotism.[23]

In the long interval, however, ill fortune had overtaken Jehudi Ashmun. When the *Cyrus* landed more than one hundred settlers, bringing only small quantities of food, he ordered the colony on half-rations. This step, greeted as an unwarranted act of oppression, signaled rebellion. Lott Cary and his men armed themselves with weapons from the colonial arsenal. They were an unanswerable challenge to Ashmun's authority. The colonial agent now decided that the time had come for a sea voyage. On April 1, 1824, he fled to Cape Verde Islands to await further instructions. The society's authority in the colony ebbed so low that as the ailing colonial agent departed on a stretcher, surly, hateful colonists robbed him of his money and personal belongings. Surveying these humiliating events from a distance, the exile ruefully evaluated his office as "a service replete with danger, sufferings, mortification, and toil." [24]

IX

THE EMERGENCE OF MR. GURLEY

———◆•••▶———

THE REVOLT at Cape Mesurado threatened to destroy the Colonization Society's purpose, power, and prestige. Fuming with anger, the managers determined to subdue the rebellious objects of their benevolence and smite the ingrates with patriarchal justice. At their urging, President Monroe sent a warship to Africa for the ostensible purpose of protecting government stores. He commissioned Ralph R. Gurley government agent in charge of the expedition, and in June, 1824, Gurley hastily sailed from Norfolk on the U. S. S. *Porpoise*. He did not intend to reside at Cape Mesurado. He really represented the Colonization Society and went to Africa for the sole purpose of restoring its control. The managers sent him away with the warning not to spend a single night on African soil, lest the dread fever destroy him. He prudently followed their advice, and spent each night on the *Porpoise*. He visited the colony for a week.[1]

The special mission gave Gurley an extraordinary opportunity to demonstrate his capacities beyond the clerical duties assigned to him by Secretary Caldwell. As the society's special envoy, he carried broad powers to arbitrate the colonists' complaints and penalize the malcontents. His success or failure in redeeming the colony promised to increase or decrease his prestige in the society. The apprentice was facing the most important examination of his career.

Before investigating the situation at Cape Mesurado, Gurley called on Jehudi Ashmun at Porto Praya, Cape Verde Islands. They spent three weeks thoroughly discussing colonial affairs. From their first meeting Gurley cherished a deep respect for

Ashmun. The exile's "stateliness of sorrow" made a lasting impression on the special envoy, and he quickly became convinced that neither the colonists nor the managers understood or appreciated Ashmun. He sympathetically appraised him as a "storm-shaken but self-contained spirit" who possessed a selfless soul "towering like an eagle against the storm and thundercloud, and already catching glimpses of the purity and brightness of the Heavens." [2]

Although certain the managers would object, Gurley reinstated Ashmun as colonial agent. With Ashmun's assistance, he framed a new colonial constitution which he judged "beneficent, durable, and capable of an expansion." The new constitutional provisions brought a small revolution to the colonial government. Though final power rested with the board of managers, Gurley permitted colonists to hold certain appointive offices under the colonial agent. He thought this provision gave a more republican air to the government and assured greater loyalty.

Ashmun, remembering the menaces and insults leading to his downfall, disagreed with Gurley. He expressed misgivings about the creation of a colonial advisory council, insisting that what he really needed was an armed guard to overawe unruly elements. But military rule was contrary to Gurley's basic ideas about administering the colony. Coercive measures would breed new grievances and foment political unrest, he argued. Persuasion was better than threat. He tried to convince Ashmun of the "excellence of authority 'extending more over the wills of men than over their deeds and services.' " [3]

Gurley went to Cape Mesurado and listened to the colonists' complaints. He decided that most of the friction came from the distribution of the town lots, the "turbulent and malicious temper" of a few discontents, accumulated hardships due to the want of a physician, the old government's weakness to restrain "the first tendencies towards insubordination," distrust of Ashmun's link with the Baltimore Trading Company, a generally low level of intelligence among the colonists and their lack of preparation for their new responsibilities, and finally grave doubts about the "disposition or ability" of the managers to provide "adequate aid and protection." Gurley propitiated the colonists by meting out no penalties to rebel leaders. He assembled all the inhabitants and read the new constitution, hoping it would dispel "despairful darkness" and "light up that whole land with . . . constellated glory." He secured its ratification *viva voce,* lectured them on their duty to uphold the laws, and left Africa convinced that Ashmun's regime would thrive.[4]

Ralph Gurley was alone in this expectation. The managers waspishly refused to ratify his arrangements at Cape Mesurado, doubting the wisdom of including colonists in the government and disapproving his liberal pardon for the rebels. They provided for banishment of rebels, confiscation of property, and long terms of forced labor for those who did not achieve "recognizance for good behavior." They regretted Gurley's championing of Ashmun's fallen fortunes. For several months they refused to confirm Ashmun's appointment, and they invited another man to replace him.[5]

In January, 1825, the managers abruptly countermanded this decision. A large bundle of dispatches arrived from Liberia with reports of order and prosperity in the colony. In the intervening months, Ashmun had been remarkably busy. He submitted massive reports on all details of the colony and offered extensive plans for improvements. He built a stone pier for visiting merchantmen, put up more fortifications, composed a treatise on Liberian agriculture, and sketched a map of the coast. In all communiques he emphasized the colony's progress and he unstintingly praised Gurley's wisdom. Influential colonists now held posts in the new government, and the advisory council shielded Ashmun from numerous burdens. After Gurley's visit, "wonders of Divine Goodness" occurred. There was an "increased sense of the sacredness of the Law" and a new attention to religion. These were favorable omens that Africa was nearing "the Fold and the City of God." He ranked religion as an indispensable commodity for teaching industriousness, assuring loyalty, encouraging obedience, and instilling "good character." He begged the managers to send more missionaries.[6]

Ashmun noted that Lott Cary underwent a total reform. He was no longer victim to "his own corroding tempers" and the source of "turbulent passions." He conquered his "revolting and unfeeling churlishness" and now bore "an inimitable air of sweet and profound humility." After his change of heart, he led dawn-hour prayer meetings in which he preached hard work, good behavior, and loyalty. Ashmun rewarded Cary's constructive attitude with a high post in the new government. Cary swiftly rose to vice-colonial agent. Three years later, when Ashmun returned to the United States, Cary became acting colonial agent. A fatal gunpowder explosion, which occurred while he and his followers were preparing to attack an enemy tribe, cut short his career.[7]

Profoundly impressed by Ashmun's success in winning the loyalties of the settlers, the managers belatedly praised Ashmun's "prudence and propriety," ratified the provisional constitution, and, after exonerating Ashmun for wrong-doing with regard to his unpaid debts in the United States, appointed him permanent colonial agent.[8] Afterwards, Jehudi Ashmun's position was secure and the board never again questioned his decisions or superseded his authority.

Ashmun's vindication also assured Ralph Gurley's pre-eminence in the colonization movement. Ashmun and Gurley now ruled their respective provinces in tandem. As the architect of the new constitution, loyal defender of the once friendless Ashmun, and conscientious resident agent of the parent society, Gurley now was able to formulate many of the society's policies with only token interference from the managers. Not long after Gurley returned from Africa, Caldwell ceased to attend board meetings. His paralysis worsened, and after a desperate illness, he died in June, 1825. He had but one logical successor, and the managers formally voted to make Gurley the new Secretary. He received $1,250 a year.

Ralph Gurley had many qualifications. He was youthful, zealous, and capable. He was experienced as traveling agent and lecturer, as Caldwell's clerical assistant in Washington, D.C., and as special envoy to Liberia. Though a quiet, not entirely self-assured man in ordinary life, he was a brilliant lecturer. Speaking without notes, he began in a timid, low voice "tremulous with emotion," but he gradually gained confidence. As he spoke he twined his fingers in his long black hair and threw it back from his "noble white forehead." His listeners remembered a flow of "words of purest English formed into sentences of the rarest harmony and force." He admiringly studied English classics, including Bacon, Milton, and Shakespeare, and his writing and speaking style reflected "pure old English eloquence." [9]

Office routine consumed a great part of Gurley's time. Not by habit methodical and systematic, he made special effort to wade through his clerical tasks, concentrating on one problem at a time. Routine matters bored him, but he found patience and tenacity to hack away at mounds of letters that were always piled on his desk. His replies, written in a brisk, angular scrawl, were direct and businesslike. During the winter months his office on Pennsylvania Avenue was cold and drafty. Finally, the board of managers ordered the fireplace "to be so altered as the better to subserve the purpose for which it was designed." [10] Eventually the board hired an assistant for Gurley, but there was always more work than Gurley could handle with ease, for he scrutinized all matters and impressed his personality on every transaction.

For fifty years Gurley's career centered around African colonization. He was one of a handful of dedicated laymen and clergymen who piloted the great religious and benevolent societies of the day. He ranked with such men as Jeremiah Evarts, first corresponding secretary and treasurer of the American Board of Commissioners for Foreign Missions; Rufus Anderson, who devoted forty-two years to the American Board; William A. Hallock, secretary of the American Tract Society for forty-five years; Frederick A. Packard, for thirty-eight years editorial secretary of the American Sunday School Union; and Absalom Peters, Gurley's step-brother, secretary of the United Missionary Society of New York and later secretary of the American Home Missionary Society. The men who devoted full time to the secretarial and executive concerns of the numerous meliorative societies constituted a new professional class. They managed great, nation-wide movements that affected thousands of people and handled hundreds of thousands of dollars. Besides supervising hosts of agents, remembering hundreds of local leaders by name, and understanding the vagaries of finance, they had to develop skills as orators, impromptu speakers, publicists, money raisers, and auxiliary builders. They were experts in manipulating the "public mind" or what the Reverend Calvin Colton called the "dynasty of opinion."

Gurley's appointment as Secretary inaugurated a new era for the American Colonization Society. His authority now extended beyond the daily routine of running an office. He viewed his principal task as that of enlarging the colonization cause into "a great national movement." It was the obligation of the parent society to build a popular movement throughout the Union. "There must be a central spring here," he said, "which, if touched, will be felt . . . as certainly as electricity, in the extremities of our land." His Washington office would be "a heart whose pulsations should send life and vigour into every part of the system" and coordinate the society's accumulated energies. He called for building numerous auxiliaries and distributing literature everywhere.

Gurley intended to build the national movement with appeals to benevolence. In his maiden address before the society in 1825, he implored colonization chieftains to pitch their appeals to "moral principle" and the "moral opinions of the country" rather than to "interest or expediency." In the public mind, the principle of moral duty outweighed that of self interest, even if it concerned the "wealth and public good" of the nation. "Interest [is] narrowly confined," but moral duty embraces all mankind and promises better things for posterity. The "great doctrine of expediency" was not antagonistic to "holy and benevolent purposes" but the public sometimes misunderstood the delicate relationship. The appeal to moral duty was strong enough to "set a man to work and keep him to work with unrelaxed resolution." It planted deep, lasting motivation. He urged colonization leaders to spare no effort "to affect by our writings, the public mind" and thus reach "those higher Powers upon which depends the success of our operations"—the federal and state governments. He also called for candor in revealing the society's ills, for "if we state none . . . we shall awaken little sympathy and gain little credit." [11]

In the next months Gurley followed his own prescription. In speeches and writings he told Americans that they lived in an age of benevolence, an era "distinguished by its systematic charity, by institutions for the relief of human misery, and for the improvement of human condition, and character, almost as various as that of misery or the defects and errors of mankind." Charity was the moral duty of every man. He embroidered this imperative with the corollary that citizens of a republic mutually shared the guilt for social wrongs—especially slavery. He repeated Robert Finley's theme that national guilt called for national atonement to forestall "those judgments which the Almighty inflicts for National crimes." It was a great act of charity to colonize "ignorant, vicious and unhappy" free Negroes in Africa. There they could enjoy civilization, freedom, and religious instruction without being "injurious or dangerous to our social interests." Colonization would obstruct the blood-splattered slave trade and pave the way for the end of slavery, the "flaw in the iron pillar of our constitution." [12]

Gurley ranked systematic publicity as the first step in building a national movement. "A change in public opinion," he said, comes only with the "repeated and striking exhibition of certain truths and facts." He persuaded the managers to launch a monthly journal. The job of editing the periodical became one of his many duties. The first issue of the *African Repository and Colonial Journal* came off the press in March, 1825. It promised to "furnish the public with accurate information concerning the plans and propects" of the society and to provide a "minute report . . . of the condition and progress of the colony." In format the *Repository* was octavo size with heavy colored wrappers and thirty-two double column pages. Gurley deliberately modeled it in "style and execution" after the *Christian Observer,* the foremost organ for British benevolent societies. Subscriptions were two dollars a year, and at the end of the first year, Gurley claimed four hundred subscribers.[13]

Every number was a testimonial for colonization. Gurley relied on letters of praise, extracts from African travel books, and reprints of newspaper articles. True to the journal's pledge to "communicate any new and interesting intelligence . . . relating to the Geography, Natural History, Manners and Customs of Africa," Gurley published pieces entitled "Observations on the Early History of the Negro Race," "Traits of the African Character," "Specimens of African Genius," "Moral Qualities of the

Africans," "An Account of the Kroomen, on the Coast of Africa," "Customs of the Gold Coast," and "Some Account of the Soosoos." One essay described the wildly "destructive ravages" of the dread Harmattan, a hot, brisk fury of wind that periodically swept out of the Sahara and burned all vegetation in its path. Another detailed the breeding and uses of the dromedary, "an extraordinary creature . . . peculiarly adapted, by Divine Providence, for the service of man in the sandy deserts of Africa and Asia." [14]

Each copy of the *Repository* was a salvo for Liberia. Gurley printed generous portions of Ashmun's official correspondence. Colonial dispatches usually stressed the steady prosperity and rhythmic growth of the colony. The *Repository* greeted the steady rise in population, increased church and Sabbath school membership, and peaceful relations with African tribes as evidence that colonization was triumphant. Ashmun took time to compose essays about the colonists, agriculture, topography, and history. In 1826, the founding of the *Liberia Herald* at Monrovia prompted Gurley to remark that the "Americo-African" newspaper measured the colony's remarkable growth and progress.[15]

Even the *Repository*'s short stories and poems shaped colonization sentiment. Charles C. Harper of Baltimore, son of Robert G. Harper, contributed a short story entitled "Liberia—Fifty Years Hence," the tale of a saintly preacher leading a group of brave, pious free blacks to Africa. Another piece, about an African chieftain who was captured, sold into slavery, and reduced to insanity, caught the eye of William Cullen Bryant, then co-editor of the *New York Review and Athenaeum Magazine* and fast becoming the nation's leading poet. He flattered the Colonization Society by converting the tale into "beautiful and pathetic stanzas" which Gurley happily reprinted. The last verse of "The African Chief" described the dissolution of the maddened prince:

> His heart was broken—crazed his brain—
> At once his eye grew wild,
> He struggled fiercely with his chain,
> Whispered, and wept, and smiled;
> Yet wore not long those fatal bands,

And once, at shut of day,
They drew him forth upon the sands,
The foul hyena's prey.[16]

Gurley seized every opportunity to execrate the slave trade and to reaffirm the claim that African colonization would destroy the "nefarious traffic." He published Ashmun's lamentation for the "multitudes of human beings . . . immolated on the altars of avarice" and "crowded to death in the dungeons of a slave ship." He found room also for an excerpt from a British explorer's lurid description of places "strewed with human skeletons" and shriveled mummies of murdered slaves. From the Sierra Leone *Royal Gazette* he borrowed the grisly account of a slaver who dumped "sixty-five miserable beings" into the sea to avoid detection. He approvingly quoted the Baltimore *Gazette*'s assertion that "the only way to abolish the Slave Trade is, by invading its sources with settlements." [17]

The *Repository* also recorded and encouraged the building of a national movement. Gurley unwearyingly published endless testimonials from friends of colonization in several states, and he curried support by listing names of individual donors in each community. Clergymen, church societies, sewing circles, and small auxiliaries in obscure villages had the pleasure of seeing their names in print, regardless of the size of the contribution. Occasionally, Gurley singled out and saluted a specific auxiliary. "Another donation of thirty dollars, has been forwarded by the Female Liberian Society of Essex county, Virginia," he noted. "This makes an amount of one hundred and seventy dollars, in little more than six months! An example of liberality worthy of imitation." [18]

Gurley carried out his pledge to reveal adversities as well as successes at the colony. He printed accounts of the disease that ravaged newcomers, taking the view that a bout with the "acclimating fever" was routine for new arrivals. Colonizationists repeatedly explained that the death rate at Liberia was far lower than among colonists at Plymouth and Jamestown. Gurley followed Ashmun's custom of blaming most fatalities on the fever victims themselves. In case after case the colonial agent attributed death to foolish mistakes, such as leaving bed too soon after the initial attack, taking too much sun, or eating too much raw fruit. He insisted that the climate at Liberia was basically healthful, but he did concede that colonists from a line north of Elkridge, Maryland, were more subject to fatal attacks than emigrants from the southeastern states. In 1829, Ashmun's successor blamed the deaths of twenty-six new colonists on their own folly. They "owe their death, to imprudent exposure during convalescence, and a free indulgence in the fruits of the place, particularly the pineapple, than which nothing can be more deleterious." Gurley conceded that this was a "very remarkable mortality" but steadfastly maintained that Plymouth and Jamestown had higher death tolls. The managers cheerfully noted that once emigrants recovered they enjoyed "more vigour and exemption from disease than in countries without tropics." [19]

Gurley loved his work and spent long hours each day in the Colonization Society's offices. He believed in the society's principles, and on one occasion when the society needed funds he sold his furniture and books at public auction to pay its debts. On another occasion he sacrificed his property to prevent a slave family from being sold and separated. "He came nearer than any man I ever knew to the example of Christ," his pastor admiringly remarked. After his marriage in 1827 to his fourteen-year-old cousin, Eliza McLellan Gurley of Portland, Maine, he made his home in Georgetown. There he entertained numerous traveling agents, lecturers, and dignitaries of the society. The urbane Mrs. Samuel Harrison Smith admired the couple. She described Mrs. Gurley as "very young, very beautiful and ingenuous and simple as a child,—not much mental strength or improvement but truly lovable." In all, the Gurleys had ten children, three of whom grew to adulthood. Gurley loyally named the first-born Felicia Liberia Heneaus Gurley, and two sons bore the names of leading colonizationists, William Henry Fitzhugh Gurley and John McDonogh Gurley.[20]

With an indefatigable administrator, editor, and publicist to prod the managers and direct a national movement, the Colonization Society was equipped to send its message into every corner of the Union.

X

BUILDING A MOVEMENT

————◆•••◆————

AFTER Ayres and Boyd discovered that New England was waiting for the southern states to take the lead, the Colonization Society redoubled its efforts to win support in Virginia, Maryland, North Carolina, and Delaware. In speeches, writings, and meetings, friends of colonization tailored their appeals to southern interests and southern fears. One argument sounded the alarm of servile insurrection. Dire prophecies that one day the two races would become locked in a monstrous death struggle became a standard colonization theme. "Noyades, fusillades, the gallows or the guillotine," cried one colonizationist, would "blot out . . . all differences and distinctions" between the races. The celebrated Santo Domingo massacres of 1802–1804 exemplified "intemperate and visionary schemes of enfranchisement" and the catastrophic influence of "religious zealots" who ranged their blind faith above "all human considerations." Another pointed to Santo Domingo as "a terrible demonstration, of the susceptibilities of the race." Santo Domingo became a shibboleth of colonization.[1]

Other publicists called for the gradual death of slavery. In his last address before the Colonization Society, General Harper denounced slavery as "a great social evil" and "a cancer on the body politic" that was eating at the vitals of American society and destroying "the entire mass of our social strength and happiness." He warned fellow colonizationists that emancipation must be gradual in order to prevent "a void . . . occasioned by the precipitate subduction of so great an amount of effective labour." Like many other gentlemen in Maryland and Virginia, Harper expected slavery to die, but colonization was the only "safe" means of removing it.[2]

The Frederick County Auxiliary echoed these sentiments, saying slavery was a British curse left over from colonial days. It denied northern charges that southerners wished to "rivet more strongly the fetters of slavery" by removing free blacks. Contrarily, colonization would "prepare the way for gradual emancipation." Only the complete extirpation of slavery could assure Virginia's prosperity and save the country from "impending ruin." The end of slavery was "essential to the improvement of agriculture and the increase of national wealth" as well as the rescue of large estates already "reduced to a wretched cultivation." [3]

To sow colonization sentiment systematically and build auxiliaries in southern states, the managers commissioned the Reverend William McKenney traveling agent. Within a few months in 1824, dozens of local societies marked his path through Delaware, Maryland, Virginia, and North Carolina.

McKenney successfully played upon the emancipation theme, calling colonization a matter of "policy" and not merely a puff of benevolence. He drew dark pictures of free Negroes improverishing landowners and crowding cities. In Delaware he directed the formation of two large auxiliaries, the Union Colonization Society of Wilmington, which had the support of leading Quaker abolitionists, and a female auxiliary. At its first annual meeting in 1825, the Union Colonization Society solemnly declared that the Negro population "depreciates our soil, lessens our agricultural revenues, and like the lean kine of Egypt, eats up the fat of the land."

In Maryland McKenney repeated his emancipation arguments and won additional adherents. He formed auxiliaries in Kent, Queen Anne, Talbot, and Dorchester counties. He assured audiences that African colonization was "the only way" to end slavery "without injury to the domestic relations of Society." If the Colonization Society sank into oblivion for want of funds, all chance for removal would instantly perish and slavery's curse of "confusion, distrust, immorality, and destruction" would remain forever entailed upon the suffering land. With such arguments he gathered donations from "many gentlemen of the highest order of society." [4]

Carrying his message to the lower counties of Virginia, Mc-

Kenney found equally warm receptions for colonization. He repeated that the Colonization Society *"properly enough"* abjured any direct interference with slave property, but its effect was to open "a safe and wide door to all who may be disposed to emancipate." The Norfolk auxiliary, echoing McKenney's arguments, declared that free labor was "incontestably cheaper and more productive than slave." The gradual removal of slavery through colonization ought to invigorate appeals to Christian benevolence by "adding the weight of interest." [5]

McKenney spoke in Presbyterian, Episcopal, and Methodist churches and, occasionally, in a Quaker meeting house. Through his efforts, auxiliaries sprang up in Norfolk, Petersburg, Portsmouth, Hampton, and Lynchburg. Nansemond, Isle of Wight, Sussex, Albemarle, King William, Augusta, Powhatan, and Fluvanna counties supported local societies. Another flourished at Hampden-Sydney College.

Touching parts of North Carolina, McKenney collected money from men, churches, and auxiliaries. Though the Haiti craze still lingered, "many warm-hearted and influential" citizens endorsed African colonization. He collected $25 from a group of Murphreesborough ladies, and he organized an auxiliary headed by General Thomas Winns. The Hertford County Auxiliary presented $48. One gentleman "whose heart is full of kindness and charity" offered one hundred slaves and enough money to transport them to Africa.

McKenney happily reported that hundreds of Virginians and North Carolinians were eager to adopt colonization "for the double purpose of new modelling their domestic economy" along free labor principles and conferring freedom on those who could never enjoy it in the United States. Everywhere he went, he found encouraging signs that colonization would eventually triumph. The movement's prospects were "daily brightening," he told the managers, and they were at last "realizing *all* their predictions in regard to the cordial cooperation of the *South*." Between July and December, 1824, McKenney forwarded more than $2,000 to Washington. [6]

By far the most spectacular growth of African colonization sentiment occurred in Virginia. The foremost men of the day accepted principal offices in local societies. General John Hart-well Cocke, wealthy proprietor of the plantation "Bremo" and patron of several benevolent societies, was president of two county auxiliaries, in Albemarle and Fluvanna. He confidently asserted that colonization was "a good cause and must finally triumph." It promised to remove a stain that defaced "our national eschuteon" and avert "the future horrors of servile War." The scheme was essential to Virginia's prosperity.[7] Others who lent their names were Jefferson's protégé, Congressman William Cabell Rives; Thomas W. Gilmer, rising young lawyer and politician; and Congressman John Roane. James Monroe accepted the presidency of the Loudoun county auxiliary. McKenney could justifiably boast that the "most enlightened" men of Virginia advocated colonization.

No society in the United States could match the Richmond and Manchester Auxiliary for prestige. The most distinguished names of the Old Dominion adorned its roster. Chief Justice John Marshall was president. He gave handsome donations to the state and national organizations, privately believing that colonization would strengthen the Union and relieve the country from "a danger whose extent can scarcely be estimated." He urged free Negroes seeking his advice to go to Liberia.[8] Vice-presidents of the auxiliary included James Madison, James Monroe, ex-governor James Pleasants, Senator John Tyler, Richmond lawyer William Maxwell (afterwards president of Hampden-Sydney College), and Congressman Hugh Nelson, son of ex-governor Thomas Nelson. The Richmond society, soon to become the Colonization Society of Virginia, customarily held its annual meetings in the House of Delegates, and it reminded Virginians that "the first momentum to this benevolent enterprise" originated there in 1816.[9] The legislature gave $500 to the society, and Abel Upshur sponsored a bill to grant the organization larger sums.

In Virginia colonization was the moderate position. The Petersburg society calmly remarked that extremists in the north charged that colonizationists merely wished to "rivet more closely the chains of the unhappy slave" and, at the same time, extremists in the south railled at the scheme for "madly breaking down" class lines. Such contradictory charges were proof that colonization was moderate and judicious, it said. Flinging moderation at all critics, the auxiliary declared that colonizationists were "visionary enthusiasts" to the degree that Monroe, Marshall, Pleasants, Washington, or Crawford were guilty of the charge. The Norfolk *Beacon* called colonization the embodiment of "moderation and prudence." [10] The Richmond auxiliary loftily warned critics that "unnecessary and groundless alarms" would bring just opprobrium on their heads.

McKenney had made an auspicious beginning, and Secretary Gurley did not allow his work to fall into disrepair. Each year he sent more agents to refresh lagging auxiliaries and stimulate new ones. The Reverend James Nourse, grandson of Benjamin Rittenhouse and a recent graduate of Princeton Theological Seminary, continued McKenney's work in North Carolina. Preferring appeals to benevolence over appeals to expediency and "policy," Nourse formed auxiliaries in Cumberland, Randolph, and Rowan counties. James Iredell, son of Justice Iredell, and that year elected governor of the state, was president of the auxiliary at Edenton. The Raleigh auxiliary reorganized as the North Carolina Society for Colonizing the Free People of Colour of the United States, with Colonel William Polk, Governor Hutchins, Gordon Burton, Chief Justice John L. Taylor, and the Reverend William McPheeters, eminent Presbyterian divine, as officers. One of the members called Liberia "a glorious beacon, beaming with a broad, and vivid, and constant splendor" and blessing Africans "enveloped in the night of witchcraft and superstition." [11]

McKenney and Nourse prodded Quakers in North Carolina to give money. The yearly meeting of North Carolina Friends had supported the ill-fated Haitian project, but its members were willing to help the Liberian cause. In 1827, they offered several hundred dollars to help buy a colonial schooner. One Quaker woman prayed that the "cause of colonization and emancipation" would triumph and Liberia flourish "as the cedars of Lebanon so that conscientious men may not die hampered with their Slaves." [12]

As important as the traveling agents were the men and women who promoted colonization in each community. They were as

necessary as the traveling agents or the famous men who served
as national officers. In community after community, friends of the
cause clasped the links in Gurley's lengthening chain. They collected money, gave colonization orations, inserted publicity in the
weekly newspaper, and encouraged local free blacks to consider
emigrating. The traveling agents used their homes and their
churches as way stations.

In Richmond, David I. Burr, a New England-born iron foundry
owner who catered to wheat farmers in Virginia, was a strong
adherent of colonization. He kept up a correspondence with
Gurley which informed the parent society of the auxiliary's work.
An active Presbyterian, he induced his church to support colonization. Benjamin Brand of Richmond applied himself to routine
duties of the auxiliary, serving as treasurer. Contributions
gathered in surrounding counties went to Brand for transmission
to Washington. William Crane, another loyal colonization worker
in Richmond, created the African Baptist Missionary Society as
an adjunct of the Richmond Baptist Foreign Missionary Society.
The free Negroes elected Crane corresponding secretary and
sought his advice on emigration. He used Burgess's glowing report
to induce Lott Cary and Colin Teague to go to Africa as missionaries of the little society. At Crane's urging, the Baptist General
Convention ordained them, and the Reverend Obadiah Brown, a
manager of the parent society and Baptist minister in Washington,
arranged their transportation to Africa. "I am an African," Cary
declared. "I wish to go to a country where I shall be estimated by
my merits, not by my complexion; and I feel bound to labour for
my suffering race." Crane persuaded other free blacks to follow
the Richmond missionaries to Liberia.[13]

In Petersburg, William M. Atkinson served as resident agent,
corresponded with Secretary Gurley, and nurtured colonization
sentiment in his community. William Maxwell Blackford, owner
of the Fredericksburg *Arena,* sponsored colonization among his
neighbors and filled his newspaper with colonization propaganda.
The agent in Lynchburg was Jesse Burton Harrison, a brilliant
young lawyer and orator. In Norfolk the managers depended on
the talents and energies of John McPhail, a Scottish-born Presbyterian elder who also served as treasurer of the local Bible

society. McPhail had the important duty of chartering ships and preparing expeditions from Norfolk. He gathered supplies and looked after the emigrants who trickled into the city before—and sometimes after—the departure of colonist ships.

Virginia gave the colonization movement its most famous female exponents. Miss Margaret Mercer, prim, sickly, spinster school teacher and daughter of a Maryland governor, emancipated fifteen slaves inherited from her father. At her home near Lynchburg, Virginia, she championed colonization by raising funds, sponsoring education projects at the colony, and arguing the merits of the scheme with friends or foes.[14] Mary Berkeley Minor Blackford, wife of William M. Blackford of Fredericksburg, joined her husband in colonization activities. She freed her household servants for emigration, and he sent his colored newspaper apprentice to Liberia where he subsequently became the printer of the *Liberia Herald*. Mrs. Blackford's brother later served as a missionary in West Africa. Her female auxiliary raised money by selling home-made articles of clothing. She kept a private notebook, "Notes Illustrative of the Wrongs of Slavery," which recorded her loathing for the institution.[15]

In Baltimore, Robert G. Harper, until his death in 1825, was colonization's best friend. He gathered promising young men around him and taught them to cherish the project. His protégé Virgil Maxcy was a charter member of the parent society. His son, Charles C. Harper, and his law student, John H. B. Latrobe, son of the famous architect, were his most devoted apprentices. Harper's friend Dr. Ayres kept him informed about African matters. It was Harper who invented the name "Liberia." He often said African colonization and internal improvements were the "two leading topics of his life." He was so convinced that Africa promised great commercial riches that he sent mulatto seaman Abel Hurd to explore the Niger river to confirm or disprove the theory that it was an extension of the Congo. Hurd reached Cape Mesurado and promptly died of fever, leaving the mystery to British explorers to solve.[16]

After Harper's death, Charles C. Harper and John H. B. Latrobe carried on his work. In 1827, they reorganized the Maryland society to include every auxiliary in the state. At the head of this alliance they placed the venerable Charles Carroll, a signer of the Declaration of Independence and young Harper's grandfather. For vice-presidents they chose Philip E. Thomas, Hezekiah Niles, Bishop James Kemp, Roger B. Taney, Isaac McKim, General Samuel Smith, and the principal officers of each auxiliary. The board of forty managers included the Reverend John Breckinridge, well-to-do Benjamin C. Howard, merchant Solomon Etting, shipowner Richard H. Douglass, and Dr. Eli Ayres. Controlling power was in the hands of an inner group composed of John H. B. Latrobe, Charles C. Harper, Edward J. Coale, a prosperous bookseller, Francis S. Key's brother-in-law Charles Howard, Judge Brice of the Criminal Court, and John I. Lloyd, a young lawyer and friend of Latrobe.[17]

Harper and Latrobe were indefatigable workers for colonization. They devoted much time to money-raising campaigns and publicity. With John Hoffman, the treasurer of the Maryland society, they called on Baltimore clergymen and persuaded them to take collections in their churches. When Methodist parsons declined, saying they could make no promises without the permission of church trustees, Harper beseiged the trustees. He urged Secretary Gurley to smooth the way for widespread Methodist support by making Bishop Soule a vice-president and adding "some other popular clergyman or religious layman" to the board of managers. "Such an arrangement would, I know, promote the success of our annual collections," he said. It was Harper's plan to annex the entire Methodist organization to the Maryland auxiliary. He wanted to make each minister the colonization agent in his circuit with a general agent, roughly comparable to a bishop, over all.[18]

Harper and Charles Howard canvassed the wealthier citizens of Baltimore for donations. On one occasion they collected over $100 in three hours. In 1826, Harper addressed the Baltimore electorate and called for donations to remove five thousand free Negroes from the city. Their departure would open jobs for "fellow citizens who were in want of employment," he said, and assure "a white and more wholesome species of population." [19]

Latrobe tried to annex Masonry to colonization. His lodge, Winder Lodge No. 77, was composed of Baltimore's leading men.

He urged them to circularize Masonic lodges throughout the United States to contribute to colonization. The letter drafted by Latrobe declared that the "utility of removing this portion of the inhabitants of our country" was "plain and undoubted." The Colonization Society was not an abolition society and it did not approve schemes "trenching on the right of property." It was a project of "extensive benevolence and permanent charity" that accorded with Masonic principles of promoting "the happiness and improvement of mankind." Colonization expressed the sentiment of thousands who regretted "the existence of such a population" and wished to wipe a "stain and a nuisance" from the "chosen soil of freedom." [20]

Lodges at Hagerstown, Princess Anne, Georgetown, Cumberland, and Baltimore's Cassia Lodge of Ancient York Masons obligingly sent small donations. A few lodges in Pennsylvania, Maine, Massachusetts, and Mississippi also answered the call. The Grand Lodge of Vermont contributed $100 and four of its subordinate lodges sent $50. They urged the formation of a Grand Lodge at Liberia.

The parent society was pleased with the Masonic donations and hoped they would swell. At the next annual meeting the Reverend Mr. William Hawley, a manager of the parent society and Grand Chaplain of the Grand Lodge of the District of Columbia, sponsored a resolution thanking the lodges who contributed and invited others to match their donations. Secretary Gurley broadly hinted that the Grand Lodge of Massachusetts, with $50,000 at its disposal, could shower its liberality on the Colonization Society.[21]

Another source of support was the female auxiliary. The "age of benevolence" spawned hundreds of ladies' auxiliaries for missionary, Bible, education, Sunday school, and charitable movements.[22] By 1825, the female auxiliary was a standard device in national movements. Beginning that year, ladies in Delaware, Virginia, and Maryland formed small colonization circles. Many succeeded in raising money for the parent society. The wife of ex-Congressman James Mercer Garnett of Essex county, Virginia, organized the "Liberian Society" among her school girls and neighbor ladies. They devoted Saturday afternoons to sewing and knitting "various little articles." Proceeds from sales made up the contributions to the parent society. The initial gift of the Richmond female auxiliary was $170. The Fredericksburg and Falmouth Female Colonization Society gathered $500 in its first year. In Baltimore, colonization ladies staged a gigantic fair that netted $2,500. In Charlottesville, a smaller fair earned $500.[23]

Secretary Gurley greeted the female auxiliaries as "a most propitious omen to the future hopes and prospects of the Society." He observed that woman's tender nature, more sensitive to emotional appeals, was a fitting ingredient in a movement that aimed at elevating and civilizing the Negro race. Henry Clay gallantly thanked "our fair countrywomen" who gave "their cheering countenance and encouragement" to the movement. He welcomed the combination of female assistance and Divine approval as peculiarly auspicious.[24]

Several slaveowners underscored the colonizationists' assertion that the scheme opened the door to manumission. In Virginia, where manumission was contingent on prompt removal of freedmen, slaveowners seized the opportunity to send their slaves to Liberia.[25] Nathaniel C. Crenshaw near Richmond offered to free sixty servants for immediate removal. The Reverend John D. Paxton, a Presbyterian clergyman in Prince Edward's county, liberated a family of eleven and shepherded them to Norfolk for embarkation. Episcopal clergyman Cave Jones, Navy chaplain and principal of the Navy seminary at Brooklyn, New York, owned two Virginia slaves whom he volunteered to free for colonization. He offered to pay their passage. Colonel David Bullock of Louisa county, Virginia, manumitted twenty-three slaves for Africa. He asked the society to take extra precautions that none ran away before they were safely embarked. Former Congressman Edward Colston of Berkeley county freed six. The Reverend Thomas P. Hunt of Brunswick county sent twenty. At his request Hunt became the society's agent in Delaware, Maryland, Virginia, and North Carolina.[26]

Ralph Gurley greeted these and additional offers of manumitted slaves as evidence that the movement prospered among "intelligent citizens" who wised to remove slavery. He attributed the rise in manumissions to the influence of the society. He privately predicted that as colonization sentiment spread, manumissions would "become more numerous and striking." He carefully listed in the *Repository* the names of men who sent their slaves to Liberia. Additional offers came from gentlemen in Maryland, North Carolina, South Carolina, and Georgia. W. H. Robbins of Cheraw, South Carolina, offered twenty-five slaves representing the substance of his property. Wealthy Joel Early of Greene county, Georgia, the son of a rich planter and brother of Governor Peter Early, freed thirty slaves. In turning them over to the Colonization Society, he told them that they went to a better life in Africa.[27]

Some friends of colonization provided for manumission and colonization in their wills. In many cases the master freed his slaves on the explicit condition they emigrate to Liberia. Emigration was less than voluntary in such cases. Executors of the estate of Henry B. Elder of Petersburg, Virginia, found that he had ordered twenty slaves to Liberia. Henry Robertson of Hampton left $50 to each of seven slaves to pay their passage. A spinster in Louisa county left a legacy of $500 to transport her sixteen slaves to Cape Mesurado. Another slaveowner in Frederick county liberated ten slaves and left $1,000 for their removal. William H. Fitzhugh of Fairfax county, a vice-president of the national society and a vigorous exponent of colonization, suddenly died in 1830, leaving a will that provided for the manumission of his many slaves in 1850. At that time they were to choose whether to go to Liberia. To encourage them to emigrate, his estate was to pay their transportation plus a $50 bonus for each who reached Africa. Gurley urged other Virginians to imitate Fitzhugh's "bright, beneficent, exalted" example.

The society continued to receive legacies of slaves and offers for manumitted emigrants. At a public meeting in Philadelphia in 1829, manager Francis S. Key exultantly declared that Gurley's office was processing offers totaling six hundred slaves for removal to Liberia.[28]

Raising emigrant expeditions was a major undertaking for the society. As Leonard Bacon remarked, they injected more excitement and enthusiasm than scores of meetings, speeches, and sonorous resolutions. Agent McKenney found that the task of recruiting colonists and gathering supplies focussed interest in colonization, inspirited the local auxiliaries, and shook generous donations from men in Virginia and Maryland. He assured audiences wherever he went that their donations would speed shiploads of free blacks to Africa.

Before long, the *Cyrus* left Norfolk with one hundred free Negroes. Thanks to McKenney's collections, the parent society was able to lay out $2,600 for the expedition. Most emigrants on the *Cyrus* came from Richmond, Petersburg, and the lower counties of Virginia. One of them, the Reverend Colston M. Waring, a Baptist preacher, had previously visited the small settlement and returned to fetch his family and friends who wished to emigrate. In February, 1825, McKenney and McPhail loaded sixty-six more on the brig *Hunter*. Two were from North Carolina, two from the District of Columbia, and the rest from Virginia. McKenney collected over $2,000 from individuals, churches, and auxiliaries. The Petersburg auxiliary donated $264, the Norfolk auxiliary $186, and the Richmond society $352.[29]

In the next few years several more emigrant ships sailed from southern ports. In February, 1826, the *Indian Chief* carried over 150 from Norfolk. All but a few were free Negroes from North Carolina. The federal government paid a substantial portion of the cost because the ship also carried rescued Africans. A year later, the *Doris,* owned by Baltimore shipper Richard H. Douglass, an officer of the Maryland Colonization Society, left Hampton Roads with more than ninety emigrants and returned before the year ended to take one hundred more.[30]

Colonizationists used each departure to dramatize their work. An embarkation was a solemn occasion that called for divine invocation. When the brig *Strong* sailed from Baltimore in May, 1822, hundreds of spectators crowded the wharf to say farewell to the emigrants and rescued Africans. Bishop Kemp, a member of the state society, blessed the vessel, cargo, and crew. The passengers sailed in "high spirits." At the sailing of the *Indian Chief,* Norfolk clergymen from several denominations raised their voices in a "parting prayer" for the emigrants. Spectators found the ceremony "very solemn and impressive." The passengers on the *Doris,* which left Baltimore in 1827, heard the Reverend John P. K.

Henshaw, rector of St. Peter's Church and later Bishop of Rhode Island, deliver an "eloquent and affecting" farewell. When he finished, a gun boomed, other vessels in the harbor hoisted their flags in salute, and the *Doris* slid down Chesapeake Bay.[31]

With emigrant ships leaving southern ports, collections flowing from churches, sewing circles, and new auxiliaries flourishing in Virginia, North Carolina, Maryland, and Delaware, donations rose from the record low of $800 in 1822 to $4,700 in 1824, $10,000 in 1825, $15,000 in 1826, and nearly the same amount in 1827. The colonization movement was at last gaining momentum. "The God of Heaven . . . is with us," Henry Clay declared in surveying the new prosperity. "With zeal, energy, and perseverence we shall subdue all difficulties and ultimately realize every hope." [32]

XI

NORTHERN BENEVOLENCE

———◄••►———

NEW ENGLAND's Leonard Bacon long held that the Colonization Society, properly administered and heralded, could match any of the great benevolent societies whose agents swarmed the thriving commercial centers of the north and whose panoply of auxiliaries enriched the parent institutions. Sharing Bacon's conviction, Ralph Gurley, while cherishing endorsements in Maryland, Virginia, and North Carolina, aggressively sought eastern support. From the day he took direction of the Society, Gurley laid plans to carry the movement to New England and the middle states. Here was a populous and wealthy region unclaimed for colonization.

Gurley's primary propaganda instrument, the *African Repository,* played to northern ears. In every issue Editor Gurley strummed the dulcet theme of benevolence. Pointing to northern cities he lamented that a shroud of degradation and uselessness enveloped their free Negroes. The Colonization Society, like many charitable institutions of the day, would strive to "raise up the fallen" in those cities. Though numerous associations cared for the poor, the deaf-mute, the insane, the fallen female, the aged and infirm, the orphan, and the decayed mariner, none ministered to masses of "notoriously ignorant, degraded and miserable, mentally diseased, broken-spirited" free blacks. Gurley pictured them as friendless, bewildered wanderers whose only freedom was licentiousness and for whom "restraint would prove a blessing." His editorials hammered at their need for benevolence. "Their bodies are free, their minds enslaved," he declared. "They can neither bless their brethren in servitude, nor rise from their own obscurity, nor add to the purity of our morals, nor to our wealth, nor to our political strength." [1]

Gurley's call for northern aid was a step in the larger plan to wring large subsidies from Congress. Voluntary donations merely measured the movement's broadening popularity. "We candidly acknowledge that private charity is inadequate to the consummation of our design," Gurley asserted. "But as these powers are controlled by popular opinion, it is this which constitutes the medium through which the Society must communicate its influence and secure to its purpose the resources and energy of the nation." The fostering of "moral rectitude and benevolence" was as much the duty of government as of individuals.[2]

To impress the eastern states that free Negroes were "legitimate objects for benevolent exertion," Gurley noted that their prisons and penitentiaries were overflowing with colored convicts. The *Repository* carried startling data compiled by the Pennsylvania Prison Discipline Society showing that in most northern states the ratio of Negro convicts to white convicts was far larger than the ratio of Negro citizens to white citizens. In Pennsylvania the white population numbered 800,000 and the Negro population only 30,000, but fifty percent of the prison inmates were black. In Massachusetts, Connecticut, Vermont, New York, and New Jersey the ratios were almost as striking. The Prison Discipline Society frankly ascribed high crime rates to the "degraded character" of free Negroes. Gurley declared that the Colonization Society could offer no "more impressive or affecting" proof that removal would be greatly beneficial to American society.[3]

Appeals to nationalism played a role in the campaign. Gurley and his co-workers frequently invoked memories of national heroes and national deeds. It was a day of triumph when the aging Lafayette adorned the annual meeting of 1825 and accepted an honorary vice-presidency. The old revolutionary hero, sitting next to Chief Justice Marshall in the red draped hall of the Supreme Court, voiced his "great respect and affection" for the society. Its "laudable and benevolent views" accorded with his life-long principles, he said. Though he never donated a cent, his praises and his name were substantial gifts. When he died, Gurley and the managers paid grateful tribute to the "illustrious benefactor of the human race." [4]

At the same annual meeting, George Washington Parke Custis, proud of his name and easily the society's most eloquent speaker, used revolutionary fervor to thaw anti-colonization prejudices "which still existed in northern sections." He reminded northerners that southern patriots were at their side when they "braved the Canadian snows, and scaled the icy bulwarks of Quebec." Just as the south rushed to the rescue at the heights of Cambridge, now it was time for eastern states to help save their southern brethren from ruin. He asked them to remember the southern warriors "hailing the spark of freedom that northern hands had kindled, and crying out—'Go on, we are coming to support you!' " [5]

In the quickening campaign for eastern support Gurley repeatedly probed at New England's favorite benevolence—missionary work. He asserted that African colonization was a "powerful influence for the Gospel among the Pagan tribes. . . . In this day of mighty effort for men, when the light of Divine truth is kindled, and growing brighter in almost all the dark regions of the world, Africa should not, and will not be forgotten; for the decree hath gone forth, Ethiopia shall stretch forth her hands unto God."

Gurley combined benevolence and patriotism by asking clergymen to devote their Independence Day sermons to colonization and to earmark church collections that day for the parent society. Scores of eastern clergymen, mostly Congregationalist and Presbyterians, promptly took up the cause. "Ethiopia shall stretch forth her hands unto God" became a ceaseless roundelay that chorused through many Fourth of July sermons, essays, and orations. The Reverend Leonard Bacon of Center Church, New Haven, gave a brilliant colonization sermon in Boston in 1824 and repeated it the following year in New Haven. He condemned slavery and demanded its extinction "not by some sudden convulsion, demolishing the fabric of society, but by the tendencies of nature and the arrangements of Providence, slowly yet surely accomplishing the happiness of man." He invoked New England's trustee tradition, reminding his neighbors that they were "almoners of his love." "The institutions of our age," he said of the numerous benevolent societies, "are a republic of benevolence, and all"—the Hindu, the Indian, and the African—"may share in the unrestrained and equal democracy." [6]

Bacon and his Yale colleagues, Theodore Dwight Woolsey and Alexander Catlin Twining, organized the New Haven Antislavery Association, pledging to popularize colonization in New England. Bacon ominously predicted that the one and one-half million slaves in 1820 would multiply to twelve million in 1880. He wondered "how much terrour and anxiety must be endured, how many plots must be detected, how many insurrections must be quelled" in those sixty years. "A Touissant, or a Spartacus, or an African Tecumseh" would surely hoist the standard of insurrection. The only way to avert the danger, he warned, was by eradicating slavery as well as the free blacks' political and moral degradation. The Reverend Nathaniel Bouton in his Fourth of July address in Concord, Massachusetts, also dwelt on the insurrection theme. "Plots will thicken! servile insurrections spring up! and flames be kindled, which can be quenched only with blood!" [7]

Bouton and the Fourth of July preachers repeatedly declared that bland, unyielding prejudice obstructed efforts to meliorate the condition of the free blacks. A quarter million free Negroes, Bouton observed, live in the United States—"the most ignorant, degraded and vicious class" in any community. "Public opinion has set her brand of infamy and exclusion upon them. . . . As long as they retain the complexion which the God of nature has given them, their condition among us cannot be essentially improved." Nathaniel Scudder Prime of the First Presbyterian Church in Cambridge, New York, said that prejudice, not racial inferiority, was the "grand reason of all that present dullness and stupidity." "This is not their country, nor their home," the Reverend Mr. Philip C. Hay told colonizationists in Newark, New Jersey. "Visit our jails and penitentiaries, and you will find them crowded with coloured convicts. Beyond a doubt their moral character is far more debased than any part of the white population." Negrophobia was everywhere, excluding Negroes from the colleges, professions, and business world and condemning them to be "ignorant, degraded, and depraved." Under like circumstances, William McMurray told his congregation at a Dutch Reformed church in New York city, white men "would naturally sink into the same state of bodily and mental torpor." [8]

Besides the themes of latent insurrection and uneradicable prejudice, the Fourth of July speakers pictured colonization as the only hope of abolishing slavery. They stoutly denied that it was an abolition scheme to deprive the owner of his property or foist freedom on the Negro. Rather, it was a device for encouraging systematic manumission, an attempt to end slavery through persuasion, not force. "This day commences the 50th year of freedom to American white men," the Reverend Mr. Prime observed, "and yet a million and a half of our fellow men, within our own dwellings, are this moment groaning under the chains of bondage. Tell me not . . . that they are incapable of providing for themselves; and are therefore happier in their present dependent condition. . . ." Only voluntary consent could end slavery. Colonization was a judicious method by which "these deeply-rooted evils may be branded with disgrace, and thus gradually but effectually eradicated." "Slavery wherever tolerated, is . . . a national evil," warned McMurray. "While we have exulted in our national freedom, the sighing of the captive has passed by unheeded on the wind, and the supplications of the oppressed among us have been heard in vain." Slavery is "a solemn mockery" of the Declaration of Independence and a contradiction of "the first principles of our Constitution," Bouton declared. [9]

The missionary aspects of colonization won the approbation of the Boston *Recorder,* New England's foremost mouthpiece of benevolence. It urged Christians to use the nation's birthday as a day of dedication. "When you assemble to hear your pastor's plea for suffering humanity, will you not bring with you some small portion of that abundance with which Providence has crowned your labors . . . ?" Even the smallest offering "will ere long soften some bed of sorrow, mitigate some pain, or put a Bible into the hands of some miserable African who is now a heathen!" Colonization, it said pontifically, "is very dear to the heart of Everlasting Love." Gurley was delighted when in 1825 the

American Board of Commissioners for Foreign Missions voted to establish a mission in Liberia. "No measure would have so great an effect in drawing the affections of northern people to the Colonization Society," he remarked.[10]

Religious assemblies and colonization auxiliaries also invited churches to set aside the Fourth of July for colonization. The General Assembly of the Presbyterian church and the General Synod of the Reformed Dutch church urged member churches to participate in the drive, and the New Jersey, Vermont, and New Hampshire auxiliaries circularized ministers in those states for aid. On July 4, 1825, many churches responded generously. Boston churches collected almost $200. Salem, Providence, Newport, Bristol, and Bath and many small communities brought the total collected in a two month period to nearly $3,800. In the following months the society's special agents canvassed outlying villages to pick up unreported donations. Between January and March, 1826, they harvested another $1,600.[11]

The success of the Fourth of July drive brought Gurley's thankful praise. He exalted the clergy as "the watchmen of the church—the guardians of public morals—the expounders of human rights and social duties—the reprovers of unrighteousness—the friends of man, be he civilized or rude, bond or free." From that day forward, the Colonization Society depended on Independence Day contributions as one of its chief sources of revenue. At last the *Repository* could boast that the "principles and plans and operations of our institution" were inspiring "an extensive change in public sentiment." [12]

While the clergymen prepared the ground and taught their parishioners to give to colonization, the parent society was sending its agents into many corners of New England. The agents gathered money held by ministers who waited for their coming, and they attempted to raise auxiliaries in communities that showed a disposition to give. In 1825 and 1826 the more important agents stationed in New England were three young clergymen: William Watson Niles, son of the Reverend Nathaniel Niles of West Fairles, Vermont, the "Athenian on the east side of the Green Mountains"; Myron Tracy, of Hartford, Vermont, who was waiting for a church to call; and Horace Sessions, of Pomfret, Connecticut, a graduate of Yale and Andover. Niles traveled through Maine and eastern Massachusetts, Tracy concentrated on western Massachusetts and Vermont, and Sessions toured Rhode Island and Connecticut. David Hale of the Boston Correspondence Committee served as depository for their receipts.[13]

Thirty-two-year-old Sessions was the most promising of the three. In a few weeks, late in 1825, he collected $1,000. The sale of life memberships—a standard practice among benevolent societies—proved to be a successful device. He guessed that "not less than $50,000 have in this way been poured into the treasury of the Lord." Women were especially eager to buy $30 life memberships for their ministers. He sold certificates in Providence, Newport, New Bedford, Nantucket, Plymouth, and Duxbury, while Niles sold them in Boston, Hallowell, Augusta, Kennebunk Port, Brunswick and Portland.[14]

Sessions learned that he could collect even larger sums by pledging to outfit a colonist ship from Boston. With the blessings of the parent society he chartered the *Vine* and set the sailing date for late December, 1825. He solicited donations, announcing that he would personally shepherd the settlers to Liberia. All colonization activity in New England focussed on the first emigrant ship to leave a northern port. The Clarkson Society at Salem urged New England's free Negroes to emigrate, and Sessions screened sixty applicants "presenting testimonials of good character." Among the thirty-three accepted were Newport Gardner and Salmar Nubia (alias Jack Mason), two aged blacks from Newport, Rhode Island, who had planned to go to Africa in the 1780s with the Reverend Dr. Hopkins's followers. Eighty-year-old Gardner, a manumitted slave who was once tutored by Hopkins, was the pastor of the Colored Union Church and Society in Newport. The *Vine* also carried the Reverend Calvin Holton, who went as a missionary for the American Board, one Dr. Hunt, "a respectable physician," and Charles L. Force, a printer hired at $416 a year who intended to establish the first Liberian newspaper. Colonial supplies included fonts of print, paper, and ink, given by Boston friends plus a $50 bell for the proposed Lancasterian school, books collected by Chester Wright of Montpelier, blacksmith tools, scales, farm implements, clothing, and kegs of nails.

At the embarkation ceremonies January 4, 1826, the aged Gardner sang a hymn he composed for the occasion. A Boston psalmist added to the festivities with an inspirational account of the sailing:

> . . . Delightful scene!
> I view it still.—Divine philanthropy
> Smil'd on the glorious work. The church of God
> Bless'd the propitious hour. A multitude
> Stood in the stillness of entranced hope—
> Of breathless expectation.

But breathless expectation in Boston soured when news came back that Holton, Force, and twelve emigrants died of fever as soon as they touched the promised land, and Sessions, hastily fleeing the pestilence, succumbed on the return voyage. Newport Gardner and Salmar Nubia died a few months later.[15] It was five years before Boston formed an auxiliary.

Though Boston men were stunned by this cruel denouement, the parent society did not relax its drive for eastern support. It sent its ablest agents to build auxiliaries in the middle and New England states. During the fall of 1826, Ralph Gurley and Francis S. Key toured the Atlantic coast from Philadelphia to Montpelier, Vermont. With the aid of Chauncey Langdon and Chester Wright, Key converted Middlebury's commencement exercises into a colonization rally and urged churches to send money to the Vermont Colonization Society at Montpelier. He proposed that the legislators carry the funds to the state headquarters. Congressmen going to Washington, in turn, could carry the money to the parent society.

Gurley held a rally at Gardiner Spring's Brick Presbyterian Church, center of benevolent society work in New York city, in an attempt to revive the auxiliary that Haitian emigration had split and demoralized. The New York *Observer* rejoiced "that the friends of Africa are becoming daily more numerous and active" and announced that the New York city colonizationists would try to send two emigrant vessels to Liberia "if adequate means are obtained." A committee that included John Nitchie of the American Bible society went among the churches to collect money.[16]

"The sentiments of the Quakers have, I believe, changed much in our favour," Gurley happily reported from Philadelphia. In October, 1826, he inspired the formation of the Colonization Society of the State of Pennsylvania with Dr. Thomas Chalkley James, Gerard Ralston, and William B. Davidson as officers. The new auxiliary promptly sent $600 to the parent society. Ralston accepted the chief responsibility for overseeing the society's growth and management. In the next months he recruited more Quakers. They are "extremely clannish," he commented, but follow their leaders as a body if "induced to make enquiry into the plan calmly and free from bias." The endorsement of North Carolina Quakers, he told Gurley, "gave you a hold on the whole sect, which you probably would not have possessed otherwise." Following this move in Philadelphia, a smaller society was organized at West Chester with fifty "influential men of the different religious and political sects." One of the Quaker members explained, "We experience the evil of a free coloured population to its fullest extent. We have tried an Abolition Society and given it up; all seem now disposed to join heart and hand with the Colonization scheme." Wealthy Philadelphia Quaker, Elliott Cresson, a county director of Negro schools, said the time was ripening for petitioning the Annual Meeting at Baltimore for its assistance in removing free blacks. He thought the argument that "a manumitted slave is much better, both for himself and the community, sent to Liberia, than into the already over-numerous blacks in our Cities" would triumph over all objections.[17]

Gurley trained a steady barrage of propaganda on Philadelphia. In 1828 he sent his young assistant, John H. Kennedy, to give a Fourth of July sermon in the Sixth Presbyterian Church. Kennedy tailored his speech to Quaker abolitionists, praising their pure motives but questioning their long-range effects. All that had resulted, he lamented, was southern enmity. "The mind of the master at the South has been embittered, the cords have been tightened, the chains riveted." Thus abolition proved impractical by "rushing direct upon the set pikes" of its opponents. Colonization, he promised, will bring the "extinction of Domestic Slavery" by overcoming the slaveholder's belief that Negroes did not benefit from freedom.[18]

The following year Francis S. Key again journeyed to Philadelphia. He urged Quakers to swing behind the Colonization Society because it was actually promoting manumission in southern states. Slaveowners who were willing to manumit without compensation "deserve assistance in executing their benevolent intentions. . . . This is the cheapest and most direct method of promoting Abolition," he declared. Such appeals succeeded in enlisting support from Roberts Vaux, Quaker opponent of colonization in previous years. Ralston suggested the parent society add Vaux to its vice-presidents for he was the executor of a large estate and could direct part of it to the Colonization Society. Scores of Philadelphia Quakers, including William Short, John Elliott, Joseph Hemphill, and Sarah M. Grimké, pledged money.[19]

Early in 1827, Gurley happily reported that the Colonization Society had added twenty auxiliaries, and there were prospects for more. That year he pushed into Connecticut and Massachusetts. He spoke before conventions of Congregational clergymen meeting in Hartford and Boston, persuading them to collect money on July Fourth. He hoped to form state auxiliaries in both places, but his only immediate success was in his native Connecticut. During April, 1827, while "several religious and benevolent societies" were holding annual meetings in Hartford, he created the Connecticut Colonization Society. Leonard Bacon, Seth Terry, and Joel Linsley helped. Members included Governor Gideon Tomlinson, Lieutenant Governor John S. Peters, Bishop Thomas C. Brownell, Thomas H. Gallaudet, and Benjamin Silliman, professor of "Chymistry" at Yale. Silliman gave his warm endorsement. "It is both a *private christian* duty and a *public national* duty, to give it *efficient aid*. . . . It is our duty to provide an asylum beyond the ocean," he declared, "and beyond the reach of scorn and contempt, for those coloured people who are willing to emigrate." [20]

The new Connecticut auxiliary set in motion a whirl of publicity, repeating the arguments formulated earlier by the parent society and recapitulating in microcosm the work of auxiliary building, publications, endorsements, and money collecting. Leonard Bacon issued more sermons and pamphlets, the state society printed and distributed its annual reports, and new converts took up their oratorical cudgels. The Reverend Orin Fowler of Plainfield who preached colonization to his congregation asserted that "A deep interest is beginning to be felt among us." He offered to give $20 a year for ten years if 499 men promised to match his gift. On Independence Day,1829, Samuel J. May, Unitarian minister of Brooklyn, Connecticut, and members of the local temperance society organized a colonization auxiliary. May was certain that support would grow as information spread, and he promised to use his pulpit to push the cause. In New Haven, Simeon S. Jocelyn, a painter and engraver soon to be ordained pastor of a Negro Congregationalist church, urged the parent society to speed its missionary work in Africa. He was collecting money for it. "The field now opening for the introduction of Christianity through out Africa is vast," he warned impatiently. "Must not more be done here to raise up coloured men to preach the Gospel to their brethren in this land, and also to the millions of Africa[?]" [21]

Two volunteer workers who aided colonization in Connecticut were lawyer Chauncey Whittlesey of Middletown and Hartford's ready poetess Mrs. Lydia H. Sigourney. Whittlesey organized the Middletown Juvenile Colonization Society, gave impromptu colonization speeches on steamboats and stagecoaches, and sent his former slave, Nugent Wicks, to Liberia. Mrs. Sigourney, a pious worker in many benevolent causes, became New England's most famous lady colonizationist. Though she had no slaves to send to Liberia, she aided the cause by dashing off verses celebrating colonization's benevolent and missionary motives. She was a leading figure in Hartford's Female African Society, and in 1827 she induced her school girls to donate a box of books to Liberian school children. She personally selected books offering "useful knowledge and religious instruction" rather than "those which feed the imagination . . . and might awake in African bosoms a sigh of discontent, for luxuries in which they might not participate." The girls sewed neat covers, and she composed a set of rules for using the books, providing catalogue numbers and explicit directions for the Liberian school teacher charged with keeping the collection. Mrs. Sigourney also requested the Liberian children to write thank-you letters, and she directed Gurley to list her donation in the *Repository* at $50.[22]

In Peterboro, New York, rich Gerrit Smith studied African colonization's claims and agreed that it was the best plan "for ridding our country of its black population." "My heart is fully set on discharging the patriotic duty of contributing to relieve our country of its black population and on the christian duty of uniting with others in the attempt to raise Africa from death to life," he declared. In 1827 he offered to give $100 a year for ten years if one hundred wealthy men matched his donation. Gurley delightedly announced the munificent "Gerrit Smith Plan" and within a year some of the nation's wealthiest men subscribed. Among them were Jasper Corning of Charleston, Theodore Frelinghuysen of Newark, Elliott Cresson of Philadelphia, William Crane of Richmond, Robert Gilmor of Baltimore, General Edward Carrington of Virginia, Arthur Tappan of New York, and Mathew Carey of Philadelphia. Carey confessed that at first he had deemed colonization "almost as Utopian as it would be to attempt to drain Lake Erie with a ladle." But he now declared that no other benevolent society "promises so copious a harvest of blessings." In later years he loyally wrote and printed numerous colonization tracts and pamphlets. Invited to become a subscriber to the Smith plan, Colonization Society president Bushrod Washington peevishly replied that he would never consent "to entail upon my heirs or estate the payment of so large a sum." Southerners depending wholly on the "profits of agriculture" could not match the rich northern philanthropists whose wealth came from "more certain sources."[23]

Lewis Tappan thought it was time to summon a large meeting in Albany and organize a state auxiliary when the legislature met. "On such occasions gentlemen of intelligence and character, in the various professions, are assembled from all parts of the state," he noted, and they could diffuse colonization among all the citizens. Gurley took the hint and hired one of his college classmates to go to Albany. The Reverend Isaac Orr, a native of Bedford, New Hampshire, graduated from Yale in 1818, and for five years taught in Thomas H. Gallaudet's Deaf and Dumb Asylum in Hartford, Connecticut. He also preached in Tyngsboro and Amherst. Gurley commissioned him General Agent and Assistant Secretary for the territory stretching from Philadelphia to Portland.

In the spring of 1829, Orr spent a month among the New York legislators, but he found that President Andrew Jackson's New York followers were reluctant to sign a call for the formation of an auxiliary. They were afraid of alienating their South Carolina brethren. "It gives a party aspect to the Society in its very commencement," Orr lamented. The circular called slavery "a blot, or at least a glaring and discreditable inconsistency" and demanded "an act of charity to nearly two millions of people, that have been kidnapped and shackled by the hand of violence." [24]

At the meetings held April 9 and 11 in the Senate Chamber, President Eliphalet Nott of Union College, the chief speaker, warned ominously that by 1900 the Negro population would reach twenty-four million. He shuddered at the thought of "such an appalling amount of ignorant, vicious, degraded, and brutal population." The time has passed, he said, when slavery "sat as easy on the conscience of the puritan of the North, as the planter of the South." African colonization was a "timely expedient" and a boon to commerce. Gerrit Smith added that it was necessary to implant the desire to emigrate by teaching the misfit Negroes that America was not their true home. He assured the legislators that slaveowners were "as kind-hearted and as generous" as those who sat before him. They too were "impatient to emancipate." [25]

Officers of the New York society included Justice John Savage, Harmanus Bleecker, John T. Norton, and two Democrats, Nathaniel P. Tallmadge and Benjamin F. Butler. They resolved to keep "separate from all local and party considerations." Orr was disappointed that most New Yorkers, excepting Smith, Nott, and a few others, were reserved and cautious toward colonization. He sneered that "the general coldness will give me a *fever*." [26]

His pessimism quickly passed. In May, 1829, Orr attended the benevolent societies' anniversary meetings in New York city and came away with the conviction that "New York is to be the chief foundation of our future resources, and future prosperity." He gathered names of ministers attending the anniversaries and asked Gurley to give them free subscriptions to the *Repository*. He also asked the American Tract Society to publish a colonization tract, but Corresponding Secretary William A. Hallock did not wish to put his tracts in "jeopardy in the south." The Presbyterian *National Preacher* declined to aid for the same reason.

During the summer and fall of 1829 both Isaac Orr and Francis S. Key labored in New York city. Key called a large meeting in Middle Dutch Church at which Mayor Walter Bowne presided. He predicted colonization efforts in Virginia and Maryland would touch off a chain-like emancipation movement that would spread into all slaveholding states. Slaveowners would manumit their slaves, he said, "as fast as they could be sent away." Only money was needed, and every $25 contribution sent another Negro to Africa.[27]

Joshua Leavitt, one of the committee appointed to raise funds for the society in New York city, volunteered to send his colored servant girl to Liberia. The general agent of the American Seamen's Friend Society described her as being an unwed mother and probably pregnant a second time. He wished to get her out of his house and away from his growing boys. "In these circumstances," he said, "I thought of Liberia." She is "strong and healthy, tolerably skillful in the ordinary work of a New England family, honest, willing to work." He offered to pay her way.[28]

Of the eastern states, Massachusetts lagged the most. Gurley repeatedly begged friends of colonization to build a state auxiliary, but William Roper and John Tappan of the Boston Correspondence Committee said the time was not ripe. Massachusetts needed more work and publicity. Unfortunately, Gurley could not find an agent as efficient or as persistent as the late Horace Sessions. Myron Tracy drifted to the Western Reserve, and William W. Niles resigned his agency to take a pulpit in the Unitarian church at Malden. "If I *now* abandon this Society I probably abandon it to unitarianism forever," Niles explained. "If I remain a while longer . . . I expect to save it to orthodoxy." Leonard Bacon turned down the job of general agent, refusing to give up his large church in New Haven. In 1827, David Hale, depository for all money collected in Massachusetts, Vermont, New Hampshire, and Maine, moved to New York city to work for Arthur Tappan's *Journal of Commerce*. Niles warned that "Boston is the place of deposit for all public charities from the states above named," and those who carried money to Boston would send it back to the donors rather than direct the funds to New Yorkers. Gurley promptly designated Charles Tappan to be the new depository. His brother John described Charles as "zealous in your cause and will do all that any man can effect for you." [29]

Short-term agents occasionally touched parts of Massachusetts and its neighboring states, but no general agent supervised the entire field. Gurley's brother-in-law, Eliphalet Gillet of Hallowell, secretary of the Maine Missionary Society, served as regional agent for eight dollars a week plus expenses. At his suggestion, Gurley commissioned the Reverend Jonathan Greenleaf of Wells, "a man of respectability and influence" and a Royal Arch Mason, to collect money from the Masonic fraternity. Another agent, the Reverend George W. Campbell of South Berwick, Maine, toured northern New York and Vermont. He was the author of a plan for selling "transportations." For $30, payable in five and ten year installments, a subscriber could designate a "beneficiary" or colored person who was to go to Liberia. After completing payments, the purchaser became a life member of the parent society. Eliphalet Nott subscribed along with scores of lesser-known men, including a young editor in Bennington named William Lloyd Garrison.[30]

Well-wishers in many villages of the east piled praises on the society. The venerable advocate of peace, William Ladd of Minot, Maine, organized an auxiliary, stating that "all the benevolent exertions of the day, like the strands of a rope, mutually strengthen each other." He was eagerly looking for the day "when the people of this country will be willing to be taxed, to rid ourselves of the opprobrium under which we now suffer." Another peace advocate, Noah Worcester of Brighton, Massachusetts, organized a joint temperance and colonization society and sent $20. He hoped that "what is saved by abstinence, to avoid becoming enflamed by strong drink, may be appropriated to the pr[oject] of improving the condition" of the free blacks.[31]

In Vermont and New Hampshire local auxiliaries were headed by former governors Chief Justice Skinner and Jonas Galusha. The Reverend Calvin Yale urged Vermonters to redouble their efforts, insisting that colonization "may ultimately lead to the extinction of slavery," and the Reverend Silas McKeen soberly declared "the spirit of those immortal men who rejoiced to fall as martyrs in this benevolent enterprize" blessed the whole movement. Slavery was a fire "long confined under a mountain; which heaving and groaning for a while, at length bursts out with a terrible explosion, darkening the sun with its smoke, and overwhelming all the adjacent region with its burning deluge." [32]

A few colleges and academies joined the crusade. Pupils of the Classical School at Bangor, Maine, agreed to distribute colonization, peace, and temperance tracts "to excite the spirit of moral enquiry." At Amherst, President Heman Humphrey collected $31 in chapel. Colonization, he said, was "one of the noblest [plans] that can be presented to the patriot and christian." His distinguished colleague, Professor Samuel M. Worcester, volunteered to serve as the society's agent. He tripled Humphrey's donation with funds solicited in the college, Mt. Pleasant Academy, and the Andover churches. He also wrote colonization essays for the Boston *Recorder*. Methodism's Willbur Fisk, principal of the Wesleyan Academy at Wilbraham, Connecticut, and soon to become president of Wesleyan University, sent money and godspeed to the parent society.[33]

Fervent support came from Andover Theological Seminary students. They wrote to Gurley to ask for "a *brief, connected* view of the whole subject" on which to base thirty or forty colonization sermons for the Fourth of July. Some asked for vacation employment as agents. "I have always heartily approved of the object" of the Colonization Society, Amos A. Phelps declared in his job application. Gurley had larger plans. He asked for a band of twenty-four volunteers to devote a year or two as agents in every state. In this way, "the whole Union would experience a revolution in [colonization's] favor and the resources of the Federal Government be applied to conduct it forward to a glorious consummation." The seminarists also wrote and published an unsigned colonization pamphlet. Young Bela B. Edwards, a member of the student committee on Africans and assistant secretary of the American Education Society, warned Gurley not to reveal the tract's authorship. "We thought it best not to have mentioned that it was prepared at Andover, as there are prejudices against whatever comes from this place in some parts of N. England." The pamphlet declared that "when slaveholders and slaves, generally, become Christians, slavery will cease." To New Englanders it declared, "We are under weightier obligations than any other portion of the human family to spread far and wide the blessings of freedom and Christianity. Blessed, thrice blessed, shall we be, if we fufill these obligations." [34]

With support growing steadily, Gurley renewed his call for a Massachusetts auxiliary. He sounded out Professor Worcester on the matter. Worcester replied that colonization was still unknown in the backcountry and needed a weekly newspaper "which could be widely circulated—could be thrown into our stores and public houses, as well as into our dwellings." He did not think a state auxiliary could thrive if colonization was "superficially presented to the minds of the people." They had already been "so much addressed and exhorted" and "cannonaded" by hosts of foreign and home missionary, Bible, and Sabbath school agents that "unless *very special* efforts are made" the whole effort would fall flat. Agent Orr reported disconsolately that there was a "pressure for money . . . such as the north has seldom experienced." And when money tightened, only the well-established societies thrived. "Our cause," he complained, "is as yet what New England children would very vulgarly call the *titman*." [35]

Besides the crush of competition, another obstacle blocked the way. "It arises from the state of religious parties," Worcester explained. "The orthodox and unitarians seldom unite in the promotion of a benevolent object." "All our leading political men" are Unitarians, and "it is not to be disguised that the influence of these men is wanted to give a State Society . . . a certain kind of popularity." Yet "efficient and permanent patronage" comes largely from orthodox Trinitarians. Whether the two groups would unite in a colonization society he could not predict, but he counseled delay. Dr. Lyman Beecher volunteered to aid the cause, but he saw no purpose in waiting for the Unitarians. "They have uniformly proved a dead weight to such enterprizes," he snorted.[36]

At Gurley's direction colonizationists bombarded Boston with sermons and editorials asking for a Massachusetts auxiliary. New Haven's Leonard Bacon used his *Christian Spectator* to launch some of the missiles. "I have good reason to believe that there the people are ahead of the clergy in this matter," he privately remarked. "So indeed it is generally in N. England." The Boston *Courier* stressed the commercial value of African trade, suggesting that large profits would repay emigration costs while at the same time building a prosperous colony. On July 4, 1830, John Newland Maffit, New England's spell-binding Methodist preacher, begged Bostonians to hasten African colonization. Rhapsodically he compared its "radiant influence" to a rainbow, "insufferably bright, spanning . . . sombre clouds of human wrong, that have accumulated on the horizon of our country's prosperity." And, he noted less lyrically, removal was cheaper than a war of extermination. Not long after, Ezra Stiles Gannett gave a Thanksgiving discourse in the Federal Street Church in which he warned that a deadly crisis caused by slavery was stalking the land. "A most rare union of firmness and moderation alone can avert bloodshed," he asserted. "A rash hand is on no account to be preferred to an eye blind to its character." [37]

The key men in organizing the Massachusetts State Colonization Society were two Connecticut men, Thomas H. Gallaudet, recently resigned principal of the Hartford Deaf and Dumb Asylum, and Leonard Bacon of New Haven. Gallaudet's sympathies were firmly attached to benevolent society work and colonization in particular. In 1830 he was seeking employment in some association. Bacon persuaded him that "a breeze might be raised in Boston" among the state's "great political characters." The two visited Boston during the legislature's session and called a meeting for February 10, 1831, in the hall of the House of Representatives. State Senator Stephen C. Phillips and General Henry A. S. Dearborn spoke. Members of the new society included Samuel Lathrop, presiding officer of the senate, Speaker William B. Calhoun, Bishop Alexander V. Griswold, and Alexander H. Everett, editor of the *North American Review*.[38]

Bacon and Gallaudet's victory in Boston came late in the drive to capture eastern support. Philadelphia and New York were far ahead in their plans and operations. Following Key's visit in 1829, the Pennsylvania society launched a drive to raise $2,000 to sponsor an emigrant ship. The appeal quickly succeeded, and early in 1830, the *Liberia,* owned by John Hanson of Philadelphia, left Hampton Roads with fifty-nine emigrants. Hanson agreed to carry the emigrants for $30 a head. The auxiliary swiftly raised an additional $3,200 to send the *Montgomery* with seventy emigrants, mostly manumitted slaves. Within a year the Pennsylvania society gathered enough money to sponsor four ships. The *Carolinian* sailed in October, 1830, with 107 emigrants, and a few weeks later, the *Volador* took eighty-two more. In April, 1831, Philadelphians contributed $3,000 to build a "beautiful, fast-sailing" copper bottom vessel to serve as the colonial schooner. The parent society christened it the *Margaret Mercer*.[39]

Meanwhile, the New York city colonizationists reorganized and strengthened their auxiliary. Officers included President William A. Duer of Columbia College, the Reverend Dr. Nathan Bangs, Mayor Walter Bowne, editors William L. Stone and Gerard Hallock, and wealthy Anson G. Phelps. In August, 1831, they sponsored the *Criterion* which carried forty-six emigrants, most of whom were manumitted slaves.[40]

By 1832 Secretary Gurley and the managers of the parent society could look with deep satisfaction on their work in the eastern states. After fitful starts and missteps, the colonization enterprise, now one of the nation's major "benevolent" societies, was prospering. Like her sister associations the society also looked to the expanding west for supplemental assistance. Her agents found westerners responsive to their calls for removal and colonization of free blacks.

XII

THE WESTERN CRUSADERS

---◆•••◆---

A LARGE, cumbersome mail coach was bumping along from Marietta to Wheeling on the narrow, curving road high on the hillside overlooking the Ohio river. The drowsy passengers felt a warning lurch and gasped as the coach horses plunged over the precipice. The vehicle hurtled through brush and trees, rolled over and over, and finally stopped in an unright position. Its wheels were smashed, coach bed crushed, passengers stunned and wounded, and the wheel horses killed. The lead horses, wild with fright, dragged the helpless driver into the river. Tangled among the battered, senseless passengers was the Reverend Henry Bidleman Bascom, former president of Madison College in Uniontown, Pennsylvania, and now serving as the Colonization Society's agent. Bruised and bleeding, he pulled himself from the wreck, lifted the injured to the ground, and hobbled to the river to fetch water with his hat for the unconscious. He regretted the boat captain's decision at Marietta to transfer his passengers to the stage, but such were the hazards of a traveling agent in the west.

In July, 1826, the managers of the Colonization Society decided to canvass the western states for support. Two auxiliaries in St. Louis and Cincinnati, organized by public-spirited citizens, were asking for guidance and encouragement. Though the managers expected the Atlantic seaboard to provide the greater support, they recognized that the west was growing both in wealth and political power.

Its Negro population was also growing. In the southwest the slave population was the fastest growing in the nation. In the northwest free blacks were flocking to towns in western Pennsylvania, southern Ohio, Indiana, and Illinois. Almost overnight many new communities acquired Negro residents who abandoned eastern states for a home in the west. Colonizationist Benjamin Brand of Richmond, Virginia, noted that many free blacks in that city were leaving for Ohio. "Why they will not go to Liberia I do not know." North Carolina Quakers also discovered that their manumitted slaves preferred Ohio and Pennsylvania to Haiti or Liberia. Ohio's restrictive laws against free Negroes were not enforced and more Negroes came. "Their fecundity is proverbial," one Ohio newspaper complained. "They are worse than drones to society, and they already swarm our land like locusts." Henry Clay expressed the sentiments of many apprehensive westerners when he observed that free blacks usually dwelt in the "lowest state of social gradation—aliens—political—moral—social—aliens, strangers, though natives." Echoing this, a colonizationist in Chillicothe declared that "with few exceptions" they were "little less than a nuisance." With dismay a Brown country resident estimated that nearly five hundred free blacks now lived in his neighborhood. As a whole, they lived on the poorest lands, stole from their neighbors, and looked upon white men as a "common enemy." When he joined the colonization movement he candidly asserted, "It is not to be disguised that most of us in this undertaking are influenced more by interested motives than otherwise." [1]

The Colonization Society's first agent to the "Western country" was Benjamin Orrs Peers, a graduate of Transylvania University and of the Reverend Mr. Wilmer's Episcopal Theological Seminary at Alexandria. On Wilmer's motion, the Colonization Society's managers commissioned young Peers to raise auxiliaries, advertise colonization, and gather money in Pennsylvania, Ohio, and Kentucky. They paid him $25 a month plus expenses to be deducted from his collections. [2]

In the next two years, Peers organized dozens of auxiliaries and filled local newspapers with propaganda. "I am determined that there shall be scarcely a press west of the Mts. not pressed into our service," he declared extravagantly to Secretary Gurley. In Pennsylvania his opponents were free Negroes and Quakers. The free Negroes dreaded deportation, and the Quakers resented rivalry with their moribund abolition societies. The day after he organized the Pittsburgh auxiliary, two Negroes, "decidedly frightened by our meeting," begged him to endorse their petition for a federal land grant at the mouth of the Columbia river. They proposed to take Pennsylvania and Ohio's Negro population to their colony. Denouncing the idea as "folly," Peers urged them to go to Africa. Privately, he blamed the Quaker abolitionists for stirring up Negro opposition. But not all Quakers were hostile. In Brownsville and Washington, Quaker abolition leaders joined the colonization societies. "Though 'Quakers sly' I find their risible muscles recover their flexibility at a compliment," he confided.[3]

While Peers crossed Ohio, forming auxiliaries in Cleveland, Canfield, Canton, and a state society at Columbus, Moses Montgomery Henkle, a Methodist clergyman in Springfield, labored in smaller communities. Soon societies sprang up in Bellbrook, Lancaster, Full Creek, Germantown, Eaton, Bainbridge, and at Oxford where Miami University students and faculty pledged to assist colonization. The Grand Jury of Ross county urged citizens to join the local auxiliary. Henkle won endorsement from the Ohio Methodist conference which promised to collect money on the Fourth of July, and Peers specialized in enlisting well-known Ohio politicians. Governor Jeremiah Morrow, ex-governor Edward Tiffin, Supreme Court Justice Jacob Burnet, Thomas Corwin, a rising attorney in Warren county and high official in the Ohio Masonic Lodge, and several Ohio congressmen pledged their support. In January, 1828, the state legislature approved resolutions instructing senators and congressmen to "induce the Government of the United States to aid the American Colonization Society." "The fire of Colonization has at length broken out in our country," one Ohio colonizationist exclaimed. It is spreading everywhere "with the most unparralled rapidity." [4]

In Xenia, Ohio, Independence Day was a solemn holiday for colonization. The Sabbath school children and their teachers marched in procession from the court house to the picnic grove behind the Associate Meeting House where the local auxiliary and its female auxiliary jointly met. After opening prayers and annual reports, men, women, and children ceremoniously marched forward to drop their contributions into the "Colonization Box." [5]

Agent Peers found strong colonization sentiment in his own Kentucky. He reported that among Kentucky's foremost men there was a "growing disposition for gratuitous manumission," and some vowed to press "with all their might" for an emancipation scheme if a new state constitutional convention met. However, in 1828 when Peers created the state society in the senate chamber at Frankfort, emancipation was not an avowed goal. Robert Wickliffe, a defender of slavery, was president and Henry Clay's general endorsement of colonization assured the society's prestige and growth. Other Kentuckians who supported colonization were Governor Thomas Metcalfe, Lieutenant Governor John Breathitt, Cave Johnson, the Reverend Gideon Blackburn, and Dr. Luke Munsell. In 1829 Henry Clay addressed the parent society and predicted that by 1929 there would be eighty million whites and sixteen million Negroes in the United States. "What mind is sufficiently extensive in its reach, what nerves sufficiently strong, to contemplate this vast and progressive augmentation, without an awful foreboding of the tremendous consequences?" These dire results, "now wrapt in futurity," would be economic in origin. As population grew and labor became more plentiful, slavery would be uneconomical, and slaveowners would turn loose their surplus workers. This social upheaval in turn would lead to "shocking scenes of carnage, rapine, and lawless violence" and followed by a reign of martial law and mass executions. The Kentucky society petitioned the legislature to ask the federal government to aid colonization, citing as a precedent the "millions of dollars . . . annually expended for the maintainence and comfort of the North American Indians." The Africans' claim is "at least of equal dignity with that of the savage," they contended.[6]

Similar fears of the Negro prevailed in Cincinnati. In 1829 its rapidly growing black community reached 2,200, about ten percent of the city population and the greater part of Ohio's entire black population. Former slaves and mulattoes were jammed into "Little Africa," a cluster of shacks and shanties sprawling over two wards. They are "a great and manifest drawback on the prosperity of this city," one Cincinnati man complained, "as they make it difficult for the labouring poor white people to obtain employment." The colonization auxiliary organized in 1826 and reorganized from time to time, claimed the city's foremost men, including Justice Jacob Burnet, Peyton S. Symmes, the Reverend Asa Mahan, and President Lyman Beecher of Lane Seminary. The society's secretary, Robert Smith Finley, was the son of the Reverend Robert Finley of Baskingridge, New Jersey. Another son of the parent society's founder, Dr. James C. Finley, was a manager of the Cincinnati auxiliary.[7]

Both Finleys were ardent colonizationists. Professing "an hereditary attachment" to the movement, James volunteered for service in Liberia, and his brother became a traveling agent. Robert began his career by organizing many auxiliaries in Ohio, including societies in New Lancaster, Newark, Lebanon, and Lane Seminary. Then he made annual tours of the eastern states and concentrated on building the movement in Kentucky, Louisiana, and Mississippi. Another brother, Josiah F. C. Finley, a Princeton graduate, later went to Liberia as a missionary and was killed by natives.[8]

Cincinnati's frank dislike for its black population burst forth in the form of harsh legal pressures and violence. In 1829 local authorities ordered the free Negroes to post $500 good behavior bonds or leave the city within thirty days. Negro leaders begged for a time extension and sent Israel Lewis and Thomas Cressup to find a haven in Canada. They did not return before the deadline passed, and whites rioted in "Little Africa," causing a few deaths and many injuries that dramatized ugly race tensions. Lewis and Cressup finally returned and led more than one thousand free blacks to Upper Canada. In the next years more followed. Even this substantial exodus raised angry voices. The Cincinnati *Gazette* complained that the "sober, honest, industrious, and useful" had migrated, leaving behind the idle, indolent, and vagrant. Two hundred settled on a fertile, wooded tract purchased from the Canada Company and named the Wilberforce Colony. The Canadians were not pleased with their new neighbors. The House of Assembly of Upper Canada censured the company for "introducing large bodies of negro settlers into this province." [9]

Cincinnati colonizationists, disappointed that the Negroes did not choose to go to Liberia, vainly tried to persuade them that Africa was not really "pervaded with a monstrous gloom."

Lawyer Salmon P. Chase, calling colonization a noble cause deserving the "smiles of Heaven and the support of men," urged free Negroes to subscribe to the *Repository* and make plans for emigrating to Liberia. But Cincinnati Negroes were divided among themselves. The mulattoes shunned the blacks and demanded a separate colony.[10]

From 1829 to 1835 many agents crossed and recrossed the western states. Some were seasoned diplomats and persuasive speakers. Others were underpaid refugees from seminaries and colleges and had only superficial knowledge of colonization principles. Cornelius Moore, agent in Ohio in 1834, was "scarcely acquainted with the rudiments of the subject" and depended on his "strong antipathy to abolition" for success. Every agent faced perils, frustrations, and disappointments. In Illinois an Indian war and an uncommonly hard winter slowed one agent's progress. In many western communities epidemic cholera drove strangers away and closed meeting halls. An agent in Mobile could not find enough people to attend his meetings because "an actress of more than common celebrity had just arrived in town." One of the society's better agents, Josiah F. Polk, succeeded everywhere he went except among the Pennsylvania Dutch. He left them, exclaiming bitterly, "O the Dutch! the Dutch! The Lord deliver me from the Dutch!" [11]

The most energetic and eloquent western agent was thirty-seven-year-old Methodist clergyman and educator Henry Bidleman Bascom. In 1829 he gave up the presidency of a hardscrabble college in Pennsylvania and gratefully accepted the Colonization Society's agency for western Pennsylvania, New York, and Ohio. With the toughness of a Methodist circuit rider, Bascom set out from Pittsburgh and stopped at Buffalo, Batavia, Canandaigua, Geneva, Rochester, Erie, Meadville, Wheeling, Steubenville, St. Clairsville, and Mt. Pleasant. The following spring he dipped into Kentucky and Tennessee. He lectured by day and read works on colonization and Africa by night. Half a year later, he could boast that he had addressed seventy thousand people.

Only his patience was exhaustible. The Presbyterian minister at Canandaigua, New York, flatly refused to open his church to a

Methodist. "The blue stocking parson," Bascom snorted, "treated me with boorish incivility. I had no sooner announced myself a Methodist preacher, than he bristled almost into a swine, and grunted his negative most becomingly." Bascom stormed away, "hating bigotry more implacably than ever before." He deplored western New York's inferior inns. "Dined on fat middling and fried eggs," he noted with distaste, "and passed the night at a tavern where I was annoyed by the noise and vulgarity of a parcel of Irish wagoners—half beast—half devil, from whom I was relieved only by their getting too drunk to continue their revel." He left the region, declaring that "on the score of solid comfort, cordial welcome, and generous hospitality" it was the least attractive he visited.[12]

Bascom infused his colonization lectures with Methodist fervor. Dark, handsome, and dressed in clothes cut in the latest fashion, he made a striking figure on the platform. His eyes seemed to "dart arrows of flame" over his audience. His voice modulated with his mood—rolling, pealing, ringing, and sometimes sinking into the "wild wail" of a funeral chime. One listener remembered his words as "successive thunder-claps, causing the very hair to rise on the hearer's head, and the warm marrow to creep . . . in his bones." His lectures, sometimes lasting more than two hours, dwelt on the standard slave-trade theme, and his limitless imagination embroidered the usual description of blood-thirsty pirates worshipping at the "shrine of avarice," wrenching helpless men from their families and homes, and murdering protesting innocents. He also painted rich pictures of ancient African culture, arguing that "this condemned race" claims a "brighter ancestry than our own." "They found Egypt a morass, and converted it into the most fertile country of the world." The pyramids, obelisks and granite pillars of ancient cities were monuments to their architectural skill. Egypt was the bridge of civilization.[13]

Bascom used his tours for more than trumpeting the principles of colonization. Occasionally he played the tourist. In New York he tramped over battlefields of the War of 1812, donned an oil cloth raincoat and walked below Niagara Falls, "the most magnificent spectacle that ever chained the eye of a beholder," and crossed into Upper Canada to visit relatives. In each state he made political soundings for his friend Henry Clay. He cautioned the presidential aspirant on two topics, "the *Masonic* excitement, which is, strange as it may appear, agitating *large* portions of the country, and . . . the *Purchase of Texas.*" He also used his tour to hunt a new position in the west. In 1832 he settled in Kentucky as professor of Moral Science and Belles-lettres in Augusta College, later becoming president of Transylvania University and then bishop of the Methodist Episcopal Church, South.[14]

While Bascom worked New York and Pennsylvania, the managers directed Josiah F. Polk to push farther west and southwest. Through letters Henry Clay introduced him to influential men there. Starting in Maryland, Polk labored in Pennsylvania, Ohio, Indiana, and then concentrated on Tennessee and northern Alabama. He visited nearly every county in Tennessee and organized the state auxiliary at Nashville with branches in Memphis, Franklin, Murphreesborough, Knoxville, Jonesboro, Kingsport, and many smaller communities. He also created the Alabama state society at Tuskaloosa and several local groups. He was astonished to find that many men in the southwest had never heard of Liberia, but they quickly endorsed colonization as the best plan to rid themselves of free blacks. In a few months he traveled 6,700 miles, mostly on horseback, organized 40 auxiliaries, sold 150 subscriptions to the *Repository,* and collected $500 and pledges for hundreds more.[15]

In Indiana Polk organized five auxiliaries and the state society at Indianapolis. Supporters of colonization hoped to prevent further free Negro migration into that state. The editor of the Richmond *Public Ledger* criticized North Carolina Quakers for unloading social misfits on the west, and Isaac Newton Blackford of the Indiana Supreme Court and once a student in the Reverend Mr. Finley's academy, ominously warned that "a low, ignorant, debased multitude" of free blacks soon would swarm to Indiana. Two distinguished Illinois citizens, Cyrus Edwards, brother of Governor Ninian Edwards, and ex-Governor Edward Coles, presented colonization to their neighbors as a plan to reduce the state's free black population. Pointing to the growing numbers of free Negroes in Ohio, Edwards insisted that Illinois also has "an immediate, a peculiar, and a pressing interest" to avoid being "overborne by an evil of such magnitude," especially if the free blacks driven from other states decided to seek a haven in the Illinois prairies.[16]

In Kentucky colonization was undergoing an important transformation. In 1829 the state society had pledged to relieve the commonwealth from "the serious inconvenience resulting from the existence among us, of a rapidly increasing number of free persons of colour." But in 1830 some supporters were boldly calling their scheme an emancipation project. The extinction of slavery had been a lively political topic since the state constitutional conventions of 1792 and 1799. Antislavery advocates periodically called for a new convention to abolish slavery, but in 1830 they switched strategy and advertised colonization as a constitutional vehicle for ridding Kentucky of slavery. State Senator Robert Wickliffe, president of the Kentucky society and a defender of slavery, quit the society in disgust. Afterwards, Robert J. Breckinridge, a family friend of Jefferson and a lawyer turned Presbyterian minister, became the society's foremost spokesman in Kentucky. He declared that emancipation was the ultimate aim of African colonization. He argued that the federal government would assist in removing freedmen once Kentucky or another slave state took steps to end slavery. "The political moral of the Colonization Society is strikingly plain," he declared. "It has taught us how we may be relieved of the curse of slavery in a manner cheap, certain and advantageous to both the parties. It now remains for those who say they are its friends to go whither the light of its example points them." [17]

As a member of the state legislature, Breckinridge insisted that the lawmakers already possessed sufficient authority to regulate slavery. They could use the tax power to destroy it. "The power is complete and the right to exercise it perfect," he said. Also, the state could buy and liberate slaves. "Domestic slavery cannot exist forever," he declared. "It cannot exist long, quiet and unbroken, in any condition of society, or under any form of government. It may terminate in various ways; but terminate it must." [18]

Certain that Kentucky's decision to abandon slavery would launch a nation-wide movement, agent Robert S. Finley hurried to Kentucky to bolster the emancipationists. He worked closely with Breckinridge in building auxiliaries and popularizing colonization. He assured Gurley that emancipation in Kentucky was not far off. "I have no hesitation in saying that there are *thousands* of slaves in this state who are merely held by their masters *in trust*" for colonization. Some slaveowners allowed their servants to listen to Finley's addresses on Africa, for they "wish their minds to be prepared for it." With "proper exertions" that year the Mississippi valley would furnish no less than one thousand emigrants and as much as $50,000. "This calculation may appear extravagant," he conceded, but it was the opinion of "some of the wisest and best men" in Kentucky. He chided the doubting managers, saying "public opinion is at least five years in advance of the *operations* of the Board." [19]

To hasten the work, Finley commissioned the Reverend George C. Light and the Reverend Edward Southgate agents for Kentucky, and the Reverend Orramel S. Hinckley, Gurley's brother-in-law, agent for Tennessee. Commending Robert J. Breckinridge as "a man of superior talents, and an excellent public speaker," he urged the managers to schedule speaking engagements for Breckinridge in Philadelphia and Baltimore. The managers did not act, fearing they would be affixing the cachet of approval to his bold pleas for emancipation. Breckinridge was furious. He complained that the managers treated him as "one of the two dollar a day agents" and a raving "ultra." Furthermore, it was wrong to "inveigle the friends of Slavery into a short-lived friendship" for colonization, for they quickly discovered that its real goal was emancipation. Finley placated him with a commission as agent for Kentucky. Breckinridge promised thirty thousand emigrants in a ten-year period if political moves to secure emancipation in Kentucky succccdcd.[20]

A large block in the legislature favored measures restricting if not ending slavery. Breckinridge's friend John Green offered a bill to tax every slave to raise a colonization fund, but it failed to pass. Kentucky colonizationists drew attention to antislavery arguments, but they came no nearer to emancipation than placing restrictions on the domestic slave trade. Non-importation bills came before the legislators in 1828 and 1830. Breckinridge,

Green, and other colonizationists filled the weekly press with essays that portrayed non-importation of slaves as the first step in ridding the state of slavery. Opponents attacked the bill as an invitation to slave states to retaliate against Kentucky's exports —mules, horses, and hogs. In 1830 the bill failed by one vote, but in 1833 it passed. Until its repeal in 1849 it was the fulcrum of political discussion of slavery in Kentucky.[21]

Meanwhile, Finley and his co-workers advertised African colonization in Kentucky by outfitting emigrant expeditions. In 1831 the parent society contributed $5,000 to send the schooner *Crawford* from New Orleans with twenty-one Kentucky free Negroes and manumitted slaves. In 1832 and 1833 agents in Tennessee and Kentucky collected $1,500 and gathered seventy emigrants at Louisville and thirty-three more at Shawneetown. The steamboat *Mediterranean* gave them free passage to New Orleans where an agent waited to load them on a ship destined for Liberia.[22]

Kentucky's frank avowal of emancipation disturbed slaveowners of the southwest. When Agent Bascom visited Mississippi in 1832 he found many men believed colonization to be an emancipation scheme—as it was rumored among their Negroes. Bascom succeeded in allaying their fears. He collected $700 and organized a few auxiliaries. He crossed Alabama and gathered a few hundred dollars more in Florence, Tuscumbia, Athens, and Huntsville, but he told Gurley he could have done more if cautious slaveowners had not regarded him as an "outsider." [23]

A few months later, the managers appointed an Alabama slaveowner to tour the southwestern district and confidently looked forward to larger revenues. James Gillespie Birney was a native of Kentucky and a family friend of Henry Clay. He had quit planting, sold his field hands, and turned to the practice of law in Huntsville, a fast-growing, prosperity-seeking town in northern Alabama. As an attorney he owed more to his "industry and fidelity" than to "any overmastering ability or . . . richness of legal attainments." At forty his practice was modest and his family large. He hinted that he would accept an agency.[24]

Birney first brought himself to the attention of the Colonization Society in 1828 by collecting $20 and sending it to his father's friend, Henry Clay, and from time to time thereafter he transmitted larger sums to Washington. The local Presbyterian minister recommended Birney as a devout Christian and loyal supporter of the Bible Society. All in all, he seemed a logical choice, and in 1832 Gurley offered him $1,000 a year to canvass Alabama, Mississippi, Louisiana, Arkansas, and Tennessee.[25]

Birney termed the offer providential for he was on the verge of moving to Illinois to find a new career. He set aside this plan and accepted the commission. In his meticulous way, he spent several weeks studying colonization literature and the duties of an agent. With a convert's zeal he began writing cogent essays defending colonization as a boon to slave states, and he planned an ambitious tour to revive languishing auxiliaries started by Polk and Bascom. "If I mistake not, *facts* are strong weapons," he said hopefully, "and will, if properly presented, command success." He assured Gurley that he did not approve of slavery and that if he ever moved to Illinois he would send his household slaves to Liberia.[26]

Though eager and methodical, Birney was less successful than his experienced predecessors. In the southwest caution was hardening into hostility. Chilly receptions in Mobile and New Orleans cooled his ardor. Judge Alexander Porter, president of the almost defunct Louisiana auxiliary, discouraged him from holding public meetings, saying that disfavor was too great. But Birney forged ahead and called a meeting; it was a dud. Birney was depressed. "I am afraid, that our cause will languish unto death here.—I know not what to do to raise it." He blamed his failure on the city's complete disregard for benevolence. "I have seen no place where men are so exclusively occupied with private business," he complained. "Day or night—Sunday not excepted—seems to offer no repose from its toils." He also blamed Robert S. Finley's blunt antislavery remarks for his unfavorable reception. He condemned Finley for calling opponents "enemies." Hard names only pushed dissenters into the "ranks of an unrelenting opposition," he admonished. The proper way to deal with critics is to use "forbearance, and kindness, and sober argument, that they are wrong, and thus persuade them to be our friends and cooperators." [27] In future years he ignored his own advice.

One of Birney's duties in New Orleans was supervising the sailing of the emigrant ship *Ajax* with funds collected in Kentucky and Tennessee. He chartered the ship for $3,600 and tried to thaw apathy in New Orleans with publicity about the expedition.

Just before the ship sailed, two emigrants died of cholera. With no thought of the consequences, Birney decided to "say nothing publicly upon this matter," led the remaining emigrants on board, and sent the ship off with the customary fanfare. The ship's departure deeply moved him. He thought of Africa " 'robbed and spoiled'—'weeping for her children—refusing to be comforted'—now I saw her rejoicing at their return;—I thought of the shriek of phrenzy, the stifled groan of death in the slave-ship,—now, I saw the sober job of the restored and in their countenances the beams of an elevating and glorious hope. . . . Sir, Sir, if it be weakness to sympathize with the miserable made happy—to rejoice, even to tears, at the contemplation of my country's true glory—to feel an overmastering expansion of heart at this practical exhibition of benevolence so like God's, then I am most weak indeed." Several months passed before word returned from Africa that a large portion of the *Ajax*'s 150 passengers had come down with cholera and 30—mostly children—had died of cholera and whooping cough. Birney objectively commented that this "disastrous intelligence" would probably delay another expedition planned that fall.[28]

By that time, Birney had again decided to quit Alabama and return to his father's home in Kentucky. Gloomily he told Gurley that in twenty years Alabama, Mississippi, and Louisiana "must be overrun by the blacks" because men of the southwest steadfastly refused to give up slavery. By 1833 Kentucky seemed a "better field for operations than that in which I have been laboring." There he joined Finley, Breckinridge, and Green in speaking boldly for emancipation through colonization, but his efforts to launch a separate society, "The Kentucky Society for the gradual relief of the State from slavery," were abortive, and he looked elsewhere for employment.[29]

By 1835 traveling agents had penetrated every region of the United States, advertised African colonization principles, and formed numerous auxiliaries. In that year the managers counted seventeen state societies and more than two hundred local auxiliaries plus many female, college, academy, and juvenile affiliates. Top-ranking leaders in nation, state, and community endorsed colonization. Hundreds of emigrants were crossing the Atlantic. The robust Cincinnati auxiliary spoke for its sister societies when it declared that "the success of the parent Society has fully demonstrated that the system is expedient and practicable." [30] While the managers were perfecting their organization and weaving a national movement, they approvingly watched Liberia grow large and strong. Their dreams of an American empire in Africa seemed to be nearing fulfillment.

XIII

VISIONS OF EMPIRE

———◆•••◆———

WHILE the Colonization Society was building a national movement, Jehudi Ashmun strove to make Liberia a working model for a vaster enterprise. After his triumphant restoration in 1825, the colonial agent reigned supreme at Monrovia. He enjoyed the trust of the board of managers, the partnership of Secretary Ralph Randolph Gurley, and the protection of the United States government. Under Ashmun's direction, the ragged thatch village hugging Cape Mesurado grew rapidly and extended its authority up and down the coast. Ashmun's dream of a vast tropical colony guided his work. He envisioned the high, narrow cape wrested from King Peter's people in 1821 as the nucleus of an American empire in Africa. With this goal he set about to strengthen colonial agriculture, exploit commercial opportunities in the interior, and annex neighboring tribal lands. His mind's eye wandered down the Atlantic littoral to the native kingdoms of Little Bassa and Grand Bassa and beyond to Cape Palmas where the African coast turns sharply eastward. In time, these would become part of Liberia.

In his second capacity as the United States government's agent for rescued Africans, Ashmun commanded virtually unlimited access to funds set aside by the Slave Trade Act of 1819. Both Monroe's and Adams's administrations permitted a broad interpretation of the act, enabling Ashmun to use federal funds to enlarge the colony as well as the government agency. At the same time Ashmun built a loyal following in Monrovia by creating salaried posts and appointing influential colonists to them. His civil list included Assistant Agent, Storekeeper, and Assistant

Superintendent—all drawing salaries from the United States treasury. Ample supplies of arms from government arsenals permitted him to drill a 90-man militia, and in 1825 and 1826 he raided slave depots along the African coast. After one notable expedition, he carried 170 confiscated slaves to Monrovia and added them to the government's accounts as rescued Africans.[1]

The colonial agent also launched a vigorous program for constructing public buildings and fortifications at Monrovia—all at the expense of the United States. In this way he provided work and wages to carpenters, joiners, plasterers, stonemasons, and common laborers in the colony. Under his supervision they completed his headquarters and residence, the Agency House, a frame building sixty-four by forty feet, made of yellow pine imported from the United States. Its double piazza was finished with "Venetian work of excellent workmanship and materials." In 1827 he estimated its worth at $7,500. With government funds he built two warehouses, the Central Receptacle for rescued Africans, plus smaller dormitories, a granary-storehouse, a stone magazine, and a new schooner. Nurtured by the United States treasury, the village grew into a town, and the town into a colony.

At first glance, visitors could have mistaken Monrovia, with its stout forts and forbidding batteries, for a military station. Ashmun replaced Fort Stockton, heart of the town's defenses in the hectic days of 1822 and 1823, with Central Fort, a triangular battery of three pentagonal towers dotted with port holes and joined by long walls ten feet thick. To protect the outer roadstead from pirates and unfriendly ships, he built Fort Norris Battery near the summit of Cape Mesurado and equipped it with four twelve-pounders. At Crown Hill on the eastern side of Monrovia he began another fort, a hexagonal tower with thick walls and eight gun mounts. Ordnance supplied by the Monroe administration included five long twelves, two eighteen-pound gunnades, three mounted nines, plus smaller swivel pieces and Ashmun's favorite—a brass six-pound field piece mounted on a traveling carriage.[2]

Ashmun had not come to Africa to design forts, mount cannon, raid slave depots, or beat off intruders. When he sailed from Baltimore in May, 1822, as the representative of the Baltimore

Trading Company, he intended to become a rich merchant dealing in ivory, gold dust, palm oil, camwood, and beeswax. He shared the dreams of the Reverend Robert Finley, General Robert G. Harper, and Dr. Eli Ayres that Africa would one day become a bounteous commercial haven for Americans. Before going to Africa, Ashmun hoped to persuade the managers to grant a monopoly to a single mercantile house—his firm—with absolute bans against foreign merchantmen and prohibitive duties for unlicensed American bottoms. His company would send four ships a year, charging the Colonization Society 100 percent on outward shipments and 200 percent on return cargoes. He warned the society not to turn merchant itself and launch its own shipping line. "Such an appendage would prove most unpopular at home" and absorb all the profits.[3]

Upon taking office as colonial agent, Ashmun changed his views radically. He now advocated agriculture, not commerce. But he discovered that the colonists preferred trade to farming and planting. Contrary to the Colonization Society's vision of a large tropical plantation rivaling the West Indies, the colonists displayed slight interest in planting coffee, sugar, or cotton. The managers tried to stimulate the production of staples by fixing low prices for land, offering large land grants to prospective planters, and promising premiums to farmers. Few colonists attempted to carve plantations out of the tropical thickets, and one plantation was wholly fictitious. In 1828 Lott Cary, posing as a planter, sent 6,000 pounds of "Liberian" coffee to the Richmond market and attracted public notice. After his death it was discovered that he had purchased the beans from a visiting merchantman and passed them off as his own crop.[4]

Token efforts at farming proved a failure too. The hot rainy climate as well as soils, crops, and pests were unfamiliar to the North Americans. Seasons varied from dry to wet, the temperature usually hovered in the low eighties, soil around Monrovia was thin and hard to work, and dense forests were sturdy obstacles to a colony without a single draft animal. Ashmun's carefully prepared handbook on Liberian agriculture pleased the managers in Washington, D.C., but it did not overcome the Liberian farmer's hazards, nor could it wipe out the colonists' prejudices against African food.[5]

The settlers preferred pork, ham, wheat flour, and Indian corn imported from the United States at great cost to native-grown cassada, plantain, bananas, or yams. The latter grew quickly, and harvesting two crops a year from the same ground was not unusual. An American visitor found the yams "tough and tasteless, and [bear] much the same relation to an excellent or common potato as codfish or shark meat does to a well-dressed pike or trout." Disdaining African dishes as well as African agriculture, the colonists turned to petty barter with near-by tribes and bought American food with their profits. When necessary, they supplemented their American diets with cheap rice gathered by the natives. In short, the colonists found it easier to obtain food by trade than to hoe the soil themselves. Ashmun tried to salvage colonial agriculture by converting rescued slaves into farmers and settling them on new farms in outlying areas where the lure of trade was less obvious.

Agriculture was drudgery compared to the beckoning riches of trade and petty barter. Increasingly, the colonists turned to trade which quickly became the major economic activity in Liberia. Any shrewd colonist could enter the "country traffic" with a barrel of rum, a hogshead of tobacco, or a few bolts of bafta or cotton cloth. Success in petty barter depended on skill in bargaining with neighboring tribes. Several colonists enriched themselves by exploiting the native gatherers of ivory, camwood, palm oil, and rice—all readily marketable commodities. On one occasion, angry tribesmen tried to throttle the ivory and camwood trade, complaining that the colony's prices were too low. Their boycott failed, and operations continued much as before. "Without single exception," Ashmun lamented in 1826, "the mechanics of the Colony, even the most skilful, have repeatedly sacrificed the profits of their proper business to the precarious gains of this country traffic." In 1831 a new colonist observed that swarms of Liberians were "eager in the pursuit of traffic." He was astonished to discover "what little time is necessary, to qualify even the youngest, to drive as hard a bargain, as any

roving merchant from the land of steady habits, with his assort-
ment of tin ware, nutmegs, books, or dry goods." [6]

One of Liberia's wealthy merchants, Francis Devaney, was
once the slave of Langdon Cheves, Speaker of the House of
Representatives, and later an apprentice to Samuel Forten, free
Negro sailmaker in Philadelphia. In 1823 Devaney earned $200
as the captain of a small public vessel that plied the African coast
for food supplies. With his earnings he became the consignee of
a mercantile firm in the United States. By 1830 he could place
his fortune at $20,000. The prosperous firm of Roberts, Colson,
and Company was a partnership between Joseph Jenkins Roberts
and William Nelson Colson of Petersburg. Roberts had inherited
some property from his parents, and Colson was a barber. Roberts
went to Liberia and Colson consigned cargoes to him from Petersburg, Philadelphia, and New York. They were soon able to buy
their own schooner, the *Caroline*. Roberts later became president of the Liberian republic.[7]

The charms of "an immediate, and certain profit" seduced the
preachers as well. The Reverend Lott Cary and the Reverend
Colson M. Waring each tried to raise rice, cassada, and vegetables, but a host of pests—including rice birds, ants, and mon-
keys—destroyed their crops. Thereupon each surrendered to
"such pursuits as promised a surer return on much smaller dis-
bursements." Cary became the Liberian representative of a Richmond trading house, and Waring formed a partnership with a free
Negro in Petersburg. In 1830 Waring's business grossed $70,-
000.[8]

Ashmun deplored the virtual extinction of agriculture. Reminding the colonists that Liberia had to win self-sufficiency, he exhorted them to clear their lands, raise food, and plant staples.
Trade is precarious, he warned, and "liable to be affected by a
thousand circumstances over which the colony itself can exercise
no control." He attempted to restrict trade to a few men by creating licensed trade factories with exclusive rights among certain
tribes. The penalty for interlopers was forfeiture of goods and
wares. These regulations, he assured the managers, made trade
more profitable to a few individuals and "less prejudicial" to
agriculture. After one colonist borrowed $5,000 from a Boston

firm without consulting Ashmun, the Colonial Agent issued rules of "the most positive nature" to prevent any repetition of this "imprudence." In addition, he forbade all purchases on credit.[9]

At Ashmun's behest, the managers tried to regulate petty barter by clamping restrictions on the distribution of rum and whiskey, age-old ingredients in African commerce. Without stringent rules, Ashmun complained, the colony would soon swarm with "tippling shops, tipplers, and drunkards." Agreeing that "much injury may be sustained by the Colony, if ardent spirits be permitted to be sold by Retailers without limitation," the managers gave the colonial agent a liquor wholesale monopoly. In turn he distributed rum and whiskey, at a maximum of 300 percent profit, to a few licensed retailers. The society's assured profits were to buy "fresh provisions or such necessaries as the settlers need." [10]

Closely related to Ashmun's commercial policies were his frequent attacks on slave factories along the coast. With arms supplied by the United States Navy and a militia subsidized by the federal government, Ashmun invaded and demolished towns operated by French and Spanish traders, accusing them of "piratical depredations" on American shipping. In 1826 he destroyed Trade Town in the Young Sesters territory below Monrovia. A few days later, plundered cotton goods sold in Monrovia at bargain prices. Monrovia's extensive fortifications discouraged reprisals and drove off unwanted foreign ships. "A piratical Spaniard . . . came into our waters strongly armed," Ashmun reported on one occasion, "and being refused in his saucy application to trade ashore, he uttered certain threats of retaliation . . . which made it necessary to chase him out of our roads, and keep him off by force." Ashmun begged the United States Navy to "subdue and crush such formidable combinations" and remedy the "exposed state of American commerce on this coast." [11]

Intertwined with this lively sense of competition was the impulse to extend the colony's political control beyond the confines of Cape Mesurado. During 1825 and 1826, Ashmun took steps to lease, annex, or buy tribal lands along 150 miles of the Grain Coast and on major rivers leading inland. Not all tribes welcomed these expansionist steps. Some resisted proffered treaties of commerce and peace. From the experience of neighboring tribes they learned that commercial agreements were preliminary to outright annexation. Ready to honor peace if the natives complied with his demands for virtual monopoly of their trade, Ashmun was just as ready to employ force to secure his ends. He justified force, saying that it was necessary to protect trade routes and factories from "lawless violence and savage rapacity." The Colonization Society's managers applauded his reasoning and held up Sierra Leone as the condoning example. In 1825 the British had concluded a treaty with warring natives, thereby adding 120 miles on the coast and 5,000 square miles of "the most fertile land in this part of Africa." The Sierra Leone *Gazette* had joyously welcomed the destruction of the "abominable traffic in human victims" as well as the "immense commercial advantages which must accrue from this happy stroke of policy." [12]

Ashmun's similarly aggressive acts swiftly increased Liberia's power and dominion over its neighbors. In May, 1825, King Peter, former owner of Cape Mesurado, surrendered control of Cape Mount, a large area above Monrovia. Ashmun promptly opened a trade factory there and issued regulations "to close the door still more effectually" to foreign traders who frequented the place. He predicted Cape Mount's trade would be worth $50,000 a year to Americans. Six years later, Cape Mount became part of Liberia. King Peter also gave up a large island just north of Monrovia which Ashmun christened Bushrod Island in honor of the Colonization Society's first president. A small war wrenched the Young Sesters territory below Monrovia from the recalcitrant Little Bassa tribesmen. In 1826 Ashmun installed a trading post on the Junk river, and King Joe Harris gave up the strategic Factory Island. Soon after, tribesmen farther up the St. Paul's river ceded an extensive tract which Ashmun named Millsburg in honor of Samuel J. Mills and Ebenezer Burgess, the Colonization Society's first agents in Africa. There he built a log factory to receive the interior trade, predicting that one day "a large body of farmers" would follow trade up the river and open the new lands to agriculture. Harried tribesmen learned to respect the colony's power and prestige. They came to look upon the Liberian colonists as "white men." To be "acquainted with the white man's fashions and to be treated as one, are considered as marks of great distinction, among the Bassas and other nations," an observant colonist noted.[13]

In the United States the colonizationists unreservedly applauded Ashmun's expansion policy. They hailed it the first step in building an American empire. The Virginia Colonization Society frankly asserted that "the great problem of a new empire is about to be solved." William M. Blackford of Fredericksburg, Virginia, assured fellow colonizationists that "the germ of an Americo-African empire has been planted" and would "flourish and expand until it overshadows a continent." Samuel L. Knapp of Boston, a Masonic editor and spread-eagle orator, boasted that the Colonization Society was reversing the "tide of empire" from west to east. It was building "an empire more enlightened than any time in his course has seen." African soil, he rhapsodized, "is the most fertile on earth, where every luxury grows spontaneously, and where the rivers roll upon golden sands." Captain Robert F. Stockton reminded loyal Americans that national destiny called them to this noble work. "National responsibility . . . behooves every patriot to look and see, if possible, how he can best fulfill the trust reposed in him." A steady stream of ships and colonists will link the African and American continents as roads and canals link cities, hamlets, bays, and rivers. "You are invited to reclaim Western Africa" and "open the resources of that immense continent to the enterprise of the civilized world," he exclaimed.[14]

John H. B. Latrobe of Baltimore was the Colonization Society's most outspoken expansionist. His dreams of empire surpassed even Ashmun's. He urged the Colonization Society to work for the day when it would control a one thousand mile arc extending from the Senegal river north of Sierra Leone to Cape Palmas— an area embracing the mouths of the Senegal, Gambia, Grande, Nunez, and Pongos rivers. He said Cape Palmas was the key to the commerce of the entire southern coast of Africa and the natural site of a great "Americo-African" city. In time the United States would supplant all its European rivals in Africa because it could pour forth thousands upon thousands of "pilgrims" for whom the African climate "is as genial as was that of New England to our forefathers." [15]

Commerce with the colony grew gradually, but hopes grew faster. The colonists needed tobacco, rum, arms, and cotton textiles for the interior trade and lumber, pork, ham, beef, molasses, Muscovado sugar, flour, and ironware for themselves. Less than a dozen ships visited Monrovia in 1825, but next year the number tripled. In the first half of 1826 ships from Portland, Boston, Providence, Norfolk, Baltimore, the Barbados, England, and France loaded Liberian camwood and ivory. These cargoes were worth $44,000 at African prices. The *African Repository,* always ready to boast of Liberia's trade potential, noted that the gross profit to the colonial exporters was $30,000. Of particular interest to American merchants was Ashmun's success in persuading Sierra Leone officials to allow Liberian ships to call at Freetown. Here was an opportunity to open a trade forbidden to American ships since Paul Cuffee's day. Such prospects inspired *Niles' Register* to comment that regardless of its effect on the nation's fast growing Negro population, African colonization promised one day to employ "a greater amount of American tonnage than is now employed" in the European trade.[16]

Orators, pamphleteers, and traveling agents freely predicted that enterprising American merchants would find great riches in Africa. The Maryland Colonization Society declared that Maryland men could "reasonably expect a great accession to our commerce and a boundless market for our products." A committee of the Virginia legislature agreed that "any new avenue for our productions, must be greatly desirable, in the present embarrassed state of our commerce." Certain that southern emigrants would carry southern tastes to Africa, Virginia expected a brisk demand for its tobacco and flour. The Reverend Thomas H. Gallaudet, speaking to New York city colonizationists, hailed the colony's commercial growth as "astonishing." Even the British, he insisted, conceded that Liberia was better poised than Sierra Leone to garner the unfathomed interior trade. He urged New York merchants to export the Bible along with trade articles. Commerce will be the instrument for diffusing the "blessings of freedom, civilization, and Christianity" among the "millions of that benighted and degraded continent," he intoned. "What a theatre of benevolent action!" Captain William A. Weaver of the brig *Henry Eckford* returned from "our sable colony" with predictions that southern states would find prosperity in exporting tobacco to Africa and the east "will find a vent for her surplus manufactures." "There are millions to be clothed in Africa," he declared hopefully.[17]

Lured by such reports, several American shipowners and merchants directed their ships to Liberia. Boston merchant William Roper sent an occasional vessel freighted with textiles and molasses, but unlike other merchants he refused to trade in rum. Philadelphia colonizationists proudly applauded John Hanson's growing trade with the colony. He had two ships in the Liberian trade and planned to engage more. Richard H. Douglass of Baltimore, "one of our richest and most respectable merchants," repeatedly sent the *Doris* to Monrovia and proposed launching a regular packet line. John McPhail of Norfolk, Benjamin Brand of Richmond, and John H. B. Latrobe of Baltimore occasionally consigned hogsheads of tobacco to Liberian agents. In 1829, free Negroes in Baltimore led by Hezekiah Grice, "a coloured man of some intelligence . . . and considerable respectability among that class of people," asked Charles C. Harper to aid in forming a Liberian trade association. With capital promised by free Negroes in Baltimore, Philadelphia, and New York, they planned to charter a schooner and freight it with $2,000 worth of "suitable merchandize." [18]

Plans to establish a regular packet received Ashmun's approval. He frequently complained of the irregularity of ship arrivals and shortages of needed supplies, such as lumber, paint and nails. He had discovered that some merchants were unreliable in filling specific orders. Others demanded exorbitant prices for scarce goods. The colonial agent urged the Colonization Society to establish its own packet line to guarantee a steady flow of needed items, full warehouses, and reasonable prices. He argued that the society's power to regulate commerce would insure it against loss and at the same time cut the cost of transporting colonists. "You have, Sir, founded an empire," he reminded Secretary Gurley.

"Heaven help you to the means of sustaining the happy beginnings." [19]

Ashmun's proposals were cogent, but the managers hesitated to launch their own shipping line. They feared that merchants in New York, Philadelphia, Boston, and Baltimore would abandon the society if it grasped the entire trade. In effect, the colonizationists would be forsaking one of their potent arguments: rich trade opportunities in Africa. In 1827 the managers unveiled a tentative plan to raise $10,000 to buy a 250-ton ship. Gurley, faithfully echoing Ashmun, declared that a "regular intercourse" with Liberia would be "economical, and, for numerous other reasons, of great advantage." As the managers feared, nettled shipowners promptly warned that only experienced merchants and shippers understood the vagaries of international trade. John H. B. Latrobe, a spokesman for Baltimore shippers, suspected that Ashmun had personal interests in the Liberian trade. He urged the managers to send an additional agent to Monrovia to watch him. "I do not think Ashmun a saint," he admitted. "We want a second eye in the colony—which without being a direct spy may be a check upon the agent—an *honest child* would do." [20]

The managers found it prudent to suspend their plans for a packet line, and they were still considering Ashmun's recommendations long after Ashmun gave up his post. Meanwhile, individual merchants in New York, Philadelphia, and Baltimore repeatedly sought special concessions. Some wanted a franchise to engross the entire Liberian trade. Others wanted exclusive rights to carry emigrants for the society, believing they would gain commercial advantages over their competitors. For the same reasons the managers hesitated to operate their own vessels, they hesitated to commit themselves to a single firm. In 1826 Ashmun took it upon himself to make a packet line agreement with John Cox, a Portland merchant. Cox agreed to limit prices to 100 percent on American invoices for tobacco and lumber, 75 percent on rum, flour, butter, and lard, and 50 percent or less for all else. Though Ashmun had no authority to grant a monopoly, Cox was free to "engross the trade of the Colony" by means of "fair competition." Not long after, John

H. B. Latrobe privately urged the managers to grant all passenger contracts to his friends, Richard H. Douglass and William P. Matthews of Baltimore. "This establishment of a regular trade from Baltimore," Latrobe declared, *"I* deem *all important,* and even if the Society strains a little to encourage it by sending emigrants I think it would be well." Charles C. Harper endorsed the same firm, saying "no other ship-owner's offers should be accepted before his, even though they should be a little lower," because Douglass could establish a regular trading packet. "He was partly induced to enter into the trade by our offer of supplying passengers; and any neglect to do so now, might appear to him a disregard of his past services," Harper warned.[21]

Similar demands came from John Hanson's influential friends in Philadelphia. In New York city, Arthur Tappan sounded out Secretary Gurley for pledges of patronage if he entered the Liberian trade. "It has at times crossed my mind that it would be a good thing to have a vessel or rather vessels forming a line of packets to sail regularly from this city for Liberia for the double purpose of transporting coloured people and carrying on a trade with the Colony." The hard-pressed managers studiously avoided any commitments, and in 1831 they declared that they would not confer a franchise on any firm. The flow of colonial supplies may be uncertain and irregular, they conceded, but only "unrestricted individual interest" assured Liberia's eventual prosperity. "The nearer Liberia can be approximated to a free port, the stronger and broader will be the foundations of a prosperous colony." [22]

Three years before this policy took shape, poor health forced Jehudi Ashmun to resign as colonial agent. On March 26, 1828, he said farewell to the colonists, boarded the brig *Doris,* and sailed for the West Indies, hoping the long voyage would save him. It did not. Continuing to New Haven, he reached Professor Silliman's house in a state of collapse, and died a few days later. The colonizationists bewailed "the great martyr of Africa's salvation," the Reverend Leonard Bacon preached his funeral sermon, the managers ordered a red granite stone for his grave, and Lydia Sigourney dedicated a poem to the "friend of misery's race." Secretary Gurley had watched over the colonial agent's deathbed and soon after began collecting materials for a massive biography of his friend.[23]

Forewarned that Ashmun would not live, the managers promptly selected a new colonial agent, Dr. Richard Randall of Washington, D.C., a member of the board. Born in Annapolis, he attended St. John's College and the Philadelphia Medical School. For seven years he served as an Army surgeon, and in 1827 he was professor of chemistry in Columbia College. The managers were confident that a physician could withstand the dread "acclimating fever" and perhaps find a cure as well. They were also satisfied that Randall's experience as a board member and his military knowledge fitted him to continue Ashmun's work in Liberia.[24]

Following Dr. Randall to Africa was an elderly freedman whom the managers and a number of American merchants fervently hoped would be useful in opening a rich trade with unknown but fabled central African kingdoms. His name was Abduhl Rahahman, and he was known as Prince. He was well past sixty and had been a slave for forty years. Describing himself as a Mohammedan prince and the son of the founder of Teembo in the kingdom of Footah Jalloh, he said that he had been born and educated in the palace of his grandfather, king of Timbuktu. When captured and sold into slavery by a rival nation, the prince was a colonel in his father's cavalry. The State Department under Henry Clay accepted his story as authentic. In 1826, his owner, Colonel Thomas Foster of Natchez, Mississippi, manumitted Prince and urged him to go to Liberia.[25]

Of all the colonists destined for Africa, Prince promised to be the most valuable. The Colonization Society broadcast its plan to use Prince to open trade with Teembo and its metropole, the fabled Timbuktu, "the principal emporium of the Moorish commerce in Africa." Teembo lay three hundred miles north of Monrovia and Timbuktu seven hundred miles beyond. The Reverend Thomas H. Gallaudet, Prince's champion in the eastern states, pictured Footah Jalloh as larger than New England and capable of furnishing "a variety of productions that constitute a very considerable part of our trade; and ready to take our own manufactures in return." Gallaudet discovered that Prince's nephew, Alam Boorbahkar, was now the king of Footah Jalloh, and Prince's son, Allusine, was a general. The king was "a peaceable man, carrying on a considerable trade with Sierra Leone." Once Prince returned to his grateful kin "is it not most rational to conclude, that a friendly intercourse would thus, at once, be established between his country and our own," Gallaudet asked his listeners. "It may be the means of securing advantages to our trade, to scientific curiosity, and to benevolence." [26]

Gallaudet easily enlisted Arthur Tappan in the project of returning Prince to his rich relatives and launching trade with Africa's interior. Tappan's wealth and commercial instincts made his aid invaluable, and Gallaudet vouched for "his character for piety & energy." "His interest must be kept alive," he warned the parent society. The New York merchant made plans for "training up, in this country, some coloured youth, to go to Africa, even to its very interior, to become *Commercial Agents.*" He intended to ask the federal government to send a consul to Teembo, Prince's home. "Only imagine the influence of such a man, in connexion with Prince & your Colony," Gallaudet exclaimed, "& especially if we could be as happy as to procure the appointment of *one who is truly pious.*" Tappan's newspaper, the *Journal of Commerce,* noted editorially that if Great Britain "had possession of Abduhl Rahahman, and he stood in the same relation to her that he does to us, she would prize her good fortune beyond almost any sum." It urged the federal government to underwrite Prince's return voyage as a project "favourable to the interests and honourable to the character of the American people." [27]

The Colonization Society extracted full advertising value from their unique colonist. During the fall and winter of 1828, the managers paraded the old man before audiences in Baltimore, Washington, Philadelphia, New York, Hartford, New Haven, Providence, and Boston. To the doubting he showed a "recommendatory certificate" signed by Secretary of State Henry Clay. The Reverend Mr. Gallaudet accompanied Prince on his tour of New England and collected $2,500 from well-wishers. In all, Rahahman needed $7,000 to buy his numerous progeny from Colonel Foster and take them to Liberia. Arthur Tappan headed a committee in New York that served as depository for donations. He handled negotiations for Prince's children. "I have customers in Natchez whose assistance in negotiating with Mr. Foster I can depend on," he assured the parent society. "My object is the spiritual good of the Africans, and my project has from the first been predicated on Abduhl Rahahman's being able, through his family connexions [and] with the aid he might receive from us, to open a friendly intercourse with the interior and thus prepare the way for the introduction of the blessings of Civilization and Religion." [28]

Early in February, 1829, Abduhl Rahahman and his wife sailed on the brig *Harriet* with 160 emigrants. Secretary of State Clay consented to pay "a reasonable sum" for Abduhl's passage and subsistence in Liberia. Tappan corresponded with Dr. Randall about the "proposed commercial enterprise" and waited for the colonial agent to open diplomatic relations with Teembo and Timbuktu. "My interest in this subject is in no degree abated," he assured Secretary Gurley several weeks after Prince sailed for Africa, "and as soon as we learn the reception that Prince's letter by Dr. Randall has met with from his kinsmen I shall be better able to decide on the course I will take." [29]

Randall's reply never came. Reaching Liberia late in 1828, he pronounced Monrovia ideally situated for commercial purposes. "Whatever may be the final success of our colonizing operations, nothing but some most unfortunate disaster can prevent this from becoming one of the most important commercial cities on the African coast." Exports in 1828 had risen to $60,000, and the new agent planned to triple that amount. But fever intervened. Soon after landing, Dr. Randall ridiculed "this much-talked-of African fever," saying it was no worse than Carolina or Georgia fever and not half as bad as the Alabama fever. He died April 19, 1829, of "an inflammation of the brain" following a desperate bout with the vengeful fever. Soon after, Abduhl Rahahman succumbed to its ravages. Dr. Joseph Mechlin, acting colonial agent, lamented the "great loss," for the Footah country abounded in gold, and had Prince lived, Liberia would have become the "most important [settlement], in a commercial point of view, on the whole Western Coast of this continent." [30]

When this news reached the United States, Arthur Tappan's interest in Liberia vanished. "The death of Abduhl Rahahman, in addition to that of Doct. Randall, appears to put far off the day when a commercial enterprize, such as I have contemplated, can be engaged in with a prospect of success," he declared. "And I feel obliged to relinquish all thoughts of it for the present." For the first time he complained that Liberian trade was drenched in rum. William Roper of Boston convinced him that he had suffered irreparable financial losses in African trade *in consequence of his refusing to send out ardent spirits.* The Society must discountenance & if possible prohibit the introduction of distilled Spirits into its Settlements before I can ever feel it my duty to aid it," Tappan growled. Shortly after, he canceled his $1,000 subscription to the "Gerrit Smith Plan" and left the Colonization Society forever.[31]

The uncertainties of trade chilled the ardor of other merchants and seeded rivalry among them. The Douglass interests of Baltimore, discovering that large ships were uneconomical in the African trade, dropped out. John Hanson of Philadelphia took over the greater share of the remaining commerce, but he was "somewhat soured" when the managers of the parent society continued to commission other lines to carry passengers. Isaac Lea, "an Enterprising gentleman" and Baltimore merchant, complained bitterly that Hanson "will only fetch and carry for himself" and that Hanson set difficult terms for other merchants. Lea offered to operate a rival schooner if the managers promised passengers. A Richmond merchant cautioned the managers that Hanson's new brig *J. Ashmun* was "an unlawful trader" known to stop at African slave stations to sell cargoes originally consigned to Liberia. A rival merchant in New York peevishly warned that Hanson's agent, a free Negro who was about to go to Liberia, "is not a pious man, and probably from what I learn, not entirely chaste in his intercourse with women." [32]

Though Liberian trade did not grow as rapidly as the managers wished, they did not lose confidence in its future prosperity. Meantime, they placed all their hopes on finding a second Jehudi Ashmun. After Randall's sudden death they appointed Dr. Mechlin colonial agent, and he conscientiously followed Ashmun's policies. During his four-year term he added another one hundred miles to the colony's coastline and annexed Grand Bassa, Grand Cape Mount, and a "considerable tract" on the St. John's river. He ordered tribesmen on Bushrod Island to break their connections with other tribes and henceforth "consider themselves as Americans." He built small forts in the new territories because "there is no great reliance to be placed on the good faith of the natives." Small wars broke out. In 1832, when the Dey tribesmen insisted on collecting revenue from traders passing through their land, Mechlin led a surprise attack on their fort and destroyed it. He forced their humiliated chieftains to sign the peace treaty in Monrovia.[33]

Mechlin planned to increase the colony's exports, which in 1830 amounted to $88,000, by substituting an anchorage fee for tonnage duties. At the same time his attempts to stimulate agriculture and planting were no more successful than Ashmun's. Despite his pleas and offers of bounties, the 1,200 colonists raised almost nothing of trade value. Mechlin questioned the wisdom of colonizing manumitted slaves, arguing that they contributed nothing to colonial agriculture. "In point of industry and intelligence," he asserted crisply, they are "far below the free people of colour" and, being "too ignorant to appreciate the advantages that will accrue from the cultivation of the soil," they refused to work on Liberian farms. The need for farm laborers was obvious to visitors. Captain Edward F. Kennedy of the United States frigate *Java* suggested using orangoutangs of the Malay archipelago in rice and corn fields. He once saw the beasts "acrabbing with a rude basket and crab stick." As long as they "are not considered human beings, I see no reason why they should not be made to work as well as a Horse or an Ox." [34]

In his dealings with the board of managers, Mechlin did not prove as tactful as Ashmun. His reports carried complaints rather than paens of hope and faith. When he became agent, he found the colonial treasury empty, provisions low, and many bills overdue. In the following months he sharply criticized the managers for failing to send sufficient supplies promptly and regularly. This oversight, he said, forced him to draw on their treasury to a "ruinous extent" for items sometimes purchased at triple cost from visiting merchantmen. Disturbed by rising colonial expenses, the managers wondered how Ashmun had operated on a small budget. They continued to believe that if they could find another Ashmun all difficulties would vanish. In 1833 they recalled Mechlin and appointed the Reverend John B. Pinney in his place. Pinney was in Liberia as Presbyterian missionary for the Foreign Missionary Society at Pittsburgh. He attempted to arrest decaying finances, stimulate agriculture, and augment commerce, but his program for building hospitals and storehouses and repairing the rotting colonial schooner only added to the managers' pyramiding debts. Another Ashmun was an elusive dream.[35]

Despite the managers' gloom over mounting debts and never-ending responsibilities for a growing colony, visitors were impressed by the steady if slow progress made by the colonists. In 1836, the Reverend Charles Rockwell, an agent of the United States Navy, found that domestic agriculture had greatly improved since Ashmun's day. The colonists now raised Indian corn, rice, cassada, sweet potatoes, and pumpkins. He saw bean vines that had mushroomed into "strong and firm bushes" because no frost halted their growth. An English visitor, F. Harrison Rankin, praised Liberia, saying that she had surpassed her larger and older neighbor, Sierra Leone, in learning "the arts of civilised life." Liberia valued education and training. Above all, the American emigrants—even the slaves—brought with them "a stock of civil and social knowledge, as well as an impulse to improvement" that the typical Sierra Leone inhabitant, "fresh from his native bush," did not share.[36]

Rankin's praise for Liberian progress was too extravagant in one respect. In Monrovia, freedom of the press was unknown. In 1831 the *Liberia Herald*'s motto proclaimed "Freedom is the brilliant gift of Heaven." But this sentiment did not suit the new editor, John B. Russwurm, a graduate of Bowdoin College and formerly coeditor of *Freedom's Journal,* the first Negro newspaper in the United States. In February, 1831, Russwurm remarked editorially that demands for a free press were senseless. "As fire is a very useful servant when properly cared after, but unheeded, becomes a dangerous one," he argued, "so would the press be, unless under the wholesome restraint of the law." He declared to fellow colonists that "the experience of past ages demonstrates most conclusively, that no country could long exist with what is vulgarly called a free press, under the guidance of unprincipled men." The motto disappeared from the next issue.[37]

Between 1825 and 1835, the growth, complexity, and expense of colonial administration sharpened the managers' desire for federal aid. A decade's trial convinced them that only the federal government could fulfill the larger task of developing and protecting the nucleus of an American empire in Africa. As auxiliaries multiplied and colonization became the popular solution to the tangled problems of race and slavery, the leaders of the movement again pressed Congress to accept African colonization as national policy.

XIV

POLITICAL FORTUNES

———◆•••◆———

INSPIRED by dreams of an American empire stretching across the Atlantic and tantalized by President Monroe's assistance in 1820, the colonizationists again looked to Congress for aid. But the national mood of the country was fading. Sectional jealousies unleashed by the Missouri debates and acerbated by the tariff controversy soured the southern politicians' brief romance with nationalism. Before Monroe left the Executive Mansion proposals to extend federal authority—especially in areas touching directly or indirectly on slavery—evoked hostile criticism.

Some of the society's friends in Congress, sensing the change in attitude among some southern politicians, urged colonizationists to postpone their campaign for federal aid. In February, 1824, at the seventh annual meeting, Charles F. Mercer of Virginia, the society's spokesman in the House of Representatives, warned that a new plea for federal aid would only raise the hurtful cry of "enthusiasm." The society must move with "utmost caution and prudence" and must not ask Congress for aid in "direct form" lest it fail. After all, Mercer contended, President Monroe was already giving "all we could have expected to obtain" from Congress. The society, however, did not heed Mercer's warnings. A committee headed by General Robert G. Harper of Baltimore deemed it expedient to petition Congress immediately.[1] In seeking governmental aid, the society was offering a political solution to the free Negro problem, and it could not escape becoming a topic of political debate in the Capitol, in many state houses, and in newspapers and tracts.

Hoping to spur Congress to action, the colonizationists sought state endorsements. In 1824 the Ohio legislature called for federal aid to colonization, and at the same time branded slavery a national evil. The Ohio lawmakers begged Congress to adopt colonization as the means of eradicating slavery.[2] They sent their antislavery declaration to the legislatures of other states, thereby setting off a prolonged debate in southern as well as eastern and western capitals.

Following Ohio's example, the Connecticut legislature called slavery a "great national evil" to be removed by colonization "under the patronage of the General Government." In 1825 New Jersey grandly predicted that colonization will "effect the entire emancipation of the slaves in our country, and furnish an asylum for the free blacks, without any violation of the national compact or infringement of the rights of individuals." Delaware blessed colonization as "one of the grandest schemes of philanthropy" ever presented the American people. Without mentioning emancipation, the Kentucky legislature in 1827 insisted that "no jealousies ought to exist, on the part of this or any other slaveholding States, respecting the objects of this society, or the effects of its labor." [3]

Some slaveholding states, however, did harbor jealousies. The Ohio declaration boldly linking colonization with emancipation goaded the South Carolina legislators into denouncing the resolutions as "a very strange and ill-advised communication" and warning other states that South Carolina would never permit slave property "to be meddled with, or tampered with, or in any manner regulated, or controlled by any other power, foreign or domestic, than this legislature." [4]

The Georgia, Louisiana, Alabama, and Missouri legislatures underscored these sentiments, and on two occasions angry Mississippi legislators assailed the Ohio resolutions. The Richmond *Enquirer* printed a letter reviling colonization as "the most insidious and least suspicious mode of attack on us." An angry South Carolina pamphleteer denounced the resolutions as "paroxysm of their folly and their fanaticism . . . phials of wrath." No longer friendly to colonization, the *Georgia Journal* tartly advised the society to concentrate on the "private munificence of the citizens" and not the United States treasury for aid in its emancipation plot.[5]

The society's secretary, Ralph R. Gurley, unhesitantly waded into the fray and defended the society from its traducers. His editorials in the *African Repository* pleaded for national aid in removing the free Negro population. The society's goals were too large for private benevolence alone. "Compared to the whole work to be effected, no private association can accomplish more than a very small proportion." The state legislatures and the Congress, he declared, "can alone consummate the proposed design." Repeatedly he denied that the Colonization Society plotted to abolish slavery. "This Society promulgates no new and dangerous doctrine," nor is it gripped by the "ungovernable spirit of fanaticism." It aims only at removing "a people which are injurious and dangerous to our social interests, as they are ignorant, vicious, and unhappy." As for constitutional authority, he reasoned that "If Congress has no right to save a State against its will, it is most sacredly bound by every law, to exhibit the means, if such exist, by which such State may secure its own salvation." The work has begun auspiciously; only money is needed to complete the task. "The object is *national*," he argued, "it demands *national* means." [6]

A suggestion from Monticello indicated that national means might be accessible. In the seclusion of old age, Thomas Jefferson followed the Colonization Society's career and privately applauded its aims. In a letter to Jared Sparks, editor of the *North American Review* and a friend of the society, Jefferson suggested an improvement in the society's operations. The wiser policy was removal of the young only, thereby reducing the number of "breeders." As for federal funds, "why not from . . . the lands which have been ceded by the very States now needing this relief?" he queried. "I am aware that this subject involves some constitutional scruples," he admitted. "But a liberal construction, justified by the object, may go far, and an amendment of the constitution, the whole length necessary." There was another point to consider. "The separation of infants from their mothers, too, would produce some scruples of humanity," he conceded.

"But this would be straining at a gnat, and swallowing a camel," the eighty-two-year-old sage mused.[7]

In February, 1825, Jefferson's proposal to use money from public land sales came before the United States Senate. Rufus King of New York proposed to reserve "the whole of the public lands of the United States, with the net proceeds of all future sales thereof," as a special fund for the emancipation and colonization of slaves. Ten days later, Senator Robert Y. Hayne of South Carolina entered his *"solemn protest"* to King's plan and declared that Congress "possesses no power to appropriate the public land" for either emancipation or colonization. Such a measure, he complained, was "calculated to disturb the peace and harmony of the Union." [8]

"Officious and impertinent intermeddlings with our domestic concerns," Governor George M. Troup of Georgia hissed when he read King's plan. In a sharply worded message to the Georgia legislature Troup charged that the federal government was plotting to usurp state power. "Soon, very soon, therefore, the United States' Government, discarding the mask, will openly lend itself to a combination of fanatics for the destruction of everything valuable in the Southern country." He exhorted Georgia's lawmakers to "temporize no longer—make known your resolution that this subject shall not be touched by them, but at their peril." [9]

Henceforth congressmen from Georgia, South Carolina, Alabama, and other slaveholding states of the lower south fought colonization proposals whenever they appeared in either house. In March, 1825, Representative George Tucker of Virginia proposed that the United States examine and purchase Indian lands "lying west of the Rocky Mountains, that may be suitable for colonizing the free people of color." The vigilant James Hamilton, Jr., of South Carolina, promptly demanded that Tucker withdraw his "extraordinary" resolution touching upon a subject brimming with "distempered enthusiasm." [10] A year later, Congressman John Forsyth of Georgia, soon to be governor of his state, aimed a dart at the colony when he demanded the repeal of provisions of the Slave Trade Act of 1819 stationing agents on the African coast.[11]

As colonization grew controversial, insults and accusations

flayed its officers. President Bushrod Washington received his share of the attacks. In 1821 several newspapers censured the squire of Mount Vernon for allegedly selling fifty-four slaves. The Baltimore *Morning Chronicle* published an eyewitness report charging that after the sale "husbands had been torn away from their wives and children, and that many relations were left behind." Editor Hezekiah Niles of Baltimore found "something excessively revolting in the fact that a herd of them should be driven from *Mount Vernon,* sold by the nephew and principal heir of George Washington, as he would dispose of so many hogs or horned cattle." [12]

Washington confirmed the reports by replying, indignantly, that he had every right to sell his slaves, that he had unsuccessfully "struggled for about twenty years to pay the expenses of my farm," and that his slaves had become useless because of their "total disregard of all authority." Mount Vernon, he complained, was overrun with sightseers, some of whom "have condescended to hold conversations with my negroes, and to impress upon their minds the belief, that, as the nephew of General Washington, or as president of the colonization society, or for other reasons, I could not hold them in bondage, and particularly that they would be free *at my death.*" He had already spent $250 retrieving runaways, and by selling his slaves he had merely anticipated "the escape of all the laboring men of any value, to northern states, so soon as I should leave home." [13]

In 1824 and 1825, when colonization was being denounced in southern legislatures and Congress as a thinly veiled abolition plot, Washington again was the butt of criticism. "Gaius Gracchus" in the Richmond *Enquirer* warned Washington that the Colonization Society was the "repository of all the fanatical spirits in the country" and was now in fact an abolition society. It was goading slaves to revolt and helping ruthless politicians to augment federal powers. Doubting that he could "overthrow an *old man's opinions,* thus supported by his pride and his prejudices," Gaius Gracchus insolently demanded that Washington prove himself a "Patriot and a Virginian" by resigning from the Colonization Society. [14]

Another letter in the *Enquirer* offered proof that the Colonization Society nurtured abolition. By combing the society's annual reports, "Philo-Gracchus" could quote colonizationist George W. P. Custis, George Washington's grandson, as saying to the federal government, "Lend us your aid to strike the fetters from the slave and to spread the enjoyment of unfettered freedom over the whole of our favored and happy land." He also quoted Robert G. Harper of Baltimore as saying that the total eradication of slavery "would alone complete the scope of our design." [15]

William H. Fitzhugh of Ravenswood, Virginia, a vice-president of the society, replied to these critics in essays signed "Opimius." He asserted that the society deserved federal assistance because it promoted the "common defence and general welfare." Congress needed no more authority than that, he insisted. Internal improvements, road appropriations, and similar projects had already set the precedent.[16] At Fitzhugh's behest, the society at its next annual meeting declared that it desired neither to destroy nor to perpetuate slavery. The society repeated this principle in its 1826 memorial to state legislatures. Colonization, it explained, opened the way to manumission, not emancipation.[17]

With this noninterference principle the society hoped to avoid further political controversy. But the tornadic election campaign of 1828 sucked colonization into its churning vortex and transformed it into a partisan issue. As the election approached, states' rights men in the southern states rallied to Andrew Jackson's candidacy and scrutinized all schemes invoking national power. Already hostile to colonization, they viewed the society as an ally of the Adams-Clay party.

After 1825 Henry Clay succeeded William H. Crawford as the Colonization Society's most influential political friend in Washington, D.C. He frequently pleaded its case for national assistance and identified it with his own nationalist program. As early as 1827 some of Jackson's friends looked upon the society as a "political engine" for Clay. "The consequence of it is," agent John H. Kennedy reported sadly from Pennsylvania, "that the partizans of the Gen. view us with some suspicion." From Tennessee came the warning that in Jackson's state Clay "is considered by the few who know any thing about the society, to be its leader and to be making use of it for political purposes—for gaining popularity in the North." The Colonization Society's leaders were not unaware that Clay "has been helping himself to a ride on our shoulders," but with John H. B. Latrobe of Baltimore they reasoned that Clay "has no doubt been a service to us." [18]

Some colonizationists urged the parent society to wait until the election storm had passed away before pleading for national funds. Kennedy reported that a Jackson congressman in Pennsylvania privately approved the society but dared not support it openly until the votes of the southern states had been counted. The society's leaders chose not to wait. The tenth annual meeting gave the board of managers a free hand in initiating petitions to Congress, and in 1827 the managers boldly called for the "immediate and effectual interposition of the Government of the country." Though making explicit the society's "real and only design" was the removal of free Negroes, the memorial enraged the states' rights partisans. The Georgia legislature protested to Congress that African colonization was "wild, fanatical, and destructive." The enemies of the southern states, Georgia warned, are "preparing a mine, which once exploded, will lay our much-loved country in one common ruin." [19]

A South Carolina writer was even more vehement. Robert J. Turnbull, in 1828 an influential Jackson man, reprobated colonization in a thick pamphlet significantly entitled *The Crisis: or, Essays on the Usurpations of the Federal Government*. He scornfully ranked colonizationists with high tariff and internal improvements advocates who were employing the "general welfare" interpretation to transform the federal government into a "firm *consolidated* national government." The Colonization Society, Turnbull asserted, was an abolition plot, a "dangerous association," a "midnight assassin," and "an insidious attack meditated at the domestic tranquility of the South." He implored South Carolina's congressmen to forestall any discussion of slavery. "Discussion will cause *death* and *destruction* to our negro property. Discussion will be equivalent to an act of emancipation, for it will universally inspire amongst the slaves, that hope." [20]

In Virginia friends of the society hesitated to circulate the society's petition. "Opposition and indifference prevail generally," a Norfolk colonizationist lamented. Agents would find it "most prudent" to press the cause lightly for now. The Petersburg auxiliary, usually reliable, flatly refused to peddle the "injudicious" petition, and newspapers in Richmond would not print it. "Should it be known that the present Administration are in favor of it, I am sure it would immediately create a host of enemies to the views of the Society," one Virginian commented. "The enemies of the President of the U. States," Benjamin Brand of Richmond warned, "are catching at everything within their reach trying to injure him." [21]

Any mention of colonization in Congress stirred partisan debate. Party jangling broke out in the House of Representatives when a Clay congressman from Kentucky sought to present his state's resolutions applauding federal aid to colonization. A Jackson congressman from Alabama demanded that the House ignore the Kentucky resolutions, but Clay's friends fought to send them to a select committee presided over by Clay's fellow colonizationist, Charles F. Mercer. Mercer brought in a report emphatically declaring that "the Government of the United States has the constitutional power to acquire territory," confer "moral protection" on Liberia, and transport colonists at public expense. In an unusual move, congressmen from South Carolina and Georgia tried to prevent the printing of the report, but the House defeated their move, 70-41.[22]

When Senator Ezekiel Chambers of Maryland presented the Colonization Society's memorial begging for federal aid, South Carolina's Robert Y. Hayne jumped to his feet and excoriated the society and its friends. "Of all the extravagant schemes that have yet been devised in this country, I know of none more wild, impracticable, or mischievous than this of Colonization." So saying Hayne produced a sheaf of papers purporting to show that Liberia annoyed European powers and bullied native Africans. "Under their gallant leader, the Reverend Dr. Ashmun," Hayne sneered, colonial militiamen "made war upon the Spaniards and the French, as well as on the natives." In short, Liberia proceeds "as all such Colonies always will proceed, with a high hand, to extend their influence and power by the sword." Constitutional limitations ruled out such a scheme, and the Senate, Hayne pleaded, should not waste its time on such "an odious and un-profitable subject." [23]

Chambers hastily withdrew the Colonization Society's memorial when its critics gleefully discovered that it was unsigned. Two days later Chambers returned with arguments prepared in the Colonization Society's offices, and this time the memorial bore the clerkly signature of Bushrod Washington. Chambers stoutly denied that the society had "ulterior views, inimical to the Southern or slave-holding States," defended Jehudi Ashmun as the sworn foe of pirates and slavers, and professed great shock at Hayne's "sweeping denunciation" of an association claiming the support of so many distinguished men.

Hayne scoffed at the Society's "large and respectable class of paper members" and popularity seekers. In an oblique attack on Henry Clay, Hayne observed that some men "never hesitate to throw themselves on the popular tide, in the expectation of being carried safe to the haven of their hopes." With aid from Senator Thomas Hart Benton of Missouri, Hayne tabled the colonization memorial.[24]

A few months before the 1828 election, senatorial enemies of colonization again assailed the society. Led by Clay's foe, Littleton W. Tazewell of Virginia, the Senate Committee on Foreign Relations issued a long report resolutely denying that the United States had the constitutional authority to acquire an African colony. Tazewell insisted that erecting "new empires" was contrary to the "genius and spirit of all our institutions." Besides, African colonization would bleed the treasury and still fall short of its goal. Tazewell reached beyond the realm of foreign relations when he insisted that the federal government was powerless to "intrude within the confines" of any state for the purpose of removing a portion of its inhabitants. To do so would "impair the political weight of the States" and "derange the equilibrium of political power" in states where five slaves counted as three whites in apportioning congressional representation.[25]

Tazewell's report, one colonizationist shuddered, "will have the charm of oracles in the South." Such fears spurred Secretary Gurley and Vice-President Fitzhugh to prepare elaborate replies, but before the *African Repository* had printed their essays, the election was over.[26] At once colonization debates in Congress subsided, and neither the society's petition of 1830 begging for "immediate and effectual" aid nor Mercer's bill to pay $25 for the "passage of every colored emigrant who may leave America" stirred significant debate. In the inventory-taking after Andrew Jackson's inauguration, Amos Kendall, the new Fourth Auditor of the Treasury department, discovered how far previous administrations had stretched the Slave Trade Act of 1819. In amazement he reported that since 1819 the United States treasury had paid out $264,710, ostensibly to repatriate and care for less than 260 Africans rescued from the slave trade. Kendall urged a drastic revision of policy, but Jackson made no move to terminate the government agency or deprive Liberia of naval protection. Secretary Gurley persuaded himself that Jackson was "a kind hearted old man who [has] very good feelings towards us." [27]

Acting on instructions from the parent society, colonization agents again besieged state legislatures for endorsements. Between 1828 and 1832 lawmakers of Ohio, Indiana, Pennsylvania, Massachusetts, Maryland, Kentucky, and New York urged Congress to give federal aid to colonization. New York colonizationists conciliated Jackson men by enlisting the support of Benjamin F. Butler, a Van Buren partisan. Butler obligingly commended colonization as the "only neutral ground upon which the northerners can meet the Southrons for candid interchange of sentiments on the delicate subject of slavery, & the situation of the free blacks." The Massachusetts General Court had to wait until the excitement over the Foote resolution debates and the "stir lately made in the Virginia legislature" over *Walker's Appeal* had cooled, but in 1831 it joined the chorus of state legislatures demanding federal aid to colonization.[28]

Meanwhile, colonizationists worried about the eclipse of colonization sentiment in Virginia. They had hoped that the Old Dominion would unravel the slave states' scruples against federal aid. But the states' rights furor crippled the movement in Virginia. Her auxiliaries languished, applications for passage to Liberia diminished, and once confident friends begged the parent society to use moderation and caution in framing policy. They reported that federal aid was unthinkable, and state support doubtful.

William Atkinson of Petersburg privately warned Secretary Gurley that a new petition seeking federal aid would destroy the movement below the Potomac. William M. Blackford of Fredericksburg cautioned that the smallest allusion to colonization in the constitutional convention of 1829 would seriously damage the cause. In the bitter struggle for supremacy, he observed, the delegates representing eastern Virginia would gladly seize any mention of colonization as proof that their opponents in western Virginia plotted emancipation.[29]

Suddenly, in August, 1831, the mood in Virginia changed. Nat Turner's insurrection in Southampton county shocked all who heard the lurid descriptions of massacres and brutalities. The prolonged "excitement" following the insurrection swept away the gloom gripping Virginia's colonizationists. The affair amply dramatized the society's long-standing prophecy that servile wars would erupt in every slaveholding state. "These insurrections will form a grand subject of appeal," a clergyman in Romney, Virginia, correctly predicted. The Colonization Society's board of managers grimly warned that "without the most strenuous efforts, the late afflicting scenes, flagrant and calamitous as they are, will be followed by events still more appalling." [30]

Overnight African colonization revived in Virginia. Defunct auxiliaries returned to life, new auxiliaries sprang up, and in the state capital Benjamin Brand of the Richmond society reported that many former opponents now endorsed colonization. He noted that Lieutenant Governor Peter V. Daniel openly favored colonization, and Dr. Carr Bowers, "the eldest magistrate" in Southampton county, became a life member of the society. From Hanover county came word that "many of the principal slaveholders" were signing a petition calling for a state tax on slaves and free Negroes to raise funds for colonization. "Under the existing circumstances," John McPhail of Norfolk remarked, the Norfolk and Portsmouth auxiliaries alone could raise $1,000. Atkinson of Petersburg cautioned that Virginians would consider colonization, but that they were more sensitive than ever to the topic of abolition. The parent society risked every shred of popularity if it uttered a sentence in defense of emancipation.[31]

The severities of the "excitement" induced hundreds of free

Negroes to seek immediate passage to Africa. In Southampton
county many frightened free Negroes agreed to depart instantly
if a ship could be chartered and outfitted at Norfolk. "A loud call
of providence," McPhail piously remarked, compelled colonizationists to offer the blacks "an opportunity of escaping to the
land of their Fathers." Additional emigrants came from Elizabeth
City, North Carolina, where "under the present state of excitement," a Quaker resident observed, "the free blacks are badly &
in many instances cruelly treated." Early in December, 1831, almost 350 emigrants, mostly from the lower counties of Virginia,
crowded aboard the *James Perkins* and fled to Liberia.[32]

Besides stimulating emigration, the Nat Turner affair renewed
demands for state appropriations for colonization. A few years
earlier, the legislatures of Maryland and Virginia had given token
sums, but colonizationists now hoped that the "excitement" would
wring fat appropriations from frightened politicians. On the eve
of the Virginia legislature's session, Ralph R. Gurley enjoined
the lawmakers to give colonization their *"deep and solemn deliberation."* He bolstered his plea with new endorsements gathered
from famous Virginians. Chief Justice John Marshall avowed that
through colonization "the whole Union would be strengthened
. . . and relieved from a danger, whose extent can scarcely be
estimated." Ex-president James Madison donated $100 and ap-
provingly noted that "the spirit of private manumission" was
quickly spreading and that "prospects in Africa seem to be expanding in a highly encouraging degree." [33]

In the fall of 1831, Virginia colonizationists called public
rallies, circulated petitions, and filled the newspapers with pleas
for state aid to colonization. About 180 citizens of Southampton
county angrily branded free Negroes "a most prolific source of
evil." Resolving to discharge all free Negro employees and to
evict free Negro families from rented houses and lands, the
Southampton whites begged the legislature to transport the unwanted population to Liberia. When the lawmakers gathered in
Richmond, a large bundle of colonization and emancipation
petitions were waiting for them.[34]

Early in 1832 the Virginia state house became the scene of a
full dress debate on slavery. Some delegates demanded a frontal

assault on slavery, while others pleaded for laws easing manumission procedures. Both groups joined in condemning slavery as an economic and social handicap. John Marshall's son, Thomas Marshall, an advocate of colonization, asserted that slavery was "ruinous to whites—retards improvements—roots out our industrious population—banishes the yeomanry from the country —and deprives the spinner, the weaver, the smith, the shoemaker, the carpenter, of employment and support." Thomas Jefferson Randolph refurbished his grandfather's *postnati* scheme for emancipation, and the lawmakers who wished to end slavery by legislative enactment rallied behind a bill to free slaves gradually.[35]

William H. Broadnax of Dinwiddie county, the Colonization Society's foremost advocate in the Virginia legislature, agreed that slavery was a "mildew which has blighted in its course every region it has touched, from the creation of the world." But he opposed any direct interference with private property. In an east-west split, the lower house voted down emancipation. Broadnax then presented a bill granting $100,000 to colonization. Friends of the measure argued that it would encourage manumission and thus whittle away at slavery without violating property rights. Western delegates who had favored emancipation complained that the colonization bill would compel free Negroes to emigrate. As revised and finally approved, the bill appropriated $35,000 for 1832 and $90,000 for 1833 and applied only to free Negroes who volunteered to emigrate. Colonizationists could not rejoice at their victory, for the upper house killed the bill by a vote of 18-14.[36]

The narrow defeat postponed the issue to the next legislature. In the interim, colonizationists canvassed Virginia for support of a new bill. They called public meetings, circulated more petitions, composed newspapers essays, and distributed colonization tracts arguing for the removal of all free Negroes.[37] At the same time, proslavery men took alarm at the growing colonization sentiment in Virginia. They were dismayed by the antislavery indictments written into the lawmakers' journal. They found small comfort in the colonization bill as an alternative to emancipation, for colonizationists had agreed with emancipationists that slavery was an economic and social blight. Before the new legislature convened, however, an effective and persuasive pleader for slavery rallied opponents of colonization and emancipation.

In an unsigned article in *The American Quarterly Review,* twenty-nine-year-old Thomas R. Dew, professor of history, metaphysics, and political law at William and Mary College, castigated the Virginia slavery debaters, declaring that the legislature was "composed of an unusual number of young and inexperienced members." Acting under the spell of "misguided philanthropy," the lawmakers had "boldly set aside all prudential considerations." With scholarly arguments, Dew spurned both colonization and emancipation, labeling one unworkable and the other dangerous. Drawing from Thomas Malthus's gloomy predictions that population growth was outrunning society's ability to feed itself, from Adam Smith's dictum that governmental interference stunted national and local wealth, and from Senator Littleton W. Tazewell's estimate that colonization would require fantastic expenditures, Dew sought to destroy the colonizationists' arguments. He predicted that systematic removal of the colored population would merely drive up the price of slaves, encourage slave breeding, stimulate greater growth of the Negro population in the United States, and bring "irremediable ruin" to the southern states. "There is nothing more dangerous," he warned, "than too much tampering with the elastic and powerful *spring* of population," a mysterious force that would produce Negroes more rapidly than colonizationists could remove them. Colonization, the professor exclaimed, was a *"stupendous piece of folly,"* and he adjured the next legislature to "ponder well" before embracing a scheme sure to "destroy more than half Virginia's wealth, and drag her down from her proud and elevated station among the mean things of the earth." [38]

Colonizationists both in and outside Virginia viewed Dew's article as a serious threat to a new colonization bill. Gerard Ralston of Philadelphia lamented to Gurley, "You may well call it an able article—it says more against our favorite scheme of colonization than I was aware could be urged against it." He implored the parent society to enlist the "most talented friend of the Colonization scheme" to refute Dew's indictment—Robert J.

Breckinridge, Kentucky's antislavery colonizationist. Editor Robert Walsh promised space in the next issue of *The American Quarterly Review*, and Mathew Carey, busily sending his own colonization pamphlets throughout Virginia, volunteered to answer Professor "Dewey" at "Charlottesville College." While the Colonization Society searched for a champion, Dew enlarged his article into pamphlet form. Appearing on the eve of the legislature's meeting, it caused consternation among Virginia colonization leaders. General John H. Cocke of Fluvanna county begged Gurley to "clear our skirts from the charge of the slave trade made in the overwrought zeal of the Professor against our cause." [39]

Secretary Gurley selected a Virginian to answer Professor Dew. He turned to the society's loyal friend, the orator, lawyer, and politician, Jesse Burton Harrison of Lynchburg. Three years before, Harrison had helped to answer sharp criticisms leveled by South Carolina's Robert J. Turnbull. In the fall of 1832 Harrison hurriedly composed a forty-seven page answer to Dew, ostensibly reviewing Thomas Marshall's twelve-page speech. Harrison did not attempt to meet Professor Dew's scholarly indictment. Ignoring Dew's Malthusian forebodings, Harrison repeated Marshall's arguments that slavery was the real cause of Virginia's economic decay, lauded the parent society and its colony, and blandly asserted that the Colonization Society in seeking federal and state funds "has no share whatever in the abolition question. . . . It is no propagandist of agitating opinions." [40]

Just as the Virginia lawmakers gathered to discuss colonization, the parent society made a final bid for state-wide popularity. In February, 1833, Secretary Gurley notified the eighty-two-year-old James Madison that he had been elected president of the Colonization Society to succeed the late Charles Carroll of Carrollton. Promptly accepting the post, the ex-President sent word from Montpelier that it was his "earnest prayer, that every success may reward the labors of an Institution . . . so noble in its object of removing a great evil from its own country." [41]

With Madison's blessings the Virginia colonizationists renewed their battle for state appropriations. Early in March, 1833, William Broadnax with the aid of Thomas W. Gilmer, secretary of the Albermarle auxiliary and later governor of the state, won final approval for a bill appropriating $18,000 a year for five years. Emigration was voluntary, and the funds applied only to Negroes free at the time the bill became law. The act created a special colonization board, including the governor and lieutenant governor, to pay the Colonization Society the maximum of $30 a head "upon proof of the actual transportation to the colony at Liberia." General Cocke spoke for many colonizationists when he exulted that the new act gave "signal proof that Professor Dew's elaborate efforts against our Cause, have failed of their object." [42]

While Virginia was preparing to help colonization, new efforts to secure federal money were in the making. As the presidential election of 1832 approached, Henry Clay again took up colonization and tied it securely to his political kite. In March, 1832, amidst tariff and bank debates, Senator Clay presented the Kentucky legislature's memorial endorsing federal aid to colonization. Senator Hayne of South Carolina again asserted that the federal government lacked the necessary constitutional authority to make such an appropriation, but Clay countered that African colonization was a national, not a sectional, matter.[43]

The incident warned Clay's opponents that he was preparing more colonization moves. A few days later, Clay's friends in the House presented two colonization memorials, one from the Kentucky legislature and the other from forty inhabitants of Cirencester, England. James K. Polk of Tennessee objected that this was the first time that "foreign subjects" had submitted memorials interfering in the "internal concerns of the States." He urged the House to reject the English memorial and thus discourage "similar annoyances in the future." A dozen congressmen debated the matter. Representative James Blair of South Carolina, losing all patience, hoarsely denounced Charles F. Mercer, the sponsor of the English memorial, as a "recreant to the cause" of slavery. Ignoring the Speaker's demand for order, Blair vehemently condemned colonization as the first step to abolition. It was an issue, the South Carolinian shouted, that would be settled in "the open field, where powder and cannon would be their orators, and their arguments lead and steel." "A general burst of laughter," the clerk noted, punctuated Blair's dramatic threat. The debate now turned into an exchange of recriminations. New England congressmen did not laugh when Blair turned upon them and blamed southern slavery on eastern slave traders who subsequently invested their profits in "vast stone" factories. He charged that Rhode Island Senator James DeWolf had once "thrown into the sea a living African in a state of disease, for fear the smallpox should spread to the rest of his cargo." A congressman from Rhode Island dryly retorted that DeWolf was "an eminently good Jackson man" whom he did not wish to defend.[44]

These skirmishes were preparatory to the debates on Clay's Distribution Bill reported from the Senate Committee on Manufacturers in April, 1832. The bill made colonization a joint beneficiary of funds from public land sales. Clay tried to dodge states' rights scruples against federal aid by distributing the money among the twenty-four states and letting them apply the funds to "education, internal improvements, or colonization," according to the preference of each. Assuming that land sales would continue to bring about $3 million a year into the federal treasury, Clay offered to distribute in a five-year period nearly $2 million to New York, more than $1 million to Pennsylvania and Virginia, and lesser amounts to other states—in all, a total of nearly $12 million.[45]

Clay's political enemies saw the Distribution Bill as a way of subsidizing internal improvements while at the same time keeping tariff schedules high. The Public Land Committee led by Alabama's Senator William R. King attacked the colonization feature of Clay's bill. Colonization was a "delicate question" connected "indissolubly with the slave question" and sure to rekindle the "fires of the extinguished conflagration which lately blazed in the Missouri question." When the bill came before the House, Clement Clay, King's Alabama colleague, avowed that those who accepted colonization would eventually accept abolition as "necessary, nay, indispensable, to the 'general welfare.' " While the politicians fought, colonizationists privately cheered Clay. An agent of the society freely assured his English friends that "on the elevation of . . . the Honourable Henry Clay . . . to the Presidency, there cannot be a doubt that funds adequate to the fulfilment of this glorious design will be granted by the general government." [46]

On June 20, 1832, Clay delivered a long speech defending colonization as a national benefit. The brimming galleries and lobbies heard him assert that "The evil of a free black population is not restricted to particular States, but extends to, and is felt by, all." He agreed with southern politicians that the "General Government has no constitutional power . . . in regard to African slavery," but colonization was a separate matter. Eight days later, attacking Clay's Distribution Bill, Senator Thomas Hart Benton of Missouri complained that westerners and purchasers of the public lands would be subsidizing the eastern shipping interests which stood to benefit from mass emigration. Benton ridiculed African colonization, commenting that Britain's Sierra Leone was a costly venture both in lives and money, and that every governor had died of fever, except one who had been killed by natives. "The soldiers and sailors sent there were swept off in crowds," he observed. "Troops from the West Indies, from the Cape of Good Hope, the East Indies, all shared the same fate. The only difference was, that the drunkards died the first season, and the sober ones the second or third." Who was prepared, he demanded, to send American mariners and soldiers to "perish on that pestilential coast?" [47]

The Distribution Bill passed Congress, but Jackson, victor over Clay in 1832, vetoed it. Secretary Gurley, hinting at the colonizationists' sorrow, wistfully noted that Clay's bill, had it passed Jackson's approval, "would have enabled States interested in the subject to prosecute the work of African Colonization with great energy and on a large scale." A hostile Jackson administration now began to reevaluate the limited government assistance made possible under the Slave Trade Act of 1819, and in 1834 Secretary Levi Woodbury of the Navy Department ordered a "very reduced compensation" for the American agent at Liberia.[48] Jackson's administration did not abolish the agency for the sole reason that the colony was useful to the Navy in disposing of Africans captured from slave ships. This informal partnership of convenience fell far short of the society's undiminished desire for federal aid.

Jackson's veto in 1833 crushed the colonizationists' most serious attempt to secure federal aid, and for nearly three decades afterwards the issue rarely came before Congress. After 1833 antislavery agitation usurped colonization as a controversial topic in Congress. Instinctively the society moved closer to Henry Clay and so shared his political fortunes. In 1836 Clay became president of the Colonization Society to succeed James Madison. By that time congressional resistance to colonization had stiffened so much that Clay could not secure a congressional charter for the society. When Clay brought the matter before the Senate, John C. Calhoun sternly reminded the Kentuckian that African colonization was a "question of much delicacy" and that nine-tenths of the southern people unalterably opposed it. It was not merely a matter of constitutional scruples. "A mysterious Providence had brought the black and white people together from different parts of the globe," Calhoun remarked, "and no human power could separate them." [49]

The dream of federal aid dimmed with each successive Democratic victory. Henry Clay remained president of the Colonization Society until 1849, but he had long before lost hope that colonization would become national policy. The society managed to limp along on private benevolence and restricted state funds, and in a short time the unsuccessful contest for federal aid grew small in importance compared with the bitter contest for public opinion stirred up by an angry Boston editor in gray steel spectacles— William Lloyd Garrison.

XV

FIRE-BRANDS FROM BOSTON

———◆◆◆◆———

AFTER fifteen years of proselytizing, the American Colonization Society had won a large measure of public approval. Many distinguished and influential men looked to colonization as the only practicable solution to the race and slavery questions, but among the 300,000 free Negroes in the United States there was little enthusiasm for the society's goals. Undying rumors of mistreatment, disease, and hardship scotched any impulse to go to Africa. By 1830 the society's managers were well aware that African colonization evoked little less than hostility among most free Negroes. Reports of Negro antipathy flooded the society's Washington headquarters and perplexed the managers, for they saw that their project of benevolence, lacking the voluntary consent of the beneficiaries, was doomed.

Anticolonization sentiments thrived in cities and towns where free Negro communities were large and well informed. In New York city free blacks complained that Liberian authorities withheld trading privileges from colonists, denied settlers a voice in the government, and refused return passage to dissatisfied emigrants. Similar complaints hardened Philadelphia's large free Negro community against colonization's blandishments. A colonization worker there lamented that "their clergy and influential men have imbued them with very strong prejudices." In 1827, free Negro spokesmen in New York and Philadelphia, including James Forten, Richard Allen, and Samuel Cornish, stubbornly vowed that the free colored are "by birth entitled to all the rights of freemen and ought to be admitted here to a participation of the enjoyment of Citizenship." They blamed the Colonization Society for a new wave of anti-Negro feeling. Africa, they warned their brethren, is "a land of destruction where the Sword will cut off the few wretched beings whom the climate spares." [1]

Agents of the society strove to erase the many "false notions" about colonization. But they frequently discovered that free Negroes steadfastly held that "the scheme originated with slave-holders, not from motives of benevolence, but with the hopes of rivetting the chains more firmly on their slaves." In 1828 Elliott Cresson of Philadelphia complained that "not a man will listen to the scheme, much less emigrate." The same complaint echoed in Baltimore, Richmond, Cincinnati, Charleston, and lesser communities. John H. B. Latrobe of Baltimore found that "Many here have an idea that they work all for the agent—and are more slaves in Africa than here." Benjamin Brand of the Virginia society, noted that Negroes flocked to Ohio but refused to go to Liberia. In North Carolina free Negroes balked at emigration because they had heard a rumor that the captain of one ship sold Africa-bound passengers into slavery. Occasionally even a slave being manumitted for Liberia objected to emigration. With dismay a Virginia gentleman discovered that two of his newly freed Negroes had jumped ship at Savannah and fled to New York city. [2]

Sometimes a dissatisfied colonist drifted back to the United States and sowed anxiety among colonizationists, as in 1830 when one Gilbert Hunt returned to Richmond and frightened prospective emigrants with uncomplimentary pictures of colonial life. David I. Burr of the Virginia society called Hunt "a complete croaker" who was doing "his utmost to prejudice the minds of the col[ore]d free among us." The *African Repository* discredited another troublesome ex-colonist with Agent Mechlin's brutal comment that he had been "one of the most indolent and good for nothing characters in the Colony." But Mechlin confided that disillusionment was not unusual among the newcomers and that it sprang from extravagant promises of "every comfort, and many of the luxuries of civilized life" made by "over-zealous" colonizationists. In 1834 Gurley estimated that as many as fifty colonists had returned to the United States. [3]

Friends of colonization tried several expedients to overcome

Negro resistance. Charles C. Harper blandly assured Baltimore free Negroes that emigration was the only hope for ending slavery in the United States. The guileful Elliott Cresson of Philadelphia tried to lure influential free Negroes with flattery and promises of riches. He urged the parent society to offer "great commercial advantages" to the respected Negro leader James Forten if he would establish a trading line between Philadelphia and Liberia. "His coming into the measure would do great good in our City," Cresson reasoned. "His opinion has great weight with our coloured population." [4]

Meanwhile, the parent society gathered and published colonization testimonials from Negroes both in the United States and Liberia. In December, 1826, a group of Baltimore free Negroes meeting in the Sharp Street African Church hailed Liberian settlers as "the pioneers of African Restoration" and accepted the principle of removal as both necessary and just. The free blacks abjectly conceded that they were "a distinct caste" and "an extraneous mass of men" in American society. "We reside among you," they said to the white inhabitants of Baltimore, "and yet are strangers; natives, and yet not citizens; surrounded by the freest people and most republican institutions in the world, and yet enjoying none of the immunities of freedom." The parent society greeted their statement as evidence that free blacks were becoming "more generally and decidedly favourable" to colonization.[5]

At the behest of John H. B. Latrobe the managers solicited similar declarations from Liberian settlers. Latrobe hoped that their testimony would forever silence the "discontents among the blacks" as well as those who "harp upon our cruelty, selfishness, &c. in sending the blacks to a certain grave in Africa." In September, 1827, "a numerous meeting of the citizens of Monrovia" proclaimed that Liberians enjoyed every liberty once denied them in the United States. "We know nothing of that debasing inferiority with which our very colour stamped us in America." This "moral emancipation—this liberation of the mind from worse than iron fetters" repaid the hardship and suffering of the early years. The stories that the African climate was murderous or that settlers starved to death were merely "malicious misrepresentations." The Reverend George M. Erskine, Joseph Shipherd, and other contented colonists sent additional testimonials to the Boston *Recorder,* Norfolk *Herald,* and the Richmond *Southern Religious Telegraph.* Erskine knowingly declared that a settler with $500 could easily build a fortune, and Shipherd avowed that he had gone to Africa at the "direction of the Lord." [6]

The society scored an important point when John B. Russwurm embraced colonization. As coeditor of the New York *Freedom's Journal,* first Negro newspaper in the United States, Russwurm had criticized African colonization, declaring flatly that "we are all, to a man, opposed, in every shape" to the society. Early in 1829, however, he privately informed Secretary Ralph R. Gurley that his views had turned about and he was now prepared to go to Liberia. When he announced his conversion, "a violent persecution" stormed about him. Old friends disowned him. In his farewell to colored readers he declared that full citizenship in the United States was "utterly impossible in the nature of things" and all Negroes who "pant for this, must cast their eyes elsewhere." Several months later, Russwurm landed at Monrovia and soon after revived the Liberia *Herald.* With great delight Cresson noted that the reappearance of the colonial newspaper "has quite *staggered* some of our opponents." [7]

Looking far into the future, several colonizationists reasoned that education would imbue free Negroes with "an earnest desire to emigrate." Using the colonists' testimonies as the core, Latrobe composed and published a small primer for colored children in which he emphasized that Africa was their "natural home" and the only place where they could "ever hope to attain the full enjoyment of the rights of free and independent men." The primer concluded with a hymn:

> Land of our fathers, Af-ri-ca,
> We turn our thoughts to thee—
> To gain thy shores we'll gladly bear
> The storm upon the sea.

Latrobe privately assured Gurley that "African Emigration will yet become so popular among the blacks that they will . . . furnish their own passage money to Liberia." Gurley promptly bestowed blessings on "this very judicious method of instructing the Free People of colour in the design of our Institution." [8]

The Colonization Society often voiced its approval of Negro education projects in the United States, and in 1826 and 1828 it specifically endorsed efforts to build schools at Parsippany, New Jersey, and Hartford, Connecticut. But the tiny schools did not thrive, and late in 1829 Secretary Gurley organized the African Education Society to train "persons of color destined for Africa" in subjects "as may best qualify them for usefulness and influence in Africa." The first meetings, held in December, 1829, in Washington, D.C., showed that colonizationists controlled the new society. Its officers included Bishop William Meade of Virginia, Theodore Frelinghuysen of New Jersey, Gerrit Smith of New York, Francis S. Key of the District of Columbia, Elliott Cresson of Pennsylvania, and Arthur Tappan of New York—all prominent colonizationists. Ralph R. Gurley sat on the board of managers, Treasurer Richard Smith of the Colonization Society also served as treasurer of the new society, and Isaac Orr, former colonization agent, became secretary. Orr was confident that the ancillary society "will increase the income of the Col[onization] Society." [9]

The founders planned to build a manual labor school in the District of Columbia. This system, they noted, would not only "make constant and untiring inroads" into the students' "wrong habits and propensities," but would "ultimately aid in the support, and diminish the expense, of the establishment." They hoped also to procure $25,000 from a fund established in 1798 by General Thaddeus Kosciusko for the liberation and education of slaves. Benjamin L. Lear, executor of the fund, was a manager of the new society. With the launching of the African Education Society, Secretary Gurley exclaimed with satisfaction, "What if the colored people in these states are now prejudiced against emigration to Africa?" Education would soon change their views and persuade them to "bear across the Atlantic the means of freedom, prosperity and happiness" to their African cousins. [10]

Despite all, the Colonization Society failed to subdue Negro opposition. In September, 1830, a convention of free Negroes meeting in Philadelphia launched the American Society of Free

Persons of Colour, for Improving their Condition in the United States; for Purchasing Lands; and for the Establishing of a Settlement in Upper Canada. Led by James Forten, Hezekiah Grice, the Reverend Samuel Cornish, and the Reverend Peter Williams, the forty delegates publicly condemned African colonization. A year later, an anticolonization convention of free Negroes in New York city flatly asserted that "This is our home, and this our country. Beneath its sod lie the bones of our fathers: for it some of them fought, bled, and died. Here we were born, and here we will die." [11]

The waves of anticolonization sentiment crested when a new voice angrily declaimed against "expatriation" and "expulsion." On January 1, 1831, a penniless young typesetter and editor in Boston brought out a small newspaper dedicated to the immediate abolition of slavery and the destruction of African colonization. In 1829 William Lloyd Garrison had been a lukewarm colonizationist when he delivered the annual Fourth of July colonization address in Boston's Park Street Church. After joining Quaker Benjamin Lundy as coeditor of the *Genius of Universal Emancipation*, then published in Baltimore, Garrison rejected colonization for immediate emancipation. But his pen was too quick and his rhetoric too sharp to win friends or convert enemies. Criminal and civil libel suits growing out of his attack on alleged African slave traders abruptly ended the twenty-three-year-old crusader's Baltimore career. Forty-nine days after Garrison entered the Baltimore city jail, Arthur Tappan of New York, hearing of the young man's plight, paid his fine.[12]

Free to find a new berth, Garrison wandered first to Washington, D.C., Philadelphia, New York, and then to Boston, looking for work, gathering plaudits for his martyrdom to slavery, and planning a new antislavery sheet. At Washington he considered buying Walter Colton's *American Spectator and Washington City Chronicle*, the African Education Society's organ. "For heaven sake," Elliott Cresson nervously commanded Ralph R. Gurley, "do not let Colton sell out [to] that Bedlamite Garrison." Shortly after, the Reverend Thomas H. Gallaudet met Garrison in Hartford and hastened to warn the parent society that the young zealot "lacks wisdom & prudence exceedingly. I should think the best course was, to maintain a perfect silence with regard to him." [13]

But silence, however perfect, was not to stop Garrison. He moved toward Boston, giving anticolonization speeches en route to free Negro audiences. At Boston he tried to organize an antislavery society, and shortly afterwards, with scrap type and a hired press, he launched *The Liberator*. Garrison designed the small weekly paper to appeal chiefly to free Negroes in Boston, Philadelphia, New York, and other eastern communities. *The Liberator* carried Negro news, praised Negro achievements, and defended Negro claims to full citizenship in the United States. Its small columns burgeoned with anticolonization sentiments. Garrison reserved his most abrasive rhetoric for the Colonization Society, denouncing it as hypocritical, unjust, unchristian, proslavery, and antirepublican. He spent ten times more space on anticolonization than on immediate emancipation. Garrison's ardent courtship of free Negro readers sold many subscriptions. Within six months, Garrison had procured five hundred Negro subscribers. The number of white subscribers was negligible.[14]

Even in Boston few men knew *The Liberator* or its editor. In October, 1831, Boston's Mayor Harrison Gray Otis, once Garrison's Federalist idol, was surprised to learn from the Washington *National Intelligencer* that an "incendiary" paper operated in his city. At Otis's orders city officers "ferreted out" the editor in his "obscure hole" and reported that "a very few insignificant persons of all colors" were his only supporters. Otis assured South Carolinians and Virginians alarmed by the recent Nat Turner insurrection that *The Liberator* commanded only "insignificant countenance and support." [15]

In the spring and summer of 1831, Garrison toured the eastern states, giving addresses to Negro audiences in which he decried African colonization as odious, contemptible, antirepublican, and anti-Christian. The libel-conscious editor blasted the principle of melioration through wholesale removal as "a libel upon humanity and justice—a libel upon republicanism—a libel upon the Declaration of Independence—a libel upon christianity." He condemned colonizationists as apologists for the "crime of slavery," enemies of Negro education, and tools of cunning slaveholders seeking to rid themselves of useless slaves. "Why, my friends," Garrison exclaimed in horror, "hundreds of worn-out slaves are annually turned off to die, like old horses." Their masters consign them to a certain death in Africa, claiming to be their benefactors. Garrison solemnly promised free Negro listeners that, with the Bible in one hand and the Declaration of Independence in the other, he would lead a crusade against "these promulgators of unrighteousness." [16]

Negro meetings in Boston, Hartford, Providence, Pittsburgh, Harrisburg, Rochester, Trenton, Baltimore, Cincinnati, and Washington, gratefully recommended *The Liberator* and pledged their "utmost endeavors to get subscribers for the same." Boston free Negroes agreed with Garrison that the Colonization Society was a "clamorous, abusive and peace-disturbing combination." In June, 1831, *The Liberator*'s editor repeated his invectives before the annual free Negro convention in Philadelphia and approvingly watched the fifteen delegates castigate the Colonization Society for seeking to "perpetuate slavery" and "many of our unconstitutional, unchristian and unheard-of sufferings." [17]

Meanwhile, Garrison was taking steps to win over white supporters as well as Negro adherents. In the winter of 1831–1832 he organized the New-England Anti-Slavery Society, persuading its twelve founders to discard the proposed title, "Philo-African Society." The address, written by Garrison, espoused immediate emancipation and repudiated colonization. He enlisted some Quaker abolitionists, including Arnold Buffum, George Benson, James and Lucretia Mott, and John Greenleaf Whittier. In addition he persuaded the Reverend Simeon S. Jocelyn, pastor of a Negro church in New Haven, the Reverend Samuel J. May of Brooklyn, Connecticut, Deacon Ebenezer Dole of Hallowell, Maine, and Joseph C. Lovejoy, principal of the Hallowell Academy, to renounce their support of colonization and join his growing band. Both Garrison and Buffum, president of the small association, toured the New England states, seeking converts and soliciting money for the new society.[18]

News of Garrison's triumphs quickly reached the Colonization Society's Washington offices. Charles Tappan of Boston warned the managers that the young editor "is doing us all the harm he can." In an interview with Tappan, Garrison declared himself an implacable enemy and vowed to oppose colonization even "if he knew it would evangelize the whole of Africa!" The Boston agent observed sadly, "I sometimes wish Arthur Tappan had let him lay in [the] Baltimore jail." [19]

From New York city, merchant-philanthropist Gabriel P. Disosway reported that "Garretson" had bitterly assailed colonization in a Negro Baptist church. "At this moment," he wailed, "his visit and his eloquence are calculated to do our cause very great injury in this city." The Reverend Leonard Bacon of New Haven was fearful that Garrison's repeated charge that the Colonization Society was a plot to perpetuate slavery would persuade whites as well as Negroes. Another Connecticut colonizationist begged the parent society to send able agents to answer Garrison, for he was already "prejudicing the minds of N. Eng. people against Colonization." [20]

Driven by this fear, the board of managers dispatched the Reverend Joshua N. Danforth to Boston to be permanent agent for New York and the New England states. The thirty-four-year-old Danforth, a graduate of Williams College and Princeton Theological Seminary, at the time of his appointment was pastor of the Fourth Presbyterian Church in Washington, D.C. In May, 1832, Danforth attended the New York anniversary meetings of various benevolent societies, visited colonizationists at Providence, Newport, and Bristol, and opened his headquarters at Boston. Concentrating on churches, he addressed ministerial associations and spoke from the pulpits of Baptist, Congregational, and Unitarian churches in many towns near Boston. The energetic agent supplied colonization sermon topics, data, and arguments to hundreds of clergymen in his district, urging them to take up collections for the parent society on Independence Day. On that day the Reverend Lyman Beecher of Boston led a host of New England clergymen in proclaiming the merits of African colonization and asking God to prosper the cause.[21]

Danforth quickly collided with Garrison and Buffum. When Danforth addressed the congregation of Boston's Second Baptist Church, Buffum boldly interrupted the collection and denounced the Colonization Society as a proslavery engine. "And that too on a Sabbath evening," Danforth indignantly snarled. Soon after, Buffum and Garrison challenged Danforth to meet them in debate. Finding their invitations "exceedingly bitter and spiteful," Danforth yearned to answer the "braggart challenges." Perhaps the antislavery agitators, having "thoroughly disgorged themselves of the venom which was rankling in their hearts," would gain new respect for "one of the most benevolent institutions that ever adorned and blessed mankind." But Boston colonization leaders strongly advised against giving the New-England Anti-Slavery Society free advertising. Danforth, however, thirsted for a fight, and not long after he crossed swords with Buffum at Northampton. By agreement they debated one evening. The Colonization Society's agent claimed victory, exalting that Buffum decamped "without a cent of Northampton money in his pocket." [22]

Danforth's tireless excursions from Boston led him into many small communities in Massachusetts and upstate New York. By mid September, 1832, he had personally collected nearly $800, mostly in village churches. He had organized new auxiliaries, including the Hampshire county auxiliary led by President Heman Humphrey of Amherst College and George Bancroft, historian. In his travels Danforth assured audiences that the Colonization Society favored gradual emancipation. Danforth's two assistants, the Reverend Charles Walker of Rutland, Vermont, and the Reverend Cyril Pearl of Bolton, Connecticut, canvassed Vermont and Maine. While Walker solicited endorsements from Vermont's ministerial associations, Pearl scoured Maine, traveling 624 miles in five weeks and giving twenty-seven addresses in churches and camp meetings. [23]

While Danforth battled Garrison in New England, the *African Repository* grandly ignored the mounting crusade to label colonization a slaveholder's plot to perpetuate slavery. Editor Gurley rarely alluded to Garrison. In April, 1831, Gurley casually acknowledged the existence of "the rash and deluded youth, who is scattering fire-brands from Boston." Later, he frowned on immediate emancipation as an infringement on property rights and declared, "We have no sympathy with the man, who professing to condemn war, is doing all in his power to kindle hostile feelings, and the fiercest passions" among Negroes. Colonization, Gurley asserted, is the middle ground between the heartless who would reopen the African slave trade and the foolhardy who courted civil disruption. Garrison's name did not appear in the *African Repository* until October, 1832, and only then in a footnote slapping the New-England Anti-Slavery Society: "A few men in Boston (chiefly young, and of course ardent), with A. Buffum a Quaker, for their President, and Garrison for their Secretary, have associated and assumed this larger title, than which none could be more inappropriate. New England disavows them." [24]

Despite his editorial shyness, Gurley had already met and listened to the fiery Boston editor. In June, 1832, he confronted Garrison at the annual Negro convention in Philadelphia. But Gurley's trip was in vain. Despite his eloquence, the twenty-nine delegates resoundingly condemned African colonization. Garrison once more demonstrated that his hold on free Negro opinion was unbreakable. The *African Repository* prudently overlooked the incident.[25]

While the *African Repository* closed its eyes, Garrison was slowly building the tiny New-England Anti-Slavery Society into a regional association with several auxiliaries. His press was relentless and his cohorts active. Hoping to convert many colonizationists to anticolonization, Garrison prepared a 240-page book innocently entitled *Thoughts on African Colonization, or an Impartial Exhibition of the Doctrines, Principles and Purposes of the American Colonization Society*. Unlike *The Liberator,* which appealed primarily to free Negroes, Garrison's *Thoughts on African Colonization* aimed at a white audience. At the outset he apologized for using "very plain, and sometimes very severe language," but he assured his readers that he approached the topic with "an unbiassed mind." Then he set out to prove that the Colonization Society was an ardent defender of slavery and a "creature without heart, without brains, eyeless, unnatural, hypocritical, relentless, unjust." [26]

In page after page he bludgeoned the society with invectives, linking excerpts from reports, resolutions, speeches, essays, and editorials by the society or its friends. The *African Repository* was his prime source, and Garrison treated any statement in it as official colonization doctrine. Taking as his motto, "Out of thine own mouth will I condemn thee," he selected passages showing the society recognized slaves as property, shielded slavery from direct attack, raised the value of slaves by removing the free Negroes, exploited racial prejudices, slandered and terrorized free blacks, obstructed Negro advancement, and blinded citizens to the impracticability of removing the entire Negro population. In short, the society's motives were not only mistaken, they were evil. "Jesuitism was never more subtle—Papal domination never more exclusive," he hissed. Exclamation marks leaped from every page. "Ye crafty calculators! ye hard-hearted, incorrigible sinners! ye greedy and relentless robbers! ye condemners of justice and mercy; ye trembling, pitiful, pale-faced usurpers! my soul spurns you with unspeakable disgust!" [27]

Garrison wailed that the Colonization Society's deceitful principles had "shamefully duped" many men of good intentions. In a pointed appeal to Quakers, he reprobated Jehudi Ashmun's "murderous warfare" against native Africans and contrasted it with William Penn's pacific Indian policy. Liberia, he dramatically asserted, was "conceived in blood, and its footsteps will be marked with blood down to old age—the blood of the poor natives." He appealed to humanitarians, arguing that the society drugged the national conscience against slavery as sin and fed the "fires of persecution" in overemphasizing "intemperance, indolence and crime" among the free Negroes. As a whole, he insisted, the free blacks were superior in their habits to the "hosts of foreign emigrants who are crowding to our shores, and poisoning our moral atmosphere."

He appealed to missionary and temperance-minded Americans, arraigning the society for permitting the sale of rum as well as tobacco, "two poisons which are exactly adapted to destroy both soul and body." Contrary to all predictions, Liberia will "obstruct the progress of christianity" in Africa, the colonists being "illiterate, degraded and irreligious" and the missionaries "avaricious and unscrupulous foreigners" preying upon ignorant natives. One hundred inspired missionaries who truly "abhor dishonesty, violence and treachery" could easily evangelize all Africa, but sending groups of men, women, and children to an insalubrious colony was no less than "murderous." [28]

The last seventy-six pages listed anticolonization resolutions by free Negro groups. Free blacks, Garrison declared, were as "unanimously opposed to a removal to Africa, as the Cherokees from the council-fires and graves of their fathers." As for Africa being the Negroes' natural home, he doubted that the Creator "has immovably fixed the habitations of any people within a boundary narrower than the circumference of the globe." [29]

By the time Garrison had finished his exposé he sincerely believed all he had written. The infallible conscience had spoken. Colonization was virtually synonymous with slavery. "I look upon the overthrow of the Colonization Society as the overthrow of slavery itself," he assured a relative, "—they both stand or fall together." [30] Henceforth, the Colonization Society was to be his whipping boy, for he needed a tangible foe with whom he could battle and upon whom he could heap epithets. In the absence of a slaveholders' association dedicated to preserving and extending slavery, Garrison turned to a nationally known association which consorted with slaveholders and dealt with the slave question indirectly. His assault on the Colonization Society was courageous only to the extent that his thesis—that the society was the handmaiden, ally, and apologist of slavery—was true. His *Thoughts on African Colonization* sought to prove his boldest allegations. As polemic it was without peer.

The Boston editor's zeal in distributing his anticolonization pamphlet easily matched his zeal in pummeling colonizationists. He secured money from Arthur Tappan who, after 1830, was disgusted with colonization. In time Tappan would dramatically renounce his membership in the society. With Tappan's secret aid, Garrison placed free copies of *Thoughts on African Colonization* in the reading rooms of several colleges and seminaries. He sent free copies to scores of New England editors and clergymen and, during the summer of 1832, he toured New England from Providence, Rhode Island, to Bangor, Maine, distributing many more copies.[31]

By the end of 1832 the arraignment had found its way into many hands. Its documented revelations stunned many once confident colonizationists. The parent society had never offered so succinct a compilation of colonization information, and few readers of the *Thoughts* were able to check Garrison's sources: numerous back issues of the *African Repository,* assorted pamphlets, and obscure newspaper articles. An alarmed Princeton seminary student cried, "We are deluged in this place with Garrison's 'Thoughts' & 'Liberator.' " Some students had already switched allegiance and the rest needed "a forcible, concise" denial that the Colonization Society perpetuated slavery. From faraway Hudson, Ohio, two colonizationists reported that Garrison's works had caused a "revolution of sentiment" at Western Reserve College. "A large portion of the students . . . have become, 'all of a sudden,' thorough-going *Abolitionists.*" Not only that, two professors were now "bold, & even warring, advocates of this newfangled theory." The students wanted "facts, indisputable facts" to hurl at their opponents. Speaking for many friends of colonization, the New York *Genius of Temperance* demanded a full reply to Garrison's charges. "We confess ourselves brought to a stand. . . . If *he* is correct, *we* have been going wrong." [32]

Like demands poured into Gurley's office. From all sides agents and friends urged Gurley to meet Garrison's unrestrained assaults and to seize the offensive. Temperance leader Edward C. Delavan, a life member of the Colonization Society, prescribed an inexpensive weekly paper modeled after his *Temperance Recorder* which each week turned out fifty thousand copies. The press, Delavan said, was the "most efficacious means" of hastening a "moral revolution" in America. Gerrit Smith of Petersboro agreed with his friend Delavan. "More printing—a thousand times more printing, is what we need." A young writer for the *North American Review,* Benjamin B. Thatcher of Boston, seconding the call for a weekly paper, lamented that antislavery agitators were daily winning adherents. Gorham D. Abbott, agent of the American Tract Society and a friend of Thatcher, warned Secretary Gurley that further silence would cost colonization its New England supporters. [33]

Agents in the field were more aware of Garrison's inroads into colonization than Secretary Gurley and the board of managers at Washington. The hardworking Joshua N. Danforth was assessing

Garrison's impact on New England. Publicly he declared that New Englanders rejected "the crude and fantastic notions of a few *radicals* and *ultras*," but privately he warned Gurley that Garrison's "bold pamphlet" had riddled many churches and auxiliaries with grave doubts. He tried to convince Gurley that the colonization movement faced a severe crisis in New England, and prompt, unequivocal countermeasures had to come from Washington.

During the summer and fall of 1832 he piled example on example to prove his point. One of the society's early friends, the Reverend Nathaniel Bouton of Concord, New Hampshire, was "so staggered" by Garrison's revelations that he forthwith closed his pulpit to colonization agents. Danforth forwarded corroborating reports from his assistants in Maine, Vermont, and New Hampshire who attested that colonization's motives were under heavy fire. One desperately cried, "Something must be done to check the errours and false statements of those mad men. Something should be done immediately." Another reported that several influential Maine clergymen were "on the poise" and perhaps already converted to immediate emancipation.[34]

By 1833, Danforth had lost all patience with Gurley's unperturbed attitude. He complained that Gurley was not giving him editorial support, while Garrison's press gushed anticolonization propaganda and antislavery agents were spreading Garrison's *Thoughts on African Colonization*. Danforth asked the managers of the parent society to relieve Gurley of his duties as editor of the *African Repository*. Only vigorous action could save New England, and he doubted that Gurley had the time or inclination to infuse the *African Repository* with a fighting spirit. The magazine needed someone who could bring it out promptly each month and see to its immediate delivery. Danforth assured the managers that they faced a "critical period" in northern states and bold steps were urgently needed. In Boston alone it would require great exertion to "repress the influence of the abolitionists, who are endeavouring to get possession of the pulpits in the City." [35]

Late in 1832 the parent society begrudgingly broke its self-imposed silence. Ralph R. Gurley, both in the *African Repository*

and in a small pamphlet entitled *Letter on the American Colonization Society,* charged Garrison with unfairness in tearing sentences and phrases out of context and distorting meanings. He
insisted that it was unfair to treat every article appearing in the
African Repository as an expression of colonization doctrine.

In a kindly and forebearing manner, Gurley rebuked Garrison the reformer for using methods certain not to reform any-
thing. "The language of reproach and vituperation" will not "win
men over to the love and belief of the truth," Gurley chided.
Garrison vilifies the South, reproaches the North, and stigmatizes
the Colonization Society and its followers because they do not say
that slavery—admittedly an "evil system" but deeply intertwined
with the roots of American society—ought to be "entirely, and
completely, and instantaneously demolished." What, Gurley
asked, did this gadfly hope to accomplish with his "notes of
alarm, his unqualified, and reiterated denunciations?" In the
South he had forfeited any moral influence over slaveholders who
universally regard him as "dangerous to the public safety, and
attempting to scatter the firebrands of war and death." Even if
Garrison's "delusive and blazing lights" succeeded in turning the
whole North from the "practical and sober scheme" of colonization, immediate emancipation would still require the consent of
southern men.

Patiently and politely, Gurley repeated the maxim of benevolence that safety of the community was superior to "any unsub-
stantial theory of the rights of man." Nor was it right, he added,
"that men should possess that freedom, for which they are entirely
unprepared, and which can only prove injurious to themselves
and others." He pledged the Colonization Society would continue
to improve the lot of free Negroes by colonizing them in Africa
and through moral influence induce "an extensive and judicious
voluntary manumission of slaves." [36]

Gurley's belated remarks heralded the battle against Garrison.
The Boston editor had waited nearly six months for a reply after
handing Gurley a copy of the pamphlet. When *The Liberator*
jeered that the long-awaited remarks were "flimsy and irrelevant,"
an annoyed Gurley responded less gently with proof that Garrison had used garbled evidence to vilify the society. Denying the

Colonization Society had duped good men with wrong principles, he read Garrison a lesson in theology: benevolence, or good intentions, went hand in hand with good principles. "Will Mr. Garrison tell us how benevolent men shall effect a good object by righteous means, from wrong *principles?*" [37]

Colonizationists in the eastern states, and particularly the harried agents, greeted Gurley's remarks as the long overdue signal to attack Garrison. Their attacks easily surpassed Gurley's mild rebuke. In a scholarly salvo in *The Quarterly Christian Spectator*, the Reverend Leonard Bacon asserted that Garrison's "wrath and railing, such recklessness and coarseness of vituperation" could neither enlighten nor convince. Indeed, the Boston editor's ferocity would merely help in "disastrously delaying" the hour of emancipation. Proclaiming himself a friend of the slave, he was in fact doing the poor creature great harm. *The Methodist Magazine and Quarterly Review* of New York commented that Garrison wrote "as though goaded by a feeling of malevolence and revenge," and rebuked him for his "censorious, vulgar, and abusive epithets" and cant "bordering even on profanity." It accused him of seeking racial amalgamation in the United States.[38]

The hardhitting Joshua Danforth, preferring fist blows to Gurley's judicious finger wagging, pounded Garrison in the Boston *Recorder,* New York *Observer,* and the New York *Commercial Advertiser*. Garrison's *Thoughts on African Colonization,* he growled, displayed "the most disgusting egotism," "the grossest misrepresentations," and "a cataract of abuse." Danforth's expositions bristled with angry words: "reckless fanatic," "incendiary publication," and "lunatic." Danforth's assistant, Cyril Pearl, issued a forty-eight-page pamphlet that answered Garrison's sensational charges point for point but "without railing and needless declamation." [39]

In Boston, heart of the anticolonization swirl, a group led by Gorham D. Abbott, Benjamin B. Thatcher, Henry T. Tuckerman, Horace Mann, and the Reverend Ezra S. Gannett, organized the Young Men's Colonization Society of Boston, and, in April, 1833, brought out *The Colonizationist and Journal of Freedom,* a monthly magazine that focussed on New England's role in the movement. At the outset Editor Thatcher promised "common decency in the use of language." Emphasizing the antislavery aspects of colonization, the magazine sought to answer the New-England Anti-Slavery Society's monthly *Abolitionist,* but at the same time *The Colonizationist* was a rebuke to Gurley's *African Repository.* Hinting that the *Repository* was too dilatory in its handling of the antislavery question, Cyril Pearl frankly told Gurley that *The Colonizationist* better suited New England tastes and ought to take over the *Repository*'s subscription lists in that region.[40]

Editor Gurley faced a dilemma—one seriously aggravated by Garrison's relentless assaults. Gurley personally wished to emphasize the antislavery mission of the Colonization Society, but he feared loss of all support south of the Potomac if the parent society too boldly embraced antislavery. Friends in Virginia were imploring the parent society to proceed with greatest caution, while northern friends were demanding less reticence. "A *little thing* now, would prevent us from making the great progress we might otherwise hope for," a Virginia colonizationist cautioned. Connecticut's Leonard Bacon counterbalanced this with a plea that Gurley declare the society "looks to the voluntary and peaceful abolition of slavery . . . as one of the ultimate results of its labors." [41]

In private letters and conversations, Gurley favored the latter course. "The great question in regard to the perpetuity of gradual abolition of slavery, we believe, must be decided by the *Southern States* themselves," Gurley assured a Mississippi contributor, "yet we do hope that our plan will exert a *moral influence* favourable to *voluntary* emancipation." Emboldened by the Virginia legislature's open arraignment of slavery, Gurley remarked to Jesse B. Harrison of Lynchburg, Virginia, that the question of slavery "cannot fail to come more & more into discussion as we advance, & the great matter seems to be, to move as fast as we can, and carry public sentiment with us, yet not so fast, as to produce reaction at the South." He urged Harrison and "all who are willing that emancipation should proceed, as fast as it can take place in justice & with benefit to all parties concerned," to pledge their support to this policy of gradualism.[42]

Gurley's dilemma symbolized the dilemma that confronted all

colonizationists. Antislavery objectives voiced by the Reverend Robert Finley at the society's founding were now colliding with the narrower objective of merely removing free Negroes from the land without touching slavery itself. The growing divergence between the two positions became apparent when the nationalist mood faded. Garrison's assaults both aggravated and advertised the colonizationists' predicament.

After 1832 Gurley was far less reluctant to trade blows with the persistent Boston adversary, for he now realized that Garrison was striving for more than Negro support in eastern cities. He was attempting to divert the mainstream of antislavery sentiment to his embryonic movement. He was fighting for control of public opinion. During 1833 and 1834 antislavery and colonization proponents, shouting their war cries in churches, public halls, and the press, would meet in desperate battle. Agents in search of allies would scour the eastern and western states, and some would carry the campaign to the British isles.

XVI

THE UNQUENCHABLE TORCH

———◆•◆•◆———

ON JANUARY 20, 1833, delegates and guests of the Colonization Society's sixteenth annual meeting assembled in the taper-lit hall of the House of Representatives. Charles Fenton Mercer, sitting at the Speaker's desk, gazed down upon the dignified faces of Henry Clay, Theodore Frelinghuysen, Thomas Corwin, Edward Everett, William Cabell Rives, Gulian C. Verplanck, George Washington Parke Custis, and Ezekiel Chambers. Following the invocation, Secretary Ralph R. Gurley recited the society's accomplishments for the previous year. The inventory was impressive. In 1832 the society spent $37,000 to send five ships with 645 colonists, among them 229 manumitted slaves. From Maine to Arkansas Territory agents were gathering funds and raising more auxiliaries. Bequests for one year totaled more than $12,000. Gurley enumerated Liberia's achievements: exports reached $125,000, the colonial agent had annexed new territories, and new churches and schools had opened their doors to the God-fearing colonists. Agent Joseph Mechlin happily reported that throughout the colony there was "cheering evidence of enterprise and improvement." [1]

The optimistic summary gave scant notice to the society's enemies multiplying both in the north and in the south. The managers complacently declared that, opposition notwithstanding, the Colonization Society's demonstrated benevolence and its moral influence in fostering manumission "place the character of this Institution on grounds inaccessible to the boldest assailant." Nor did the managers allude to the rumblings within the society itself and the growing despair among some of its friends in the north.

The rumblings burst into tumult when Secretary Gurley, waiting until the close of the customary speeches and resolutions applauding colonization, proposed drastic changes in the officers and government of the society. In a bold attempt to wash away any stain of proslavery, Gurley engineered the deposal of five members of the board of managers, including the distinguished chairman, Francis S. Key, owner of many slaves. Unquestioningly, the delegates approved Gurley's list of nominations in a routine manner, and only afterwards discovered that Francis S. Key, General Walter Jones, Samuel Harrison Smith, Colonel Henry Ashton, and Judge William Cranch were no longer managers of the society. By way of consolation, Key, Jones, and Smith, long-time members of the society, were now vice-presidents.

Secretary Gurley also asked the delegates to reduce the managers to the status of servants of a powerful board of directors who would formulate policy and oversee their work. Under this plan, the directors, including all officers of parent and state societies, guardians of state colonization funds, and all donors of $500 or more, would be mostly northerners, for the north had more state auxiliaries and gave more money. Gurley's plan gave no credit to slaveowners who gave their slaves for removal.

The troubled delegates debated Gurley's revolutionary proposals in four long and "boisterous" meetings. At length they turned down Gurley's constitutional revisions, and by a close vote of 63 to 57, reinstated the deposed managers.[2]

Rumors of a "commotion in the society at Headquarters" quickly spread among gleeful antislavery men as well as dejected colonizationists. The Boston *Atlas* and the New York *Moral Advertiser* reported that the deposed managers had bitterly fought their banishment and had accused Gurley of leading a "secret combination to let the North to overshadow and blast the peace of the South." They charged that "radical abolitionists" would seize the society and make it a "machine for breaking the fetters of the slave population." [3]

The New-England Anti-Slavery Society's monthly journal, *The Abolitionist,* greeted the colonizationists' bickerings as proof that the rival society embraced two "diametrically opposed" factions —one seeking eventual abolition, the other wishing to make slave property more secure. The antislavery journal complimented the Colonization Society's leaders for skill in avoiding an "open rupture" by arguing both objectives, and it expressed "deep regret" that sincere, well-meaning enemies of slavery were "so deluded as to support such an institution." [4]

In the weeks following the stormy sixteenth annual meeting, Secretary Gurley made bolder antislavery pronouncements that placed him on the side of gradual emancipation. In a widely distributed essay addressed to a British antislavery leader, Gurley unhesitantly preempted emancipation for the colonizationists. He declared that "All or nearly all Americans, cherish the desire and expectation" that slavery "will one day be abolished." Slavery was as doomed as a stray iceberg "amid the sunny tropics." Colonization's "gentle, persuasive, but *mighty*" moral influence would slowly and safely melt slavery. The Colonization Society, he pleaded, offered the only safe middle ground for both northern and southern men. But two forces were working against emancipation: southern fears of *"rash and dangerous interference from the North"* and apprehensions of *"evils greater than slavery itself"* if the free Negroes remained in the United States. Referring to William Lloyd Garrison, Gurley warned that "to thunder forth denunciations" would only bring a "conflict between the North and the South, more appalling than any ever witnessed in our country." [5]

Meanwhile, Garrison's thunderclaps grew louder. In January, 1833, the New-England Anti-Slavery Society held its first annual meeting and boasted that in the past year it had stimulated "more public addresses on the subject of slavery, and appeals in behalf of the contemned free people of color . . . than were elicited for forty years prior to its organization." In February, Garrison and Buffum invaded an organizational meeting of the Boston Young Men's Colonization Society arranged by Joshua N. Danforth, permanent agent of the parent society. By interrupting Danforth's speech in Old South Church and jeering at the society's fellowship with slavery, they compelled Danforth to call off the rest of the meeting. [6]

Angered and insulted by these bold tactics, Danforth readily accepted a challenge to debate with Buffum in Salem. Buffum argued that the Colonization Society's measures gave "increased security" to slavery and the domestic slave trade and tended to "excite and perpetuate unholy prejudices" against free Negroes. To Buffum's charge that some managers of the parent society owned many slaves, Danforth lamely replied that Francis S. Key's slaves had voluntarily spurned manumission. To Danforth's chagrin, the Salem audience adopted Garrison's resolution that the Colonization Society's "authentic publications . . . demonstrate that the institution originated with slave-holders, and that it does not appear that they have manumitted their own slaves." Danforth came away from the meeting, thinking Buffum "a rough, disagreeable, reckless man." [7]

Danforth countered Garrison's repeated charge that colonization fostered slavery with a parade of distinguished New Englanders. Early in February, 1833, a crowd of 1,500 men gathered in Boston's Park Street Church to hear lawyer-politician Caleb Cushing declaim against slavery and against those who foolishly endangered the Union by antagonizing the south. Alexander H. Everett, editor of the *North American Review,* flatly asserted that colonization slashed at the roots of slavery by crushing the African slave trade at its source. The renowned crusader for peace, William Ladd, avowed that the Colonization Society "deserves the patronage of all who are, from principle, opposed to slavery." [8]

Through the spring and autumn of 1833, colonization agents labored to stamp out the antislavery contagion. In March the staid Boston Lyceum opened its forum to a colonization debate that lasted two nights. Oliver Johnson, newly elected secretary of the New-England Anti-Slavery Society, argued against and Cyril Pearl, agent of the parent society, pleaded for African colonization. Charles C. Beaman, Benjamin B. Thatcher, and Bela B. Edwards, of the Young Men's Colonization Society, contended that only colonization could destroy slavery without shaking the Union. The Lyceum agreed, 108 to 46, that the Colonization Society's measures tended to "remove the evil of slavery from this country." A few weeks later, Robert S. Finley, agent of the New York society, debated with Professor Elizur Wright, Jr., of Western Reserve College, in Boston's Park Street

Church. Finley assured the audience that his father, the founder of the society, envisioned the gradual extinction of slavery, and that colonizationists over the country shared this goal.[9]

In Portland, Maine, colonizationists met strenuous opposition from the small Maine Anti-Slavery Society when they attempted to organize an auxiliary. General Samuel Fessenden spent three hours berating the colonizationists as friends and proponents of slavery. His chief source was Garrison's *Thoughts on African Colonization*. Agents Danforth and Pearl denied the charges, ridiculed Garrison's inaccuracy, and argued that irresponsible immediate abolitionists were in fact goading southerners to oppose emancipation in any form. Colonial Vice-Agent Anthony D. Williams spent another evening demolishing Fessenden's harsh picture of Liberia. After the debate had continued for a week, two hundred men, led by ex-governor Albion K. Parris, joined the new colonization auxiliary.[10]

Meanwhile, the anticolonization whirlwind was sweeping westward. At Western Reserve College in Ohio a small band of antislavery students shouted down an agent of the Colonization Society, and a few months later the college shook with a prolonged debate between colonization and antislavery champions. The contest grew so intense that the professors who espoused immediate emancipation left the college. Beriah Green became president of Oneida Institute in Whitesborough, New York, and Elizur Wright, Jr., became secretary of the American Anti-Slavery Society. The *African Repository* rejoiced that the "firmness of the Trustees" had thwarted a plot to subvert Western Reserve into a "Seminary for educating Abolition Missionaries." [11]

In the southwest the parent society's permanent agent grew alarmed at the "baleful influence of the abolition-propagandists," for slaveowners confused colonization with abolition. James G. Birney labeled Garrison a dangerous incendiary whose views were completely opposite to the Colonization Society's concepts of gradual emancipation. Beginning in the spring of 1833, Birney published a series of seven colonization essays in the Huntsville, Alabama, *Democrat*. Shaping his arguments to the prejudice of fellow slaveowners, Birney argued that the removal of free blacks would stimulate "good conduct" among the slaves, and thus predispose the satisfied owner to manumit his well-behaved servants. In this subtle, imperceptible way, colonization fostered emancipation.[12]

While colonization agents were deprecating Garrison's "rashness and mischievousness," shrewd antislavery men were preparing a new attack. In the spring of 1833, merchant-philanthropist Arthur Tappan, for more than a year Garrison's secret supporter, dramatically renounced the Colonization Society and accused it of drenching Africa with "ardent spirits." In a letter to the Anti-Slavery Society at Andover Theological Seminary, Tappan charged that in one year "no less than *fourteen hundred barrels* of the liquid poison" entered Liberia. He had learned this fact as a merchant in the Liberian trade. The grievous discovery, Tappan avowed, induced him to reexamine Garrison's exposure of the Colonization Society as a "device of Satan." Tappan's newspaper, the New York *Emancipator,* underscored this testimony with a dissatisfied colonist's complaint that rum and wine were forced upon him, and that tiny Monrovia sheltered more drunkards than either Philadelphia or New York.[13]

Tappan's accusations were sensational enough to terrify the friends of African colonization, for many clergymen and reform spokesmen throughout the north were growing acutely sensitive to the liquor question. Joseph Tracy, editor of the *Vermont Chronicle* and a loyal colonization advocate, termed the new charge the "heaviest gun of the Garrisonites." Unless the society was completely exonerated, he warned, the African colonization movement faced certain disaster in the northeast.[14]

Gurley grieved over Tappan's unexpected thrust, for he looked upon the New York philanthropist as a "truly good, though greatly mistaken man." In a kindly, forthright reply, Gurley denied that the society itself shipped liquor to Liberia or that the colony encouraged intemperance. But he conceded that private mercantile firms used rum in the native trade. Rejecting Tappan's statistics, he asserted that only two confirmed drunkards lived in the colony. In an effort to rid the society of opprobrium, the managers publicly promised to inspire temperance among the colonists, restrict the liquor traffic with the natives, and impose heavy liquor licenses on wholesalers. But they declined to "try the experiment of prohibition, till the commercial prosperity of the Colony should be fixed on a stable basis." Otherwise, the entire native trade would quickly revert to slavers. Gerrit Smith chided those who demanded prohibition, saying "surely, our countrymen should not denounce us for omitting this measure, until, at least, some one of their own civil governments has set the example." [15]

Before long, the *African Repository* announced that temperance societies were springing up in Liberia. Vice-Agent Anthony D. Williams, touring Boston, New York, and Philadelphia, testified that the sober, God-fearing colonists were laboring to persuade the natives to accept prohibition. In its zeal to picture Liberia's new devotion to temperance, the *African Repository* prudently declined to print one colonist's account of "the practice heare in the time [of] the elections for the Candendats to treet And for many days the hole Colony is rum mad. . . . And the hole place is in an unroar fighting and quarreling—and careing durks, swords and P[olice] clubs." [16]

Despite the society's denials, demurrers, and promises, the liquid-poison theme, as a coda to the riveting-the-chains-of-slavery indictment, recurred as often as antislavery orators and pamphleteers execrated African colonization. Delegates at the next annual meeting, betraying their profound sensitivity to the rum charge, voted to "found all future settlements on temperance principles." Agent Robert S. Finley branded the rum traffic "a greater crime than the slave trade" and pledged that in the future "not a single barrel of liquid damnation shall pollute the soil" of Africa. [17]

As the contest between colonization and antislavery grew hotter, Secretary Gurley decided to enter the field as general agent. For three months he labored in the cities of the northeast. At Philadelphia friends of colonization, under Bishop William White's chairmanship, hailed the society's "powerful inducements to effect a safe, gradual, *voluntary* and entire emancipation of slavery." At a meeting in New York's Masonic hall, Gurley gathered $1,200. At Boston, his success was greater. A public meeting sponsored by Alexander H. Everett, the Reverend Ezra S. Gannett, and the Reverend George W. Blagden, yielded $10,000 in pledges.[18]

Gurley's long tour opened his eyes to the antislavery foe. Within a short time he was sending the managers alarming reports that the movement faced an unprecedented crisis. Confronted with Garrison's *Thoughts* and unable to answer the grave charges, many friends were waivering and falling away. The society needed "large measures" and "great energy" to combat the influence of the antislavery attacks, or "thousands will desert us, north of the Potomac." In amazement he declared, "You can hardly conceive the zeal & energy of the ultra abolitionists." Their pamphlets were everywhere. "They print, I have not a doubt, *ten times* as much as the Colonization Society, & send their publications gratuitiously to all the Clergy, & to a large portion of all respectable men in the Union." [19]

Besides Garrison's *Liberator,* antislavery forces now employed the New York *Emancipator,* the Brooklyn, Connecticut, *Unionist,* and the Boston *Christian Soldier.* The New-England Anti-Slavery Society issued the monthly *Abolitionist,* plus annual reports and tracts. At New York, John G. Whittier was editing the *Anti-Slavery Reporter.* Joshua Leavitt's *Evangelist and Religious Review* gave antislavery a friendly hearing. Garrison's *Thoughts on African Colonization* was merely the first of many powerful anticolonization pamphlets. In 1833 Elizur Wright, Jr., produced the widely circulated diatribe, *The Sin of Slavery;* Lydia Maria Child, *An Appeal in Favour of that Class of Americans called Africans;* and John G. Whittier, *Justice and Expediency.* The English abolitionist, Charles Stuart, helped knot the anticolonization noose with *Prejudice Vincible* and *Liberia Unveiled.* The antislavery leaders relied more on the written word and less on the visiting agent.

By contrast, the Colonization Society published few pamphlets and one monthly—frequently late in its delivery. It depended largely on traveling agents to call attention to the *African Repository,* annual reports, and an occasional pamphlet. The *Repository's* circulation never exceeded five thousand, and the parent society neglected to maintain subscription agents in all large cities. In 1832 the managers issued fifty thousand copies of their annual report, but this was their greatest effort. The Boston *Colonizationist,* begun in 1833 under the auspices of the Young Men's Colonization Society, lasted a year. Cyril Pearl's *Remarks on African Colonization* and Mathew Carey's *Letters on the Colonization Society,* both privately printed, were the only well-known pamphlets explaining colonization principles. While colonizationists printed their pamphlets on fine paper and sold them for twelve or twenty-five cents, the antislavery writers chose large printings on cheap paper and gave away their works.

Printing propaganda, an essential in the antislavery movement, was only incidental to the Colonization Society's work. In 1832 the society allotted only $3,300 to printing and ten times that amount to colonial expenditures. The following year, hard-pressed by the abolitionists, the society raised its printing fund to $4,000 and spent $24,000 for transportation, supplies, and colonial salaries.[20] Compared with antislavery's light and easy maneuvers, the Colonization Society was an unwieldly behemoth burdened with a voracious progeny. It needed large sums each year to nourish its colony. At a critical moment in the society's existence, Liberia was absorbing thousands of dollars that may well have gone into cheap pamphlets and tracts explaining the purposes of the colonization movement.

The Colonization Society ignored its friends' appeals to launch a weekly newspaper. Unlike the men favoring immediate abolition, colonization writers had easy access to many newspapers. Chief among these in 1833 were the New York *Commercial Advertiser;* Boston *Recorder;* Windsor *Vermont Chronicle;* Philadelphia *United States Gazette, American Centinel, Daily Chronicle,* and *Intelligencer;* and the *National Intelligencer* at Washington, D.C. But newspaper articles were often ephemeral and rarely passed from hand to hand. Many times antislavery agitators succeeded in forcing themselves into hostile newspapers simply by drawing the abuse of indignant or pugnacious editors.

Colonization essays found ready acceptance in monthlies, quarterlies, and other serial publications, such as the Portland *Christian Mirror,* New York *Observer,* Princeton Seminary's *Biblical Repertory,* Boston's *New-England Magazine,* and *North*

American Review, Philadelphia's *American Quarterly Review,* and New Haven's *Quarterly Christian Spectator.* But articles and reviews appearing in their columns, even when signed by such men as William Ladd, Henry Clay, or Leonard Bacon, did not attain extensive circulation except among a class of men already favorable to colonization.

While colonizationists in the United States gaped at the avalanche of anticolonization propaganda, Elliott Cresson was canvassing the British Isles. Hopeful that an American could collect large sums in Great Britain, Cresson set his goal at £10,000. Lydia Sigourney, Hartford's colonization poetess, gave the eager agent an appropriate send-off:

> Go forth—God's peace possessing!
>   To all mankind a friend—
> Full be thy cup of blessing,
>   Where'er thy wanderings tend.

Working among fellow Quakers, antislavery men, and leaders of British benevolent societies, the wealthy Philadelphian freely depicted the Colonization Society as seeking "the final and entire abolition of slavery." Cresson lectured in England, Scotland, and Ireland, gathered testimonials from such famous men as Thomas Clarkson, venerable foe of the African slave trade, sold seventy-five life memberships in the American society, and solicited large sums, as at Edinburgh, where he promised a special colonial village to be named "Edina." During his first year abroad Cresson collected $4,000. By the time he returned to the United States, late in 1833, he had gathered £2,200.[21]

At first Cresson expected the aid of the British Anti-Slavery Society, and he carried letters of introduction to Zachary Macaulay, one of the society's principal leaders. But Macaulay, erstwhile governor of Sierra Leone, refused to give African colonization a hearing in the *Anti-Slavery Reporter,* and Cresson decided that "the old Turk" secretly envied Liberia's progress. "Old Macaulay is a great boor," he sniffed. He quickly discovered that many British antislavery men were "as thorough-paced Abolitionists as Garrison himself." They resented Cresson's intrusion just as they were campaigning for West Indian emancipation.

One antislavery man bluntly told the American agent: "John Bull does not like to have his cow milked by strangers; England is the preserve of the Anti-Slavery Society, and you are a poacher in it." [22]

Cresson's disillusionment was complete when he encountered the eccentric Charles Stuart, the spirited antislavery pamphleteer who had visited the United States and who abhorred the Colonization Society. Stuart promptly convinced the horrified Cresson that he wanted intermarriage and amalgamation. "With such men, reason is thrown away & argument pointless," Cresson hotly exclaimed. [23]

Unable to win over the British Anti-Slavery Society, Cresson singlehandedly made war upon it. In his lectures he discredited the British antislavery men as "ultras" or extremists. In some places he organized miniature colonization societies that competed with local antislavery groups. Noting that antislavery men claimed their greatest strength in the dissenting churches, Cresson was careful to speak only in the Anglican churches and often with the blessings of the local bishop. "Our great hope must after be from the *Church* (where the wealth lies)." [24]

The British antislavery men accepted Cresson's impudent challenge and plagued him with Charles Stuart. The two soon collided in a debate, and Cresson found his eloquent opponent "very canting, hypocritical & abusive—calling us once 'Ministers of Hell'—he is a 2nd Garrison." Stuart continued to flay Cresson in pamphlets and broadsides, charging that the Colonization Society fostered race hatred. [25]

By May, 1833, Cresson was thoroughly weary of his private war. Abuse, illness, and disappointment turned him into an embittered, tortured creature. He saw himself as the symbolic victim of anti-American feelings. Everywhere he went insult and accusation mocked him. One Sunday on a street in Manchester a total stranger berated Cresson for fomenting anti-Negro prejudice. His visit, he wailed, had deteriorated to "guerrilla warfare." An "epidemic insanity," he plaintively remarked to Gurley, "prevails throughout Britain." [26]

In May, 1833, just as Cresson was about to organize a British Colonization Society, William Lloyd Garrison arrived in England. The Boston editor intended to raise money for a Negro manual labor school, and he also planned to "correct the views of the British public in regard to the Colonization Society." Arriving just as the West Indian emancipation movement was climaxing, he wisely agreed not to compete with the British Anti-Slavery Society and set aside the task of soliciting money. Instead, he challenged Cresson to debate the merits of African colonization. The agonized Cresson haughtily refused to meet Garrison in public, but Garrison and James Cropper of the British Anti-Slavery Society called public meetings in London's Wesleyan Chapel and denounced African colonization as the "brazen hand-maiden of slavery." Garrison belabored Cresson for "abusing the confidence and generosity of the philanthropists of Great Britain" and publicly labeled him an "impostor." [27]

Cresson burned with rage and frustration, but he feared Garrison and his brilliant invective. Convinced that his foe was far more agile in debate and better equipped with the latest Colonization Society reports and journals, Cresson vented his anger in long, painful letters to Secretary Gurley. He blamed Gurley entirely for his humiliation before Garrison, for the secretary had neglected to send him the newest issues of the *African Repository*. "Do you mean to drive me mad?" he asked petulantly. He never forgave Gurley.[28]

Early in July, 1833, Cresson launched the British African Colonization Society with the Duke of Sussex as Patron. Distinguished titles, including Lord Bexley, the Duke of Bedford, the Archbishop of Dublin, Lord Advocate Jeffrey, and the Marquis of Westminster, adorned the list of officers. The small society proposed to "introduce the blessings of Christianity and of civilization" among African natives, abolish the slave trade, and establish new colonies. After private conversations with the Lord Advocate, Cresson was hoping the British government would grant £100,000 to the American Colonization Society to weld Sierra Leone with Liberia and form the "Empire of Liberia." [29]

Cresson's grandiose dreams suddenly exploded when Garrison's friends in the British Anti-Slavery Society published the brief but chilling "Protest" signed by eleven leading antislavery advocates, including the dying William Wilberforce, venerable symbol of British benevolence. Wilberforce, Thomas Fowell Buxton, James Cropper, Samuel Gurney, Daniel O'Connell, and others solemnly declared that the American Colonization Society's claims to be an abolition association were "wholly groundless" and "altogether delusive." A few days later, Wilberforce died, and antislavery spokesmen revered the "Protest" as his last will and testament. The "Protest" climaxed Garrison's visit and harried Cresson out of Great Britain. Though failing to collect any money for the Negro manual labor school, Garrison exulted that the "Protest" was "alone worth a trip across the Atlantic." When Secretary Gurley read the name Wilberforce at the bottom of the "Protest," he deeply regretted that "a denunciation so flaming should have proceeded from authority so grave." Colonizationists sorrowfully agreed that Wilberforce was sick and demented when he signed the fateful document.[30]

Garrison's triumphal return from Britain coincided with efforts to form the New York City Anti-Slavery Society. Early in October, 1833, Lewis Tappan, William Goodell, Joshua Leavitt, and John Rankin summoned friends of immediate emancipation to a meeting in Clinton Hall. Excited foes of the "ultras" promptly assumed that Garrison was behind the move. On the eve of the meeting one newspaper exhorted "all good citizens" to put down the fanatics. Secretary Gurley, by coincidence on a visit to New York colonizationists, noted that "prodigious excitement" filled the city. Another New York visitor, John Neal, secretary of the Portland Colonization Society, was eager to meet Garrison face to face. Neal was on his way to Washington, D.C., to apply for the society's agency in England. Avowing himself an enemy of slavery and a still greater enemy of immediate emancipation, Neal told Gurley that he and a group of New York colonizationists intended to invade the antislavery meeting. He vowed to denounce Garrison's "calumnies & expose his misrepresentations, or put a stop to his further proceedings, *for the present* at least." [31]

On the appointed evening antislavery leaders, finding Clinton Hall closed to them, quietly gathered at the Chatham Street Chapel, quickly organized their society, elected Arthur Tappan president, and after only thirty minutes slipped out the rear door. Fifty-three men and women had attended the hurried, hushed meeting. Meanwhile, two thousand men jammed Tammany Hall and the street around to hear John Neal deride immediate emancipation. The crowd loudly resolved that it was "improper and inexpedient to agitate a question pregnant with peril and difficulty to the common weal." Afterwards, a mob of rowdies trooped to the antislavery meeting place, broke down the iron gates, and staged a mock meeting in the empty hall. The rioters amused themselves by insisting that a frightened Negro, derisively dubbed "Arthur Tappan," deliver an antislavery speech.[32]

The brush with violence incensed many New York men. The *Journal of Commerce,* exonerating the Colonization Society from any blame, sternly condemned the charade at Chatham Street Chapel as an insult to the right of free assembly. "The essence of toleration is, to bear with those who differ from us," the newspaper admonished, even if the advocates of immediate emancipation were "of the feeblest intellect and the most worthless character." To persecute them would only make martyrs and recruit more abolitionists. Secretary Gurley discovered that "our most sober & wise Friends deem the *course pursued unjustifiable,*" and he warned his assistant at Washington to disavow the riots in the next *African Repository.* At Gurley's behest, the managers declined to give the excitable John Neal a commission to labor in England.[33]

By the end of 1833, colonizationists began to see that systematic exposition of principle, appeals to benevolence weighted with reason, face-to-face encounters, and threats of violence would neither chasten nor silence the antislavery agitators. To meet them in public debate or to answer their publications merely advertised their charge that African colonization was the secret spouse of slavery. Moreover, in trying to answer Garrison by claiming that colonization was the only true means of destroying slavery, colonizationists risked splitting the movement.

In Virginia, where colonization sentiment was strong, opinion was divided. Some observers assured the managers that Garrison and followers "are rendering essential service to the Colonization cause" by making colonization seem safe and sane. But others, including John Marshall's nephew, Edward Colston of Martinsburg, Virginia, cried that Garrison was demolishing the emancipation movement in the south. No one, he complained, "cares to open his mouth on the subject for fear of being branded as an ally of Garrison's, & of doing evil instead of good to the cause he would advocate." It vexed him to see "all our hopes of finally eradicating this evil, spoiled & marred by the intemperance & folly, not to say wickedness of those, who are perfectly ignorant, of the subject, its difficulties, & dangers." Farther south, in Savannah, Georgia, agent John Crosby discovered that many men assumed that Garrison and colonizationists were "coadjutors" and equally reprehensible.[34]

By contrast, many northerners now accepted Garrison's thesis that colonization and emancipation were diametrically opposed. Gerrit Smith, referring to Garrison's relentless campaign, ruefully noted that "the belief has of late obtained pretty rapidly at the North, that our Society is an obstacle in the way of emancipation, in the way of the precious cause of universal freedom." Northern men would no longer accept African colonization as the only road to ultimate emancipation. The society erred in taking this ground. Let antislavery societies fight slavery; let the Colonization Society colonize the free. Smith urged the parent society to seek neutral ground, say no more of slavery, and allow individual members to be slaveowners or antislavery men "without doing violence to their connexion with the Colonization Society." After this plea for coexistence, the society reaffirmed that it sought only to "execute a plan for colonizing (with their own consent) the Free People of Colour, residing in our country." [35]

Despite Smith's demand for truce, antislavery partisans continued to flay colonization, and colonizationists belabored immediate emancipation. The campaign was reaching its peak. Late in 1833 the American Anti-Slavery Society—with Arthur Tappan as president—organized in Philadelphia and immediately unleashed a new flood of agents, pamphlets, and petitions calling for the end of slavery and the death of African colonization. At length, one weary defender of colonization gloomily conceded that antislavery agitators would thrive as long as they could brandish the "unquenchable torch of excitement." [36]

Meanwhile, troubles more urgent than antislavery outcries nagged at the Colonization Society. Toward the end of 1833, the society's finances were drooping. The exertions of 1832 had strained the treasury and left a small but stubborn debt. Privately assuring the managers that the size of the debt was unimportant "if we preserve our credit & go forward," Secretary Gurley urged them to borrow more money and rely on "public liberality" for repayment. But the annual Fourth of July collections, after reaching a record $12,000 in 1832, unexpectedly sank to $4,000 in 1833. Monthly receipts were dropping too. Just at this critical moment, a brief panic, growing out of President Jackson's war with Nicholas Biddle, froze the springs of charity. As one agent in New York city observed, "whenever the counting-house thermometer falls below Zero," a commercial city's "good spirits" congealed.[37]

Anticipating larger returns, the managers had borrowed $10,-000 and delayed paying bills held by mercantile firms. Suddenly, in June and again in August, a flurry of drafts drawn on the society by Colonial Agent Joseph Mechlin assailed the managers. Having no forewarning, the managers repudiated the drafts. Angry creditors showered them with protested drafts totaling $10,000. Thomas Bell of New York, recently appointed commission agent for the society, cried, "something ought to be done & that quickly, or the Society will lose friends *on all sides* & their credit be *utterly & irretrievably prostrated* for *ever*." Among the holders of protested drafts were two loyal colonizationists, Gerard Ralston and John Hanson of Philadelphia. Hanson's claims on the society reached $20,000. The Samuel Trainer company of Boston ominously warned that dishonored drafts could have "a very unfavorable effect upon subscriptions to be raised when such facts are known." [38]

In the fall of 1833, Secretary Gurley again visited the eastern cities and begged friends of colonization to raise large sums immediately. He frankly admitted that "never were the pecuniary wants of the Society greater than at this moment. Without an increase of funds, it will be incapable of sending expeditions to Liberia during the present year." Many free Negroes and slaves "ready to be liberated" would be disappointed. "Shall they appeal in vain to a generous and magnanimous people?" [39]

Boston, New York, and Philadelphia colonizationists tried to

dissuade Gurley, saying that during the panic appeals for contributions would surely fail. Benjamin B. Thatcher of Massachusetts lamented that money had vanished: "It is really distressing all
over the commonwealth in a great degree." Nevertheless, Boston
and Philadelphia men pledged $10,000, and New York city colo-
nizationists grandly promised $20,000. Gurley's cash collections
were smaller, but late in October he sent $5,000 to Washington.
In the following weeks many pledges matured and traveling agents
remitted their collections. Between November 4 and December
31, 1833, $19,000 poured into the Society's famished treasury.
During the last weeks of 1833, the society chartered two ships
and sent 108 emigrants of whom 79 were manumitted slaves.[40]

The crisis was not over. As the panic tightened, many who had
pledged in September and October were too pinched to pay in
December and January. When the seventeenth annual meeting
convened, the managers confessed that the society's debt exceeded
$40,000 and monthly receipts were slipping. Gurley talked of
resigning. "The crisis has arrived," the managers conceded.
"Thought, inquiry, feeling, are awake, and while the mind of the
whole nation is fast making up its permanent judgment in regard
to this Society, Providence is pleased to darken its way," they intoned. "But let no man's heart fail him. A good cause may seem
to be in danger; it can never suffer a lasting defeat." [41]

XVII

"WE ARE A NULLITY"

———◆◆◆◆▶———

THE COLONIZATION SOCIETY faced 1834 with considerably less optimism than it displayed in 1833. Debt gnawed its strength, antislavery jeers and epithets beclouded its reputation, and disease and crop failures beset the Liberians. For four days worried delegates at the seventeenth annual meeting examined the society's "unprecedented and alarming" financial afflictions. At length they prescribed new rules and policies. "To guard against such heavy embarrassments in the future," the delegates directed the managers to send out no emigrants "whilst they are under a debt exceeding $10,000." They urged the Colonial Agent to build a workhouse for the "improvident and idle," and they called for greater emphasis on agriculture to make the colony self-sufficient. Complaining that "friends of this Society do not give enough money," Gerrit Smith generously offered $5,000 if other men subscribed $45,000. Promptly, sixteen men, including Elliott Cresson, Benjamin F. Butler, and Chief Justice John Marshall, together pledged another $5,000.[1]

The board of managers, slightly reorganized, grimly resolved on retrenchment as the antidote to mismanagement. But their economies came perilously close to liquidation. To save $5,000 they declined to pay the salaries of all colonial officials, save the Colonial Agent, Physician, Secretary, and Storekeeper. In special acts revising the colonial regulations, they directed the Liberians to elect and support their own public officials. This measure, the managers proudly declared, pushed the colonists "a step nearer to the point where the Society will leave them entirely to self-government."

In addition, the managers ordered drastic economies in the

headquarters office. They discharged Secretary Gurley's assistants, cut the printings of the *African Repository* and annual reports, and pruned delinquent subscribers from the society's mailing list. They refused to hire new agents or replace those who resigned. For two years the society had no agent continuously in its employ. Finally, they ordered a complete analysis of the society's accounts, noting that "the absence, to some extent, of vouchers, or suitable explanations . . . and the general want of care and economy" made it impossible to determine the exact condition of the prostrate treasury.

With a bankrupt's hope that frank disclosure would absolve him of wrong-doing, the managers published the full story of their embarrassment in the *African Repository*. They confessed that they had overextended their treasury in chartering ships, buying supplies, and transporting hundreds of emigrants, and they conceded that they overestimated the "public liberality." In all, they owed $45,645.72. Though Theodore Frelinghuysen generously avowed that this amount was trifling and Gerrit Smith labeled the "general impression that there has been a great waste of funds . . . very erroneous," the public disclosures armed the antislavery press with evidence of mismanagement. They were gleeful over the managers' astonishing confession that 1,857 gallons of whiskey, brandy, and rum had been sold to natives by the colonial agent. The revelations did not ease the unhappy creditors. Throughout 1834, holders of worthless paper besieged the managers and demanded prompt payment.[2]

Frank confessions did not restore public confidence or increase collections. As the national panic tightened, the society's monthly receipts plummeted. Gerrit Smith's plan to raise $50,000 aborted. Only Smith honored his pledge. The managers thereupon conceived a plan to borrow money by distributing $50,000 in scrip among creditors and friends of the society. The scrip bore six percent interest and was redeemable in twelve years. In May, just as the panic hit bottom, the board desperately appealed to all auxiliaries for "their aid and influence in freeing it from pecuniary difficulty." Response was so poor that delegations of board members traveled from auxiliary to auxiliary, begging them to buy scrip and send donations.[3]

In the spring of 1834, Philip R. Fendall, the society's Recorder, toured Virginia, while Secretary Gurley traveled northward to Philadelphia and New York. Fendall's collections netted only $1,500. In Richmond he found that colonization sentiment had cooled because the free blacks staunchly refused to volunteer for transportation. The failure of the Virginia colonization appropriation of 1833 convinced many Virginians that the scheme was not practicable, and Fendall sourly concluded that many had favored colonization "only as a means of ridding the state of free people of colour." [4]

Gurley's tour was no less dismal. On all sides he saw the colonization movement in shambles. The society's monumental debt and the confusion sown by the antislavery forces had "weakened the confidence of the Northern public." At Philadelphia Gurley sadly observed that "the cause has lost ground greatly in the good opinion of the people here." Not one man would buy the society's scrip. Gurley heard whispers that "licentiousness & adultery" ruled the colony and that Colonial Agent Joseph Mechlin was the chief offender. "I can see too that people look coldly at us because we are poor, & hundreds who would have given when we were in prosperity, would not lift a hand to save us from ruin. Poor Human nature!" Greater humiliation followed. When Gurley asked to speak in a Presbyterian church, the elders haltingly replied that, "the church being new, & the seats not all sold, & a difference of opinion in regard to the merits of the Society," they deemed it inexpedient to grant permission.[5]

In New York city, prospects were just as dim. Merchants hard pressed by the panic frowned on poor credit risks. Banker Samuel Ward, "one of our richest & most liberal Friends," bluntly told Gurley not to expect a cent from the city. The New York city auxiliary, complaining that the parent society's debt resulted from mismanagement, declined to pour good money after bad. Angered managers of the local society spoke of founding their own settlement in Liberia. At the May anniversary meetings of various benevolent societies, Gurley discussed African colonization's prospects with delegates from the New England states. Some wanted a general convention to reorganize the society; others talked of forming a third society that would be broader than the Colonization Society but less "wild and raging" than the antislavery societies. The north was far ahead of the south in its demands for emancipation, Gurley recorded. Somehow the society had to reconcile the two sections. "What is most important, I think, is to induce the South to act with vigour, & the north not to act at all on slavery except as the South consent." But he admitted that "to control the rising elements of opinion & feeling on this great subject will require vast wisdom & energy." [6]

Repeatedly Gurley pleaded with the board of managers to appoint "judicious & powerful" agents for New York and the New England states. After Danforth's resignation early in 1834 and Finley's return to the west, the society had no agent in the whole northeast "to explain and defend the principles of the Society and counteract the well-organized opposition that has been rising against it." A John Breckinridge or a Leonard Bacon could raise from $30,000 to $50,000 in New York alone. Gurley urged the managers to offer a salary of $1,700 or more. "I am convinced it is the worst policy in the world to employ *cheap* agents." But the managers declined to burden their treasury with new agents. [7]

Painful forebodings gripped Gurley as he saw antislavery agents taking undisputed possession of the northeast. In speeches and conversations Gurley warned that the antislavery crusade threatened the "most fearful results." Antislavery agitators were ceaselessly stirring the "deepest and most terrible elements of society—elements which once wrought into fury, will shake the land, if not cover it with blood." Pointing to the French Revolution, he drew the grim lesson that "reason is powerless in the hurricane of the passions." These fears again assailed the troubled secretary when he attended the anniversary meeting of the American Anti-Slavery Society and listened to its leaders excoriate African colonization. "The tempest of passion on a question of deep, universal, & fearful interest," unless halted, "will sweep with fury over the land." [8]

Not long after Gurley left New York his predictions seemed to come true. During the summer heat violent antislavery riots exploded in New York city. On July 4, 1834, noisy disturbers broke up an antislavery meeting in Chatham Street Chapel. Four days later, members of the New York Musical Society battled a group of Negroes for possession of the hall. Fired by lurid newspaper reports, the tempo of riot quickened. On the next night a slavery debate in Clinton Hall ended with a mobbing. And the day after, rioters invaded Chatham Street Chapel and passed colonization resolutions, swarmed at the Bowery Theater to avenge anti-American insults lisped by an English actor, and then furiously demolished Lewis Tappan's house on Rose street. Armed clerks kept the shouting mob from the Tappan store, and pistol-carrying men protected the home of the Reverend Samuel H. Cox, recent convert to immediate emancipation. Negro dwellings and three churches were sacked or torn down, including St. Philip's, where pews and organ burned like a funeral pyre in the street.[9]

Horrified, the New York City Colonization Society's officers denied any responsibility for the riots or the colonization vows shouted in Chatham Street Chapel. Secretary Gurley agreed that violence and lawbreaking deserved "strong censure," but he drew the lesson that antislavery men had abused the privilege of free speech "by endeavouring to inflame the public mind" against the Constitution and the "peace and permanency of our happy Union." The riots were the natural consequences of antislavery's "offensive doctrines and proceedings." [10]

The riots reinvigorated antislavery men and stamped them with the zeal of martyrs. William Jay, son of the famous John Jay, hesitated no longer to take a place on the American Anti-Slavery Society's executive committee. Shortly after, he produced his probing, thoughtful *Inquiry into the Character and Tendency of the American Colonization, and American Anti-Slavery Societies.* Abandoning his earlier view that the Colonization Society was neither "a wicked conspiracy" nor "a panacea for slavery," Jay now asserted that colonization "vitiated the moral sense of the community, by reconciling public opinion to the continuance of slavery, and by aggravating those sinful prejudices against the free blacks." Coming from a man so highly placed in society, the charges stunned Chancellor James Kent and momentarily benumbed Theodore Frelinghuysen.[11]

The contagion of renunciation was spreading. The Reverend Amos Phelps publicly repented colonization—"I now see the error and my sin"—and eagerly propagated the doctrines of antislavery. In 1834, as the agent of the American Anti-Slavery Society he gathered the signatures of 125 American clergymen who willingly branded slavery a sin and colonization a false remedy. "The time has now come when the friends of God and man ought to take a higher stand, and adopt and act on principles which lay the axe *directly* at the root of the tree." [12]

The most sensational renegade proved to be James G. Birney, the Colonization Society's permanent agent for the southwest. In the fall of 1833, Birney quit his agency and left Alabama, saying gloomily that the southwestern states would do nothing for colonization or emancipation. After his return to Kentucky, the state colonization society there elected him a vice-president, but Birney's zeal had greatly diminished. In the spring of 1834 he renewed his acquaintanceship with Theodore Dwight Weld, who, as a temperance lecturer, had visited Birney's home in Huntsville, Alabama. Weld was now a student at Lane Seminary near Cincinnati and one of Tappan's antislavery agents in the west. Through Weld's labors, the seminary had gained notoriety in the east for its prolonged debates over antislavery and colonization that culminated in the formation of an antislavery society among the students. Without difficulty Weld persuaded Birney to renounce African colonization. Many influential men, he told Birney, were daily abandoning the movement, and Birney's defection, if well advertised and properly timed, would hurry many more who still hesitated. "Upon that class of mind your communication will tell with *prodigious force*." [13] Weld secured promises from the Tappans that they would find work for Birney. "I am now ready, my dear brother, to take my stand for life for the cause of God and liberty in our country, if I can see a fair prospect of providing for my family," Birney told Weld. The Tappans offered Birney $1,500 to become an agent of the American Anti-Slavery Society for one year. [14]

Declining to put his letter in the New York *Evangelist* because it would impute some connection with northern antislavery men, Birney printed his blast in the Lexington *Intelligencer*. African colonization, Birney charged, was merely "an opiate to the consciences" of many Americans who would otherwise "feel deeply and keenly, the injustice and the sin of slavery." The "union of

benevolence and selfishness" was incongruous and "mutually destructive." Antislavery clichés filled Birney's chastisement of
colonization: "heartless and grinding oppression," "open and
crushing injustice," "a mockery of all mercy." Weld and other
antislavery men had gone over the whole manuscript line by line
and offered several suggestions. Weld was especially anxious that
Birney "command and encourage the formation of Anti-Slavery
Societies" and discredit the "hue and cry about the dissolution of
the Union being effected by the foundation of such societies." But
Birney declined to announce his conversion. Instead, he untruth-
fully claimed that he had no acquaintance "either personally or
by literary correspondence with any of the northern abolitionists." [15]

Antislavery students at Lane bundled extra copies off to the
east, and special editions of Birney's *Letter on Colonization* soon
splashed from antislavery presses. The New York edition knowingly asserted that "no man has a better knowledge of colonization, and its practical effects at the south. . . . Such a man has a
right to be heard, and his arguments should be weighed with respect by every citizen of this nation." Lewis Tappan read the turn-
coat confession "with tears of joy and gratitude." Elizur Wright,
Jr., was "electrified" and exclaimed that Birney *"must be supported."* [16]

Colonizationists were stunned. Cresson angrily declared that
Birney's colonization essays, recently reprinted in the *African
Repository,* offered "good evidence that *he never understood* the
system." He called for an "exposure of his duplicity." Walter
Lowrie of the board of managers answered Birney in the *African
Repository,* saying that Birney's friends had been preparing to
defend him against the charge of *"pro-slavery* tendency" and then
suddenly found it necessary to defend the society "against the
Parthian warfare of the fugitive officer." He was shocked by the
"charge of combined duplicity, cruelty and malignity . . . by
an accuser whose lips were almost warm with vows of affection." [17]

Colonization was losing its charm for another noted colonizationist. Gerrit Smith, the society's largest contributor, was slip-
ping away. At Weld's bidding, Birney solicited Smith's conversion. "If that man could be divorced from the delusive sorcery of

Colonizationism, an immense and incalculable influence would be secured to the cause of Abolition," Weld had assured Birney. After a year of inner struggle, Smith gave up the society as a lost cause. Late in 1835, Birney persuaded him to make a *"formal separation*—somewhat in the way I did—and giving your reasons for it." In his valedictory, Smith accused the Colonization Society of being more interested in fighting antislavery men than in colonizing free Negroes. Being a gentleman, he paid the Colonization Society $3,000 pledged years before. Margaret Mercer, Virginia's lady colonizationist, preemptorily ended her friendship with Smith, saying, "This very morning I have prayed that your dogmatical, opinionated, persecuting spirit might be changed for one more calculated to do good." [18]

Meanwhile "third organizers" gathered in Boston to form the American Union for the Relief and Improvement of the Colored Race. Organized by one hundred men from ten states with the single purpose of uplifting the Negro race, it sought a common ground for antislavery colonizationists and mild abolitionists. Arthur Tappan contributed $5,000. Willbur Fisk, Lyman Beecher, and Leonard Bacon gave the new society their blessings. Secretary Gurley expected no serious competition from the new association, because many of its members were "decided Friends of African Colonization." But he chided the managers of the Colonization Society, saying the American Union organized because no colonization agent had visited New England in nearly two years. The American Union appealed to moderate antislavery men, but Garrison's attacks and a general lack of enthusiasm for a fusion society quickly smothered the unwanted infant.[19]

In July, 1834, the Reverend Robert J. Breckinridge and his brother John visited Boston to inspect the state of colonization sentiment. His report was somber. "Colonization is dead, in all this region; and the principles of our parent society, will never revive here any more." The society's reluctance to become vigorously antislavery had alienated friends. Many New Englanders, he warned, "will very soon become rampant abolition men. Thousands are so already; thousands more on the fence; and all our friends silenced—by the war." Robert S. Finley, touring Ohio and Kentucky, sent corroborating reports of colonization's downfall. "The abolitionists are gaining ground very rapidly both in Kentucky & in this State," he reported. "They are deluging the country with their publications, and are sending their travelling agents everywhere." With dismay he noted that "the principles that we act upon are becoming generally popular" but antislavery's "ceaseless *calumnies*" had destroyed all confidence in the parent society. "What ought to be done, I know not," Finley confessed. Unable to collect enough to pay expenses, he resigned his agency.[20]

Single defectors and "third organizers" betokened decay, but the defections of large and wealthy auxiliaries revealed that the movement, as a national, united force, was moribund. The first symptom of paralysis was the withdrawal of the Maryland State Colonization Society. As early as 1831, Maryland colonization leaders discovered that they could raise more money in the state by outfitting their own expeditions. With the parent society's permission, the auxiliary sent out the *Orion* with thirty-one passengers. Early in 1832, during the Nat Turner excitement, the Maryland legislature incorporated the state society and granted it $20,000 a year for ten years to remove Maryland's manumitted slaves. Those who refused to emigrate could be ejected from the state or returned to slavery. Officers of the state society became managers of the state fund. Shortly after, the Maryland society, aided by state money, sent the *Lafayette* to Liberia with 144 colonists.[21]

Serious differences arose between the parent society and its auxiliary when the *Lafayette's* crew brought back stories of illness, mismanagement, and poverty at Liberia. The Maryland managers, sharply complaining that such woeful reports would destroy public support, declared they would not "incur the responsibility of advising another emigrant to go out, whilst such a shape of things exist." In addition, the question of emancipation beclouded relations between the parent and offspring societies. Unlike the national society, which refused to broaden its constitutional objectives to include the gradual abolition of slavery, the Maryland society declared emancipation to be one of its principal goals. John H. B. Latrobe, one of the state fund managers, frankly explained that the parent society had proved that "colonies of colored people, capable of self defence, self support, and self government could be founded on the coast of Africa," and the Maryland society now sought to prove that African colonization could make slave states into free states. Maryland's example would open the way to emancipation for all slave states.[22]

Alarmed by Maryland's drift toward separation, the board of managers at Washington tried to persuade Latrobe and his colleagues that independent action would prove "very injurious," "pernicious," and perhaps fatal to the entire colonization movement. The success of the scheme, they argued, depended on a "systematic course of measures" flowing from central headquarters at Washington, D.C. After experimenting with formulas for sharing costs, the Maryland society dissolved its formal connections with the national body. The parent society had no power to prevent the divorce and no will to compromise. After 1833, there were two societies, two movements, and two colonies. The independent society hired its own agents to collect funds in Maryland, and later, competing with the parent society, it commissioned agents to scout funds in New England and the western states.[23]

In 1834, with the Colonization Society's grudging permission, the errant auxiliary began its own colony at Cape Palmas, a high peninsula separated from the mainland by a narrow sandy isthmus. The natives sold it for muskets, powder, cloth, kettles, cutlasses, beads, pots, looking glasses, and other trinkets. In many respects, Maryland in Liberia was a small scale replica of the older colony, but it eschewed commerce for agriculture and embraced total abstinence. Dr. James Hall, former colonial physician at Monrovia, recruited settlers at Monrovia and moved to Cape Palmas as colonial agent of the Maryland society. Plagued by hostile natives, shortages of supplies, and disagreements over land distribution, the colonists ignored agriculture, demanded food rations from the colonial storehouse, and grumbled at the "stingy" policies of the Maryland managers.[24]

The appearance of the Maryland scheme and its bold antislavery pronouncements baffled William Lloyd Garrison. Colonization, he wryly observed, "is wondrously 'given to change'; sometimes urging itself on us in one form and with one set of reasons, and then again in a new form and with newer and better reasons." But he maintained that colonization even in this unfamiliar garb "drained off" the emancipation spirit in Maryland, compelled manumitted Negroes to emigrate, and fostered race prejudice. Lauding the Maryland plan, Robert S. Finley exultingly told John H. B. Latrobe that the abolitionists *"squirm* under the new announcement of your scheme. 'It pulls all their teeth out.' " [25]

With Maryland as bellwether, New York and Pennsylvania colonizationists scanned the paths of independent action. Angered and embarrassed by the parent society's financial indiscretions, they resolved to retain part of their funds for their own use. In Philadelphia, the energetic Young Men's Colonization Society superseded the older Pennsylvania Colonization Society and emerged an aggressive exponent of local action. Elliott Cresson, secretary of the Young Men's auxiliary, led the clamor for separation. After his ignominious return from Great Britain late in 1833, Cresson nursed his grudges against Secretary Gurley and the board of managers. He blamed them for his difficulties in Britain and jeered that the burdensome debt was evidence of "suicidal" mismanagement. He collected grievances and urged Philadelphians to establish their own settlement to be named Penn or Benezet and stocked with *"pious, temperate"* colonists.[26]

Meanwhile New York city colonizationists agreed that "there has been an extravagant and heedless expenditure of money in the colony," "injudicious . . . and unfortunate management," and a "want of attention and efficient supervision." In February, 1834, they announced that they were about to found a new community in Liberia that was to be distinctly agricultural and temperance-minded. Prospective colonists would have to undergo strict examination for moral character.[27]

Secretary Gurley watched these moves with great alarm, exclaiming "if our Board gives up the control of the funds raised for colonization, it gives up every thing. If the state societies take colonization into their hands, we are a nullity." But Gurley's pleas and the managers' exhortations could not stop the determined auxiliaries. By the end of 1834 Philadelphia and New York colonizationists had joined forces and founded a new settlement on the St. John's river. The tiny Bassa Cove community was dedicated to temperance and Quaker peace principles.[28]

The Philadelphia and New York societies pledged continued loyalty to the parent society, but they declined to remit any money until Bassa Cove was thriving. The parent board angrily complained that "every one acquainted with the expense of founding a new colony . . . must regard such a proposal as significant of little more than kindness and good will to the Parent Society." The managers bluntly accused the Philadelphia society of styling itself an auxiliary but in fact operating "an independent colony to be governed exclusively by its own laws" and strangling the parent society by withholding needed funds. After elaborate negotiations in Washington, both Philadelphia and New York societies agreed to remit 30 percent of their collections and to raise immediately $15,000 in each city. In addition, they promised to increase their annual contribution to 50 percent after Bassa Cove was securely planted.[29]

To raise funds the Philadelphia and New York societies argued that their colonization principles embraced emancipation. A Philadelphia orator boldly claimed that *"Ten thousand slaves would at this moment be released from thraldom, if they could be transported from the country."* John Breckinridge, president of the Philadelphia society, told a New York audience that he was an abolitionist "of the good old school of John Jay and Benjamin Franklin" and that "every consistent Christian was an abolitionist, in the right sense of that much abused term." He urged the parent society, burdened by southern auxiliaries, to remain neutral on the slavery issue, while the New York and Philadelphia auxiliaries tried to *"stave off* the *goths & vandals* of Garrisonism, in a way which you cannot." [30]

At Washington the managers worried over this obvious deviation from the parent society's constitutional objective, and they worried even more when the Philadelphia and New York auxiliaries failed to transmit the promised funds. Treasurer Joseph Gales, Sr., and the Reverend William Hawley hurried to New York when Walter Lowrie and the Reverend James Laurie failed in their mission to get money. Public meetings "respectably and numerously attended" had raised only a fraction of the $15,000 promised by both auxiliaries. Unexpected disasters were swallowing all funds raised by New York and Philadelphia.[31]

The New York and Philadelphia colonizationists quickly learned the heartaches of colonial management. The pacific Bassa Cove settlers were poorly prepared for a surprise attack led by the native subjects of King Joe Harris. Twenty colonists perished in a midnight massacre, and the screaming warriors drove the rest away at spear point. Sick, wounded, and bewildered, the survivors stumbled into the forest and fled to Monrovia. In 1836, at great cost and labor, the disheartened Philadelphia board sent out a mercy vessel laden with military stores, arms, clothing, and food. It abandoned earlier professions of peace principles. New York cooperated with the Philadelphia colonizationists in sending nearly two hundred additional colonists to rebuild Bassa Cove. By 1838, the colony was restored but it was not prosperous.[32]

Unperturbed by these examples, the Mississippi Colonization Society, spurred on by Robert S. Finley who served briefly as its agent, announced in 1836 that it would establish a separate colony on the Sinou river, 130 miles south of Monrovia. Composed of wealthy slaveholders in southwestern Mississippi who wished to rid themselves of an infinitesimal free Negro population, the state society withheld its funds to the parent society because of a disagreement over the fate of a loan entrusted to the Washington headquarters. At Finley's urging Louisiana colonizationists pledged cooperation to the Mississippi society, and in 1838, they launched their colony, Mississippi in Africa, a small, poverty-stricken settlement centering around Greenville, the village capital. Mississippi's colonization zeal soon evaporated. Economic depression crippled the society's treasury and natives killed Governor Josiah F. C. Finley, Robert S. Finley's brother. After 1840, the tiny colony lived in perpetual poverty.[33]

Faced with secession on all sides, the Colonization Society languished. Its income dropped disastrously. Receipts totaling $48,000 in 1835 dropped to $35,000, then to $27,000, and by November, 1838, the parent society had gathered only $10,000. The severe panic beginning in 1837 and extending into the early 1840s merely aggravated the society's financial paralysis. By August, 1838, the society had succeeded in selling only half of its loan scrip. Creditors angrily called for their money. Some threatened lawsuits. Merchant-shipper John Hanson of Philadelphia, claimant for $20,000, retired from the Liberian trade, calling Africa "that *Golgotha* of the white man." A Boston creditor complained of the society's "want of *Christian* honesty," and a Philadelphia merchant bitterly exclaimed, "we think it is high time the Society was broken up as it has been begging and swindling the American people long enough." [34]

Meanwhile, the Philadelphia and New York auxiliaries, ignoring their agreement to pay 30 percent of their collections, paid no money to the parent society on the pretext that the colonial agent at Monrovia had incurred a debt to the New York society. Moreover, they proposed to sever all ties with the parent society after paying $4,000 toward the debt. The Washington managers surrendered. After January, 1837, the auxiliaries agreed to pay 10 percent on all future collections, and the parent society drastically remodeled its government to give the northern auxiliaries the dominant voice in its affairs. [35]

Under its new constitution, adopted in 1838, the American Colonization Society became a federation of state auxiliaries. Each state was entitled to representation on the new board of directors in proportion to its contributions and the size of its colony. The state societies reserved the right to appropriate their own collections and to "enjoy all the proprietary rights, authorities and jurisdiction" not specifically delegated to the directors. Amendments to the new constitution could originate only with the state societies and required approval of two-thirds of the directors. [36]

The new constitution revolutionized the society. The only elected officers were the president and vice-presidents. The board of managers disbanded, and Ralph R. Gurley became an appointee of the new board of directors. He continued as secretary at their discretion. Pennsylvania and New York representatives dominated the board and controlled the society. Their instrument was Judge Samuel Wilkeson, a wealthy real estate promoter from Buffalo, New York, and a relative by marriage of Secretary Gurley. As president of the board and chairman of the executive committee, Wilkeson exercised vast power over all aspects of the

Colonization Society. Declining any salary, the bluff, gouty businessman sternly set about to save the ailing society. He looked upon his mission as akin to that of a receiver for a bankrupt concern. With the zeal of a military dictator, he discharged clerks, reduced salaries, promulgated new rules for the headquarters offices, drew up strict orders for a host of new agents, and ordered a cease-fire in the war with antislavery agitators. Agents were to collect money and ignore time-consuming controversy.[37]

Until his resignation late in 1841, Wilkeson ruled with a firm hand. His businesslike procedures succeeded in restoring the society's broken finances. By 1842 he had paid off most of the "old debt," sometimes by compelling weary creditors to accept fifty cents on the dollar. In his gruff, no-nonsense manner, he persuaded the errant auxiliaries to remit larger sums to the parent society. Under his regime, the Mississippi and Louisiana societies returned to their auxiliary status and surrendered control over the Sinoٸ settlement. For two years Wilkeson personally owned the *African Repository* and under his proprietorship it prospered. When he retired, the society's annual receipts had risen to $54,000.[38]

During Wilkeson's regime, Ralph R. Gurley spent most of his time canvassing the United States for funds. He made two long tours of the west, labored in the south without success, and revisited New England. Meanwhile, Wilkeson assumed all of Gurley's former duties at the headquarters offices, reduced Gurley's salary, and insisted on constitutional revisions excluding the secretary from the executive committee. In 1840, with Wilkeson's grudging consent, Gurley secured funds from New York colonizationists to go to England to collaborate with the British African Civilization Society and to survey the British government's intentions in west Africa. During Gurley's prolonged absence, Wilkeson and the directors summarily deposed the absent secretary.

Undaunted, Gurley returned and vindicated himself. In his long account of his British tour, Gurley aired his grievances against Wilkeson and exposed the political maneuvers used to remove him from office. After Wilkeson's retirement, Gurley returned to his old post. But his tenure was brief. In 1844, his enemies, led by Elliott Cresson of Philadelphia, replaced him with the Reverend William McLain, a traveling agent. Cresson, urging the headquarters be moved to Philadelphia, branded Gurley a "modern Machiavelli, destitute of all energy save but for purposes of mischief." [39]

Gurley's second dismissal splintered the society. It alienated the New York city and District of Columbia auxiliaries who withheld further donations. Philanthropist John McDonogh of New Orleans coldly refused to give the parent society any aid. The Mississippi society bickered with the new secretary. Calling Gurley a "traitor" and a "miserable, soulless ingrate," Cresson threatened to take the Pennsylvania society out of the organization if it returned to "his wilful & imbecile sway." [40]

Plagued with internal bickerings, the society lingered on. Wilkeson's counting-house nostrums restored the society's finances, but they did not recapture the vitality of the movement. Despite all, the movement had died. The spirit of growing and doing was still. The forward thrust had wilted, and revitalizing it was a task that exceeded the ability and imagination of the Buffalo real estate merchant. Ironically, the idea of colonization as a solution to the race question was still popular, but the society and its friends were not. Through the 1850s the forlorn hope for a miraculous revival of public confidence animated the faithful few who still clung to the aging Colonization Society.

XVIII

RETREAT TO EMIGRATION

DURING THE 1840s the strife-torn, debt-ridden American Colonization Society fought for its existence. Public interest had reached bottom. The "war" with the antislavery forces had shorn away friends and confused others. Debt and mismanagement had shriveled the society's credit. As an effective, forceful movement African colonization was virtually dead. But despite all obstacles, the parent society still labored to revive it. Under the leadership of William McLain, John B. Pinney, Elliott Cresson, Anson G. Phelps, and Joseph Tracy, the society resumed sending small groups of colonists to Liberia. A few agents tried to gather donations, but annual receipts fluctuated unpredictably. In 1846, after a harvest of large legacies from "several valued friends and liberal contributors" the parent society finally paid off its thirteen-year-old debt, but the directors' doxology—"the cause is in a healthful and vigorous condition"—still rang hollow. The following year receipts dropped precipitously and the directors mournfully noted that "our present report opens with no such record of departed friends." [1]

The troubled society still had one great liability—Liberia. It was a dead weight on the society's finances. In addition, its management was complex and puzzling. By the late 1840s Liberia's population, not counting the native inhabitants, reached 3,000. Dissatisfaction with colonial laws sometimes exploded into riot. Native wars broke out along the borders when the aggressive colony absorbed neighboring territory. Exploited by the American emigrants and their descendants, natives living in the colony's back country grew restive. Confusion over political jurisdictions

pitted the independent settlements against the Monrovia government. Spurred by these grievances, the directors in 1839 proclaimed the "Commonwealth of Liberia," a union of all independent settlements, save Maryland in Liberia. They delegated
greater powers to the Colonial Council, and they dignified their
agent with the title of Governor. Symbolizing the union, Thomas
Buchanan, the Pennsylvania–New York agent at Bassa Cove, became the first governor of the commonwealth. Immediately, two
parties sprang up, Buchanan's "Government Party" and Methodist missionary John Seys's party. Disputes between them over
the exact nature of the Governor's powers came close to civil war.
At length the parent society banished Seys, and shortly after, in
September, 1841, Buchanan died of fever.[2]

Joseph Jenkins Roberts, a well-to-do Monrovia merchant who
had emigrated from Virginia, succeeded Buchanan as governor.
Under his regime Liberia faced serious problems related to its
anomalous political status. British merchants from Sierra Leone
flouted Liberian commerce regulations and colonial duties, arguing that Liberia, the possession of a private association, was
neither a sovereign power nor a bona fide colony of a nation.
British threats to seize Liberian territory and suppress Liberian
trade in retaliation for fines and punishments imposed on British
traders forced the Colonization Society to seek new arrangements.
The United States government refused to claim sovereignty over
the colony, and in 1846, just as the society was shedding its oner-
ous debt, the directors ordered the Liberians to proclaim their
independence. With restrained joy, the colonists complied, thanking the society for its generosity and kindness, and drew up a
popular constitution that excluded the vast native population. In
1848 the Republic of Liberia elected Joseph J. Roberts its first
president. Maryland in Liberia, imitating Liberia's example, also
became a republic, but, in 1857, after a native war nearly wiped
out the Cape Palmas settlement, the two republics united. Although several nations, including Great Britain and France, recognized the tiny republic, the United States withheld formal
recognition until 1862.[3]

With the shedding of its colony the American Colonization Society entered a new phase. After 1847 it no longer was a colo-

nizing enterprise. It became an emigration agency. Aware of the
radical change in the society's work, the directors warned friends
of the society not to conclude that their labors were done. Henceforth the society would serve as "helper and supporter" instead
of "planter and protector." The directors solemnly pledged to devote their future efforts to sending emigrants to help build the
Liberian republic.[4]

True to their pledge, the directors diligently gathered funds
and emigrants. From 1848 to 1854 they chartered forty-one ships
and sent nearly four thousand Negroes to Liberia. To finance
these numerous sailings they hastened agents into "fields almost
abandoned entirely as barren and unfruitful." State societies, especially in Massachusetts, New York, New Jersey, Pennsylvania,
and Kentucky, also engaged agents to gather emigrants and
money. In 1847 the aged Heman Humphrey, retired president of
Amherst College, succeeded in recapturing pulpits in the "principal churches" of Boston and New York. The directors marveled,
for the churches had refused to allow colonization or antislavery
agents to use their pulpits during their war for public support.
They saw signs of reawakening interest. Agent David Christy
labored in Ohio, concentrating his energies on the legislature,
while the Reverend James Mitchell toured Indiana, Illinois, Mich-
igan, Wisconsin, and Iowa, organizing new state auxiliaries and
soliciting small sums. In 1853 the parent society called its best
fund raiser into action. As "Traveling General Agent," Ralph
Randolph Gurley toured Georgia, New Jersey, New York, Connecticut, and Vermont.[5]

With these renewed efforts the society steadily increased its
annual receipts from $29,000 in 1847 to $97,000 in 1851. A
new era of prosperity had opened. In the next decade the society's lowest annual income was $55,000, and its highest, in
1859, exceeded $160,000. Despite these impressive sums the
directors frequently overreached their means and incurred annual deficits. In 1848 the deficit was a mere $7,000, but six years
later it had boldly grown to $32,000.[6]

As before, large legacies and gifts extinguished the Colonization Society's debt. Old friends and benefactors were dying. Their
bequests significantly augmented the society's slim income from

traveling agents and auxiliaries. In the late 1840s the Waldo family of Worcester, Massachusetts, left legacies totaling almost $24,000. At the turn of the decade William Short of Philadelphia and Augustus Graham of Brooklyn, New York, each bequeathed $10,000. In 1856 the will of David Hunt of Woodlawn, Mississippi, provided $45,000. Two years later, the bequest of John McDonogh of New Orleans, a veteran benefactor, yielded $83,-000. Smaller legacies totaling thousands of dollars proportionately aided the society's emigration work. Legacies were uncertain sources, however, and sometimes ensnarled the society in protracted legal battles with disappointed heirs. "It is melancholy to reflect how many good intentions and liberal purposes are entirely frustrated," the directors moaned, "by distant and unscrupulous heirs!" [7]

The society's new prosperity in the 1850s enabled the directors to fulfill thirty-year-old dreams. In April, 1856, the dying John Stevens of Talbot, Maryland, dramatically gave the society $36,-000 to build its own emigrant ship. Late in 1856 the *Mary Caroline Stevens* made its first voyage to Liberia. It completed a dozen sailings before the Civil War. In 1860 the society built an imposing headquarters building with surplus funds accumulated from large legacies. The four-story building on Pennsylvania Avenue at 4½ Street rested on a cement foundation. The first floor was constructed of cast iron, and the upper floors were of brick and stone. There was a convention hall, committee rooms, and offices for secretaries and officials. [8]

To the directors' manifest delight there were numerous signs that their cause was gaining ground. Annual receipts rose, the Maryland society moved to reunite with the parent society, and former friends, including James G. Birney, once again urged free Negroes to emigrate to Liberia. The country's foremost female hater of slavery, Harriet Beecher Stowe, author of *Uncle Tom's Cabin,* sent George and Eliza Harris, her fictional offspring, to Liberia. George explained that "the desire and yearning of my soul is for an African *nationality*. I want a people that shall have a tangible, separate existence of its own." [9]

More significant support came from several state legislatures that warmly advocated the early removal of "Africans" from the

United States. In 1850 the Virginia legislature set aside $30,000 annually for five years to support and encourage emigration. The grateful Colonization Society greeted Virginia's aid as "a great moral demonstration of the propriety and necessity of *state action!*" The governor of Indiana called for the removal of free Negroes from his state, and the Indiana constitutional convention urged heavy fines on all free Negroes or mulattoes who entered the state. Similar measures came before the lawmakers of Ohio and Iowa. In 1852 New Jersey's legislature voted $1,000 for two years to help Liberia-bound emigrants, and in 1855 it increased the appropriations to $4,000. Pennsylvania followed New Jersey's example and appropriated $2,000. Missouri lawmakers agreed to give the Colonization Society $3,000 for ten years to remove free Negroes from their state. The Maryland legislature renewed its aid in 1852, reserving $10,000 a year for six years for African emigration.[10]

Mindful of this growing sentiment for removal and expulsion, free Negro spokesmen reexamined emigration plans. Throughout the 1840s and 1850s they remained suspicious of the Colonization Society and Liberia, but they did not ignore other sites. Agents of planters in Trinidad, Jamaica, and British Guiana readily recruited hundred of emigrants in New York, Philadelphia, Boston, and Baltimore. In 1853 a Negro convention in Cleveland appointed agents to explore opportunities for mass emigration to Haiti, Central America, and the Niger Valley. Martin R. Delaney journeyed to Africa and concluded several treaties with African tribal chieftans in the Niger region who agreed to accept Negro settlers from the United States. James T. Holly investigated Haiti. Later Negro conventions at Cleveland in 1854 and Chatham, West Canada, in 1856, discussed the relative merits of Africa and Haiti. At length the Negro delegates turned to James Redpath, a young Scottish journalist and adventurer, for more detailed information about Haiti. Late in the 1850s Redpath, an employee of the Haitian government, launched a campaign to persuade American Negroes to seek new homes and full citizenship in the island republic. Several hundred emigrated, but the outbreak of the Civil War and reports of mismanagement and abuse in Haiti brought an early end to Redpath's work. Most of the disillusioned emigrants hastily returned to the United States.[11]

Inspired by the state legislatures' testimonials, the Colonization Society again looked to the federal government for approval and aid. Their hopes soared when prominent politicians representing all three branches of the federal government publicly applauded the society's work. Robert J. Walker, Daniel Webster, Edward Everett, Henry Clay, Stephen A. Douglas, Justice James M. Wayne, and President Millard Fillmore attended the society's annual meetings. In his famous Seventh of March speech in 1850, Webster had called for federal appropriations for African colonization. At the society's annual meeting early in 1852 he apologized for not actively working for the society after 1817, but he belatedly assured fellow colonizationists that "I have, nevertheless, never for a moment entertained a doubt that its object was useful" and that emigration to Africa "is destined to produce great good." A year later Secretary of State Edward Everett of Massachusetts repeated Webster's praise and deplored the "unmerited odium" endured by colonizationists. He commended them for their help in suppressing the African slave trade.[12]

In 1857 even the Supreme Court seemed to point to removal. The celebrated Dred Scott decision closed the door to Negro citizenship in the United States and insisted that Negroes were in reality Africans. An obscure Illinois politician, who otherwise reprobated the Dred Scott ruling as a Democratic plot to spread slavery, agreed that the Negro should not have citizenship. Abraham Lincoln, campaigning for the United States Senate in 1858, flatly asserted, "I am not in favor of negro citizenship" or "bringing about in any way the social and political equality of the white and black races." Echoing Jefferson, he declared that there was a "physical difference between the white and black races which I believe for ever forbids the two races living together on terms of social and political equality." [13]

The Colonization Society and its supporters appealed to Congress for postal subsidies to launch a steamship line to Liberia. Mail contracts would facilitate emigration, they argued. The society also pressed for diplomatic recognition of the small republic. Although it did not succeed in either of these efforts, the society did persuade Congress to appropriate money to resettle four hundred recaptives seized from the slave ship *Echo* and dumped by the Navy on Liberian shores. In 1855 Congress also agreed to station a consul at Monrovia.[14]

By 1858 the Navy's alert African squadron was rescuing hundreds of Africans from the reviving slave trade. Faced with the problem of finding homes for these recaptives, President James Buchanan unhesitatingly turned to the Colonization Society. The government contracted to pay the society $50 for every recaptive transported to Liberia and $100 to maintain each. The Society's leaders cheerfully undertook the task, believing it to be another step toward federal support in removing free Negroes as well. Unprepared for the magnitude of the work, the society's agents in one year received over four thousand recaptives from the Navy. At the insistence of Liberian officials, the society transferred the money and the contracts to Liberia. Within a short time, corrupt Liberian politicians squandered the funds entrusted to them and mistreated and starved the helpless recaptives. The society, now with no means to support its rescued slaves, appealed to the government for $380,000, but Abraham Lincoln's administration delayed payment.[15]

The Civil War and the sudden unleashing of thousands of slaves offered an unparalleled opportunity for mass colonization and emigration projects under government sponsorship. Lincoln's war administration looked for ways of disposing of "contrabands," thousands of displaced slaves who trailed after Union armies. In 1862, after emancipating slaves in the District of Columbia, Congress appropriated $600,000 to colonize the freedmen. Immediately, lobbyists representing Haitian, Liberian, and Central American schemes besieged Lincoln's "Commissioner of Emigration," James Mitchell, former agent of the American Colonization Society. Ignoring Liberia and African colonization, Mitchell investigated schemes for landing contrabands and freedmen at the Danish West Indies, Dutch Guiana, British Guiana, British Honduras, Guadaloupe, and Ecuador.

Meanwhile, Secretary of the Interior Caleb B. Smith, under orders from President Lincoln, also studied colonization and emigration projects. Resentful of Mitchell's independent commission from the president, Secretary Smith ignored the "Commissioner of Emigration" and made separate arrangements with the American-owned Chiriqui Improvement Company which held coal and railroad concessions in New Granada's Panama isthmus. Senator Samuel C. Pomeroy, serving as government agent to organize expeditions and supervise settlements, quickly spent $25,000 without being able to give a satisfactory accounting. Before Pomeroy could send an emigrant ship to the proposed "Colony of Linconia," Secretary of State William H. Seward ordered a halt to the project. Central American ministers, mindful of previous filibustering projects, angrily complained that the United States government was preparing to intrude into their territories, create alien colonies, and defy the sovereignty of the Central American republics.

A few months later, President Lincoln signed a contract with one Bernard Kock who proposed to launch a Negro colony on lands he had leased at Ile à Vache, Haiti. Commissioner Mitchell arranged the contract. At the last minute, the Secretary of the Interior interproposed to cancel the contract. Federal officials discovered, belatedly, that Kock was a crook. A few months later, Lincoln formally approved a similar contract with two prominent New York merchants, Paul S. Forbes and Charles K. Tuckerman, who agreed to colonize five hundred contrabands at Haiti for $50 per Negro. Their agent, Lincoln later learned, was the scoundrel Bernard Kock. In 1863 Kock led several hundred contrabands to Ile à Vache, confiscated their American dollars, and neglected to feed or house them. Death and disease crippled the tiny settlement, Kock fled for his life when the angry settlers discovered his perfidy, and, on Lincoln's orders, a relief vessel smuggled the survivors back to the United States. The federal government coldly refused to pay Tuckerman's and Forbes's bill for $80,000. The angry business men then attempted to compel payment by publishing their version of the fiasco.

Though the Ile à Vache disaster cooled Lincoln's interest in colonization and emigration schemes, he continued to believe that removal was the true solution to the race question. Emancipation merely sharpened the issue. Senators James Lane of Kansas and James R. Doolittle of Wisconsin spoke of making Texas a Negro state, but after 1863 the War Department found the contrabands and freedmen more useful as servants, laborers, and soldiers than as diseased colonists wasting away in some tropical exile.

The American Colonization Society's leaders watched in amazement as Lincoln's administration, spurning Liberia, toyed with first one plan and then another. In vain they urged the harried war leader to send emigrants to the African republic. Lincoln privately agreed with President Roberts of Liberia that Africa was the logical place for American Negroes, but he continued to endorse Central American ventures. In 1864 and 1865 leaders of the Colonization Society saw that confusion occasioned by the Civil War was resulting in a policy by default. Lacking a workable plan for systematic removal and a firm hand to administer it, the United States would keep its freedmen indefinitely. American Negroes, hoping for full citizenship, refused to volunteer for Liberia. The Colonization Society had to recruit its emigrants in the Barbados.[16]

With the end of the war, the abolition of slavery, and the adoption of the Fourteenth Amendment conferring citizenship on the freedmen, all schemes for wholesale removal were forever outmoded. The Colonization Society, now an emigration society, verged on extinction. In 1867 it celebrated its fiftieth birthday, proudly noting that in its effort to prove colonization practicable, it had collected $2,500,000 and transported twelve thousand Negroes to Africa. In a last effort to secure government aid, the society persuaded Thaddeus Stevens to include $50,000 in the House Deficiency Appropriation Bill to help emigrant parties reach Liberia. But there was no room in reconstruction plans for African colonization or emigration. Congress refused the request and ridiculed the society. One representative sarcastically suggested that Liberia might become the nation's sixth military district in the congressional reconstruction program.[17]

After 1865 the dwindling society lingered on, liquidating assets and feebly pleading for aid as an emigration, education, and missionary enterprise. Its servants and many devoted members grew old and died, state auxiliaries disappeared, and their delegates ceased to attend annual meetings. Legacies became rare. Entrusted with the care of certain education funds bound up in legal technicalities and nourished by tradition, pride, and a sense of sacred duty, the society clung to life. Secretary William Coppinger devoted his life to the society's declining years. In 1838 at the age of ten he had begun his long career with the Colonization Society as an office boy in the Pennsylvania society. When he died in 1892 the Colonization Society had all but disappeared. Surviving members agreed that the society's aim was the promotion of African civilization and the strengthening of Liberia. But Liberia was decaying too. Both Great Britain and France compelled the friendless republic to surrender significant portions of its territories to their adjacent colonies. By 1900 Liberia was confined to three hundred fifty miles of African seacoast with an interior two hundred miles deep. Its population consisted of twenty thousand "civilized people," the descendants of the American Negroes, and perhaps one million natives. As in Ashmun's day, agriculture was still in a rudimentary state.[18]

By 1909 five surviving members loyally kept the society alive. At last they bequeathed the association's dusty letter books and yellowed records to the Library of Congress for entombment. A skeletal organization with six members continues to exist, and as recently as the spring of 1959 it received a small legacy.

The cause of African colonization, sick and feeble after 1837, gradually had fused with emigration schemes and then had died in the Civil War. With it perished dreams of an African empire, an all-white America, and a gradual and peaceful obliteration of slavery. Its legacy to postwar America was an amalgam of racism and African nationalism that appeared in the scholarly treatises of Major Robert W. Shufeldt, exponent of Negro inferiority, or in the dynamic appeals of Marcus Garvey, advocate of Negro superiority. In the years since 1865, few voices have chanted a "back-to-Africa" refrain. The Fourteenth Amendment dictated that America's race problem was not to be settled by wholesale removal to another continent. Vote-hungry politicians, exploiters of labor, and the Negro masses who abhorred all plans to take them from the land of their birth affirmed this decision. Having

repudiated removal, Americans would grope for other solutions
—Supreme Court formulas, local accommodation, military co-
ercion, masked terrorism, intermarriage, or, in some instances,
Negro acceptance of second-class citizenship—trying to solve the
riddle African colonizationists failed to unravel.

APPENDIX

TABLE OF ANNUAL RECEIPTS AND COLONISTS SENT TO LIBERIA BY THE AMERICAN COLONIZATION SOCIETY *

Year	Receipts †	Colonists §	Year	Receipts	Colonists
1817–19	$14,031.50	—	1861	75,470.74	55
1820–22	5,627.66	156	1862	46,208.46	65
1823	4,758.22	65	1863	50,900.36	26
1824	4,379.89	103	1864	79,454.70	23
1825	10,125.85	66	1865	23,633.37	527
1826	14,779.24	182	1866	59,375.14	621
1827	13,294.94	222	1867	53,190.48	633
1828	13,458.17	163	1868	49,959.52	453
1829	20,295.61	205	1869	62,269.78	453
1830	26,683.41	259	1870	28,372.32	196
1831	32,101.58	421	1871	29,348.80	247
1832	43,065.08	796	1872	33,337.22	150
1833	37,242.46	270	1873	33,335.71	73
1834	22,984.30	127	1874	14,749.28	27
1835	36,661.49	146	1875	12,125.79	23
1836	33,096.88	234	1876	13,961.34	21
1837	25,558.14	138	1877	11,812.72	53
1838	10,947.41	109	1878	15,419.41	101
1839	51,498.36	47	1879	18,302.37	91
1840	56,985.62	115	1880	10,862.04	143
1841	42,443.68	85	1881	8,523.66	52
1842	32,898.88	170	1882	10,342.91	27
1843	36,093.94	85	1883	14,091.87	53
1844	33,640.39	170	1884	10,673.24	81
1845	56,458.60	187	1885	6,176.05	52
1846	39,900.03	89	1886	44,922.46	110
1847	29,472.84	51	1887	20,916.43	124
1848	49,845.91	441	1888	6,176.05	39
1849	50,332.84	422	1889	17,144.15	60
1850	64,973.71	505	1890	7,717.61	63
1851	97,443.77	676	1891	12,184.20	154
1852	86,775.74	630	1892	9,886.88	50
1853	82,458.25	783	1893	10,360.04	5
1854	65,433.93	553	1894	8,622.27	6
1855	55,276.89	207	1895	12,449.79	4
1856	81,384.41	538	1896	8,489.38	—
1857	97,384.84	370	1897	10,308.55	1
1858	61,820.19	167	1898	7,838.03	3
1859	160,303.23	248	1899	7,089.95	4
1860	104,546.92	316	Totals	$2,762,467.87	15,386

* Based on computations by the American Colonization Society. *Fifty-second Annual Report of the American Colonization Society, with Proceedings of the Annual Meeting and of the Board of Directors, January 19 and 20, 1869* (Washington, 1869), inside back cover, and *Liberia Bulletin*, no. 16 (February, 1900), p. 28.

† These figures do not include the independent state societies. Maryland's total receipts to 1870 were $309,759.33. The New York and Pennsylvania societies during their independence received $95,640.00, and the Mississippi Society collected $12,000.

§ This list does not include recaptives conveyed by the Colonization Society to Africa or colonists carried to Liberia by the independent state societies.

NOTES

Notes to I: TAPROOTS OF COLONIZATION

1. Thomas Jefferson, *Notes on the State of Virginia* (London, 1787), pp. 228–230, 240; Paul Leicester Ford, ed., *The Works of Thomas Jefferson* (New York, 1905), IX, 315–319, 373–375. See also, Henry N. Sherwood, "Early Negro Deportation Projects," *Mississippi Valley Historical Review,* II (March, 1916), 484–508 and Early Lee Fox, *The American Colonization Society 1817–1840* (Baltimore, 1919), *passim.*

2. Ferdinando Fairfax, "Plea for liberating the negroes within the United States," *American Museum, or Universal Magazine,* VIII (December, 1790), 285–287. Fairfax later became a charter member of the American Colonization Society.

3. St. George Tucker to Jeremy Belknap, Williamsburg, June 29, 1795, James Sullivan to Jeremy Belknap, Boston, July 30, 1795, "Letters and Documents relating to Slavery in Massachusetts," *Collections of the Massachusetts Historical Society* (Boston, 1877), Fifth Series, III, 405–410, 413; St. George Tucker, *A Dissertation on Slavery: with a Proposal for the Gradual Abolition of it, in the State of Virginia* (Philadelphia, 1796), pp. 78–79, 84, 91–92, 94–95; [St. George Tucker], *Reflections on the Cession of Louisiana to the United States. By Sylvestris* (Washington City, 1803), pp. 25–26.

4. John Parrish, *Remarks on the Slavery of the Black People; Addressed to the Citizens of the United States, particularly to those who are in legislative or executive stations in the general or state governments; and also to such individuals as hold them in bondage* (Philadelphia, 1806), pp. 41–44.

5. Ford, ed., *Works of Thomas Jefferson,* IX, 315–319, 373-375, 383–387; Stanislaus M. Hamilton, ed., *The Writings of James Monroe* (New York, 1900), III, 292–295, 336–338, 351–353.

6. Franklin B. Dexter, ed., *The Literary Diary of Ezra Stiles, D.D., LL.D., President of Yale College* (New York, 1901), I, 363–366, 414; II, 378; III, 327.

7. Gaillard Hunt, "William Thornton and Negro Colonization," *Proceedings of the American Antiquarian Society,* new series, XXX (1920), 30–39; Jacques Pierre Brissot de Warville, *New Travels in the United States of America. Performed in 1788* (London, 1792), pp. 167–168; Thornton to Brissot de Warville, Philadelphia, November 29, 1788, The Papers of William Thornton, Library of Congress.

8. Thomas J. Pettigrew, ed., *Memoirs of the Life and Writings of the Late John Coakley Lettsom* . . . (London, 1817), II, 497–507, 510–511; Hunt, "William Thornton and Negro Colonization," pp. 45, 47–48, 51; Thornton to Brissot de Warville, Philadelphia, November 29, 1788, Thornton Papers.

9. Hunt, "William Thornton and Negro Colonization," pp. 47–48.

10. Pettigrew, *Memoirs of Lettsom,* II, 518; Lettsom to Thornton, London, February 19, 1787, Thornton Papers. Thornton offered to be superintendent of the English colony, but Granville Sharp refused Thornton permission to go to Sierra Leone, saying there was "considerable risque to health" for both Thornton and his bride. Pettigrew, *Memoirs of Lettsom,* II, 532–534; Sharp to Thornton, London, October 5, 1791, Thornton Papers. As late as 1802 Thornton recommended that the United States purchase Puerto Rico and establish a Negro colony to raise sugar. Hunt, "William Thornton and Negro Colonization," pp. 53–55. Thornton was one of the charter members of the American Colonization Society in 1816 and served on the board of managers until his death in 1828.

11. Pettigrew, *Memoirs of Lettsom,* II, 270–272, 281–286.

12. *Ibid.,* I, 132; II, 236–240; Lettsom to Thornton, London, July 17, 1787, Thornton Papers.

13. Pettigrew, *Memoirs of Lettsom,* I, 133–136; II, 240–248; Sharp to Thornton, London, October 5, 1791, Thornton Papers; F. A. J. Utting, *The Story of Sierra Leone* (London, 1931), pp. 80–87; J. J. Crooke, *A History of the Colony of Sierra Leone, Western Africa* (Dublin, 1903), pp. 27–32.

14. Utting, *Story of Sierra Leone,* pp. 88–107; Crooke, *History of Sierra Leone,* pp. 32–70; Charles Booth, *Zachary Macaulay, His Part in the Movement for the Abolition of the Slave Trade and of Slavery* (London, 1934), pp. 23–52. The African Institution declared that "conquest . . . has been the harsh and more ordinary medium by which the blessings of civilization have been conveyed from one part

of the world to another" and it offered commercial penetration as a more humane method for spreading the "blessings of civilized society among a people sunk in ignorance and barbarism." Commerce, it said, was almost as powerful as Christianity in spreading civilization. African Institution, *Report of the Committee of the African Institution, Read to the General Meeting on the 15th of July, 1807. Together with the Rules and Regulations which were then adopted for the Government of the Society* (London, 1807), pp. 9–14.

15. Henry N. Sherwood, "Paul Cuffe," *Journal of Negro History,* VIII (1923), 154–159; *The History of Prince Lee Boo, to which is added, the Life of Paul Cuffee, a Man of Colour, also some account of John Sackhouse, the Esquimaux* (Dublin, 1822), pp. 154–159; Boston *Recorder,* October 21 and 28, 1817.

16. Sherwood, "Paul Cuffe," pp. 169–182, 189, 193.

17. *Ibid.,* pp. 183–197; *Annals of the Congress of the United States,* 13 Congress, 1 and 2 sessions, pp. 569–570, 572, 601, 861–863, 1150, 1195, 1256.

18. Sherwood, "Paul Cuffe," pp. 198–224; an extract from the Reverend Peter Williams's funeral sermon for Paul Cuffee, American Colonization Society, *Third Annual Report of the American Society for Colonizing the Free People of Colour of the United States* (Washington, 1820), pp. 115–120.

Notes to II: THIS SCHEME IS FROM GOD

1. Samuel Hopkins, *The System of Doctrines, contained in Divine Revelation, Explained and Defended . . .* (2d ed., Boston, 1811), I, 466–468; Oliver Wendell Elsbree, "Samuel Hopkins and his Doctrine of Benevolence," *New England Quarterly,* VIII (1935), 540–545; David Sutherland, *Christian Benevolence. A Sermon, delivered at Newbury, Vt., before the Washington Benevolent Society, at the Celebration of the Anniversary of the National Independence, July 4, 1812* (Bath, New Hampshire, 1812), pp. 10–12.

2. Clifford S. Griffin, *Their Brothers' Keepers; Moral Stewardship in the United States, 1800–1865* (New Brunswick, N.J., 1960), pp. 3–115; see also Griffin, "Religious Benevolence as Social Control, 1815–1860," *Mississippi Valley Historical Review,* XLIV (December, 1957), 423–444.

3. John B. McMaster, *A History of the People of the United States, from the Revolution to the Civil War* (New York, 1914), IV, 525–

549; Dixon Ryan Fox, "The Protestant Counter-Reformation in America," *New York History,* XVI (1935), 19–35; Charles I. Foster, "The Urban Missionary Movement, 1814–1837," *Pennsylvania Magazine of History,* LXXV (1951), 47–53; Florence Hayes, *Daughters of Dorcas, The Story of Women Home Missions since 1802* (New York, 1952), pp. 1–37, 141–156; Blanche D. Coll, "The Baltimore Society for the Prevention of Pauperism, 1820–1822," *American Historical Review,* LXI (1955), 77–87. For a discussion of the British benevolent societies and their influence on the American societies, see Kenneth S. Latourette, *The Great Century A.D. 1800–A.D. 1914: Europe and the United States of America* (New York, 1941), pp. 64–88 (Vol. 4 of *A History of the Expansion of Christianity*); Frank Thistlethwaite, *The Anglo-American Connection in the Early Nineteenth Century* (Philadelphia, 1959), pp. 76–102; Charles I. Foster, *An Errand of Mercy; The Evangelical United Front, 1790–1837* (Chapel Hill, N.C., 1960), *passim.*

4. *Condition of the American Colored Population, and of the Colony of Liberia* (Boston, 1833), p. 9; [Calvin Colton], *A Voice from America to England. By an American Gentleman* (London, 1839), pp. 11, 46, 62, 184–185.

5. Isaac V. Brown, *Memoirs of the Rev. Robert Finley, D.D., Late Pastor of the Presbyterian Congregation at Basking Ridge, New-Jersey, and President of Franklin College, located at Athens, in the State of Georgia; with Brief Sketches of some of his contemporaries, and numerous notes* (New Brunswick, N.J., 1819) p. 77. Finley manumitted two slaves. See also Robert S. Finley to Ralph R. Gurley, New York, November 12, 1830, Papers of the American Colonization Society, Library of Congress, hereafter cited as ACS papers and "Manumissions of Slaves in Somerset County," *Somerset County Historical Quarterly,* I (1912), 277.

6. *Historical Statistics of the United States 1789–1945* (Washington, 1949); Bureau of Census, *Negroes in the United States, 1920–1932* (Washington, 1935), p. 11; Census reports, 1790, 1800, 1810, 1820.

7. Brown, *Memoirs of Finley,* pp. 2–40, 53 and note; A. Van Doren Honeyman, "Notes on the Life of Rev. William Blauvelt, D.D.," *Somerset County Historical Quarterly,* VII (1918), 38–39; Jacob Magill, "Somerset Traditions Gathered Forty Years Ago," *Somerset County Historical Quarterly,* IV (1915), 30–31; Arch W. Carswell, "A Study of Robert Finley, D.D.," *Proceedings of the New Jersey Historical Society,* LVI (1938), 194–196; William B. Sprague,

Annals of the American Pulpit; or Commemorative Notices of Distinguished American Clergymen of Various Denominations (New York, 1868), IV, 128; Oscar M. Voorhees, "The Kirkpatrick Family of Somerset," *Somerset Historical Quarterly,* III (1914), 272–273.

8. Brown, *Memoirs of Finley,* pp. 31, 54–74, 237–350; George Adams Boyd, *Elias Boudinot, Patriot and Statesman, 1740–1821* (Princeton, 1951), p. 97; Sprague, *Annals of the Pulpit,* III, 222–228; *Minutes of the General Assembly of the Presbyterian Church in the United States of America from its organization A.D. 1789 to A.D. 1820 inclusive* (Philadelphia, 1847), pp. 585, 621. When he resigned as trustee, Princeton conferred on him the degree of Doctor of Divinity. Boston *Columbian Centinel,* April 19, 1817.

9. *Minutes of the General Assembly of the Presbyterian Church,* pp. 593–594.

10. James W. Alexander, *The Life of Archibald Alexander, D.D., First Professor in the Theological Seminary at Princeton, New Jersey* (New York, 1854), p. 450; Archibald Alexander, *A History of Colonization on the Western Coast of Africa* (Philadelphia, 1846), p. 79; Brown, *Memoirs of Finley,* p. 77.

11. African Education Society, *An Address to the Public on the Subject of the African School, lately established under the care of the Synod of New-York and New-Jersey. By the directors of the Institution* (New York, 1816), pp. 3–4; Isaac V. Brown, *Biography of the Rev. Robert Finley, D.D., of Basking Ridge, New Jersey; Second Edition, Enlarged; With an account of his Agency as the Author of the American Colonization Society; also a Sketch of the Slave Trade; a View of our National Policy and that of Great Britain towards Liberia and Africa* (Philadelphia, 1857), pp. 95–96.

12. Gardiner Spring, *Memoirs of the Rev. Samuel J. Mills, late Missionary to the Southwestern Section of the United States, and agent of the American Colonization Society, deputed to explore the coast of Africa* (New York, 1820), pp. 10, 13, 19–20, 37–42, 57–61, 68–72, 93, 95–97, 101–113; John F. Schermerhorn and Samuel J. Mills, *A Correct View of that Part of the United States which lies West of the Alleghany Mountains, with regard to religion and morals* (Hartford, 1814), pp. 14–52; Samuel J. Mills and Daniel Smith, *Report of a Missionary Tour through that part of the United States which lies West of the Alleghany Mountains; performed under the direction of the Massachusetts Missionary Society* (Andover, 1815), p. 47; Foster, "The Urban Missionary Movement, 1814–1837," pp. 47–53 discussing the "new missionary field."

13. James Alexander, *Life of Archibald Alexander,* p. 450; Archibald Alexander, *History of Colonization,* p. 80; Brown, Biography of Finley (2d ed.), pp. 101–102; *National Intelligencer,* December 14, 1816.

14. Brown, *Biography of Finley* (2d ed.), pp. 39, 83–96.

Notes to III: CLOSE TO THE NATIONAL VAULTS

1. Gaillard Hunt, *The First Forty Years of Washington Society, Portrayed by the Family Letters of Mrs. Samuel Harrison Smith (Margaret Bayard) from the collection of her grandson, J. Henley Smith* (New York, 1906), pp. 130–135.

2. Samuel Sitgreaves, Jr., to Jackson Kemper, Baltimore, April 13 [1822], The Papers of Jackson Kemper, State Historical Society of Wisconsin.

3. [Hallie L. Wright], "Sketch of Elias Boudinot Caldwell," *Records of the Columbia Historical Society, Washington, D.C.,* XXIV (1922), 204–213.

4. Alexandria *Herald,* November 22, 1816; Hunt, *Forty Years of Washington Society,* pp. 151–152, 159–160.

5. Edward S. Delaplaine, *Francis Scott Key, Life and Times* (New York, 1937), pp. 1–50, 194–195.

6. *Ibid.,* pp. 98–99.

7. Jesse Torrey, Jr., *A Portraiture of Domestic Slavery, in the United States: with Reflections on the Practicability of Restoring the Moral Rights of the Slave, without impairing the Legal Privileges of the Possessor; and a Project of a Colonial Asylum for Free Persons of Colour; including Memoirs of facts on the Interior Traffic in Slaves, and on Kidnapping* (Philadelphia, 1817), pp. 48–53; Delaplaine, *Francis Scott Key,* pp. 194–195.

8. "Penn" may have been William Thornton whose interest in colonization had not abated in thirty years. *National Intelligencer,* December 17, 18, and 21, 1816. One fourth of the *Intelligencer*'s December 24 issue was devoted to colonization.

9. *African Repository and Colonial Journal,* II, 335–336.

10. *National Intelligencer,* December 18 and 21, 1816.

11. Isaac V. Brown, *Biography of the Rev. Robert Finley . . .* (2d ed., Philadelphia, 1857), p. 133; Gardiner Spring, *Memoirs of the Rev. Samuel J. Mills . . .* (New York, 1820), p. 142.

12. *National Intelligencer,* December 24, 1816.

13. Brown, *Biography of Finley* (2d ed.), p. 110; *National Intelligencer,* December 24, 1816.

14. *National Intelligencer,* December 31, 1816, January 3, 1817. The memorial committee consisted of: Elias B. Caldwell, John Randolph of Roanoke, Richard Rush, Walter Jones, Francis S. Key, Robert Wright, James H. Blake, and John Peters. The constitution committee: Francis S. Key, Elias Caldwell, Walter Jones, Richard Rush, James Breckinridge, William G. D. Worthington, and Bushrod Washington. Names that appear on the original manuscript list of charter members: Henry Clay, E. B. Caldwell, Thomas Doughtery, Stephen B. Balch, John Chalmers, Jr., Thomas Patterson, John Randolph of Roanoke, Robert H. Goldsborough, William Thornton, George Clarke, James Laurie, J. I. Stull, Daniel Webster, J. C. Herbert, William Simmons, E. Forman, Ferdinando Fairfax, Virgil Maxcy, John Loockerman, John Woodside, William Dudley Digges, Thomas Carberry, Samuel J. Mills, George A. Carroll, W. G. D. Worthington, John Lee, Richard Bland Lee, D. Murray, Robert Finley, B. Allison, B. L. Lear, W. Jones, J. Mason, Mord. Booth, J. S. Schaaf, George Peter, John Taylor, Overton Carr, F. H. Wendover, F. S. Key, Charles Marsh, David M. Forest, John Wiley, Nathan Lufborough, William Meade, William H. Wilmer, George Travers, Edmund I. Lee, and John P. Todd. Bushrod Washington's name was later added.

15. Other managers: John Laird, James H. Blake, John Peters, Edmund I. Lee, Jacob Hoffman, Henry Carroll. Several were government employees. Caldwell was Clerk of the Supreme Court; Thornton was Superintendent of the Patent Office; Rev. James Laurie was a clerk in the Treasury department; Rev. Obadiah Brown was a clerk in the Post Office department and under John Q. Adams's administration became Chief Clerk. Brown was sometime chaplain to Congress.

16. Philadelphia *American Centinel,* n.d., quoted by Alexandria *Herald,* January 15, 1817; *Federal Republican and Baltimore Telegraph,* n.d., quoted by *Poulson's American Daily Advertiser* (Philadelphia), January 2, 1817; *Federal Republican,* October 21, 1817.

17. *National Intelligencer,* January 8, 9, 18, February 11, April 14, August 25, 1817; Boston *Recorder,* December 24, 1816, January 1, 7, February 4, 11, 18, 1817; Georgetown *Messenger,* n.d., quoted by *National Intelligencer,* December 31, 1816.

18. *African Repository,* IX, 226. Mercer worked with Caldwell and Key in publishing the secret proceedings. A few days after the Virginia assembly endorsed African colonization, the North Carolina legislature

passed a resolution calling for Negro colonization on the Pacific coast. William H. Hoyt, ed., *The Papers of Archibald D. Murphey* (Raleigh, 1914), II, 61–62; for Mercer's recollections, see *Thirty-Sixth Annual Report of the American Colonization Society . . .* (Washington, 1853), pp. 38–43.

19. "A Counter-Memorial proposed to be submitted to Congress in behalf of the free people of colour of the District of Columbia," *National Intelligencer,* December 30, 1816.

20. Boston *Recorder,* March 18, 1817; Ray Allen Billington, ed., *The Journal of Charlotte L. Forten* (New York, 1953), pp. 8–10; *Poulson's American Daily Advertiser,* January 10, 1817.

21. Brown, *Biography of Finley* (2d ed.), pp. 121–122; a letter undoubtedly written by Finley appears in the Boston *Recorder,* March 25, 1817.

22. Brown, *Biography of Finley* (2d ed.), pp. 116n., 178–179.

23. Carter G. Woodson, *Negro Orators and Their Orations* (Washington, 1925), pp. 51–55.

24. Pennsylvania Abolition Society, *Address of the Committee for Improving the Condition of the Free Blacks, to the Members of the Pennsylvania Abolition Society, and to the Public in General* (Philadelphia, 1800), pp. 3–7; Edward Needles, *An Historical Memoir of the Pennsylvania Society, for Promoting the Abolition of Slavery; the Relief of Free Negroes Unlawfully Held in Bondage, and for Improving the Condition of the African Race. Compiled from the Minutes of the Society and other official documents* (Philadelphia, 1848), pp. 63–65; Roberts Vaux to Thomas Clarkson, Philadelphia, May 13, 1819, Moorland Collection, Howard University.

25. Boston *Recorder,* February 18, 1817.

26. *National Intelligencer,* January 18, 1817.

27. *Annals of Congress,* 14 Congress, 2 session, pp. 481–483, 639, 939–941; *National Intelligencer,* March 28, 1817. Congressman Tucker also presented a petition from the Frederick County Auxiliary Colonization Society of Virginia which asked adoption of the plan. *Annals of Congress,* 15 Congress, 1 session, pp. 529–530.

28. *National Intelligencer,* November 17, 1817.

Notes to IV: ON AFRICA'S SHORES

1. Journal of the Board of Managers, March 14, 1817, ACS papers; *A View of Exertions Lately Made for the Purpose of Colonizing the*

Free People of Colour, in the United States, in Africa, or Elsewhere (Washington, 1817), *passim.;* Gardiner Spring, *Memoirs of the Rev. Samuel J. Mills* (New York, 1820), pp. 142–143; *Third Annual Report of the American Colonization Society,* p. 4; American Colonization Society, *Memorial of the President and Board of Managers of the Colonization Society, February 3, 1820: Referred to the Committee on so much of the President's Message as relates to the Slave Trade* (Washington, 1820), p. 4.

2. Journal of the Board of Managers, March 14, September 19, October 18, 1817, ACS papers; *National Intelligencer,* August 25, 1817.

3. Spring, *Memoirs of Mills,* p. 157; Journal of the Board of Managers, October 18, 1817, ACS papers; *Poulson's American Daily Advertiser,* July 10, 1817.

4. Baltimore *Federal Republican and Baltimore Telegraph,* July 11, 1817.

5. *A Letter from Gen. Harper, of Maryland, to Elias B. Caldwell, Esq. Secretary of the American Society for Colonizing the Free People of Colour, in the United States, with their own consent* (Baltimore, 1818), pp. 6–27. The letter is dated August 20, 1817. It also appeared in the ACS *First Annual Report,* pp. 24–49. The original MS is in the Papers of the Maryland State Colonization Society, Maryland Historical Society.

6. *National Intelligencer,* August 25, 1817.

7. *New-York Spectator,* October 29, November 11, 1817. Other members of the society included: John Murray, Jr., Thomas S. Clarkson, the Rev. Dr. Alexander McLeod, Garritt N. Bleecker, Joseph Smith, Najah Taylor, Henry Rankin, John Adams, George Griffin, George Gallagher, and G. P. Shipman.

8. Edward D. Griffin, *A Plea for Africa; a Sermon Preached October 26, 1817, in the First Presbyterian Church in the City of New-York, before the Synod of New-York and New-Jersey, at the request of the Board of Directors of the African School established by the Synod* (New York, 1817), pp. 3, 15, 20–21, 27–28, 31–35.

9. Journal of the Board of Managers, September 19, October 18, 1817, ACS papers; Spring, *Memoirs of Mills,* pp. 136–139, 141; *National Intelligencer,* August 25, 1817.

10. Spring, *Memoirs of Mills,* pp. 136–140.

11. Journal of the Board of Managers, February 5, 1818, ACS papers; ACS *Second Annual Report,* p. 10; *Address of the Board of Managers of the American Colonization Society, to the Auxiliary*

Societies and the People of the United States (Washington, 1820), p. 20; Spring, *Memoirs of Mills,* p. 146.

12. Journal of the Board of Managers, November 5, 1817, ACS papers. The board agreed to pay each agent $1,000 a year.

13. William Thornton to Joseph Banks, Washington, November 11, 1817, Papers of William Thornton, Library of Congress; Calvin Colton, ed., *The Life, Correspondence, and Speeches of Henry Clay* (New York, 1857), IV, 53–54; ACS *First Annual Report,* pp. 23–24.

14. *National Intelligencer,* May 15, 1818; Spring, *Memoirs of Mills,* pp. 146, 147–152; [Ebenezer Burgess], *Address to the American Society for Colonizing the Free People of Colour of the United States: Read at a special meeting, in the City of Washington, November 21st, 1818* (Washington, 1818), p. 8.

15. John A. Patten, *These Remarkable Men; the Beginnings of a World Enterprise* (London, 1945), pp. 11–45; *National Intelligencer,* May 15, 1818; Spring, *Memoirs of Mills,* pp. 152–154, 226.

16. Spring, *Memoirs of Mills,* pp. 160–162, 164, 175; Burgess, *Address,* pp. 8–9, 33–34, 36–37, 45, 49–52. The books the agents studied: Jean Baptiste Labat, *Voyage du Chevalier Des Marshals en Guinée* (1731), Paul Erdmann Isert, *Voyage en Guinée* (1793), Carl Bernhard Wadstrom, *An Essay on Colonization* (1794), Sylvain M. X. de Golbery, *Travels in Africa* (1802), Thomas M. Winterbottom, *An Account of the Native Africans in the Neighborhood of Sierra Leone* (1803), Philip Beaver, *African Memorandum* (1805), Mungo Park, *Travels into the Interior Districts of Africa* (1800), Henry Meredith, *An Account of the Gold Coast of Africa* (1812), and various publications of the African Institution.

17. Spring, *Memoirs of Mills,* pp. 165–167.

18. *Ibid.,* p. 182; Archibald Alexander, *History of Colonization on the Western Coast of Africa* (Philadelphia, 1846), pp. 102–104; *National Intelligencer,* September 23, 1818.

19. Spring, *Memoirs of Mills,* pp. 169–176.

20. *Ibid.,* pp. 176–198.

21. *Ibid.,* pp. 199–213.

22. *Ibid.,* pp. 187–188, 200–202, 210, 214–217; *National Intelligencer,* September 23, 1818.

23. Spring, *Memoirs of Mills,* pp. 210, 227–228; *National Intelligencer,* September 23, 1818; Burgess, *Address,* p. 9.

Notes to V: THE FOSTERING AID OF GOVERNMENT

1. *First Annual Report of the American Colonization Society,* pp. 5–8, 13–18; *Second Annual Report,* pp. 94–96, 100–106; Jefferson's letter, addressed to John Lynd and dated Monticello, January 21, 1811, appeared in the Richmond *Enquirer,* n.d., reprinted in the *National Intelligencer,* April 14, 1817. Bushrod Washington told a British traveler that he viewed colonization as an instrument in the conversion of Africa and an "important link" in the work of establishing "the kingdom of the Messiah in every quarter of the globe." Adam Hodgson, *Remarks during a Journey through North America in the years 1819, 1820, and 1821* . . . (New York, 1823), p. 58.

2. ACS *Second Annual Report,* pp. 96–100; *National Intelligencer,* June 4, 1818.

3. Unsigned letter written perhaps by Stephen B. Balch, Georgetown, November 10, 1818, Trenton *Federalist,* December 7, 1818; *National Intelligencer,* September 23, 1818.

4. [Ebenezer Burgess], *Address to the American Society for Colonizing the Free People of Colour of the United States* . . . (Washington, 1818), pp. 5–6, 7, 10–11, 22–25, 27–30, 36–52. Italics omitted.

5. *Ibid.,* pp. 10–12, 23–27; Gardiner Spring, *Memoirs of the Rev. Samuel J. Mills* . . . (New York, 1820), p. 217.

6. ACS *Second Annual Report,* pp. 14–17, 96–100.

7. Spring, *Memoirs of Mills,* pp. 218–222; *Address of the Board of Managers of the American Colonization Society, to the Auxiliary Societies and the People of the United States* (Washington, 1820), p. 4.

8. *Annals of Congress,* 15 Congress, 1 session, pp. 1771–1774; *ibid.,* 15 Congress, 2 session, pp. 2544–2546.

9. Journal of the Board of Managers, March 4, 1819, ACS papers.

10. Charles F. Adams, ed., *Memoirs of John Quincy Adams, comprising portions of his diary from 1795 to 1848* (Philadelphia, 1875), IV, 293.

11. *Ibid.,* IV, 292–293.

12. *Ibid.,* IV, 293–294.

13. *Ibid.,* IV, 298–299; Journal of the Board of Managers, March 31, 1819, ACS papers.

14. Charles F. Adams, ed., *Memoirs of John Quincy Adams,* IV, 321–322; Journal of the Board of Managers, April 7 and May 4,

1819, ACS papers; ACS *Third Annual Report,* p. 11; *National Intelligencer,* April 24, 1819, August 12, 1819; *Address of the Board of Managers of the American Colonization Society to the Public* (n.p., n.d., [1819]), note 2.

15. Charles F. Adams, ed., *Memoirs of John Quincy Adams,* IV, 355–356; *Address of the Board of Managers* [1819], pp. 2–3; ACS *Second Annual Report,* p. 142.

16. Journal of the Board of Managers, May 4, and June 21, 1819, ACS papers. Meade's biographer glosses over Meade's failure to free the Africans. John Johns, *A Memoir of the Life of the Right Rev. William Meade, D.D., Bishop of the Protestant Episcopal Church in the Diocese of Virginia* (Baltimore, 1867), pp. 120–121; ACS *Second Annual Report,* pp. 142–149; ACS *Third Annual Report,* p. 11.

17. ACS *Second Annual Report,* pp. 114–120, 150–153; ACS *Third Annual Report,* pp. 123–127; William B. Sprague, *Annals of the American Pulpit* (New York, 1868), VI, 583–584; folder of miscellaneous manuscripts, ACS papers.

18. Johns, *Memoir of Meade,* pp. 124–125.

19. Edward S. Delaplaine, *Francis Scott Key . . .* (New York, 1937), p. 203; Johns, *Memoir of Meade,* p. 124; Benjamin F. Hall, comp., *Official Opinions of the Attorneys General of the United States, advising the President and Heads of Departments, in relation to their official duties . . .* (Washington, 1852), I, 314–316.

20. Delaplaine, *Francis Scott Key,* pp. 203–204; Hall, *Official Opinions of the Attorneys General,* I, 317–320; Johns, *Memoir of Meade,* p. 124.

21. ACS *Third Annual Report,* pp. 46–49; John Gibson, ed., *History of York County, Pennsylvania, from the Earliest Period to the Present Time . . .* (Chicago, 1886), pp. 408–409; Jehudi Ashmun, *Memoir of the Life and Character of the Rev. Samuel Bacon, A.M., Late, an Officer of Marines in the United States' Service: Afterwards, Attorney at Law in the State of Pennsylvania: and Subsequently, a Minister of the Episcopal Church, and Principal Agent of the American Government for persons liberated from Slave-Ships, on the Coast of Africa; Where he terminated his Life in the month of May, 1820* (Washington, 1822), *passim.*

22. Charles Henry Huberich, *The Political and Legislative History of Liberia: a documentary history of the constitutions, laws and treaties of Liberia from the earliest settlements to the establishment of the Republic, a sketch of the activities of the American Colonization*

societies, a commentary on the constitution of the Republic and a survey of the political and social legislation from 1847 to 1944; with appendices containing the laws of the colony of Liberia, 1820–1839, and Acts of the Governor and Council, 1839–1847 (New York, 1947), I, 75–79; Amos Kendall to John Branch, Secretary of the Navy, August, 1830, in [Kennedy], *African Colonization* (27 Congress, 3 session, House Report no. 283, serial 428, Washington, 1843), p. 459.

23. Ashmun, *Memoir of Bacon,* pp. 241–242; *African Repository,* I, 340; *Niles' Weekly Register,* XVII (1820), 440.

Notes to VI: AFRICAN ILIAD

1. "Instructions of the Board of Managers to Samuel Crozier [sic]," Journal of the Board of Managers, December 10, 1819, ACS papers; instructions of the Secretary of the Navy, see Charles Henry Huberich, *The Political and Legislative History of Liberia . . .* (New York, 1947), I, 73–75.

2. Jehudi Ashmun, *Memoir of Bacon . . .* (Washington, 1822), pp. 255–258; Huberich, *Liberia,* I, 98.

3. ACS *Seventh Annual Report,* appendix, pp. 66–67; Archibald Alexander, *A History of Colonization on the Western Coast of Africa* (Philadelphia, 1846), pp. 118–119; Ashmun, *Memoir of Bacon,* pp. 260–261; Samuel Hodges, Jr., American consul at Cape Verde Islands, to Boston *Patriot,* n.d., in the *National Intelligencer,* June 13, 1820; letter of unnamed officer on the *Cyane,* off Sierra Leone, April 10, 1820, *ibid.,* June 19, 1820.

4. Journal of the Board of Managers, October 16, 1820, ACS papers; Ashmun, *Memoir of Bacon,* pp. 244, 249, 263–278.

5. Alexander, *A History of Colonization,* pp. 128–131; John Dix, U.S.S. *Cyane,* November 22, 1820, to Capt. Edward Trenchard; A. Grant, acting governor of Sierra Leone, Freetown, October 23, 1820, to Capt. Trenchard; Daniel Coker, Yonie, May 26, 1820, to Secretary of the Navy, in Huberich, *Liberia,* I, 127–136.

6. Journal of the Board of Managers, December 13, 1820, ACS papers. Some of the liberated Africans declared that they did not wish to return to Africa. Joseph R. Andrus to Elias Caldwell, Baltimore, December 27, 1820, Peter Force Papers, Library of Congress.

7. Journal of the Board of Managers, December 23, 1820, ACS

papers; letters and journals of the agents printed in Huberich, *Liberia,* I, 157–181, 183.

8. Journal of the Board of Managers, July 13 and 25, 1821, ACS papers; *A Sketch of the Life of Com. Robert F. Stockton; with an Appendix, comprising his Correspondence with the Navy Department respecting his Conquest of California: and extracts from the Defence of Col. J. C. Fremont, in relation to the same subject: together with his Speeches in the Senate of the United States, and his Political Letters* (New York, 1856), pp. 39–40; Robert F. Stockton, U.S.S. *Alligator,* Boston, July 25, 1821, to Hon. Smith Thompson, in Huberich, *Liberia,* I, 181. The cape is 6°19′N, 10°49′W.

9. *A Sketch of the Life of Stockton,* pp. 41–43; ACS *Fifth Annual Report,* pp. 59–60.

10. Robert F. Stockton to Board of Managers, U.S.S. *Alligator,* Cape Mesurado, December 16, 1821, folder of miscellaneous manuscripts, ACS papers; ACS *Fifth Annual Report,* pp. 58–59, 63, 64–66; [Newark, New Jersey Colonization Society], *A Sketch of the Colonization Enterprise, and of the Soil, Climate and Productions of Liberia, in Africa* (n.p., c.1825), pp. 2–3.

11. John E. Semmes, *John H. B. Latrobe and His Times 1803–1891* (Baltimore, 1917), pp. 141–142; ACS *Seventh Annual Report,* pp. 5–6.

12. Journal of the Board of Managers, June 26, December 23, 1820, ACS papers.

13. *African Repository,* I, 4; Ralph R. Gurley, *Life of Jehudi Ashmun, Late Colonial Agent in Liberia* (Washington, 1835), pp. 115–116; Huberich, *Liberia,* I, 199–214; ACS *Seventh Annual Report,* p. 58.

14. Huberich, *Liberia,* I, 278–292.

15. ACS *Fourth Annual Report,* pp. 66, 68–70.

16. ACS *Seventh Annual Report,* pp. 44–47.

Notes to VII: EXPLORING THE VOLUNTARY SYSTEM

1. Journal of the Board of Managers, September 19, 1817, ACS papers; H. M. Wagstaff, ed., *Minutes of the N.C. Manumission Society, 1816–1834* [James Sprunt Historical Studies, no. 22] (Chapel Hill, 1934), pp. 5, 39–42, 46–50, 57; Levi Coffin, *Reminiscences of Levi Coffin, the Reputed President of the Underground Railroad* . . . (Cincinnati, 1880), p. 75.

2. Edward S. Delaplaine, *Francis Scott Key* . . . (New York, 1937), p. 202; ACS *Second Annual Report,* pp. 136–137; *African Repository,* IX, 266; Journal of the Board of Managers, February 5, 1818, March 4, 1819, ACS papers.

3. *National Intelligencer,* September 22, 1819; Augustine C. Smith to Elias B. Caldwell, Winchester, Virginia, April 25, 1819, Peter Force Papers, Library of Congress; Frederick County Auxiliary Society, *The Annual Report of the Auxiliary Society of Frederick County, Va. for Colonizing the Free People of Colour in the United States* (Winchester, 1820), pp. 12–14; ACS *Second Annual Report,* pp. 132–134.

4. ACS *Second Annual Report,* p. 142; *Third Annual Report,* pp. 134–135; *Fourth Annual Report,* p. 67.

5. Journal of the Board of Managers, March 31 and April 7, 1819, ACS papers. Meade's salary was $1,000.

6. John Johns, *Memoir of Rev. William Meade* . . . (Baltimore, 1867), pp. 120–122; Journal of the Board of Managers, June 21, 1819, ACS papers; ACS *Third Annual Report,* p. 138; William Turner to E. B. Caldwell, Eatonton, Putnam co., Georgia, December 23, 1819, Force Papers; Putnam County Auxiliary Society, *Second Annual Report of the Putnam Auxiliary Society, for colonizing the Free Persons of Color of the United States, with their consent* (Milledgeville, 1821), pp. 40–41.

7. *National Intelligencer,* August 7 and September 22, 1819; ACS *Third Annual Report,* pp. 17, 136, 140–144.

8. Johns, *Memoir of Meade,* p. 123; ACS *Third Annual Report,* p. 17.

9. The board of managers had appointed Ebenezer Burgess agent in New England but his work was negligible. Journal of the Board of Managers, October 20, 1819, ACS papers; ACS *Third Annual Report,* pp. 138–139, 141, 145–146.

10. Journal of the Board of Managers, May 30, 1820, ACS papers; American Colonization Society, *An Essay on the Late Institution of the American Colonization Society for Colonizing the Free People of Colour of the United States* (Washington, 1820), pp. 3, 10–11.

11. *The African Intelligencer,* I (July, 1820); Ralph R. Gurley, *Life of Jehudi Ashmun* . . . (Washington, 1835), pp. 64–65.

12. Manuscript records for the Colonization Society are scanty for the period up to 1824. Caldwell kept virtually no letter file, but he inserted copies of important communications into the minute book of the board of managers. Peter Force, of the printing firm of Davis

and Force, and a collector of historical data, valued historical documents and carefully preserved many of the letters passed to him for printing. See Force Papers; Gaillard Hunt, *First Forty Years of Washington Society . . . Letters of Margaret Bayard Smith . . .* (New York, 1906), pp. 151–152, 159–160; ACS *Ninth Annual Report,* p. 26.

13. Putnam Auxiliary Society, *Second Annual Report,* pp. 6–7, 10, 19, 20–24, 44.

14. *Georgia Missionary,* n.d., quoted in *National Intelligencer,* October 22, 1819; *National Intelligencer,* October 15, 1819.

15. Archibald Alexander, *A History of Colonization on the Western Coast of Africa* (Philadelphia, 1846), p. 349.

16. ACS *Sixth Annual Report,* pp. 7–8.

17. *Ibid.,* pp. 48–52, 71.

18. Journal of the Board of Managers, March 28, May 5, June 4, 1823, ACS papers.

19. *Ibid.,* June 2, 1823. Those who attended the conference were: General John Mason, Rev. Stephen B. Balch, Rev. James Laurie, Rev. William H. Wilmer, Rev. Obadiah Brown, Dr. William Thornton, Col. Henry Ashton, William H. Fitzhugh, Charles Mercer, Elias B. Caldwell, Ralph R. Gurley, John Underwood, Joseph Gales, Sr., Joseph Gales, Jr., Rev. Luther Rice, Rev. P. Chase, Solomon Peck, and Leonard Bacon.

20. Journal of the Board of Managers, June 4, 1823, ACS papers.

21. ACS *Seventh Annual Report,* pp. 29, 103; Theodore D. Bacon, *Leonard Bacon, A Statesman in the Church* (New Haven, 1931), p. 187.

22. Bacon, *Leonard Bacon,* pp. 55–59.

23. Albert E. Gurley, *The History and Genealogy of the Gurley Family* (Hartford, Conn., 1897), pp. 51–52, 71–72; Mason Noble, *A Discourse Commemorative of the Life and Character of Rev. Ralph Randolph Gurley, by Mason Noble, D.D., Pastor of the Sixth Presbyterian Church. Published by request of the American Colonization Society* (Washington, 1872), pp. 3–4, 19–20; Hunt, *First Forty Years of Washington Society,* p. 328; Elisha Whittlesey, *An Address delivered before the Tallmadge Colonization Society, on the Fourth of July, 1833* (Ravenna, Ohio, 1833), p. 23; ACS *Seventh Annual Report,* p. 48.

24. The Papers of the American Colonization Society at the Library of Congress reflect Gurley's care in organizing and preserving the society's voluminous correspondence.

25. ACS *Seventh Annual Report,* p. 32.

26. *Ibid.,* pp. 30, 165.

27. New York Colonization Society, *First Annual Report of the New-York Colonization Society. Read at the Annual Meeting, October 29, 1823* (New York, 1823), pp. 4, 7; ACS *Seventh Annual Report,* pp. 164–165.

28. *Ibid.,* pp. 106–108.

29. *Ibid.,* pp. 108–109.

30. *Ibid.,* pp. 108–109, 164–165.

Notes to VIII: CRISIS YEARS: 1823–1824

1. New York *Columbian,* n.d., quoted in Boston *Recorder,* February 18, 1817; New York *Statesman,* n.d., quoted in ACS *Seventh Annual Report,* p. 107; *Niles' Weekly Register,* XV, 117–118.

2. [Loring D. Dewey], *Correspondence Relative to the Emigration to Hayti, of the Free People of Colour, in the United States: Together with the Instructions to the Agent sent out by President Boyer* (New York, 1824), pp. 2–11; *Niles' Weekly Register,* XVIII, 326.

3. *National Intelligencer,* November 19 and 24, 1819; Ludwell Lee Montague, *Haiti and the United States 1714–1938* (Durham, N.C., 1940), pp. 70–71; *Niles' Weekly Register,* XXVI, 272; Dewey, *Emigration to Hayti,* p. 7.

4. Dewey, *Emigration to Hayti,* pp. 15–18; John Edward Baur, "Mulatto Machiavelli, Jean Pierre Boyer, and the Haiti of His Day," *Journal of Negro History,* XXXII (1947), 325–326.

5. Dewey, *Emigration to Hayti,* p. 28n.; Journal of the Board of Managers, June 11, 1824, ACS papers.

6. Dewey, *Emigration to Hayti,* pp. 28–31n. Others who participated in the new society: Rev. Gardiner Spring, Peter A. Jay, Samuel Cowdrey, Jonathan Wainwright, John Pintard, Isaac Collins, George Newbold, Robert C. Cornell, Joshua Underhill, Stephen Allen, Thomas Eddy, John E. Hyde, James Palmer, John R. Willis, John R. Hurd, Cornelius Du Bois, Theodore Dwight, and H. Ketchum.

7. Montague, *Haiti and the U.S.,* p. 71; John Edward Baur, "Mulatto Machiavelli," *Journal of Negro History,* XXXII, 326–327; *Niles' Weekly Register,* XXVI, 373–374; letter of James Lee, a disillusioned colonist, Hartford *Times,* n.d., quoted in Richmond *Enquirer,* March 14, 1826.

8. *African Repository,* I, 150.

9. William B. Sprague, *Annals of the American Pulpit* (New York, 1868), V, 572–575.

10. ACS *Tenth Annual Report,* pp. 81–82; New Jersey Colonization Society, *Proceedings of a Meeting held at Princeton, New-Jersey, July 14, 1824, to form a Society in the state of New Jersey, to co-operate with the American Colonization Society* (Princeton, N.J., 1824), pp. 3–7, 13–17.

11. Theodore Frelinghuysen, *An Oration delivered at Princeton, New Jersey, November 16, 1824: Before the New-Jersey Colonization Society, by the Honourable Theodore Frelinghuysen* (Princeton, N.J., 1824), pp. 5, 7–14.

12. ACS *Eighth Annual Report,* appendix, p. 50.

13. *Ibid.,* pp. 14–15.

14. *Ibid.,* pp. 47–50, 68.

15. Ralph R. Gurley, *Life of Jehudi Ashmun* . . . (Washington, 1835), p. 119 and note; J. Ashmun to William A. Davis, Alexandria, April 2, 1821; Ashmun to Force, Alexandria, May 12, 1821; Ashmun to Force, n.p., May 16, 1821; Ashmun to Force, Baltimore, May 18, 1822, Peter Force Papers, Library of Congress.

16. Gurley, *Life of Ashmun,* appendix, pp. 39–42; Ashmun to Force, Baltimore, May 18, 1822, Peter Force Papers.

17. Gurley, *Life of Ashmun,* pp. 125–136.

18. Ashmun later estimated that eight hundred natives attacked on November 11 and fifteen hundred on December 2, 1822. *Ibid.,* pp. 135–142.

19. ACS *Sixth Annual Report,* p. 36; Gurley, *Life of Ashmun,* pp. 147–148, 151–152, 154–159.

20. Gurley, *Life of Ashmun,* pp. 161–162.

21. ACS *Seventh Annual Report,* pp. 115–116; Gurley, *Life of Ashmun,* pp. 162, 185–187.

22. Journal of the Board of Managers, April 1 and 18, 1824, ACS papers.

23. *Ibid.,* April 20[?], 1824; Gurley, *Life of Ashmun,* p. 207n.; the board's reply, address, and instructions are printed in Charles Henry Huberich, *The Political and Legislative History of Liberia* (New York, 1947), I, 300–312.

24. Journal of the Board of Managers, June, 1824, ACS papers; Gurley, *Life of Ashmun,* pp. 186–190, 195–196, 205.

Notes to IX: THE EMERGENCE OF MR. GURLEY

1. Ralph R. Gurley, *Life of Jehudi Ashmun* . . . (Washington, 1835), pp. 207–208; Charles Henry Huberich, *Political and Legislative History of Liberia* . . . (New York, 1947), I, 317; [Kennedy], *African Colonization* (27 Congress, 3 session, House Report no. 283, serial 428), p. 460.

2. Gurley, *Life of Ashmun,* pp. 209–211.

3. 1824 Constitution, plan of civil government, and digest of laws in force in 1824, see Huberich, *Liberia,* I, 331–338; Gurley, *Life of Ashmun,* pp. 212, 214–215n.

4. Gurley, *Life of Ashmun,* pp. 213–216; ACS *Eighth Annual Report,* pp. 11–13; *African Repository,* XI, 22–24; Huberich, *Liberia,* I, 361–362.

5. Journal of the Board of Managers, December 29, 1824, ACS papers; Gurley, *Life of Ashmun,* pp. 218–219. The board selected Dr. John W. Peaco largely because the colony desperately needed a physician. He later became U.S. agent in charge of rescued Africans. Huberich, *Liberia,* I, 627–628; *African Repository,* XI, 20.

6. Gurley, *Life of Ashmun,* pp. 221–226, 229; *African Repository,* I, 28.

7. *African Repository,* IV, 231–233.

8. Gurley, *Life of Ashmun,* pp. 243, 246–248; Journal of the Board of Managers, July 2, 1825, ACS papers.

9. Mason Noble, *A Discourse Commemorative of the Life and Character of Rev. Ralph Randolph Gurley* (Washington, 1872), pp. 7–8, 10–11.

10. Journal of the Board of Managers, October 13, 1828, ACS papers.

11. *African Repository,* I, 17–19, 129–131.

12. Ralph R. Gurley, *A Discourse Delivered on the Fourth of July, 1825, in the City of Washington* (Washington, 1825), pp. 12, 15–17; *African Repository,* I, 257–263.

13. ACS *Eighth Annual Report,* pp. 7–8.

14. *African Repository,* I, 7–21, 30–32, 43–61, 79–82; II, 15–19, 40–54; III, 110–115.

15. *Ibid.,* I, 5; II, 75, 110–119, 128, 142–152, 173–183, 211–220; III, 285, 380–382.

16. *Ibid.,* II, 320–322.

17. *Ibid.,* I, 29; II, 340, 381–382.

18. *Ibid.,* I, 320.

19. *Ibid.,* V, 271, 283–284; ACS *Twelfth Annual Report,* pp. 6–7.

20. Albert E. Gurley, *The History and Genealogy of the Gurley Family* (Hartford, Conn., 1897), pp. 72–73; Gaillard Hunt, *First Forty Years of Washington Society . . .* (New York, 1906) p. 328; Mason Noble, *Ralph R. Gurley,* pp. 5–6.

Notes to X: BUILDING A MOVEMENT

1. *An Essay on the Late Institution of the American Society for Colonizing the Free People of Colour, of the United States* (Washington, 1820), pp. 33–34, 37–59; Putnam County Auxiliary Society, *Second Annual Report,* pp. 20, 25–27.

2. ACS *Seventh Annual Report,* pp. 7–8.

3. Frederick County Auxiliary Society, *Annual Report* (1820), pp. 14–17.

4. ACS *Seventh Annual Report,* pp. 109–111.

5. ACS *Ninth Annual Report,* p. 66.

6. ACS *Eighth Annual Report,* pp. 44–45.

7. John H. Cooke, Sr., to Jesse B. Harrison, "Bremo," Fluvanna co., Virginia, October 28, 1827, J. B. Harrison Papers, Library of Congress.

8. John Marshall to F. S. Key, Richmond, October 25, 1828, ACS papers.

9. *African Repository,* I, 339.

10. ACS *Ninth Annual Report,* p. 66.

11. *African Repository,* II, 62–63; III, 349, 371, 377–379.

12. *Ibid.,* II, 289; III, 254; Mary Henderson to Gurley, James Town, Guilford co., N.C., March 17, 1827, ACS papers.

13. William B. Sprague, *Annals of the American Pulpit* (New York, 1868), VI, 578–584; Lyon G. Tyler, *Encyclopedia of Virginia Biography* (New York, 1915), II, 286.

14. *African Repository,* IV, 380; Caspar Morris, *Memoirs of Miss Margaret Mercer* (Philadelphia, 1848), pp. 114, 117–118.

15. L. Minor Blackford, *Mine Eyes Have Seen the Glory; the Story of a Virginia Lady, Mary Berkeley Minor Blackford, 1802–1896, Who taught her sons to hate Slavery and to love the Union* (Cambridge, Mass., 1954), pp. 1–2, 21–24, 27.

16. John E. Semmes, *John H. B. Latrobe and His Times 1803–1891* (Baltimore, 1917), pp. 139–141.

17. Maryland Colonization Society, *African Colonization: Proceedings of a Meeting of the Friends of African Colonization, held in the City of Baltimore, on the 17 October, 1827* (n.p., c.1827), pp. 18–19.

18. C. C. Harper to Gurley, Baltimore, July 8, 1827; Harper to Gurley, Baltimore, February 26, 1828, ACS papers.

19. Harper to Gurley, Baltimore, January 3, 1827, ACS papers; *African Repository,* II, 189.

20. *Report: The Committee of Winder Lodge, No. 77, to which was assigned the duty of communicating with Lodges throughout the State of Maryland and elsewhere, on the subject of contributing to the American Colonization Society* (n.d., c.1827), pp. 3–4; *African Repository,* II, 154–155; Semmes, *Life of Latrobe,* p. 421.

21. *African Repository,* II, 288, 353; III, 123; ACS *Tenth Annual Report,* p. 5.

22. Florence Hays, *Daughters of Dorcas* (New York, 1952), pp. 7–37, 141–156.

23. ACS *Eighth Annual Report,* p. 29; *African Repository,* IV, 311, 485; V, 317–319; VI, 29, 87–88, 369; D. I. Burr to Gurley, Richmond, February 20, 1829; Latrobe to Gurley, Baltimore, January 10, 1829, ACS papers.

24. *African Repository,* IV, 285, 311, 314–317; V, 245.

25. Benjamin J. Klebaner, "American Manumission Laws and the Responsibility for Supporting Slaves," *Virginia Magazine of History and Biography,* LXIII (1955), 443–453.

26. *African Repository,* I, 212–214, 318; III, 383; IV, 380; Tyler, *Virginia Biography,* II, 213–214; Journal of the Board of Managers, August 14, 1826; David Bullock to Benjamin Brand, Louisa County, Virginia, September 13, 1827, ACS papers.

27. *African Repository,* I, 213, 318; Gurley to J. B. Harrison, Washington, November 5, 1828, J. B. Harrison Papers, Library of Congress; W. H. Robbins to R. R. Gurley, Cheraw, S.C., October 12, 1827, ACS papers; Arthur F. Raper, *Tenants of the Almighty* (New York, 1943), p. 48; Ruth Hairston Early, *The Family of Early* (Lynchburg, Va., 1920), p. 317; *African Repository,* V, 377; VI, 30, 62. Early Lee Fox offers a table showing the number of slaves offered for emigration between 1825 and 1835. Though it contains errors and does not pretend to be exhaustive, the table shows that at least two thousand were offered to the society between 1825 and

1832, and an additional one thousand in the next three years. Early Lee Fox, *The American Colonization Society 1817–1840* (Baltimore, 1919), pp. 212–213. This computation rests largely on information offered in an index to the first ten volumes of the *African Repository,* X, 23–26.

28. *African Repository,* II, 20, 163, 352; VI, 138, 247–248.

29. ACS *Eighth Annual Report,* pp. 26, 32–33; *Ninth Annual Report,* p. 23; Charles Henry Huberich, *Political and Legislative History of Liberia* (New York, 1947), I, 342.

30. ACS *Tenth Annual Report,* p. 33; *Eleventh Annual Report,* p. 31; Huberich, *Liberia,* I, 372–373.

31. Norfolk *Beacon,* n.d., quoted by *African Repository,* I, 369–370; III, 283; P. J. Staudenraus, "Victims of the African Slave Trade, A Document," *The Journal of Negro History,* XLI (1956), 148–151.

32. ACS *Seventh Annual Report,* pp. 44–47; *Eighth Annual Report,* p. 25; *Ninth Annual Report,* pp. 28–29; *Tenth Annual Report,* pp. 51–53.

Notes to XI: NORTHERN BENEVOLENCE

1. *African Repository,* I, 36, 162.
2. *Ibid.,* I, 68, 380.
3. *Ibid.,* I, 91–92, 384; II, 152–154.
4. *Ibid.,* I, 15–17, 42; VII, 369–370; X, 190–191.
5. ACS *Seventh Annual Report,* pp. 13–14.
6. Circular signed by Gurley, dated Washington, October 15, 1823, printed at the end of the New York Colonization Society's *First Annual Report; African Repository,* I, 93; II, 8–11, 25, 124–125; Leonard Bacon, *A Plea for Africa: delivered in New-Haven, July 4, 1825* (New Haven, 1825), pp. 16–18, 22; Theodore D. Bacon, *Leonard Bacon, A Statesman in the Church* (New Haven, 1931), pp. 191–192.
7. ACS *Seventh Annual Report,* pp. 90–92; Nathaniel Bouton, *Christian Patriotism; an Address delivered at Concord, July the Fourth, 1825* (Concord, N.H., 1825), p. 19.
8. Bouton, *Christian Patriotism,* pp. 15–16; Nathaniel Scudder Prime, *The Year of Jubilee; But not to Africans: A Discourse, delivered July 4th, 1825, Being the 49th Anniversary of American Independence* (Cambridge, N.Y., 1825), p. 16; Philip C. Hay, *Our*

Duty to our Coloured Population: A Sermon for the Benefit of the American Colonization Society, Delivered in the Second Presbyterian Church, Newark; July 23, 1826 (Newark, New Jersey, 1826), pp. 7, 10–13; William McMurray, *A Sermon, Preached in Behalf of the American Colonization Society, in the Reformed Dutch Church, in Market-Street, New York, July 10, 1825* (New York, 1825), p. 19.

9. Prime, *Year of Jubilee,* pp. 7–8, 13–15; McMurray, *A Sermon,* p. 16; Bouton, *Christian Patriotism,* p. 17.

10. William E. Strong, *The Story of the American Board; An Account of the First Hundred Years of the American Board of Commissioners for Foreign Missions* (Boston, 1910), pp. 124–125; *African Repository,* I, 248–249.

11. *African Repository,* I, 64, 124–125, 223–224; II, 31.

12. *Ibid.,* I, 381; II, 25, 31, 252–253, 380.

13. *Ibid.,* I, 252–253; Sherman Weld Tracy, *The Tracy Genealogy, Being Some of the Descendants of Stephen Tracy of Plymouth Colony, 1623, also Ancestoral Sketches and Charters* (Rutland, Vt., 1926), pp. 65–66; Francis C. Sessions, *Materials for a History of the Sessions Family in America, the Descendants of Alexander Sessions of Andover, Mass., 1669* (Albany, New York, 1890), pp. 39, 61, 64.

14. *African Repository,* I, 288, 350–352.

15. *Ibid.,* I, 252–255, 287, 319, 384; X, 292; ACS *Tenth Annual Report,* pp. 32–33; George Champlin Mason, *Reminiscences of Newport* (Newport, R.I., 1884), pp. 154–159.

16. *African Repository,* II, 195–196, 221.

17. Gurley to John Kennedy, Philadelphia, October 19, 1826; Gurley to Kennedy, Philadelphia, October 25, 1826; William B. Davidson to Gurley, February 19, 1827; Gerard Ralston to Gurley, December 8, 1826; Ralston to Gurley, February 23, 1827; William H. Dillingham to Gurley, West Chester, Pennsylvania, December 1, 1827; Elliott Cresson to Gurley, Philadelphia, August 23, 1828, all in ACS papers.

18. John H. Kennedy, *Sympathy, Its Foundations and Legitimate Exercise considered, in Special Relation to Africa: A Discourse delivered on the Fourth of July, 1828, in the Sixth Presbyterian Church, Philadelphia* (Philadelphia, 1828), pp. 5–10.

19. *African Repository,* VI, 138–139; Gerard Ralston to Gurley, Philadelphia, October 31, 1829, ACS papers; Pennsylvania Colonization Society, *Report of the Board of Managers of the Pennsylvania Colonization Society, with an Appendix* (Philadelphia, 1830), pp. 7, 47–48.

20. *African Repository,* II; 291; III, 63, 92, 118–119; VI, 106; Benjamin Silliman to Gurley, New Haven, March 18, 1827, ACS papers.

21. *African Repository,* IV, 117–125; V, 252; Theodore Bacon, *Leonard Bacon,* p. 194; Connecticut Colonization Society, *An Address to the Public by the Managers of the Colonization Society of Connecticut: With an Appendix* (New Haven, 1828); Fowler to Gurley, Plainfield, Connecticut, August 5, 1829; May to Gurley, Brooklyn, Connecticut, July 5, 1829; Jocelyn to Gurley, New Haven, October 5, 1829, ACS papers.

22. *African Repository,* III, 189–190; V, 31; VI, 150–151; XI, 213, 214; Chauncey Whittlesey to Gurley, Middletown, Connecticut, May 17, 1829; Lydia Sigourney to Gurley, Hartford, January 15, 1833, ACS papers.

23. Gerrit Smith to Gurley, Peterboro, New York, October 10, 1827; Smith to Gurley, Peterboro, New York, December 26, 1827; Isaac Orr to Gurley, Washington, March 2, 1829; Bushrod Washington to Gurley, Washington, March 15, 1828, ACS papers; Mathew Carey to John H. B. Latrobe, Bordentown (?), Pennsylvania, August 16, 1828, Latrobe Papers, Library of Congress; Carey to Latrobe, Philadelphia, November 8, 1828, Latrobe Papers; Carey to Latrobe, Philadelphia, December 10, 1828, Latrobe Papers; Carey to Gurley, Philadelphia, September 7, 1829, ACS papers; *African Repository,* III, 382–383; IV, 30–31, 95, 186, 270–272, 317, 366, 379; V, 32.

24. Lewis Tappan to Knowles Taylor, New York, May 22, 1828; Orr to Gurley, March 14, 16, and 18, 1829, ACS papers; Nathan F. Carter, *The Native Ministry of New Hampshire . . . The Harvesting of More than Thirty Years* (Concord, New Hampshire, 1906), p. 58.

25. *African Repository,* V, 58–60, 277–278; New York State Colonization Society, *African Colonization: Proceedings of the Formation of the New-York State Colonization Society; together with an Address to the Public, from the Managers thereof* (Albany, 1829), pp. 3–22.

26. New York State Colonization Society, *Proceedings,* p. 22; Orr to Gurley, Albany, April 15, 1829, ACS papers.

27. Orr to Gurley, New York, May 11–12, 1829; Orr to Gurley, New York, May 15, 1829, ACS papers; *African Repository,* V, 175, 341–342; *New York Public Meeting in behalf of the American Colonization Society: The Proceedings of a Public Meeting, held in the Middle Dutch Church: Together with Addresses delivered on that Oc-*

casion, by the Rev. Mr. Gallaudet, Principal of the Deaf and Dumb Asylum at Hartford, Connecticut; Captain Stockton, of the United States Navy; Francis S. Key, Esq. of the District of Columbia; and Two Letters from Captain John B. Nicholson, of the United States Navy (New York, 1829), pp. 23–27.

28. Joshua Leavitt to Gurley, New York, October 20, 1829, ACS papers.

29. William Roper to Gurley, Boston, January 25, 1827; Leonard Bacon to Gurley, New Haven, September 13, 1828; W. W. Niles to Gurley, Boston, July 10, 1827; John Tappan to Gurley, Boston, July 24, 1827; Niles to Gurley, Malden, Mass., October 2, 1827, ACS papers.

30. E. Gillet to Gurley, Hallowell, Maine, April 4, 1828; Jonathan Greenleaf to Gurley, Wells, Maine, February 12, 1828, ACS papers; *African Repository,* IV, 378–379; V, 95.

31. William Ladd to Gurley, Minot, Maine, April 4, 1828; Noah Worcester to Gurley, Brighton, Massachusetts, July 6, 1830, ACS papers; *African Repository,* VI, 241–242.

32. *African Repository,* IV, 312; Calvin Yale, *A Sermon Delivered before the Vermont Colonization Society, at Montpelier, October 17, 1827* (Montpelier, 1827), p. 4; Silas McKeen, *A Sermon, delivered at Montpelier, October 15, 1828, before the Vermont Colonization Society* (Montpelier, 1828), pp. 19, 22.

33. *African Repository,* IV, 246–247; H. Humphrey to James C. Dunn, Amherst College, Andover, Mass., July 17, 1828; S. M. Worcester to Gurley, Amherst College, February 3, 1829; Worcester to Gurley, Amherst College, June 21, 1829; Willbur Fisk to Gurley, Wilbraham, Mass., April 7, 1829; Worcester to Gurley, Amherst College, July 8, 1831, ACS papers; [S. M. Worcester], *Essays on Slavery; Re-published from the Boston Recorder & Telegraph for 1825: By Vigornius, and others* (Amherst, Mass., 1826), pp. 5–28.

34. Amos A. Phelps to Gurley, Andover Theological Seminary, January 15, 1828; Phelps to Gurley, Andover, November 13, 1828; G. Punchard to Gurley, Andover, December 26, 1828; B. B. Edwards to Gurley, Andover, December 16, 1829; Edwards to Gurley, Boston, May 3, 1830, ACS papers; *A Few Facts respecting the American Colonization Society, and the Colony at Liberia: For Gratuitous Distribution* (Boston, 1830), pp. 15–16.

35. Worcester to Gurley, Andover, November 16, 1828; Worcester to Gurley, Andover, July 27, 1830; Orr to Gurley, Bowman's Creek, New York, June 22, 1829, ACS papers.

36. Worcester to Gurley, November 16, 1829; Orr to Gurley, New York, May 11–12, 1829, ACS papers.

37. Leonard Bacon to Gurley, New Haven, July 6, 1830; Bacon to Gurley, New Haven, October 13, 1830, ACS papers; *African Repository,* VI, 134; John Newland Maffit, *A Plea for Africa: A Sermon delivered at Bennet Street Church, in behalf of the American Colonization Society, July 4, 1830* (Boston, 1830), pp. 3–13; Ezra Stiles Gannett, *A Discourse delivered in the Federal Street Church on Thanksgiving Day, December 2, 1830* (Boston, 1830), pp. 1–24.

38. Bacon to Gurley, New Haven, July 6, 1830; Bacon to Gurley, New Haven, October 13, 1830, ACS papers; *African Repository,* VII, 28; Massachusetts Colonization Society, *American Colonization Society, and the Colony at Liberia: Published by the Massachusetts Colonization Society* (Boston, 1831), p. 15.

39. James Bayard to Gurley, Philadelphia, December 2, 1829; Gerard Ralston to Gurley, Philadelphia, December 19, 1829; John Hanson to Gerard Ralston [Philadelphia], December 25, 1829, copied by John Kennedy, January 2, 1830, ACS papers; Huberich, *Liberia,* I, 433–434; ACS *Fourteenth Annual Report,* pp. 2–3, 15; *Fifteenth Annual Report,* pp. 11–12.

40. *African Repository,* VI, 347–349; Huberich, *Liberia,* I, 434; ACS *Fifteenth Annual Report,* p. 11.

Notes to XII: THE WESTERN CRUSADERS

1. Benjamin Brand to Ralph Gurley, Richmond, Virginia, August 20, 1827; William Meade to Gurley, Millwood, Virginia, December 6, 1831; Rev. William Graham to Gurley, Chillicothe, Ohio, February 10, 1827; Robert I. Hall to R. S. Finley, George Town, Brown county, Ohio, February 3, 1832, all in ACS papers; *African Repository,* III, 157, 254; VI, 68; X, 41; Henry Clay, *Speech of the Hon. Henry Clay, before the American Colonization Society, in the Hall of the House of Representatives, January 20, 1827: With an Appendix, containing the Documents therein referred to* (Washington, 1827), p. 5.

2. Journal of the Board of Managers, July 10, 1826, ACS papers.

3. Benjamin O. Peers to Gurley, Pittsburgh, September 26, 1826; Peers to Gurley, Brownsville, Penn., October 4, 1826; Henry H. Pfeiffer to Gurley, Brownsville, Penn., December 12, 1826, ACS papers.

4. Rev. L. C. Freeman to Gurley, Cleveland, Ohio, November 16, 1826; Peers to Gurley, Canton, Ohio, November 1, 1826; M. M. Henkle to Gurley, Springfield, Ohio, May 29, 1827; Henkle to Gurley, Springfield, Ohio, August 1, 1827; B. O. Carpenter to Gurley, Bainbridge, Ross county, Ohio, March 31, 1827; William M. Thomson to Gurley, Miami University, Oxford, Ohio, May 26, 1827, all in ACS papers; *African Repository,* III, 23–24, 28, 119–120, 220–221, 252, 350–351; ACS *Tenth Annual Report,* p. 83.

5. *African Repository,* VII, 180–181.

6. Peers to Gurley, Maysville, Kentucky, December 11, 1826, ACS papers; *African Repository,* IV, 251; V, 29, 249; VI, 6–12; Kentucky Colonization Society, *The Proceedings of the Colonization Society of Kentucky, with the Address of the Hon. Daniel Mayes, at the Annual meeting, at Frankfort, December 1st, 1831* (Frankfort, [1832]), p. 5.

7. Robert S. Finley to Gurley, Cincinnati, November 9, 1826, ACS papers; *African Repository,* III, 29; IX, 88–89; Cincinnati Colonization Society, *Proceedings of the Cincinnati Colonization Society, at the Annual Meeting, January 14, 1833: Published by order of the Board of Managers* (Cincinnati, 1833), p. 2.

8. James C. Finley to Gurley, Cincinnati, September 7, 1829; Robert S. Finley to Gurley, Cincinnati, September 18, 1829, ACS papers; *African Repository,* VI, 181, 280, 339–340, 347–349; VII, 181, 185, 209; VIII, 59.

9. J. Reuben Sheeler, "The Struggle of the Negro in Ohio for Freedom," *Journal of Negro History,* XXXI (April, 1946), 211; Richard C. Wade, "The Negro in Cincinnati, 1800–1830," *ibid.,* XXXIX (June, 1954), 43–56: Fred Landon, "The Diary of Benjamin Lundy Written during his Journey through Upper Canada, January, 1832," *Ontario Historical Society Papers and Records,* XIX (1922), 110–113; *African Repository,* V, 185; VIII, 225–226.

10. Cincinnati Colonization Society, *Proceedings,* p. 14; S. P. Chase to Gurley, Cincinnati, July 25, 1831; Josiah F. Polk to Gurley, Nashville, Tenn., December 12, 1829, ACS papers; *African Repository,* VII, 208.

11. James Latta to Gurley, Greenville, Illinois, February 14, 1833; J. G. Birney to Gurley, Mobile, Alabama, December 21, 1832; Elliott Cresson to Joseph Gales, Sr., Philadelphia, April 9, 1835; Josiah F. Polk to Gurley, Harrisburg, Pennsylvania, July 19, 1830, ACS papers.

12. Moses Montgomery Henkle, *The Life of Henry Bidleman*

Bascom, D.D., LL.D., Late Bishop of the Methodist Episcopal Church, South (Nashville, Tenn., 1857), pp. 204, 206, 211–221.

13. *Ibid.,* pp. 216–221, 224; *African Repository,* VIII, 153–154.

14. Henkle, *Bascom,* pp. 207–210, 230, 276–277, 300–305; H. B. Bascom to Henry Clay, Pittsburgh, Penn., December 4, 1829, Papers of Henry Clay, Library of Congress.

15. *African Repository,* V, 220, 378–380; VI, 71–79, 130; Josiah F. Polk to Gurley, Huntsville, Alabama, January 4, 1830, ACS papers.

16. *African Repository,* III, 25–26; V, 344–345, 378; VII, 102, 105–107, 114–115; Josiah F. Polk to Gurley, Richmond, Indiana, November 21, 1829; Edward Coles to H. Clay, Secretary of State and Vice-President of the Colonization Society, Vandalia, Illinois, January 20, 1829; Cyrus Edwards to Gurley, Alton, Illinois, August 28, 1832, ACS papers.

17. J. A. Jacobs to Gurley, Danville, Kentucky, December 4, 1829, ACS papers; *African Repository,* VII, 178–181; Robert J. Breckinridge, *Hints on Slavery: Founded on the State of the Constitution, Laws, and Politics of Kentucky, Thirteen Years Ago* (n.p., c.1834), p. 11. The essays appeared in the *Kentucky Reporter* (Lexington) in April, May, and June, 1830. Asa Earl Martin, *The Anti-Slavery Movement in Kentucky prior to 1850* (Filson Club Publication No. 29, Louisville, 1918), pp. 11–62.

18. Breckinridge, *Hints,* pp. 11–12; Robert J. Breckinridge, *An Address delivered before the Colonization Society of Kentucky, at Frankfort, on the 6th day of January, 1831* (Frankfort, Ky., 1831), pp. 20–24.

19. Finley to Gurley, Lexington, Kentucky, April 12, 1831, ACS papers; *African Repository,* VII, 90.

20. Finley to Gurley, Versailles, Kentucky, April 16, 1831; Finley to Gurley, Batavia, Ohio, August 6, 1831; R. J. Breckinridge to Gurley, Brodallove [Lexington], Kentucky, August 16, 1831; Breckinridge to Gurley, Brodallove, October 4, 1831, ACS papers.

21. Martin, *Anti-Slavery in Kentucky,* pp. 88–97.

22. John T. Edgar, chairman of the Kentucky Board of Managers, to Gurley, Frankfort, Kentucky, Feb. 28, 1833; George C. Light to Gurley, Cynthianna, Kentucky, April 1, 1833, ACS papers; *African Repository,* VII, 217, 345; VIII, 343.

23. H. B. Bascom to Gurley, Blue Licks, Kentucky, August 11, 1831, ACS papers; *African Repository,* V, 138–139, 182, 206–207.

24. Gurley to Birney, Washington, June 12, 1832, Dwight L. Dumond, ed., *Letters of James Gillespie Birney 1831–1857* (New York, 1938), I, 5–7; Birney to Gurley, Huntsville, Alabama, July 12, 1832, *ibid.,* I, 9.

25. John Allan to Gurley, Huntsville, Alabama, January 13, 1829; Birney to Henry Clay, Secretary of State, Huntsville, Alabama, July 10, 1828, ACS papers.

26. Birney to Gurley, Huntsville, Alabama, August 23, 1832, Dumond, ed., *Letters of Birney,* I, 21; Birney to Gurley, Huntsville, Alabama, January 24, 1833, *ibid.,* I, 50–53; *African Repository,* IX, 171–174; William Birney, *James G. Birney and His Times, The Genesis of the Republican Party with some account of Abolition Movements in the South before 1828* (New York, 1890), pp. 125–128.

27. Birney to Gurley, New Orleans, March 18, 1833, Dumond, ed., *Letters of Birney,* I, 60–62; Birney to Gurley, New Orleans, April 15, 1833, *ibid.,* I, 70–71.

28. Birney to Gurley, New Orleans, April 8, 1833; Birney to Gurley, New Orleans, April 14, 1833; Birney to Gurley, New Orleans, April 20, 1833; Birney to Gurley, Huntsville, Alabama, August 5, 1833, *ibid.,* I, 67–68, 70–72, 81–82; *African Repository,* IX, 243, 249.

29. Birney to Gurley, Huntsville, Alabama, September 24, 1833; Birney to Gurley, Danville, Kentucky, December 3, 1833; Birney to Gurley, Danville, December 11, 1833; and "Constitution and Address of the Kentucky Society for the Gradual Relief of the State from Slavery," Dumond, ed., *Letters of Birney,* I, 88–90, 95–109.

30. For list of auxiliaries, see Index, *African Repository,* X, 8–15; Cincinnati Colonization Society, *Proceedings,* p. 4.

Notes to XIII: VISIONS OF EMPIRE

1. *African Repository,* I, 25; II, 87, 125.

2. J. Ashmun to Samuel L. Southard, Secretary of the Navy, September 1, 1827 [John Pendleton Kennedy], *African Colonization* (27 Congress, 3 session, House Report no. 283, serial 428, Washington, D.C., 1843), pp. 435–438; Amos Kendall to John Branch, Secretary of the Navy, August, 1830, *ibid.,* pp. 460–462; *African Repository,* II, 82–83, 87.

3. Ralph R. Gurley, *Life of Jehudi Ashmun* . . . (Washington, 1835), p. 119n., and Appendix, pp. 39–44.

4. *Ibid.,* pp. 128–129; *African Repository,* IV, 19–20, 318; VII, 269; IX, 185.

5. Ashmun gives his account of Liberian climate, seasons, and growing conditions in his handbook, *The Liberia Farmer; or, Colonist's Guide to Independence and Domestic Comfort: Inscribed to All the Industrious Settlers of Liberia, by their Friend and Agent, J. Ashmun* (1825), reprinted in Gurley's biography of Ashmun, Appendix, pp. 63–79; J. W. Lugenbeel provides a more detailed account of Liberian climate, crops, and geography in his *Sketches of Liberia: comprising a Brief Account of Geography, Climate, Productions, and Diseases, of the Republic of Liberia: Second Edition—Revised* (Washington, D.C., 1853), *passim.*

6. Ashmun, *The Liberia Farmer,* as quoted by Gurley, *Ashmun,* Appendix, pp. 64–67; memorandum entitled "Colonial Notices, 1826," *ibid.,* Appendix, pp. 128–130, gives Ashmun's account of the state of agriculture in Liberia; "Extracts from Sketches of Foreign Travel, (Liberia,) by Rev. Charles Rockwell, United States Navy—1836," [Kennedy], *African Colonization,* pp. 831–844.

7. Mathew Carey, *Letters on the Colonization Society, and on Its Probable Results* . . . (Philadelphia, 1833), p. 25; Luther P. Jackson, *Free Negro Labor and Property Holding in Virginia, 1830–1860* (New York, 1942), pp. 147–148.

8. Carey, *Letters,* p. 25; Gurley, *Ashmun,* Appendix, pp. 131–132; Jackson, *Free Negro Labor,* p. 148.

9. *African Repository,* II, 80–81; IV, 19–20.

10. Journal of the Board of Managers, March 28, 1825, ACS papers; Gurley, *Ashmun,* Appendix, pp. 61–62.

11. *Ibid.,* Appendix, pp. 90–92; *African Repository,* II, 125, 264–267, 270; IV, 22–23, 84; ACS *Tenth Annual Report,* pp. 44–45.

12. *African Repository,* I, 372–373; II, 94–95; IV, 22; XI, 165–166.

13. *Ibid.,* II, 93–95; IV, 21, 23–24, 85; XI, 165–166; *Liberia Herald,* November 22, 1831.

14. *African Repository,* I, 339; II, 333; IV, 76; *New York Public Meeting in Behalf of the American Colonization Society,* pp. 15–19.

15. *African Repository,* III, 326–331.

16. *Ibid.,* II, 156–157, 270–271; IV, 83–84; ACS *Tenth Annual Report,* pp. 39–41.

17. Maryland Colonization Society, *African Colonization: Pro-*

ceedings of a Meeting on the Friends of African Colonization, held in the City of Baltimore, on [17] October, 1827 (n.p., c.1827), p. 11; *African Repository,* III, 346–347; VII, 341–342; *New York Public Meeting in Behalf of the American Colonization Society,* pp. 6–13.

18. Latrobe to Gurley, Baltimore, December 23, 1826, February 13, 1827; John Hanson and Gerard Ralston to Gurley, Philadelphia, March 13, 1830; Charles C. Harper to Gurley, Baltimore, April 9, 1829, ACS papers.

19. *African Repository,* I, 219; II, 83–84.

20. *Ibid.,* III, 222, 286; Latrobe to Gurley, Baltimore, April 12, 1827, ACS papers.

21. Latrobe to Gurley, Baltimore, December 21 and December 23, 1826, the latter by private courier; Charles C. Harper to Gurley, Baltimore, September 1, 1827, ACS papers; *African Repository,* II, 268.

22. Cresson to Gurley, Washington, June 13, 1829; Arthur Tappan to Gurley, New York, September 13, 1827, ACS papers; *African Repository,* VIII, 28–29.

23. *African Repository,* IV, 182–183, 186, 214ff., 286–287; VI, 336; T. D. Bacon, *Leonard Bacon* (New Haven, 1931), pp. 195–196; Carey, *Letters,* p. 32; Benjamin Silliman to Gurley, New Haven, August 17, 1828; Gurley, *Ashmun,* pp. 384–394; Leonard Bacon, *A Discourse preached in the Center Church, in New Haven, August 27, 1828, at the Funeral of Jehudi Ashmun, Esq., Colonial Agent of the American Colony of Liberia . . . with the Address at the Grave: By R. R. Gurley* (New Haven, 1828), pp. 3–20.

24. Journal of the Board of Managers, August 25, 1828, September 8, 1828, ACS papers; *African Repository,* IV, 224; V, 122–128.

25. *African Repository,* IV, 78–81; Thomas H. Gallaudet, *A Statement with Regard to the Moorish Prince, Abduhl Rahhahman: By Rev. T. H. Gallaudet, Principal of the American Asylum for the Education of the Deaf and Dumb: Published by order of the Committee appointed to solicit Subscriptions in New-York, to aid in redeeming the Family of the Prince from Slavery* (New York, 1826), pp. 3–7.

26. *African Repository,* IV, 243–250; Gallaudet, *Moorish Prince,* pp. 5–6.

27. T. H. Gallaudet to Gurley, Guilford, Connecticut, November 8, 1828, ACS papers; *African Repository,* IV, 250.

28. Gallaudet, *Moorish Prince,* pp. 7–8; Gallaudet to Gurley, New York, October 14, 1828; Arthur Tappan to Gurley, New York,

March 2, 1829; Tappan to Gurley, New York, March 27, 1829, ACS papers.

29. H. Clay to Gurley, Washington, D.C., January 3, 1829; Tappan to Gurley, New York, March 27, 1829, ACS papers; *African Repository,* IV, 379–380.

30. *African Repository,* V, 3–8, 122–123, 150, 281.

31. Arthur Tappan to Gurley, New York, November 10, 1829, September 27, 1830; Thomas H. Gallaudet to Gurley, Hartford, Conn., June 8 and 20, 1830, ACS papers.

32. Latrobe to Gurley, Baltimore, June 25, 1830; Benjamin Brand to Gurley, Richmond, October 3, 1829; Arthur Tappan to Gurley, New York, May 28, 1829; Cresson to Gurley, Philadelphia, June 13, 1829, ACS papers.

33. *African Repository,* VI, 53, 55; VII, 260, 269, 283–284; VIII, 33–35, 46, 106, 129–135, 379; *Liberia Herald,* February 22, 1832.

34. *African Repository,* VII, 24, 157, 259–260. In 1831 the anchorage duty was $12. See broadside, "Regulations of the Port of Monrovia," bound with the *Liberia Herald,* in the newspaper division, State Historical Society of Wisconsin, Madison, Wisconsin.

35. J. Mechlin to Gurley, Washington, June, 1830, ACS papers; *African Repository,* VII, 21–22, 265–266; III, 380; IX, 283–284; X, 47–58, 108.

36. "Extracts of Sketches of Foreign Travel, (Liberia,) by Rev. Charles Rockwell, United States Navy—1836," [Kennedy], *African Colonization,* pp. 838–840; F. Harrison Rankin, "A Visit to Sierra Leone, in 1834; with Notices of the town and adjoining country, and of the colonists, their pursuits, amusements, religion, and education; also, an account of slavery, and slave liberation in West Africa," *Carey's Library of Choice Literature: Containing the Best Works of the Day, in Biography, History, Travels, Novels, Poetry, &c.* (Philadelphia, 1836), II, 280.

37. *Liberia Herald,* February 6, 1831.

Notes to XIV: POLITICAL FORTUNES

1. ACS *Seventh Annual Report,* pp. 9–12, Appendix, pp. 111–114.

2. Herman V. Ames, ed., *State Documents on Federal Relations: The States and the United States* (Philadelphia, 1900–1906), pp. 203–204.

3. *African Repository,* I, 251; Ames, *State Documents,* p. 210;

[John Pendleton Kennedy], *African Colonization* (27 Congress, 3 session, House Committee Report no. 283, serial 428, Washington, D.C., 1843), pp. 926–933.

4. Ames, *State Documents,* pp. 207–208.

5. *Ibid.,* p. 203; "Gaius Gracchus," Richmond *Enquirer,* January 21, 1826; [Robert J. Turnbull], *The Crisis: or, Essays on the Usurpations of the federal government, By Brutus* (Charleston, 1827), p. 130; *African Repository,* V, 215–216.

6. *African Repository,* I, 35–36, 66, 69, 100, 216, 261–262.

7. H. A. Washington, ed., *The Writings of Thomas Jefferson* . . . (Washington, 1854), VII, 332–335.

8. *Register of Debates,* 18 Congress, 2 session, I, 623, 696; *African Repository,* I, 249.

9. Ames, *State Documents,* pp. 208–209.

10. *Register of Debates,* 18 Congress, 2 session, I, 735–736, 740; *African Repository,* I, 249.

11. [Kennedy], *African Colonization,* p. 408.

12. Leesburg *Genius of Liberty,* August 21, 1821, and Baltimore *Morning Chronicle,* August 24, 1821, as quoted by *Niles' Weekly Register,* XXI (September 1, 1821), 1–2.

13. Bushrod Washington's letter dated Jefferson co., Virginia, September 18, 1821, *ibid.,* XXI (September 29, 1821), 70–72.

14. Richmond *Enquirer,* October 11, 1825.

15. *Ibid.,* December 10, 1825.

16. *Ibid.,* October 25, November 25, 1825, January 21, February 28, 1826; *African Repository,* II, 254–256.

17. *Ibid.,* I, 335–336; II, 60.

18. John H. Kennedy to Gurley, Philadelphia, November 27, 1827; Lyman D. Brewster to Gurley, Mt. Pleasant, Tennessee, June 26, 1828; John H. B. Latrobe to Gurley, Baltimore, January 27, 1827, ACS papers.

19. *Memorial of the American Colonization Society for Colonizing the Free People of Color of the United States: January 29, 1827* (19 Congress, 2 session, House Document no. 64, serial 151, Washington, D.C., 1827), pp. 4–5; *Resolutions of the Legislature of Georgia in relation to the American Colonization Society: February 4, 1828* (20 Congress, 1 session, Senate Document no. 81, serial 165, Washington, D.C., 1828), pp. 5–11.

20. Turnbull, *The Crisis,* pp. 7–9, 23–25, 121–125, 128–131, 137.

21. John French to Gurley, Norfolk, Va., December 9, 1826; John H. Cocke to Gurley, Hanover co., Va., February 9, 1827; W. M.

Atkinson to Gurley, Petersburg, Va., January 5, July 4, 1827; D. L. Burr to Gurley, Richmond, Va., January 22, 1827; W. M. Atkinson to C. F. Mercer, Petersburg, Va., December 2, 4, 1828; Benjamin Brand to Gurley, Richmond, Va., October 17, 1826; G. W. Taliaferro to Gurley, King William, Va., March 16, 1827, all in ACS papers

22. *Annals of Congress,* 19 Congress, 2 session, III, 1214–1215, 1532–1533; [Charles F. Mercer], *Colonization of Free People of Colour: March 3, 1827* (19 Congress, 2 session, House Committee Report no. 101, serial 160, Washington, D.C., 1827), pp. 5–7; *African Repository,* IV, 52–58.

23. *Annals of Congress,* 19 Congress, 2 session, III, 289–295.

24. *Ibid.,* III, 295–296, 318–334.

25. *Report of the Senate Committee on Foreign Relations, April 28, 1828* (20 Congress, 1 session, Senate Document no. 178, serial 167, Washington, D.C., 1828), pp. 3–10, 12–13.

26. Lyman D. Brewster to Gurley, Mt. Pleasant, Tennessee, June 26, 1828, ACS papers; *African Repository,* IV, 162–169, 257–269, 331–346.

27. [Charles F. Mercer], *Slave Trade* (21 Congress, 1 session, House Committee Report no. 348, serial 201, Washington, D.C., 1830), pp. 2–3. The appendix, pp. 4–293, contains voluminous extracts and copies of colonization literature. *Memorial of the American Colonization Society* (21 Congress, 1 session, House Committee Report no. 277, serial 200, Washington, D.C., 1830), pp. 2–29; [Kennedy], *African Colonization,* pp. 456–463; Elliott Cresson to Gurley, on *Monongahela,* crossing Atlantic ocean, April 22, 1831, ACS papers.

28. [Kennedy], *African Colonization,* pp. 926–935; *African Repository,* V, 60–61; VII, 60–61; E. N. Kirk to Gurley, Albany, New York, March 23, 1830; Charles Tappan to Gurley, Boston, March 13, 1830, ACS papers.

29. W. M. Atkinson to Gurley, Petersburg, Va., July 4, 1827; William M. Blackford to Gurley, Fredericksburg, Va., October 21, 1829, ACS papers.

30. William Henry Foote to Gurley, Romney, Virginia, September 24, 1831; W. Meade to Gurley, Millwood, Va., December 6, 1831; W. M. Atkinson to Gurley, Petersburg, Va., August 29, 1831; Laurence Battaile to Gurley, Vielleboro, Caroline co., Va., February 21, 1832, ACS papers; *African Repository,* VII, 318.

31. *African Repository,* VII, 281; VIII, 119, 190; Benjamin Brand to Gurley, Richmond, Va., October 5, 1831; John McPhail to Gurley,

Norfolk, Va., September 22 and 23, 1831; W. M. Atkinson to Gurley, Petersburg, Va., September 10, 1831, ACS papers.

32. John McPhail to Gurley, Norfolk, Va., October 10 and 28, 1831; Miles White to Gurley, Elizabeth City, N.C., October 1, 1831, ACS papers; *African Repository,* VII, 320; X, 292.

33. W. Meade to Gurley, Millwood, Va., December 6, 1831, ACS papers; [Kennedy], *African Colonization,* pp. 425–426; *African Repository,* III, 61–62; VII, 57, 281, 370–372; James Madison to Gurley, Montpelier, Va., December 29, 1831, ACS papers.

34. Charles H. Ambler, *Sectionalism in Virginia from 1776 to 1861* (Chicago, 1910), pp. 188–190; Luther P. Jackson, *Free Negro Labor and Property Holding in Virginia, 1830–1860* (New York, 1942), p. 13.

35. Ambler, *Sectionalism,* pp. 191–193; Marshall is quoted by Jesse Burton Harrison in an unsigned review of *The Speech of Thomas Marshall in the House of Delegates of Virginia, on the Abolition of Slavery: Delivered, Friday, January 20, 1832,* in *The American Quarterly Review,* XII (December, 1832), 392; Joseph Clarke Robert, *The Road from Monticello; a Study of the Virginia Slavery Debate of 1832* (Historical Papers of the Trinity College Historical Society, XXIV, Durham, N.C., 1941), 12–26, 78–80.

36. Ambler, *Sectionalism,* pp. 194–195, 199–201; Robert, *Road from Monticello,* pp. 29–35, 70–72; Theodore M. Whitfield, *Slavery Agitation in Virginia 1829–1832* (Baltimore, 1930), pp. 65–113.

37. Thomas W. Gilmer to Gurley, Charlottesville, Va., April 30, 1832, ACS papers; Jackson, *Free Negro Labor,* p. 15.

38. [Thomas R. Dew], review of *Debate in the Virginia Legislature of 1831–32 on the Abolition of Slavery and Letter of Appomattox to the People of Virginia on the subject of Abolition of Slavery* appeared in *The American Quarterly Review,* XII (September, 1832), 189–200, 203, 212–227, 235, 247–265; Robert, *Road from Monticello,* pp. 46–49; Kenneth Stampp, "An Analysis of T. R. Dew's *Review of the Debates in the Virginia Legislature,*" *The Journal of Negro History,* XXVII (October, 1942), 380–387; Whitfield, *Slavery Agitation,* pp. 135–140.

39. Gerard Ralston to Gurley, Philadelphia, September 17, 1832; Robert Walsh to Gurley, Philadelphia, September 19, 1832; Mathew Carey to Gurley, Philadelphia, January 24, 1832, September 22, 1832; John H. Cocke to Gurley, "Bremo," Fluvanna county, Va., February 22, 1833, all in ACS papers; Thomas R. Dew, *Review of the*

Debate in the Virginia Legislature of 1831 and 1832 (Richmond, 1832).

40. Gurley to Harrison, Washington, D.C., March 11, 1828; Jesse Burton Harrison Papers, Library of Congress; Harrison's review of *The Speech of Thomas Marshall* was printed by *The American Quarterly Review,* XII (December, 1832), 379–383, 388–395, 400, 404, 410–426; Robert, *Road from Monticello,* p. 49.

41. *African Repository,* VIII, 316–317; James Madison to Gurley, Montpelier, Va., February 19, 1832, ACS papers.

42. *African Repository,* VIII, 382; Thomas W. Gilmer to Gurley, Richmond, Va., February 12, 1833; William H. Broadnax to Gurley, Richmond, Va., February 14, 1833; John Rutherford to Gurley, Richmond, Va., March 20, 1833; Joseph Jackson to Gurley, Richmond, Va., April 16, 1833; John H. Cocke to Gurley, "Bremo," Fluvanna co., Va., March 31, 1833, all in ACS papers.

43. *Register of Debates,* 22 Congress, 1 session, VIII, 641–646.

44. *Ibid.,* VIII, 2332–2350.

45. *Report of the Senate Committee on Manufactures, April 16, 1832* (22 Congress, 1 session, Senate Document no. 128, serial 214, Washington, D.C., 1832), pp. 1–19; *Register of Debates,* 22 Congress, 1 session, XI, 785–791.

46. *Report of the Senate Committee on Public Lands, May 18, 1832* (22 Congress, 1 session, Senate Document no. 145, serial 214, Washington, D.C., 1832), pp. 1–20; *Register of Debates,* 22 Congress, 2 session, IX, 1907–1911; Elliott Cresson to Gurley, London, August 6, 1832, enclosing broadside printed in England, ACS papers.

47. *Register of Debates,* 22 Congress, 1 session, XI, 1096–1118, 1145–1154.

48. *African Repository,* VIII, 381; Levi Woodbury to Walter Lowrie, Washington, D.C., April 26, 1834, ACS papers.

49. *Register of Debates,* 24 Congress, 2 session, VIII, 564–566.

Notes to XV: FIRE-BRANDS FROM BOSTON

1. Chauncey Whittlesey to Gurley, New York, October 18, 1827; W. B. Davidson to Gurley, Philadelphia, February 6, 1827, ACS papers.

2. William Crane to Gurley, Richmond, January 5, 1827; John

H. B. Latrobe to Gurley, Baltimore, January 27, 1827; Gerard Ralston to Gurley, Philadelphia, February 16, 1827; John C. Ehringhaus to Gurley, Elizabeth City, N.C., June 23, 1827; C. C. Harper to Gurley, Baltimore, July 9, 1827; Benjamin Brand to Gurley, Richmond, August 20, October 27, November 3, 1827; Elliott Cresson to Gurley, Philadelphia, August 23, 1828; D. I. Burr to Gurley, Richmond, March 12, 1830; John Kennedy to Gurley, Elizabeth City, N.C., March 13, 1830; John H. B. Latrobe to Gurley, Baltimore, March 20, 1830; John Kennedy to Gurley, Petersburg, Virginia, March 17, 1830; R. Potts to Gurley, Frederick, Maryland, March 20, 1830; John Kennedy to Gurley, Richmond, March 27, 1830; John Kennedy to Gurley, Petersburg, March 29, 1830; John B. Hepburn to Gurley, Alexandria, Virginia, April 2, 1830, all in ACS papers; *African Repository,* II, 122; V, 178.

3. D. I. Burr to Gurley, Richmond, February 11, 1830; copy of Mechlin's letter, dated Liberia, February 10, 1833, addressed to C. C. Harper of Baltimore, ACS papers; *African Repository,* VIII, 42; ACS *Seventeenth Annual Report,* p. 5.

4. C. C. Harper to Gurley, Baltimore, May 30, 1832; Elliott Cresson to Gurley, n.p., January 2, 1828, ACS papers.

5. "A Memorial from the Free People of Color to the Citizens of Baltimore," *African Repository,* II, 294–298; ACS *Tenth Annual Report,* p. 48.

6. John H. B. Latrobe to Gurley, Baltimore, April 9, 1827; Howard Kearney to Gurley, St. Inigoes, St. Mary's county, Maryland, October 17, 1827, ACS papers; *African Repository,* III, 300–304; Connecticut Colonization Society, *Third Annual Report of the Managers of the Colonization Society of the State of Connecticut, with an Appendix* (New Haven, 1830), pp. 15–22; Maryland Colonization Society, *African Colonization: Proceedings of a Meeting of the Friends of African Colonization, held in the City of Baltimore, on the [17] October, 1827* (n.p., n.d.), p. 10.

7. John B. Russwurm to Gurley, New York, January 26, 1829; Russwurm to Gurley, Philadelphia, May 7, 1829; Russwurm to Gurley, New York, June 16, 1829; Elliott Cresson to Gurley, Philadelphia, May 17, 1830; Ira B. Underhill to Gurley, New York, August 6, 1831, all in ACS papers; an unsigned letter written by Russwurm, "To the Senior Editor—No. III," *Freedom's Journal,* August 17, 1827; another letter, signed "Investigator," *ibid.,* August 31, 1827; Bella Gross, "Freedom's Journal and the Rights of All," *Journal of Negro History,* XVII (July, 1932), 241–286; *African Repository,*

IV, 376–377; VI, 56, 60. *Freedom's Journal* also granted colonization a hearing. See essays signed JHK (John H. Kennedy, agent of the Colonization Society), *ibid.*, September 14, 21, 28, October 5, 1827.

8. John H. B. Latrobe to Gurley, Baltimore, April 5, 1828, ACS papers; *African Repository,* IV, 25–26.

9. Theodore Frelinghuysen to Gurley, Newark, N.J., February 3, 1827; Elliott Cresson to Gurley, Philadelphia, April 20, 1828; N. S. Wheaton to Gurley, Hartford, February 14, 1829; Hector Humphreys to Gurley, Hartford, February 24, 1829; Isaac Orr to Gurley, Philadelphia, July 5, 1830, all in ACS papers; *Report of the Proceedings at the Formation of the African Education Society: Instituted at Washington, December 29, 1829: With an Address to the Public, by the Board of Managers* (Washington, 1830), pp. 3–16; ACS *Eighth Annual Report,* pp. 18–19; *Tenth Annual Report,* p. 47; *African Repository,* II, 223; IV, 193, 205–208; VI, 46–48.

10. *Report of the Proceedings at the Formation of the African Education Society,* pp. 8, 15; *African Repository,* VI, 48–49.

11. Bella Gross, "The First National Negro Convention," *Journal of Negro History,* XXXI (October, 1946), 435–443; quotation cited by Robert Austin Warner, *New Haven Negroes, A Social History* (New Haven, 1940), pp. 49–50.

12. [Wendell Phillips Garrison and Frances Jackson Garrison], *William Lloyd Garrison, 1805–1879; the Story of his Life, told by his children* (New York, 1885), I, 124–191; Roman Joseph Zorn, Garrisonian Abolitionism 1828–1839 (unpublished doctoral dissertation, University of Wisconsin, 1953), pp. 19–32.

13. W. P. and F. J. Garrison, *William Lloyd Garrison,* I, 192–218; Elliott Cresson to Gurley, Philadelphia, September 28, 1830; T. H. Gallaudet to Gurley, Hartford, September 24, 1830, ACS papers.

14. W. P. and F. J. Garrison, *William Lloyd Garrison,* I, 219–234, 255–259; Zorn, Garrisonian Abolitionism, pp. 34–48. Zorn concludes that Garrison "blatantly courted the allegiance and financial support of the colored populace."

15. Otis to Benjamin Faneuil Hunt, Boston, October 17, 1831, and subsequent recollections of the incident, quoted by Samuel Eliot Morison, *The Life and Letters of Harrison Gray Otis, Federalist, 1765–1848* (Boston, 1913), II, 259–262; W. P. and F. J. Garrison, *William Lloyd Garrison,* I, 238.

16. William Lloyd Garrison, *Thoughts on African Colonization;*

or an Impartial Exhibition of the Doctrines, Principles and Purposes of the American Colonization Society: Together with the Resolutions, Addresses and Remonstrances of the Free People of Color (Boston, 1832), pp. 12–14.

17. *Ibid.,* Part II, pp. 17–51; *Minutes and Proceedings of the First Annual Convention of the People of Colour, Held by Adjournments in the City of Philadelphia, from the Sixth to the Eleventh of June, inclusive, 1831* (Philadelphia, 1831), pp. 5, 15.

18. W. P. and F. J. Garrison, *William Lloyd Garrison,* I, 277–290; Zorn, Garrisonian Abolitionism, pp. 67–73.

19. Charles Tappan to Gurley, Boston, August 18, 1831, ACS papers.

20. Gabriel P. Disosway to Gurley, New York, June 23, 1831; J. K. Converse to Gurley, Burlington, Vermont, August 13, 1832; Leonard Bacon to Gurley, Ellington, Connecticut, October 26, 1831, ACS papers.

21. *African Repository,* VIII, 113–115, 143–146, 285.

22. *Ibid.,* VIII, 247; J. N. Danforth to Gurley, Boston, June 10, 1832, ACS papers.

23. *African Repository,* VIII, 248–249, 282–283, 342.

24. *Ibid.,* VII, 57, 186, 194–203; VIII, 247.

25. Bella Gross, *Clarion Call; the History and Development of the Negro People's Convention Movement in the United States from 1817 to 1840* (New York, 1947), p. 19; Zorn, Garrisonian Abolitionism, pp. 80–81.

26. Garrison, *Thoughts on African Colonization,* pp. 2–3, 11.

27. *Ibid.,* pp. 38–51, 57, 61–160.

28. *Ibid.,* pp. 23, 25–32, 34–38, 129.

29. *Ibid.,* pp. 36, and Part II, pp. 5, 9–72.

30. Garrison to Henry E. Benson, July 21, 1832, quoted by Zorn, Garrisonian Abolitionism, p. 74.

31. *Ibid.,* pp. 83–84; W. P. and F. J. Garrison, *William Lloyd Garrison,* I, 286–290, 312–313 and footnote.

32. Erastus Hopkins, chairman of the committee on Africa and Colonization, to Gurley, Princeton, February 1, 1833; David O. Hudson and Horace C. Taylor to Gurley, Western Reserve College, Hudson, Ohio, October 29, 1832; H. C. Taylor, David O. Hudson, and T. H. Barr, Committee, to Gurley, W. R. College, December 10, 1832; Robert S. Finley to Gurley, New York, December 21, 183[2], all in ACS papers; *African Repository,* VIII, 271–272; [Cyril Pearl], *Remarks on African Colonization and the Abolition of Slavery, In*

Two Parts: By a Citizen of New England (Windsor, Vermont, 1833), p. 6.

33. Levi H. Clarke to Gurley, Albany, July 14, 1832; Clarke to Gurley, Middletown, Connecticut, August 8, 1833; B. B. Thatcher to Gurley, Boston, September 10, 1832; Gorham D. Abbott to Gurley, New York, January 15, 1833, ACS papers; *African Repository,* VIII, 121–122.

34. J. N. Danforth to Gurley, Boston, December 21, 1832; C. P. Russell to Danforth, Concord, N.H., December 14, 1832; printed letter, Cyril Pearl to Danforth, Dedham, Massachusetts, December 24, 1832; Asa Cummings to Danforth, Portland, Maine, December 14, 1832, ACS papers; *African Repository,* VIII, 143–144.

35. J. N. Danforth to Gurley, Boston, December 27, 1832; Danforth to the Rev. Dr. James Laurie, Boston, December 28, 1832, ACS papers.

36. *African Repository,* VIII, 272–276; Ralph R. Gurley, *Letter on the American Colonization Society, and Remarks on South Carolina Opinions on that Subject* (Washington, 1832), pp. 1–5.

37. *African Repository,* VIII, 346–347.

38. T. D. Bacon, *Leonard Bacon* (New Haven, 1931), pp. 219–222; Article VII, unsigned, *The Quarterly Christian Spectator,* V (March, 1833), 145–157; Article VIII, unsigned, *The Methodist Magazine and Quarterly Review, XV* (January, 1833), 111–116.

39. *African Repository,* IX, 81–85, 128. Pearl's pamphlet was entitled *Remarks on African Colonization and the Abolition of Slavery, In Two Parts: By a Citizen of New England* (Windsor, Vermont, 1833).

40. Henry T. Tuckerman to Gurley, Boston, October 1, 1832 and February 19, 1833; B. B. Thatcher to Gurley, Boston, February 26 and February 28, 1833; Edward Everett to Gurley, Charleston, Massachusetts, April 8, 1833; Cyril Pearl to Gurley, Windsor, Vermont, April 23, 1833, all in ACS papers; *African Repository,* IX, 92; *The Colonizationist and Journal of Freedom* (April, 1833), p. 6.

41. W. H. Atkinson to Gurley, Petersburg, Virginia, September 10, 1831, ACS papers; Bacon, *Leonard Bacon,* p. 218.

42. Gurley to John Ker, Washington, August 30, 1831, quoted by Franklin L. Riley, "A Contribution to the History of the Colonization Movement in Mississippi," *Publications of the Mississippi Historical Society,* IX (1906), 364; Gurley to J. B. Harrison, Washington, September 3, 1832, Jesse Burton Harrison Papers, Library of Congress.

Notes to XVI: THE UNQUENCHABLE TORCH

1. *African Repository,* VIII, 353–354, 356–375. The managers' report also appears in the *Sixteenth Annual Report,* pp. 2–26.

2. ACS *Sixteenth Annual Report,* pp. xviii–xxii.

3. Newspapers quoted by *The Abolitionist,* I (March, 1833), 43–44; Ebenezer Watson to Gurley, Albany, New York, April 20, 1833, ACS papers.

4. *The Abolitionist,* I (March, 1833), 44–45.

5. Ralph R. Gurley, *Letter of the Rev. Ralph R. Gurley, on the American Colonization Society; addressed to Henry Ibbottson, Esq., of Sheffield, England* (Washington, 1833), pp. 1–7. The letter also appears in the *African Repository,* IX, 51–56, and excerpts in *The Colonizationist and Journal of Freedom,* I (May, 1833), 43–48.

6. *The Abolitionist,* I (January, 1833), 2; *African Repository,* IX, 22.

7. *African Repository,* IX, 22–23; resolutions written out and signed by William Lloyd Garrison, undated note addressed to J. N. Danforth, ACS papers; substance of the note appears in the *African Repository,* IX, 23; Danforth to Gurley, Boston, February 28, 1833, ACS papers.

8. Massachusetts Colonization Society, *Proceedings at the Annual Meeting of the Massachusetts Colonization Society, held in Park Street Church, Feb. 7, 1833: Together with the Speeches delivered on that occasion by Hon. Messrs. Everett, Ladd, and Cushing, and Rev. Messrs. Stow and Blagden: Also the Letters of His Excellency Governor Lincoln, and the Hon. Samuel Lathrop, communicated to the meeting* (Boston, 1833), pp. 3–26; *African Repository,* IX, 25; Howard Malcom to Gurley, Boston, February 2, 1833; William Ladd to Gurley, Minot, Maine, January 18, 1833, ACS papers.

9. *The Colonizationist and Journal of Freedom,* I (April, 1833), 23–28, and I (June, 1833), 81–89; *African Repository,* IX, 128, 153–154.

10. *African Repository,* IX, 188, 216; *The Colonizationist and Journal of Freedom,* I (August, 1833), 121–128.

11. Caleb Pitkin to Gurley, Hudson, Ohio, March 15, 1833, ACS papers; *African Repository,* IX, 186–187, 245–246, 349.

12. Birney to Gurley, Huntsville, Alabama, June 29, 1833, in Dwight L. Dumond, ed., *Letters of Birney* (New York, 1938), I,

76–79; the essays are reprinted in the *African Repository,* IX, 172–173, 207–208, 239–240, 274–276, 310–311, 342–344.

13. *African Repository,* IX, 65–66, copied the Tappan letter from *The Liberator,* April 6, 1833; *ibid.,* IX, 183, for colonist Price's allegations. Also, Arthur Tappan to Gurley, New York [June 26, 1833], ACS papers.

14. Joseph Tracy to Gurley, Windsor, Vermont, May 16, 1833; Cyril Pearl to Gurley, Windsor, Vermont, April 23, 1833, ACS papers.

15. Gurley to P. R. Fendall, New York, July 6, 1833, ACS papers; *African Repository,* IX, 66–68.

16. *African Repository,* IX, 205–206, 307–309; X, 90, 106–107; XI, 180; James More to Gurley, Monrovia, West Africa, August 3, 1833, ACS papers.

17. *African Repository,* IX, 354–355.

18. *Ibid.,* IX, 150–151, 153, 188–190.

19. *Ibid.,* IX, 193–200; Gurley to Philip R. Fendall, New York, October 1, 1833, ACS papers.

20. "Supplemental Report" of board of managers, dated July 24, 1834, *African Repository,* X, 163.

21. For Cresson's collections, see *African Repository,* X, 30–32, ACS *Sixteenth Annual Report,* pp. 22–23, *Seventeenth Annual Report,* pp. 43–46. For Mrs. Sigourney's poem, see William Innes, *Liberia: or the Early History and Signal Preservation of the American Colony of Free Negroes on the Coast of Africa* (Edinburgh, 1831), p. 234. For Cresson's goals and methods of operation, see Cresson to Gurley, Liverpool, May 31, 1831; London, June 23, 1831; London, August 6, 1831, enclosing his broadside, "American Colonization Society: Liberia." Also, Cresson to Gurley, London, September 6, October 6, and December 5, 1831, ACS papers; Cresson to Jackson Kemper, London, September 20, 1831, The Papers of Jackson Kemper, State Historical Society of Wisconsin; Cresson to Gurley, Derby, September 2, 1832 and London, January 28, 1833, ACS papers. For *African Repository*'s accounts, see especially VIII, 212–213, 340–342; IX, 18–22, 146, 148–149. For Clarkson's endorsement, "Letter of the Venerable Thomas Clarkson, on Colonization," (an extract), *ibid.,* VIII, 257–266.

22. Cresson to Gurley, Liverpool, May 31, 1831, and from London, June 20, July 29, August 6, November 10, December 10, 1831, ACS papers; *African Repository,* IX, 174–175.

23. Cresson to Gurley, London, June 20, 1831, ACS papers.

24. Cresson to Gurley, Cheltenham, November 10, December 5,

1831; Cresson to Gurley, Norwich, July 25, September 2, 1832; Edw. Higginson, Secretary of the Hull Liberia Committee, to Gurley, Kingston up: Hull, June 22, 1833, ACS papers; *African Repository,* IX, 91–92.

25. Cresson to Gurley, London, July 29, 1831, ACS papers.

26. Cresson to Gurley, Liverpool, April 16, 1832; fragment postmarked May 5 [1833], Philadelphia but probably written from London; same to same, London, June 6, 1833, ACS papers; *African Repository,* IX, 155–157.

27. The quotation concerning Garrison's intentions in going to England are from the Cincinnati *Journal,* n.d., reprinted in the *African Repository,* IX, 29. The best accounts of Garrison's tour are: Zorn, Garrisonian Abolitionism, pp. 105–116, and W. P. and F. J. Garrison, *William Lloyd Garrison,* I, 348–379. The latter account includes lengthy excerpts from Garrison's letters and reports. Both accounts overemphasize Cresson's prowess and brilliance to magnify Garrison's victory. Actually, the British antislavery men had already neutralized much of Cresson's work before Garrison arrived on the scene.

28. Cresson to the Maryland Board of Managers, London, July 18, 1833, Letters Received, Maryland Colonization Society papers, Maryland Historical Society; Cresson to Gurley, London, June 9, June 16, 1832; Cresson to Gurley, Nottingham, August 5, 1832; London, June 28, 1833; Ipswich, August 15, August 24, 1833, ACS papers.

29. Cresson to Gurley, Aberdeen, January 29, 1833; London, July 28, 1833, July 3, 1833, enclosing circular entitled "British African Colonization Society," with Cresson's notations, ACS papers; *African Repository,* IX, 145–146, 212–215; [Thomas Hodgkin], *On the British Colonization Society: To which are added, some particulars respecting the American Colonization Society* . . . (London, 1834), 32 pages.

30. Cresson to Gurley, Ipswich, August 15 and completed at London, August 26, 1833, ACS papers; *African Repository,* IX, 211–212, 257–266; W. P. and F. J. Garrison, *William Lloyd Garrison,* I, 357–365; Zorn, Garrisonian Abolitionism, p. 114. In his report to the New-England Anti-Slavery Society, Garrison remarked, "In getting up this Protest I had no agency whatever. It was altogether unexpected by me; but to obtain it was alone worth a trip across the Atlantic."

31. Gurley to Philip R. Fendall, New York, October 2, 1833; John Neal to Gurley, New York, October 2, 1833, ACS papers.

32. *African Repository,* IX, 246–247; Henry Fowler, *The American Pulpit: Sketches, Biographical and Descriptive, of Living American Preachers, and of the Religious Movements and Distinctive Ideas which they represent* (New York, 1856), pp. 367–372.

33. *Journal of Commerce,* quoted in Fowler, *American Pulpit,* pp. 370–372; Gurley to Philip R. Fendall, New York, October 8, 1833; John Neal to Gurley, New York, November 20, 1833; John Neal to Fendall, Portland, Maine, December 4, 1833, ACS papers.

34. Edward Colston to Gurley, Martinsburg, Virginia, July 9, 1833; Benjamin Brand to Gurley, Richmond, July 22, 1833; J. Burton Harrison to Gurley, Boston, July 28, 1833; R. H. Toler to Gurley, Lynchburg, Virginia, August 22, 1833; John Crosby to Gurley, Savannah, Georgia, January 1, 1833, ACS papers; extract from Richmond *Whig,* n.d., quoted by *African Repository,* IX, 87.

35. ACS *Seventeenth Annual Report,* pp. vii–viii, xviii.

36. Gilbert H. Barnes, *The Antislavery Impulse, 1830–1844* (Gloucester, Mass., 1957), pp. 54–56; Zorn, Garrisonian Abolitionism, pp. 138–153; Daniel Newell to Gurley, Salem, Massachusetts, June 8, 1837, ACS papers.

37. ACS *Sixteenth Annual Report,* p. 15; *African Repository,* VIII, 115, 367; Treasurer's report, ACS *Seventeenth Annual Report,* p. 19; Gurley to Philip R. Fendall, New Haven, June 10, 1833; Fendall to John Underwood, Washington, June 11, 1833, ACS papers.

38. ACS *Seventeenth Annual Report,* p. 19; managers' special report, February 20, 1834, *ibid.,* pp. 29–30; letters concerning protested drafts, Gurley to Fendall, New York, June 15, 1833; Richard Wallace, Notary Public, to Fendall, New York, June 15, 1833; Gurley to Fendall, New York, June 19, 1833; Thomas Bell to Fendall, New York, June 19, 1833; Thomas W. Blight and Gerard Ralston to Gurley, Philadelphia, June 19, 1833; Gurley to Fendall, Philadelphia, June 21, 1833; Geisse and Korckhauss to Gurley, Philadelphia, August 13, 1833; Samuel Trainer & Co., to President of the Board of Managers, Boston, September 9, 1833; Michael Nourse, Notary Public, to Thomas Bell, Washington, September 7, 1833; Thomas Bell to Gurley, New York, September 11, 1833; Grant & Stone to President of Board of Managers, Philadelphia, September 16, 1833, all in ACS papers.

39. *African Repository,* IX, 199.

40. *Ibid.,* IX, 287, 313–315, 350–352; ACS *Seventeenth Annual Report,* pp. 2–3; J. N. Danforth to Gurley, New York, September 10, 1833; B. B. Thatcher to Gurley, Boston, September 17, 1833; Gurley

to Fendall, New York, October 1, 1833; same to same, Philadelphia, November 28, 1833, ACS papers.

41. ACS *Seventeenth Annual Report,* p. 17. See managers' special report dated February 20, 1834, *ibid.,* p. 31. This report appears in the *African Repository,* X, 8–17, and a supplemental report, *ibid.,* X, 162–168. Gerrit Smith pleaded with Gurley to stay with the troubled society. Smith to Gurley, Peterboro, New York, December 27, 1833, ACS papers.

Notes to XVII: "WE ARE A NULLITY"

1. ACS *Seventeenth Annual Report,* pp. iii–xxvi; the same report appears in the *African Repository,* IX, 353–376; Gerrit Smith to Gurley, Peterboro, New York, December 24, 1833, ACS papers.

2. The managers' "Special Report," dated February 20, 1834, appears in the ACS *Seventeenth Annual Report,* pp. 26–47, and in the *African Repository,* X, 8–17. A supplemental report, dated July 24, 1834, with detailed listings of creditors and expenditures in Liberia, *ibid.,* X, 162–168. For Smith's and Frelinghuysen's statements, *ibid.,* X, 17–19. For complaints of creditors: John Hanson to Gurley, Philadelphia, February 4, 1834; Gerard Ralston to Gurley, Philadelphia, February 28, 1834; Ira B. Underhill to Joseph Gales, Sr., New York, June 10, June 23, October 24, 1834, January 1, 1835. Letters on behalf of Thomas C. Brown by Lewis Tappan to President of the Board of Managers, New York, June 3, 1834; Tappan to Gurley, New York, July 18, 1834, ACS papers.

3. "Special Report," February 20, 1834, ACS *Seventeenth Annual Report,* pp. 35–36, or *African Repository,* X, 16; *Eighteenth Annual Report,* p. 21; for managers' appeal to auxiliaries, *African Repository,* X, 108–109.

4. Philip R. Fendall to Joseph Gales, Sr., Petersburg, Virginia, March 31, 1834, and Richmond, Virginia, April 5, 1834. Corroborative complaints about failure to use state appropriations: William Maxwell to Gurley, Norfolk, August 5, 1833; Benjamin Brand to Gurley, Richmond, September 19, 1833; D. I. Burr to Gurley, Richmond, September 21, 1833, ACS papers.

5. Gurley to Gales, Philadelphia, March 24, March 25, March 29, March 31, April 1, 1834, ACS papers.

6. Gurley to Gales, Philadelphia, March 31, 1834, New York, April 15, May 8, May 15, 1834, ACS papers.

7. Gurley to Gales, New York, April 15, May 15, May 17, 1834, ACS papers; *African Repository,* X, 129.

8. Gurley to Gales, New York, May 8, May 15, 1834, ACS papers; *African Repository,* X, 70–72.

9. Henry Fowler, *The American Pulpit* . . . (New York, 1856), pp. 373–376; Bayard Tuckerman, *William Jay and the Constitutional Movement for the Abolition of Slavery* (New York, 1894), pp. 54–57; circular, "To the Honorable Cornelius W. Lawrence, Mayor of the City of New-York," dated New York, July 16, 1834, and signed by Arthur Tappan, John Rankin, E. Wright, Jr., Joshua Leavitt, W. Goodell, Lewis Tappan, and Samuel E. Cornish, enclosed in Lewis Tappan to Gurley, New York, July 18, 1834, ACS papers.

10. *African Repository,* X, 190.

11. Tuckerman, *William Jay,* pp. 45, 57–62; Jay, *Inquiry into the Character and Tendency of the American Colonization, and American Anti-Slavery Societies* (10th ed., New York, 1840), pp. 5–124.

12. Amos Phelps, *Lectures on Slavery and Its Remedy* (Boston, 1834), p. 284. The "Declaration of Sentiment" appears on pp. v–x.

13. Betty Fladeland, *James Gillespie Birney: Slaveholder to Abolitionist* (New York, 1955), pp. 70–89; Benjamin P. Thomas, *Theodore Weld, Crusader for Freedom* (New Brunswick, N.J., 1950), pp. 70–84; Birney to Gurley, Huntsville, Alabama, September 24, 1833, and Danville, Kentucky, December 3, 1833, in Dumond, ed., *Birney Letters,* I, 88–90; Weld to Birney, Lane Seminary, May 28, 1834, *ibid.,* I, 112–113.

14. Fladeland, *Birney,* pp. 82–89, 92; Birney to Weld, near Danville, Kentucky, July 21, 1834, in Gilbert H. Barnes and Dwight L. Dumond, eds., *Letters of Theodore Dwight Weld, Angelina Grimké Weld, and Sarah Grimké 1822–1844* (New York, 1934), I, 161.

15. Fladeland, *Birney,* p. 84; James G. Birney, *Letter on Colonization, Addressed to the Rev. Thornton J. Mills, Corresponding Secretary of the Kentucky Colonization Society* (New York, 1834), pp. 3–8, 20, 46, and *passim.* Weld to Birney, Lane Seminary, July 8, 1834, in Dumond, ed., *Birney Letters,* I, 123–124; Birney to Weld, near Danville, Kentucky, July 17 and July 21, 1834, in Barnes and Dumond, eds., *Weld-Grimké Letters,* I, 156–162.

16. Fladeland, *Birney,* pp. 84–85; Weld to Birney, Lane Seminary, June 19, July 8, July 14, August 2, August 25, 1834, in Dumond, ed., *Birney Letters,* I, 121, 123, 127–128, 130–131; Elizur Wright, Jr., to Weld, Anti Slavery Office, New York, August 14, 1834, in Barnes and Dumond, eds., *Weld-Grimké Letters,* I, 116.

17. Elliott Cresson to Joseph Gales, Sr., Philadelphia, September 1, 1834; Elliott Cresson to Hon. W. Lowrie, Philadelphia, December 10, 1834, ACS papers; *African Repository,* X, 257–279, 293–297.

18. Weld to Birney, Cincinnati, Ohio, October 20, 1834, in Dumond, ed., *Birney Letters,* I, 146–147; Birney to Smith, near Danville, November 14, 1834, *ibid.,* I, 147–152; Birney to Smith, Danville, December 30, 1834, *ibid.,* I, 161–163; Birney to Smith, Cincinnati, November 11, 1835, *ibid.,* I, 257–263; Smith to Hon. Walter Lowrie, Albany, December 31, 1834; Gurley to Fendall, New York, November 3, November 11, 1835; Smith to Gurley, Peterboro, November 24, 1835, all in ACS papers; Bacon, *Leonard Bacon,* pp. 230–231; Fladeland, *Birney,* p. 102; Ralph V. Harlow, *Gerrit Smith, Philanthropist and Reformer* (New York, 1939), pp. 64–65; *African Repository,* XI, 65–75, 105–119; Morris, *Memoir of Margaret Mercer,* p. 133.

19. *Exposition of the Object and Plans of the American Union for the Relief and Improvement of the Colored Race* (Boston, 1835), pp. 1–23; Bacon, *Leonard Bacon,* pp. 235–236; Joseph Holdich, *The Life of Willbur Fisk, D.D., First President of the Wesleyan University* (New York, 1842), p. 329; *African Repository,* XI, 137–140; Gurley to Fendall, Boston, August 3, 1835, ACS papers; the American Union's chief accomplishment was the publication of E. A. Andrews, *Slavery and the Domestic Slave-Trade in the United States: In a Series of Letters Addressed to the Executive Committee of the American Union for the Relief and Improvement of the Colored Race* (Boston, 1836).

20. R. J. Breckinridge to Rev. Charles Hodge, D.D., Boston, July 31, 1834, Breckinridge Papers, Library of Congress; R. S. Finley to Fendall, Cincinnati, September 27, 1834; Finley to Gurley, Cincinnati, November 20, 1834, ACS papers.

21. Charles C. Harper, *An Address Delivered at the Annual Meeting of the Maryland State Colonization Society, in the city of Annapolis, January 23, 1835* (Baltimore, 1835), pp. 6–7; John H. B. Latrobe, *Maryland in Liberia, a History of the Colony Planted by the Maryland State Colonization Society Under the Auspices of the State of Maryland, U.S., at Cape Palmas on the South-west Coast of Africa, 1833–1853: A Paper read before the Maryland Historical Society, March 9th, 1885, by John H. B. Latrobe, President of the Society,* Maryland Historical Society Fund Publication No. 21 (Baltimore, 1885), pp. 14–17; *African Repository,* VIII, 25–27.

22. *Address of the Board of Managers of the Maryland State*

Colonization Society (c.1834), pp. 4, 10–11, 13–14; Latrobe, *Maryland in Liberia,* pp. 17–18, 20–21; William L. Stone to Gurley, New York, April 19, 1833; Charles Howard to F. S. Key, Baltimore, April 13, 1833; Moses Sheppard to Gurley, Baltimore, April 16, 1833; John H. B. Latrobe to Board of Managers of American Colonization Society, Baltimore, December 29, 1834, ACS papers. Also, Gurley to C. C. Harper, Washington, April 12, April 16, April 25, 1833; W. McKenney to Charles Howard, Salisbury, Somerset co., May 4, 1833; H. Teague to C. C. Harper, Liberia, July 29, 1833, Maryland State Colonization Society Papers, Maryland Historical Society.

23. *African Repository,* VII, 297–299; IX, 89–90, 282, 392; Gurley to C. C. Harper, Washington, October 10, 1832, Maryland State Colonization Society Papers, Maryland Historical Society; R. J. Breckinridge to Charles Hodge, D.D., Boston, July 31, 1834, Breckinridge Papers; Cresson to Gales, Philadelphia, August 3, 1834; Cresson to Gurley, Philadelphia, August 17, 1834, calls the Maryland agents in New England, "the Baltimore poachers." Also, Gurley to Gales, Augusta, Georgia, May 7, 1837, in ACS papers, showing contest between the societies for emigrants. The *National Intelligencer* reproved the Maryland society for sending its agents outside the state, *African Repository,* X, 243–244.

24. Latrobe, *Maryland in Liberia,* pp. 18–47; Samuel W. Laughon, "Administrative Problems in Maryland in Liberia, 1836–1851," *Journal of Negro History,* XXVI (July, 1941), 331–347; John H. B. Latrobe, Corresponding Secretary of the Maryland State Colonization Society, to the Board of Managers of the American Colonization Society, Baltimore, May 7, 1834, ACS papers.

25. [William Lloyd Garrison], *The Maryland Scheme of Expatriation Examined: By a Friend of Liberty* (Boston, 1834); Finley to Latrobe, New York, November 2, 1833, Maryland State Colonization Society Papers.

26. Philadelphia *Colonization Herald and General Register,* December 19, 1838; Cresson to the Secretary of the American Colonization Society, Philadelphia, November 20, 1833; Gurley to Fendall, Philadelphia, November 28, 1833; Cresson to Gurley, Philadelphia, December 31, 1833; circular, "Young Men's Colonization Society of Pennsylvania," enclosed in Cresson to Gurley, Philadelphia, June 25 [1834]; Gurley to Gales, Philadelphia, March 31, 1834; Gurley to Fendall, New York, May 31, 1834, all in ACS papers; *African Repository,* X, 150–152. In 1836 the Pennsylvania State Colonization Society merged with the Philadelphia Young Men's Colonization So-

ciety, with the leadership passing to the latter group but the former title being retained. James J. Barclay to Gurley, Philadelphia, October 11, 1836, ACS papers.

27. *Address of the New York City Colonization Society, to the Public: New York, February 12th, 1834* (New York, 1834), pp. 4–17; extract of the minutes of the Colonization Society of the City of New York, Ira B. Underhill, Recording Secretary, with note appended by John W. Mulligan, Corresponding Secretary, dated New York, November 21, 1833, and addressed to Gurley, ACS papers.

28. Gurley to Fendall, Philadelphia, December 2, 1833; John Breckinridge to Gurley, Philadelphia, January 15, 1835, ACS papers; Philadelphia *Colonization Herald and General Register,* December 19, 1838; *Proceedings of the Colonization Society of the City of New York, at their Third Annual Meeting, held on the 13th and 14th of May, 1835: Including the Annual Report of the Board of Managers, to the Society* (New York, 1835), pp. 4–5, 8; *African Repository,* X, 286.

29. John Breckinridge to Gurley, Philadelphia, January 15, 1835, ACS papers; *African Repository,* X, 193–198; XI, 216.

30. Job Roberts Tyson, *A Discourse before the Young Men's Colonization Society of Pennsylvania, Delivered October 24, 1834, in St. Paul's Church, Philadelphia* . . . (Philadelphia, 1834), p. 31; *Proceedings of Colonization Society of the City of New York* (1835), pp. 35–36, 42–43; John Breckinridge to Gurley, Philadelphia, January 15, 1835, ACS papers.

31. Joseph Gales to Hon. Walter Lowrie, New York, November 21, 1834; Orson Douglass, Colonization Rooms, to Joseph Gales, Philadelphia, February 28, 1837; Joseph Gales to Judge Samuel Wilkeson, Washington, August 14, 1838, ACS papers; *African Repository,* XI, 217.

32. *African Repository,* XI, 322–323, 337–339; Philadelphia *Colonization Herald and General Register,* December 19, 1838; Charles Henry Huberich, *Political and Legislative History of Liberia* (New York, 1947), I, 568–597.

33. Charles S. Sydnor, *Slavery in Mississippi* (New York, 1933), pp. 203–238; Gurley to Gales, Louisville, April 30, 1836; Gurley to managers of Colonization Society, Natchez, May 9, 1836; Gurley to Fendall, May 11, May 16, 1836; also, Gurley to Board of Managers, May [9], 1836; John Ker to Gurley, Linden, near Natchez, January 25, 1837; R. S. Finley to Gurley, steamboat *Memphis,* December 27, 1837, enclosing circular dated Natchez, 12th December, 1837, de-

scribing the Mississippi colony; John Anketell to Wilkeson, New Haven, February 27, 1839, quoting colonist James Brown, October 23, 1838, account of Governor Finley's murder; Cresson to Wilkeson, Natchez, March 12, 1840, all in ACS papers; Huberich, *Liberia,* I, 597–615.

34. Joseph Gales, Sr., to Samuel Wilkeson, Washington, August 4 and November 14, 1838; Gales to Gurley, Washington, May 14, 1837; H. V. Garretson to Gales, New York, November 18, 1837; Grant & Stone to Gales, Philadelphia, November 19, 1836; William G. Alexander to Hon. J. B. Sutherland, Philadelphia, January 4, 1837; John Hanson to Gurley, Philadelphia, February 3, 1838; Charles S. Homer to Wilkeson, Boston, August 31, 1840; James Imbree, for C. Hickman & Co., to Wilkeson, Philadelphia, March 19, 1840, all in ACS papers. Legacies enabled the society to meet its most pressing obligations: Fendall to Gurley, Washington, May 2, 1837, and Gales to Gurley, Washington, May 14, 1837, ACS papers.

35. Gurley to Ker, Washington, February 13, 1837, in Franklin L. Riley, "A Contribution to the History of the Colonization Movement in Mississippi," *Publications of the Mississippi Historical Society,* IX (1906), 367–368; Gales to Wilkeson, Washington, August 4, 1838, ACS papers.

36. Thomas Buchanan to Samuel Wilkeson, Philadelphia, September 30, 1838, ACS papers; copies of the new constitution appear in various annual reports after 1838.

37. E. Whittlesey to Wilkeson, Washington, June 3, 1838; Wilkeson to Gurley, New York, July 7, 1838; Wilkeson to Gurley, Buffalo, July 19, and July 27, 1838; Gurley to Wilkeson, Washington, July 21, July 27, August 8, August 9, 1838; Wilkeson to Gales, New York, October 22, November 2, November 7, November 30, 1838; Elliott Cresson to Wilkeson, December 18, 1838, all in ACS papers. Cresson, as usual, called for a complete housecleaning.

38. Thomas Buchanan to Wilkeson, New York, January 15, 1839; Anson G. Phelps to Wilkeson, New York, January 30, 1839; D. M. Reese to Wilkeson, New York, November 25, 1839, ACS papers; ACS *Twenty-Fourth Annual Report,* pp. 16–17, 30–32; *Twenty-Fifth Annual Report,* pp. 10, 17–18, 24. The total receipts in 1840 reached $62,000 and then slipped to $54,000 in 1841.

39. ACS *Twenty-Fourth Annual Report,* pp. 16–30; *Twenty-Fifth Annual Report,* p. 22; Ralph R. Gurley, *Mission to England, in behalf of the American Colonization Society* (Washington, 1841), pp. 1–12, 108–111, 238–264; Gurley to Wilkeson, New York, May 26, May

27, May 30, 1840; Anson G. Phelps to Wilkeson, New York, May 27, 1840; D. M. Reese to Wilkeson, New York, June 3, 1840; Gurley to Executive Committee of American Colonization Society, London, August 17, 1840, ACS papers; also, Gurley to Ker, Washington, January 29, 1844, in Riley, "Contributions to the History of the Colonization Movement in Mississippi," pp. 388–390.

40. George Barker to McLain, New York, February 15, 1844; A. G. Phelps to McLain, New York, February 24, 1834; Cresson to H. L. Ellsworth, Philadelphia, February 22, and March (?), 1844; Joseph Tracy to McLain, Boston, April 12, 1844; Cresson to McLain, Philadelphia, June 6, 1844; J. B. Pinney to McLain, March 1, 1845, ACS papers.

Notes to XVIII: RETREAT TO EMIGRATION

1. For agents' reports see Robert S. Finley to Ker, St. Louis, August 5, 1847, in Riley, "Contributions to the History of Colonization in Mississippi," pp. 397–398; circular letter by Finley, reprinted in *Journal of Illinois State Historical Society,* III (April, 1910), 93–96; Benjamin T. Kavanaugh to McLain, Mineral Point, Wisconsin, August 27, 1846; same to same, Milwaukee, September 7, 1846, Indianapolis, September 28 and November 10, 1846, February 3, 1847, Chicago, August 31, 1847; Joseph Tracy to McLain, Boston, April 6, June 19, August 29, 1847, ACS papers; ACS *Twenty-Ninth Annual Report,* pp. 8, 16–17; *Thirtieth Annual Report,* p. 14.

2. Charles Henry Huberich, *Political and Legislative History of Liberia* (New York, 1947), I, 638–728; John B. Russwurm to W. Ramsay, Agency House [Cape Palmas], September 24 and 26, 1842, in [Kennedy], *African Colonization* (27 Congress, 3 session, House Committee Report no. 283, serial 428, Washington, D.C., 1843), p. 111; D. M. Reese to Wilkeson, December 14, 1840; N. Bangs, Cor. Secty., M.S.M.E.C., to Exec. Committee of American Colonization Society, New York, October 21, 1840, ACS papers; *Trial of the Suit Instituted by the Collector of Customs for the Port of Monrovia, Against the Superintendent of the Liberia Mission of the "Missionary Society of the Methodist Episcopal Church," before the Supreme Court of Liberia, in session at Monrovia, Sept. 4th and 5th, 1840, with most of the Pleadings: Published by Request, as reported for Africa's Luminary* (Monrovia, 1840).

3. Huberich, *Liberia,* I, 737–820; II, 851–1014; John H. B. Latrobe, *Maryland in Liberia* (Baltimore, 1885), 75–84; J. H.

Mower, "The Republic of Liberia," *Journal of Negro History,* XXXII (July, 1947), 267–270; Thomas Hodgkins to McLain, London, September 16, 29, October 3, 1845; Elliott Cresson to Board of Managers (sic), London, July 19, August 18, 1841, ACS papers.

4. ACS *Thirty-First Annual Report,* p. 10.

5. *Ibid.,* pp. 15–16; *Thirty-Second Annual Report,* p. 39; *Thirty-Fourth Annual Report,* p. 9; *Thirty-Seventh Annual Report,* pp. 18–19, 22–23; "A Joint Resolution on the subject of the Slave Trade, and for the Purpose of Colonization," signed by Speaker John W. Davis and Senate President James H. Lane, Indiana Legislature, 1852, in O. B. Conover Papers, Manuscripts Division, State Historical Society of Wisconsin. Also, manuscript records of the Wisconsin Colonization Society, newspaper clippings, printed circulars for 1852–1854, Conover Papers.

6. ACS *Thirty-Second Annual Report,* p. 9; *Thirty-Eighth Annual Report,* p. 4; see table of annual receipts, *Fifty-Second Annual Report,* inside back cover.

7. For a list of donations over $5,000 see Byron Sutherland, "Liberian Colonization," *Liberia Bulletin* no. 16 (Feb., 1900), pp. 22–23; ACS *Twenty Ninth Annual Report,* pp. 6–8; *Thirty-Fifth Annual Report,* p. 6; *Thirty-Seventh Annual Report,* p. 4; *Fortieth Annual Report,* pp. 9, 21; *Forty-First Annual Report,* p. 22; *Forty-Third Annual Report,* p. 23.

8. ACS *Thirty-Ninth Annual Report,* Appendix, p. 26; *Fortieth Annual Report,* pp. 4, 44–47; *Forty-Fourth Annual Report,* pp. 23–24.

9. James G. Birney, *Examination of the Decision of the Supreme Court of the United States, in the Case of Strader, Gorman and Armstrong vs. Christopher Graham, delivered at its December term, 1850: concluding with an Address to the Free Colored People, advising them to remove to Liberia* (Cincinnati, 1852), pp. 43–47; Walter R. Fleming, "Deportation and Colonization, an Attempted Solution to the Race Problem," *Studies in Southern History and Politics inscribed to William Archibald Dunning* (New York, 1914), pp. 6–8; Harriet Beecher Stowe, *Uncle Tom's Cabin; or, Life Among the Lowly* (Boston, 1852), II, 299–303.

10. ACS *Thirty-Fourth Annual Report,* pp. 9–19, 74–78; *Thirty-Sixth Annual Report,* pp. 9–11; *Thirty-Ninth Annual Report,* pp. 5–6.

11. Carter G. Woodson, *A Century of Negro Migration* (Washington, D.C., 1918), pp. 67–80; Frederic Bancroft, "Schemes to Colonize Negroes in Central America," in Jacob E. Cooke, *Frederic Bancroft, Historian* (Norman, Oklahoma, 1957), pp. 192–196;

Ludwell Lee Montague, *Haiti and the United States 1714–1938* (Durham, N.C., 1940), pp. 74–76; Charles F. Horner, *The Life of James Redpath and the Development of the Modern Lyceum* (New York, 1926), pp. 109–110; for a fuller account of Redpath's Haitian agency, see Willis D. Boyd, Negro Colonization in the National Crisis 1860–1870 (unpublished Ph.D. dissertation, University of California at Los Angeles, 1953), pp. 87–110.

12. ACS *Thirtieth Annual Report,* pp. 25–26; *Thirty-Second Annual Report,* pp. 18–19; *Thirty-Fourth Annual Report,* pp. 42–43; *Thirty-Fifth Annual Report,* pp. 10, 27–29; *Thirty-Sixth Annual Report,* pp. 12, 20–24; *Thirty-Seventh Annual Report,* pp. 33–42.

13. Roy P. Basler, ed., *The Collected Works of Abraham Lincoln* (New Brunswick, N.J., 1953), III, 145–146, 179.

14. ACS *Thirtieth Annual Report,* p. 18; *Thirty-Fourth Annual Report,* pp. 20, 60, 74–78; *Thirty-Fifth Annual Report,* p. 6; *Thirty-Seventh Annual Report,* pp. 4, 13; *Thirty-Ninth Annual Report,* p. 7; *Forty-First Annual Report,* p. 20.

15. Boyd, Negro Colonization in the National Crisis 1860–1870, pp. 53–86; ACS *Forty-Second Annual Report,* pp. 18–19, appendix, p. 46; *Forty-Fourth Annual Report,* pp. 9–16; *Forty-Fifth Annual Report,* p. 9.

16. Bancroft, "Schemes to Colonize Negroes in Central America," pp. 196–227 and "The Ile à Vache Experiment in Colonization," in Cooke, *Frederic Bancroft, Historian,* pp. 228–258; Boyd, Negro Colonization in the National Crisis 1860–1870, pp. 144–152, 180–206, 209–249; Paul J. Scheips, "Lincoln and the Chiriqui Colonization Project," *Journal of Negro History,* XXXVII (October, 1952), 418–453; Warren B. Beck, "Lincoln and Negro Colonization," *Abraham Lincoln Quarterly,* VI (September, 1950), 162–183; Fleming, "Deportation and Colonization," pp. 18–26; Montague, *Haiti and U.S.,* pp. 76–80.

17. *Memorial of the Semi-Centennial Anniversary of the American Colonization Society, Celebrated at Washington, January 16, 1867: With Documents concerning Liberia* (Washington, 1867), pp. 182–191; Willis D. Boyd, "Negro Colonization in the Reconstruction Era 1865–1870," *Georgia Historical Quarterly,* XL (December, 1956), 372–374.

18. *Liberia Bulletin* no. 1 (November, 1892), pp. 1–6; no. 14 (February, 1899), pp. 15–16; and no. 16 (February, 1900), pp. 27–31.

BIBLIOGRAPHICAL ESSAY

THE ARCHIVES of the American Colonization Society, held by the Library of Congress, manuscripts division, are the most important source used in this study. This massive collection of several hundred bound volumes contains most of the pertinent data showing the rise of the African colonization movement as well as the growth of the organization. The volumes include letters received (after 1823) and sent (after 1844), minute books of the board of managers, and colonial reports. There are, too, folios, scrolls, and loose papers. For this work the "letters received" volumes proved to be the most useful part of the collection, and, unless otherwise noted, all letters cited, are from this section. Letters for the late 1820s, 1830s, and 1840s, from friends and agents all over the United States, constitute a rich, untapped source for ante bellum social history. Volumes for the late 1840s and 1850s, though bulky and complete, are less rich and symbolize the society's declining importance. These volumes contain many routine business letters that add no new insight into the society or the movement. Post office forms pertaining to the *African Repository*'s circulation difficulties in the 1840s and 1850s account for part of the extraordinary bulk.

The society's correspondence for the period 1817–1823 is skimpy and scattered. Secretary Elias B. Caldwell did not preserve incoming letters, but many important items appear in the minute books of the board of managers, in the *National Intelligencer* (especially 1816–1825), in the society's early annual reports, and in the Peter Force Papers in the Library of Congress. Force was the society's early printer. After Ralph R. Gurley took over as secretary, he kept all incoming letters in bound, indexed volumes. At intervals, Gurley and his assistants experimented with different filing systems, sometimes arranging chronologically and sometimes alphabetizing by sender's name and indexing by the month. In rebinding and laminating the entire collection (a worthy process that took several years), the Library of Congress staff sometimes retained the provenance and sometimes rearranged the collection to meet changing standards of the manuscript-keeper's craft. Though a few letters are misdated or wrongly arranged, the whole collection is in excellent condition. Later volumes, too tightly bound by metal pins, are difficult to use, but this is a minor disadvantage where near-perfect preservation techniques are concerned.

Some colonization data is found in the William Thornton Papers, the Robert J. Breckinridge Papers, the John H. B. Latrobe Papers, and the Jesse Burton Harrison Papers, all held by the Library of Congress. Portions of the Library's James C. Birney papers are included in Dwight D. Dumond, editor, *The Letters of James Gillespie Birney 1831–1857* (New York, 1938), volume one.

The Papers of the Maryland State Colonization Society, held by the Maryland Historical Society, form a large and complete collection that parallels and supplements the abundant data in the American Colonization Society's Papers. These papers reveal the story of the state society's emergence as an independent association with its own colony, its own problems, and its own leadership. For a detailed description of this collection, see William D. Hoyt, Jr., "The Papers of the Maryland State Colonization Society," *Maryland Historical Magazine,* XXXII (September, 1937), 247–271.

The American Colonization Society's massive collection of printed matter, which must have matched its manuscript collection, is now dispersed among the Library of Congress's thirteen million titles. It included pamphlets, journals, broadsides, reports, circulars, books, and newspapers. Early volumes of the *African Repository and Colonial Journal* (1825–1892) are especially important sources for a study of the African colonization movement. Secretary Gurley copied large portions of his correspondence and reprinted otherwise obscure articles from contemporary newspapers and journals. The tenth volume contains an index to the preceding volumes.

Annual reports of the parent society summarize data found in the *African Repository* and reveal the managers' judgments of their work and the purpose of their cause. The annual reports carry treasurer's reports, lists of officers, and minutes of the annual meetings. Though veiled and perfunctory in tone, these sketchy minutes often give evidence of the internal dissension and disagreement that plagued the society after 1830. Sometimes the annual reports carry long excerpts from speeches delivered by important figures in the movement and reports detailing the society's operations in special fields. The Library of Congress and the State Historical Society of Wisconsin have many pamphlets, reports, and addresses issued by various auxiliary societies. As a rule, the annual reports issued by the auxiliaries followed a pattern. They copied large portions of the parent society's printed data and added two or three speeches by local persons as well as the minutes of the meeting. Sometimes they included lists of local members and donors.

Two government publications are indispensable sources for the African colonization story: a three-hundred-page report by Charles F. Mercer, *Slave Trade* [to accompany bill H.R. no. 412], April 7, 1830 (21 Congress, 1 session, House Committee Report no. 348, serial 201, Washington, 1830), and John Pendleton Kennedy's *African Colonization* [to accompany joint resolution H.R. no. 44], February 28, 1843 (27 Congress, 3 session, House Committee Report no. 283, serial 428, Washington, 1843). These works contain large portions of colonization literature not available in most libraries. The latter work contains an appendix of more than 1,000 pages prepared, without doubt, by the Colonization Society itself. It has a good map of Liberia.

Charles Henry Huberich's posthumously published work, *The Political and Legislative History of Liberia* (New York, 1947), is a compendious treatise in two volumes by an eminent student of public and international law. The 1,700-page work offers a vast quantity of documentary materials culled from obscure printed and manuscript sources. It covers the period from 1820 to 1847, being arranged according to administration of each colonial agent or acting colonial agent. The second volume presents public laws, judicial decisions, and essays on specific legal questions. Though comprehensive, the work lacks brilliance or insight. Huberich's bibliography summarizes the chief books on Liberia. Volume one has a good map of Liberia.

There have been many books and pamphlets on Liberia by colonizationists or writers inspired by colonizationists. One of the earlier and more readable is William Innes's *Liberia; or the Early History and Signal Preservation of the American Colony of Free Negroes on the Coast of Africa; Compiled from the Documents* (Edinburgh, 1831). A second and longer edition appeared two years later. The appendix contains quantities of data supplied by agent Elliott Cresson, who visited Great Britain from 1831 to 1833.

Ralph R. Gurley's long and pietistic *Life of Jehudi Ashmun,*

Late Colonial Agent in Liberia (New York, 1835), offers Gurley's personal knowledge of the African colonization movement, Liberia, and Ashmun. In addition, the appendix contains many documents pertaining to Ashmun's career in the United States and Liberia, and it reprints Ashmun's rare handbook on Liberian agriculture, *The Liberia Farmer; or Colonist's Guide to Independence and Domestic Comfort.*

Four years later, Samuel Wilkeson, chairman of the executive committee of the board of directors, issued a pamphlet characteristically entitled *Concise History of the Commencement, Progress and Present Condition of the American Colonies in Liberia* (Washington, 1839). Joseph Tracy's forty-page pamphlet, *Colonization and Missions . . .* (Boston, 1845), defends African colonization as a missionary enterprise. J. W. Lugenbeel, an agent of the Colonization Society, gives a first-hand account of Liberian geography and climate in his *Sketches of Liberia: Comprising a Brief Account of Geography, Climate, Productions, and Diseases, of the Republic of Liberia. Second Edition . . .* (Washington, 1853). The most thorough study produced in this period was Archibald Alexander's *History of Colonization on the Western Coast of Africa* (Philadelphia, 1846). Professor Alexander, a Princeton friend of the Reverend Mr. Finley's, used materials in the Colonization Society's archives.

John H. B. Latrobe recorded the history of the Maryland colony in his *Maryland in Liberia, a History of the Colony Planted by the Maryland State Colonization Society under the Auspices of the State of Maryland, U.S., at Cape Palmas on the South-West Coast of Africa, 1833–1853 . . .* (Maryland Historical Society Fund Publication, no. 21, Baltimore, 1885). In 138 pages Latrobe gives a good running account of the colony's beginnings, and he reprints specimens of paper money used in the colony. A recent scholar, Samuel W. Laughon, has supplemented Latrobe's account with an able article, "Administrative Problems in Maryland in Liberia, 1836–1851," *Journal of Negro History,* XXVI (July, 1941), 325–364.

Charles S. Sydnor's chapter, "The Mississippi Colonization Society," in his *Slavery in Mississippi* (New York, 1933), is an excellent account of a small but influential and rich society. It supplements Franklin L. Riley's earlier "A Contribution to the History of the Colonization Movement in Mississippi," a collection of letters which appeared in the *Publications of the Mississippi Historical Society,* IX (1906), 337–414. The Reverend Philip Slaughter composed the less useful *The Virginian History of African Colonization* (Richmond,

1855), giving special emphasis to Virginia's early role and subsequent interest in colonization schemes.

Twentieth-century students of African colonization owe much to Walter L. Fleming and Henry Noble Sherwood. Fleming's estimable essay, "Deportation and Colonization, an Attempted Solution to the Race Problem," *Studies in Southern History and Politics inscribed to William Archibald Dunning* (New York, 1914), pp. 3–30, outlined the main story of Civil War colonization and emigration projects. Sherwood, writing in the same period, concentrated on the earlier phases of African colonization. In a series of articles appearing between 1913 and 1923, Sherwood examined eighteenth-century origins of African colonization and carried the story forward to the founding of the American Colonization Society in 1817. Sherwood's articles include: "Paul Cuffe and his Contribution to the American Colonization Society," *Proceedings of the Mississippi Valley Historical Association for the year 1912–1913,* VI, 370–402; "Early Negro Deportation Projects," *Mississippi Valley Historical Review,* II (March, 1916), 484–508; "The Formation of the American Colonization Society," *Journal of Negro History,* II (July, 1917), 209–228; and "Paul Cuffe," *ibid.,* VIII (April, 1923), 153–229.

A contemporary of Fleming and Sherwood, Early Lee Fox, while a doctoral candidate at Johns Hopkins University produced *The American Colonization Society 1817–1840* (Baltimore, 1919), which quickly became the standard reference work. The 226-page study, based on the papers of the American Colonization Society, lacks insight and interpretative analysis. Topically arranged, it overlooks the growth and complexity of the movement, ignores the society's relationship to the benevolent society network, and pours out data in a confused and chaotic way. Angered by the injustices inflicted by antislavery opponents of colonizationists, Fox sides with the maligned society to prove its enemies did not accurately portray its antislavery leanings or its influence in restraining the African slave trade. Fox's rhetorical question ending the study suggests his attitude, "Indeed, was it not worth the effort required to bring the Society into being and to preserve it for so many years?"

At the time that Fleming, Sherwood, and Fox were writing, the gentleman scholar Frederic Bancroft composed three essays on colonization, but he neglected to publish his findings. Forty years later the essays appeared in Jacob E. Cooke's memorial volume, *Frederic Bancroft, Historian; with an Introduction by Allan Nevins and Three Hitherto Unpublished Essays on the Colonization of American Negroes from 1801 to 1865 by Frederic Bancroft* (Norman, Oklahoma, 1957). The three essays are entitled, "The Early Antislavery Movement and African Colonization" (pp. 147–191), "Schemes to Colonize Negroes in Central America" (pp. 192–227), and "The Ile A Vache Experiment in Colonization" (pp. 228–258). Bancroft's first essay is the weakest, being based on printed data alone. More recently scholars have reworked the Civil War colonization schemes with greater thoroughness if not with greater insight. Willis D. Boyd's doctoral dissertation, "Negro Colonization in the National Crisis 1860–1870," completed at the University of California at Los Angeles, in 1953, tries to bring together all incidents and aspects of Negro colonization in the Civil War decade. The result is a not altogether integrated story, but a series of essays that have coherence because the topic and time period require it. Boyd does not distinguish between emigration and colonization. The latter part of his dissertation appears as an article, "Negro Colonization in the Reconstruction Era 1865–1870," *The Georgia Historical Quarterly*, XL (December, 1956), 358–382. The Ile à Vache and Chiriqui stories are adequately presented by Warren B. Beck, "Lincoln and Negro Colonization," *Abraham Lincoln Quarterly*, VI (September, 1950), 162–183, and Paul J. Scheips, "Lincoln and the Chiriqui Colonization Project," *Journal of Negro History*, XXXVII (October, 1952), 418–453.

The American Colonization Society's photograph collection is now in the Library of Congress, prints and photographs division. The principal part of the collection was gathered late in the nineteenth century, and it is almost wholly devoted to Liberian men and scenes. One group of daguerreotypes dating from the early 1850s records the faces of the principal officers of the Liberian republic. Photographs taken in the late 1890s and early 1900s vividly portray Monrovia street scenes as well as native life in the backcountry. In view of the almost imperceptible changes in Liberian life from 1850 to 1900 these photographs are virtually documents for the period covered by this study. The Colonization Society's building which stood on Pennsylvania Avenue between Fourth and Fifth streets in Washington, D.C., yielded its place to a large government building a generation ago.

INDEX